Optimizing Pianism

Optimizing Pianism

Evidence-Based Perspectives

Cameron Roberts

ROWMAN & LITTLEFIELD
Lanham • Boulder • New York • London

Rowman & Littlefield
Bloomsbury Publishing Inc, 1385 Broadway, New York, NY 10018, USA
Bloomsbury Publishing Plc, 50 Bedford Square, London, WC1B 3DP, UK
Bloomsbury Publishing Ireland, 29 Earlsfort Terrace, Dublin 2, D02 AY28, Ireland
www.rowman.com

Copyright © 2025 by The Rowman & Littlefield Publishing Group, Inc.

All rights reserved. No part of this publication may be: i) reproduced or transmitted in any form, electronic or mechanical, including photocopying, recording or by means of any information storage or retrieval system without prior permission in writing from the publishers; or ii) used or reproduced in any way for the training, development or operation of artificial intelligence (AI) technologies, including generative AI technologies. The rights holders expressly reserve this publication from the text and data mining exception as per Article 4(3) of the Digital Single Market Directive (EU) 2019/790.

British Library Cataloguing in Publication Information available

Library of Congress Cataloging-in-Publication Data

Names: Roberts, Cameron (Pianist) author.
Title: Optimizing pianism : evidence-based perspectives / Cameron Roberts.
Description: Lanham : Rowman & Littlefield, 2025. | Includes bibliographical references and index. | Summary: "Drawing on his expertise as a medical professional and active pianist, Cameron Roberts provides an understanding of how virtuosic piano playing works from an evidence-based, scientific perspective. Using accessible language, this wealth of information will help readers steer away from uncertainty, suboptimal performance, and injury"—Provided by publisher.
Identifiers: LCCN 2024059245 (print) | LCCN 2024059246 (ebook) |
  ISBN 9798881807788 (cloth) | ISBN 9798881807795 (paperback) |
  ISBN 9798881807801 (epub)
Subjects: LCSH: Piano—Instruction and study. | Piano—Performance. | Music—Performance—Psychological aspects.
Classification: LCC MT220 .R626 2025 (print) | LCC MT220 (ebook) |
  DDC 786.2071—dc23/eng/20241210
LC record available at https://lccn.loc.gov/2024059245
LC ebook record available at https://lccn.loc.gov/2024059246

For product safety related questions contact productsafety@bloomsbury.com.

∞™ The paper used in this publication meets the minimum requirements of American National Standard for Information Sciences—Permanence of Paper for Printed Library Materials, ANSI/NISO Z39.48-1992.

Dedication

To Diana, Max, and Chloe.
Thank you for making me smile.

"My piano is me."[1]—Franz Liszt

---

1. Franz Liszt, commenting in *La Gazette musicale*, 11 February, 1838.

Contents

Acknowledgments	xiii
Introduction: Myth-Busting Piano Pedagogy	xv

PART I: PIANISTIC BELIEFS — 1

1 Believing in Beliefs — 3
  I Feel It: It's True—Mistaken Truths — 8
  I Can!—Reframing Beliefs — 12
  I'm Right Because . . . —Cognitive Biases — 14
  Notes — 17

2 Mind Traps and Mental Shortcuts — 21
  Reality Evasion #1—The *I'm Right* Pianist — 23
  Reality Evasion #2—The *I Could've if I'd Wanted To* Pianist — 25
  Pianistic Implications of Your Beliefs — 27
  Notes — 30

PART II: TOUCH BELIEFS AND REALITIES — 31

3 The Touch-Tone Relationship—Performers' Perspectives — 33
  Tone Quality—What Determines Tone Quality? — 34
  Using the Body—Fat, Skinny, Curled, or Straight Fingers? — 36
    Quality Depends on Your Finger Shape and Position — 36
    Quality Comes from Your Arm Weight — 37
  Key contact—Poke, Press, Pull, or Push? — 39
    Quality Depends on the Key-Surface Contact — 39
    Quality Depends on the Velocity of the Key's Descent — 40
    Quality Lies in the Keybed — 40

Pianos, Piano-Technicians and Acoustics—Where Does the Quality Come From?	41
Sound Perception—*I Feel It; Don't You?*	42
Quality Lies in the Metaphor	42
Quality Lies in the Eye of the Beholder	43
Re-Defining the Touch-Tone Debate?	45
Notes	46
4 The Touch-Tone Relationship—Scientists' Perspectives	51
The Physics of Touch and Tone Quality	51
The Hammer Head: Speed, Felt, Compression	51
Hard-Hammer-Bright-Tone Reality Meets Piano-Pedagogy Beliefs	54
The Hammer Shaft: Flexing and Wobbling	56
Impact Noises: The Keybed and the "Thump"	58
The Keybed	58
The "Thump"	59
The Psychology of Touch and Tone Quality	64
Embodiment and the Feel of the Gesture	64
Gesture, Pleasure, and Meaning	66
Metaphors, Reality, and the Single Mental Representation	70
In the Eye of the Beholder	72
Mirror Neurons: Learning Meaning	74
Notes	78
PART III: OPTIMIZING PIANISM	**87**
5 Pursuing Excellence: Beliefs, 3 Ms, and Process	89
3M Triangle of Pianism	90
The 3M Triangle Explained	90
6 Mechanical Skills	95
The Piano Action	96
The Window of Opportunity	99
Pressed Versus Percussive Notes	102
Sliding Off the Knuckle	103
To Hit, or Not to Hit, the Keybed	103
Optimizing the Body's Movements	106
Mass Bridging, Partial Bridging and Effective Mass	107
Inertia and "The Inertia Problem"	111
Velocity and Momentum	115
Key and Hammer Facts	115
Momentum and Vectors	115

The "Momentum Chain" of Touch	115
Touch Angle and Momentum Transfer	116
Benefits of Mechanical Inefficiency	118
Momentum Transfer During Different Types of Collision	120
Coordinated and Uncoordinated Movements	123
Elastic and Inelastic Collisions	124
Minimal Volatility—an Ideal Playing Zone?	125
Force and Rebound Force	128
Combining Anatomy with Physics	130
Arches and Domes	130
Hammers and High-Knuckle Positions	133
Gravity	135
Optimizing Mechanical Efficiency: The "Triple-Stroke"	136
Finger Dependence, Interdependence and Independence	138
Forearm Muscles	138
Hand Muscles	139
Juncturae Tendinum	140
The Hand as a Functioning Unit	141
Joint Positions and Muscle Strength	141
Sitting Postures	142
The Five Fingers—Strengths and Weaknesses	145
Muscles, Pain and Injuries	150
Repetitive Motion Disorder, Focal Dystonia and Chronic Pain.	152
Notes	153
7 Mental Skills	163
Mental Practice	164
Visualization	164
Anticipatory Images	166
Learning and Neuroplasticity	170
Associations, Learning and Memorising	172
Emotionalized Movements	175
Body Language	178
Body Movements	178
Gestural Movements	178
"Learned" Emotionalized Movements	179
Mood and Movements and Expression and Pain	179
Optimizing Practicing: Improving Nerve Connections	181
Empowered Learning. Deliberate Practice. Growth Mindset.	181
Quality Practice	183
Effort and Quantity	184

	Process Optimization	194
	Leverage and Compensation Errors	195
	Incremental Gains and Compound Interest	198
	Reward-to-Risk Ratios	199
	Notes	202
8	**Musical Skills**	213
	Artistic Vision—Mind Over Matter	213
	Listening Boosts Your Learning Efficiency	216
	Be a "Sound Chef"—Mix-ing and Max-ing the Elements	217
	Make Friends with Your Medium—Work with Reality	221
	Pianist-Piano Interactions	225
	Pianist-Audience Interactions	226
	Pianist-Music Interactions	226
	Pianist-Pianist Interactions	227
	Aesthetics and Your Pianism—Sharing Expectations	228
	Notes	233

MOVEMENT OPTIMIZATION EXERCISES — 237

The "Triple-Stroke"—"Fall, Play & Roll" — 237
The Butterfly Exercise — 242
What Leap? Just Play! — 243
Chopin's Triple-Stroke and Sideways Glide — 244
Optimizing Pianism—a Working Checklist — 247
Notes — 248

Appendix A—Case Study 1: Playing *mf* with Different Touch Masses — 249

Appendix B—Case Study 2: Comparing Momentum Transfers for Elastic and Inelastic Collisions — 251

Appendix C—Ideal Touch Masses (and *m-v* Zones) for Different Dynamics — 253

Bibliography — 255

Index — 273

About the Author — 277

Acknowledgments

Prof Dr Eckart Altenmüller

Dr Di Bresciani

Dr Belinda Carne

Dr Ross Carne

Dr Michael Kieran Harvey

Dr Ashley Hribar

Ian Mansfield

Dr Lynden Roberts

Maximilian Roberts Sancho

Chloe Roberts Sancho

Dr Diana Sancho Villa

The Michael Kieran Harvey Scholarship

The Ian Potter Cultural Trust Scholarship

Introduction

Myth-Busting Piano Pedagogy

*It ain't what you don't know that gets you into trouble.
It's what you know for sure that just ain't so.*[1]—Mark Twain

THE CONFUSED PIANIST?

There are many ways to play a piano. Some will lead to virtuosity. Some will lead to injury. Some won't lead to anywhere. Before embarking on the pleasure of thousands of hours of piano practice, then, you might wish to ask some questions, like what is the pathway to take, and how are you going to know before embarking on it? Who are you going to trust to guide you and your talent? Will you trust your teacher, as famous as he or she may be, your previous teacher, your piano-playing heroes, books, videos, a course you took, your observations of other pianists, anecdotes from corridor conversations, a combination of everything, or just your own instincts?

And how will you practice? Will your approach provide you with the *best* outcomes for your pianism in both short and long terms? What is the source of your pianistic information, and why do you believe it? Are you guessing? And if so, what consequences are attached to those risks of guessing? Could you upgrade the quality of the information that you put into practice so that your risks are minimized and your gains are enhanced? What is it *exactly* that you are trying to achieve with your pianism?

This book strives to provide information that will help you answer such questions. It seeks to eliminate the guesswork from piano playing by offering an evidence-based perspective. This means applying facts and keeping an open (unbiased) mind about the reality of things.

Central to the function of any person's pianism is their touch, and the book examines this interaction in depth. The importance of mastering touch is no different to that of a tennis player or a golfer who *must* learn how to hit a ball properly should they wish to win matches at a high level—but *cannot* win if they don't. This book, therefore, examines the mechanical-physical features of touch and the psychological-perceptual aspects that provide our understanding of it. Using science, not opinion, the potential and the limits of the act of touch are explored: the goal, to steer pianists toward *understanding* how virtuosic piano playing works and away from guessing, uncertainty, suboptimal performance and injury.

What we *believe* about how touch works affects our development as pianists because, over time, these beliefs shape our decisions about touch, which, over time, shape our technique—for good or for bad. Understanding touch is, therefore, considered to play an important role in optimizing pianism as a whole, as it teaches us to recognize "what matters" from "what doesn't matter" in the world of piano pedagogy. Table 0.1 hints at the pedagogical problem that the book tries to untangle: that there are different pathways to achieving virtuosity but little clarity about *what it is* about each pathway that is actually contributing to—or preventing—it from occurring.

By learning to recognize our cognitive biases, by comparing our opinions with facts and by introducing as much evidence as possible into the pedagogical discussion, a rational view of *how pianism works* becomes possible. It is hoped that this book contributes to such an objective platform of information to which pianists can refer to make better decisions. For practical purposes, this collective information is summarized into a model— "The 3M Model of Pianism." This model does not claim to be a method but rather a guide to understanding how our, or anybody else's, pianism works, what the relationships are between its internal and external components, and how it can be optimized. It shows why seemingly different approaches to practicing, playing, and pedagog-izing about piano playing can, in reality, all be viable *if* the main ingredients needed for pianism to work are present.

To be clear, the book is written *to inform* and *to inspire*. It is not written to conform to any pedagogical status quo, nor is it a "method." If anything, it is an "anti-method" as it interrogates the diverse claims of piano pedagogy, assesses their validity and utility, and, in general, rules in favor of caution if blindly endorsing any of them. But the critical, take no prisoners discourse is not to be confused with its enthusiasm for learning about how pianists over the centuries have approached and solved the musico-technical problems of high-performance pianism.

The unbiased interrogation of opinions that this book pursues, is critical to the quality of the conclusions that it makes. For if opinions alone were to remain the source of all our pianistic doctrines, then we would remain

Introduction

Table 0.1. What Contributes What to What?

Pianist A	Pianist B	Pianist C	Pianist D
"I regularly practice Hanon and Czerny."	"I never practice Hanon or Czerny."	"I regularly practice Hanon and Czerny."	"I never practice Hanon or Czerny."
↓	↓	↓	↓
"I have a virtuosic technique."	"I have a virtuosic technique."	"I'm injured."	"I'm injured."
"I sit low and play with flat fingers."	"I sit high and play with curled fingers."	"I sit low and play with flat fingers."	"I sit high and play with curled fingers."
↓	↓	↓	↓
"I can play anything and control any sound."	"I can play anything and control any sound."	"I'm injured."	"I'm injured."
"I practice seven to eight hours a day."	"I practice three to four hours a day."	"I practice seven to eight hours a day."	"I practice three to four hours a day."
↓	↓	↓	↓
"I have a virtuosic technique."	"I have a virtuosic technique."	"I'm injured."	"I'm injured."

forever stuck inside the same pedagogical bubble: of piecemealing traditions, of imitating our idols, of hoping that what we or our teachers do, works, of endorsing pseudo-scientific beliefs, of ignoring science, and of subjecting ourselves to the risks and benefits of each. Why should we keep rolling dice? Why guess when you can know?

Talented pianists deserve better, which is why the book is devoted to them, informing and empowering them to achieve the *highest levels of pianism—artistically and technically—and not get injured.* For some, the incorporation of science into the practice room may seem unnecessary, but a quick exercise in clear thinking (not biased thinking—see Part I) shows how restrictive such a standpoint is, given that wasted talent, unmet potential, and performance-related injuries remain daily problems for thousands of pianists around the world year after year[2] *and* that scientific material is readily available to help *and* that its application does not impose upon musical-artistic goals in any way. An Olympic sportsperson would not ignore the opportunities of science.

Simply, by introducing a few facts into the practice room, using our time better, and avoiding common pitfalls, we can play quicker, more accurately, with more key control, with less fatigue, with faster learning, better memorizing, more creativity, with more engagement with audiences, with less performance anxiety and, not least, with less risk of injury. These are not insignificant areas of pianism. Knowledge from the disciplines of physics, physiology, and psychology will be applied to piano playing, with the intention of showing how much quicker our pianism can progress when ambitious artistic ideas are combined with the right pianistic tools. This is what the science would conclude, and it is what the book strongly advocates:

1. To pursue (much!) *more ambitious* artistic goals;
2. To use, as often as is appropriate, the most *effective* and *efficient* means of realizing these artistic goals;
3. To *ignore* everything else.

No musician should have any conflict with such recommendations. And if they did, the question of *why* should appear. Piano traditions are as rich in content as they are riddled with speculative theories, sound-bite anecdotes and genuine attempts by professionals to share their experience and expertise. Unsurprisingly, answers to the pianistic questions of *what to do* or *how to do it* are diverse, and not always consistent in meaning, evidence or application. Most curiously, too, the diversity of opinion seems to *increase* as it climbs up the tree of expertise, not decrease, as one might expect—or hope (see chapter 3. The Touch-Tone Relationship—Performers' Perspectives).

That such divisions exist in such an authoritative body of pedagogical information should raise warning signals as to how reliable expert opinions actually are. Student pianists who change from teacher to teacher during their studies will know the feeling of uncertainty that different teachers bring to their sense of identity as pianists—not to mention, confidence. But it doesn't have to be this way—if we all knew how to evaluate pedagogical information better and learned to appreciate that underneath the many different opinions are usually some universal truths.

Separating fact from fiction, and what is useful from what is useless in the world of piano pedagogy is not a complicated task after one learns to recognize *what matters*. Given the huge investment of time that we put into our pianism, to learn *what matters* would seem a reasonable thing to do. And for career-driven pianists, it should be considered to be even more important, so that the thousands of hours of practice that lie in waiting may be more productive.

If we were playing the piano only for enjoyment purposes, the question of how to play optimally would be largely irrelevant. For professional pianists, however, playing and practicing optimally matters a lot. The extremely competitive nature of the profession ensures that *how well we use our practice time* will be a major factor in determining how quickly, how far, and how deep our talent can progress toward artistry. By analogy, our activities as pianists may be considered to be like those of mountain climbers: where we dream of reaching peaks but can only reach them by *actions*—actions that involve many frequent, well-directed steps. The pathways to the peak performance achievements of Bach, Liszt, and Horowitz were no different either (despite any myths), as they will be for *you* too.

And so, with a better knowledge of how things work (physics and physiology) and how to be more productive (the neuroscience of learning musical motor skills), we may more confidently address our core questions: *What is the goal of our pianism, and how do we best achieve it?* Without engaging seriously with these questions, our chances of reaching our pianistic mountain peak is wishful and unlikely. It is also at risk of suffering from the negative consequences of aimless practice, which include:

- *Suboptimal pianism*—unfulfilled potential for not aiming high enough or not taking the right steps to nurturing it;
- *Wasted time and effort*—learning the wrong things or learning them incorrectly, resulting in slow progress and low productivity;
- *Wasted money*—costs on lessons, courses, and institutions that don't align with your goals or know how to train virtuosity;
- *Injuries*—for not knowing the basics of physiology or for ignoring the feedback from your body;
- *Negative emotional states*—e.g., anxiety, depression, burnout or stage-fright that may accompany such losses.

It is taken for granted that the reader of this book will already be a musically talented, ambitious pianist. This book is not trying to teach music, though it does presume that the reader will be seriously committed to improving their pianism to realize their musical ideas through it. This group of pianists—professionals and professionals-to-be—and the teachers who instruct them, are the target audience because they are involved in the highest number of learning interactions per day, per week, per year, year after year *and* who have the highest invested interest in the success of those interactions. In this group, getting things right before they go wrong can result in life-changing career outcomes altogether.

Finally, admittedly, not everything needs to be understood in order to play well. Pianists frequently operate using assumptions that are factually wrong but still work. Trial-and-error strategies work well too without ever needing to understand why. This is because virtuosic pianism will work when *what matters* is present, not what we *think* matters, but doesn't. Indeed, many of the best players and teachers operate with little factual knowledge about the physical, physiological and perceptual aspects of piano playing at all – which is fine . . . when it works.

But here lies the rub: What is one supposed to do if it doesn't work? Are pseudo-facts, historical dogma and opinion-based advice going to be your go-to sources for information? *Speculation* is never a problem in pedagogy when things appear to be working, but it is a big problem when things are not. It is also the underlying narratives of injured pianists who have confidently practiced in ways that violate the laws of physics, disregarded the physical limits of physiology or remained perceptually blind to the risks that are *actually happening* to them.

For those who seek to understand how pianism works, to optimize playing and avoid its many pitfalls, then this is your book. Everything is easy to understand and easy to apply. This book is only as long as it is because of its obligation to demonstrate why! There are three parts to the book, each part representing a stage in the pedagogical journey from biased belief systems through to clear-thinking understandings and, finally, targeted applications of science to enhance technical and aesthetic outcomes. It may help to read them in order, but it is not essential. Artists are free to choose.

Part I: Pianistic Beliefs explains why we are prone to believing in what we want to believe irrespective of their factualness or utility. It examines psychological biases and shows how these influence the decisions that we make about our pianism and the consequences that these decisions have. Ultimately, the chapter highlights how we can systematically improve our pianism by improving the quality of the information that we allow to filter into it.

In *Part II: Touch Beliefs and Realities*, the relationship between touch and tone quality is discussed. This is an area of immense pedagogical importance. Unfortunately, it is also an area in which pianists tend to mix misinformation with strong convictions. A survey of the touch-tone literature is carried out, comparing the opinions of pianists with the findings from science. The diversity of the opinions presented in the chapter highlights that neither strong beliefs nor expert pianists' opinions about the touch-tone relationship correlate with what is actually happening when we play the piano. That our interpretation of the touch-tone event is influenced by a complex web of motor-sensory and kinaesthetic interactions is shown to be one of the main reasons why such a wide range of opinions exist about the function of touch in piano playing.

Following the myth-busting information provided in Parts I and II, *Part III: Optimizing Pianism* becomes possible. It outlines evidence-based ways to optimize piano playing by focusing on three key components of pianism: *Mechanical*, *Mental*, and *Musical* skills—the *3 Ms* of pianism. Importance is also given to improving the *process* of piano practicing, a skill in itself that can be used to ensure faster progress. As an extra, a brief discussion of hand function, injuries, and how to prevent them, is included. This serves both to inform and act as a reminder of what can go wrong when "great ideas about piano playing" conflict with the realities of the physical world.

NOTES

1 Quote attributed to Mark Twain, likely derived from Josh Billings's 1874 phrase, "it iz better tew know nothing than two know what ain't so." Discussed in:Quote Investigator. "It ain't what you don't know that gets you into trouble. It's what you know for sure that just ain't so." Accessed September 20, 2024. https://quoteinvestigator.com/2018/11/18/know-trouble/#note-20795-2.

2 The point-prevalence for musculoskeletal complaints in professional musicians ranges between approximately 30–60 percent, with higher prevalences over a lifetime. See:

Bragge, Peter, Andrea Bialocerkowski, and Joan McMeeken. "A Systematic Review of Prevalence and Risk Factors Associated with Playing-Related Musculoskeletal Disorders in Pianists." *Occupational Medicine* 56, no. 1 (November 7, 2005): 28–38. doi:https://doi.org/10.1093/occmed/kqi177;

Kok, Laura M., Bionka M. A. Huisstede, Veronique M. A. Voorn, Jan W. Schoones, and Rob G. H. H. Nelissen. "The Occurrence of Musculoskeletal Complaints among Professional Musicians: A Systematic Review." *International Archives of Occupational and Environmental Health* 89, no. 3 (November 12, 2015): 373–96. doi:https://doi.org/10.1007/s00420-015-1090-6;

Zaza, Christine. "Playing-related musculoskeletal disorders in musicians: a systematic review of incidence and prevalence." *Canadian Medical Association Journal* 158, no. 8 (1998): 1019–25.

Part I

PIANISTIC BELIEFS

"Facts do not cease to exist because they are ignored."[1]
—Aldous Huxley

---

1. Dobelli, Rolf. *The Art of Thinking Clearly*. London: Sceptre, 2014, 23, quoting from Huxley's essay, "On the Relation of Reality to the Human Mind."

Chapter 1

Believing in Beliefs

"To teach superstitions as truth is a most terrible thing. The mind of a child accepts them, and only through great pain, perhaps even tragedy, can the child be relieved of them."[1] —Hypatia

When we practice the piano, we practice our beliefs about piano playing. We put into action our ideas about technique, sound, expression and musical purpose. These beliefs may be based upon facts or fiction, just as they may be useful or useless in helping us improve our pianism. However, regardless of their source, their validity or their utility, by repeatedly putting them into action, these beliefs shape our pianism. Over time, we become used to this "shape" without necessarily questioning whether such a shape was, is, or will be, the best shape for us in the future.

The sense of familiarity that is acquired from our day-to-day constancy with our environment is an example of the process of *habituation*. We become accustomed to certain patterns of thought and activity because of their existential frequency—*not* their utility—and, being more accustomed to them, repeat them with greater ease, which then further reinforces their familiarity.[2]

Recognizing our practicing habits (habituations) is a vital step toward optimizing our playing. It directs our attention to "what we are doing" and raises our awareness to the possibility that "what we are doing is maybe not as useful as what we think it is."

In the world of piano playing and practice, habituation can work in our favor or act as a restraining order against it—depending on what it is that we have habituated. Considering the wide variety of beliefs about "how to play a piano" and the high degrees of habituation that pianists develop over their years of practice, it is understandable that the world of piano pedagogy will contain a vast array of *highly conflicting* yet *highly-believed-in* methods of playing the piano. This lucky dip of ideas that (young) pianists have to choose from—or be confused by, or be subjected to, or be ruined by—is listed in the the following textbox.

Beliefs, Actions, Habits: Beliefs, Actions, Habits

How have you habituated the following aspects of pianism?

- How to sit → high, low, near, far?
- How to position the hand → high/low wrist, flat/curled fingers, high/low arch?
- How to play into the key → finger-, hand-, forearm-, arm-dominant movement?
- How to move the body → freely, minimally?
- How to practice → small/large amounts, low/high frequency, slow/fast tempi, with exercises, rhythms, from memory?
- How to change the quality of the tone → speed of keystroke, depth of keystroke, type of weight used?
- What to practice → scales, exercises, etudes, repertoire, contemporary music, improvisation, sight-reading, composing, chamber music?
- How composer X should be played → strictly/freely, narrow/wide emotional range?
- What elements of the music to prioritize → focus on details, style, emotions?
- What state of mind to adopt when playing → dutiful, ambitious, serious, creative, nervous, carefree, spiritual?
- Whom to serve → ourselves, our teacher, the audience, the composer?

Of the choices that you have made, why have you chosen to make them part of your pianistic narrative? Do they best serve your goals or are your pianistic actions just a mindless derivative of unchecked habituation?

As with other human beliefs, our pianistic beliefs serve the *Homo sapien* function of providing a stable and coherent mental framework so that we can more easily pursue goals within a specific environment.[3] This does not make our, or anybody else's, beliefs about how pianism works universally true nor objectively useful. Our assumptions are simply our mind's "best guess"—based on its accumulated experience of its previous best guesses—about how to best navigate a particular environment.

Recognizing that our beliefs about pianism are constructed out of lines that are drawn from a limited set of pedagogical data points of information explains why so much of what we are taught, adopt and habituate, will only work up to a certain point—the extent to which those previous lines of assumption *match the context* in which they are now being asked to function. For example, applying certain pedagogical advice to *your* pianism that was meant for a different student in a different context (e.g., Beethoven's advice to a specific pupil on a specific instrument within a specific aesthetic style) may not be wholly useful *to you* playing *different* repertoire on a *different* instrument to a *different* twenty-first-century audience. Some of it might be useful, but some of it might not, so how do we discriminate? The textbox below gives some examples of the problems, frustrations and comedies that can occur when the assumptions of our (previous) pianistic beliefs are exposed to the realities of (new) different contexts.

Belief-Reality Malalignment and Its Problems

- Your dutiful passing of the thumb under your hand [belief] prevented you from playing the extremely fast scale passagework in some of Liszt's etudes [reality];
- Your successful use of the sustain pedal when playing Bach [belief] in the big international piano competition did not please the experts of "The period-instrument, authentic-Bach-performance school" [reality];
- Your usual approach [belief] to memorizing a Beethoven sonata did not work [reality] when trying to memorize a Boulez sonata;
- The high finger-lift technique learned during your early years of training [belief] caused you fatigue and pain [reality] when your professional commitments increased;
- The lower-sitting, flat-fingered positions encouraged by your previous teacher [belief] were rejected for a higher-sitting, curved-fingered position by your new teacher [reality];
- The quick tempos recommended to you for playing Debussy in France [belief] were rejected by your teachers in Germany [reality];
- Your childhood beliefs about easy success as a pianist [belief] were not matched by the difficulties faced as a professional [reality];

- Dedicating all your efforts to executing all the notes and details of the score [belief] did not correlate to how the composer actually wanted the piece to sound [reality].

On the other hand, when the expectations of a belief system are well matched to the reality of the context in which they operate, their realization will seem effortless. For example, shaping your phrases exactly in the way your examiner wants, keeping an aligned posture in your Alexander-technique class, or praising Rachmaninoff's *rubato* to a "Friends of Rachmaninoff Society" is never going to receive negative criticism, irrespective of whether either party is right or wrong, or whether the actions contain any objectifiable value whatsoever.

Along the same lines, what we learn to believe about pianism in our early years of training may not be so useful in our future years. Different contexts require different ways of thinking. Understanding that there may be a mismatch between what we *believe* is useful and *the reality* of what is useful is critical to long-term pianistic success. There are hundreds of examples of how this occurs in practice—as the book describes—but the mismatch becomes most obvious to us when our habitual beliefs about technique and style are taken out of their usual context and placed into a foreign one, where, what may *previously* have worked well (and without criticism) may *now* not work well at all, or might be criticized, treated with suspicion, be misunderstood or even ridiculed. The new music that composers present to audiences routinely suffer from such evaluations—ask Igor Stravinsky in Paris.[4] And harsh

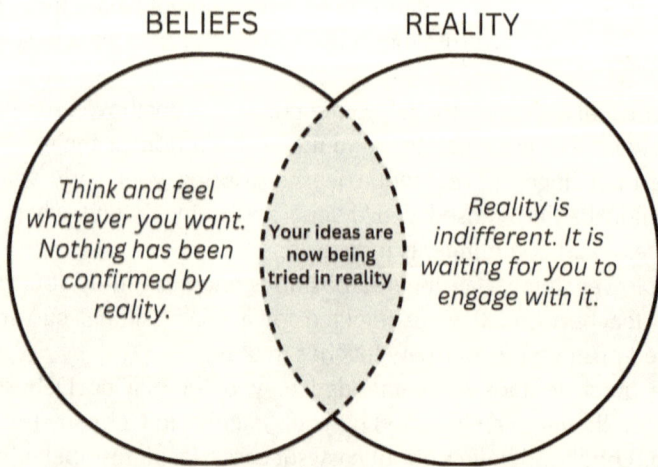

Figure 1.1. Beliefs meet Reality. Author created

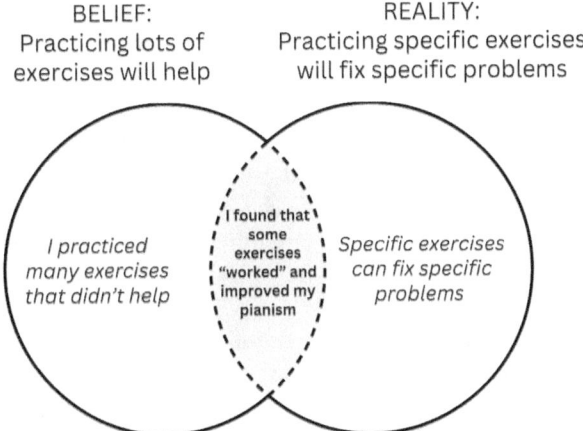

Figure 1.2. Beliefs vs Reality about Exercises. Author created

Figure 1.3. Aligning Beliefs with Reality. Author created

criticisms to creative interpretations are no different—ask Glenn Gould in New York. Could our personal views about piano technique—like how to touch the key, how to play fast, how to practice, how to learn quickly, how to memorize, how not to get injured etc.—also be living in a naive bubble of surety, until proven otherwise? We could ask an injured pianist like Leon Fleisher: "back then, no one even recognized this [risk of over-practicing and focal dystonia] as a legitimate medical problem."[5]

Potentially, a more enlightened belief-reality framework for our pianism could be used. Figure 1.3 shows how: where an optimal working space exists—improved *and* safe—where our very best thoughts about pianism are *allowed* to work because they comply with the laws of the reality of the context in which they are trying to operate.

Unsurprisingly, any belief system that remains unchallenged or resistant to change over a long time can become out of touch with reality and very distorted. To state the obvious, look at religious systems over the course of humanity where habituated rules are so entrenched among the participants of one context that they are unable (or unwilling) to be open to the alternatives of another:

> *"In order to survive, the inhabitants of a particular valley needed to understand the superhuman order that regulated their valley, and to adjust their behavior accordingly. It was pointless to try to convince the inhabitants of some distant valley to follow the same rules."*[6]—Y. N. Harari

But any musical organization will have its own rules too—which stem from its beliefs—for organizing, controlling and promoting certain thoughts and behaviors, be they technical (actions) or stylistic (thoughts), accompanied with its blessings through scholarships and prizes for those who successfully follow its laws. In piano pedagogy, antagonism between different pianistic belief systems is extremely common, and may arise when discussing *any* issue related to pianism. How touch affects tone quality (or doesn't) is one such area of conflict—the central focus of Part II.

Given the importance of choosing pianistic beliefs that are going to overlap with what reality can offer (physics, physiology, shared psychology), let us examine why our minds are so blind to the flaws in its own logic and resistant to the facts of alternative points of view.

I FEEL IT: IT'S TRUE—MISTAKEN TRUTHS

As part of its cognitive stabilizing function, the default mode of operation of our mind's belief system is *to hold as true* that in which it already believes and *to reject as false* that which challenges it. In psychology, this belief system stabilizing function is called *assumed veracity*.[7] From an evolutionary perspective, it allows us to act quickly and effortlessly with a certain degree of predictive accuracy, based on our previous experiences within such environments. Other participants, who also share the same assumed truths, can also operate quickly and effortlessly, should the context remain the same. Piano competitions are important . . . for those who believe in their utility. Playing on the pads of your fingertips is important . . . for those who believe in their utility.

Facts to the contrary of any belief systems are usually never welcomed as they require a personal admission of error of judgment (the assumed veracity of a belief has been disproven) or a remodeling of the assumptions upon which it operates i.e., "some animals are more equal than others" (Orwell). Both responses require effort—an energy cost that living organisms (i.e., us) do not readily accept unless the gain for the effort is known to outweigh it. Personal assumptions about piano technique that are protected by hardened layers of assumed veracity flourish in piano pedagogy. They are usually wrong when it comes to their explanations of causality (musicians tend to skim past the science), though, not unsurprisingly, are often useful when it comes to their applicability (because they have been tried and tested in the playing arena).[8]

Here is a typical pedagogical assumption: *the tone becomes fuller and rounder when I allow my arm weight to sink slowly and deeply into the key.* In the statement, the claim is that the combination of "arm weight," "sinking slowly," and "deeply into the key" correlate to a "full and round" tone. The assumptions appear to be logical, well-intended and may even come from an expert pianist. But apart from trying it out yourself and convincing yourself that it's true, no evidence—i.e., no verification of its truth in the physical world—is provided. Thus, such a statement represents an *opinion*: an opinion based on the experience of 1 person's assumptions. As the assumption *appears* to work, another 1,000 people may also choose to agree with the statement, adding to the assumed-veracity pedagogical-party. But 1 untested opinion shared by 1,000 people is still an opinion. Zero times 1,000 is still zero.

We must think more critically. The statement about how to produce a "full and round" tone is not evidence-based; it is experience-based, working for the pianists who believe in it, but leaving others, who disagree, no closer to knowing whether "arm weight," "sinking slowly," playing "deeply into the key," or *something else* is responsible for causing it (should any of those terms be objectively definable). In such a fashion, much of the information in piano pedagogy is accumulated: experience-based and largely unchecked—until something goes wrong.

In piano pedagogy, despite much that is useful, much *is* still going wrong: pianists still engage in high-risk activities that offer dubious pianistic gain and, almost certain, injury risk. With careers at stake, no ambitious pianist should be accepting of such inconsistency of information that they put into practice. It is not that all pedagogical advice is wrong, it is that, as a blind consumer, there is little way of knowing which of it is useful and which of it isn't. The story of the following pianist's injury, typical of many, is as lamentable as it is preventable:

> "Looking back now, the solution to fixing it was quite simple. Given a time machine I could have offered myself advice about how to heal it. I would have said, 'stop pressing so hard on the keys' [... but] Instead of teaching me how

to move my hand differently so this problem wouldn't keep coming back, what I got from faculty members included: simply resting it until it was better, playing more left handed repertoire, and even observing how my hand moved while running water over it—not one piece of practical advice on how to change my technique. And I didn't know any better as a young undergraduate student."[9]

If pedagogical advice were a medicine, it would have to pass through years of research and scrutiny, and, finally, be issued with informed consent. No such accountability exists in the world of piano pedagogy. Any advice can be freely created, freely given, with some or none of it working to any degree of benefit or harm.

And so, as pianists, how do we differentiate what is useful from what isn't? When personal opinions dominate our information sources, the process of discrimination becomes just another exercise in guessing: in ascribing value to information according to its popularity, accessibility, or our feelings toward it, which, of course, is just another spin-off of our already-established beliefs—like dogs chasing their own tails. Experts with a history of success are, logically, good starting points but should not be seen as definite sources either. Experts differ in their opinions too.

Obviously, a process of rationally evaluating information is required. A measuring stick must be used. Critical thinking must be used, and science must be introduced. Facts need to be included in the discourse, like the ones offered in this book, so that our beliefs don't sail off course.

Unfortunately, however, for many pianists, accepting facts—and change—will be a major challenge. This is, psychologically, because of the "meaning threat" that facts pose to an already well-established belief system[10] and because of the "backfire"[11] that will be triggered in our minds: of accepting information with which it already agrees (glorified as "truths") and rejecting information with which it already disagrees (discredited as "lies"). A perfect example of this meaning threat-backfire sequence occurred to me in 1995 when, as a student, I played the same Chopin *Scherzo* to a professor from the Vienna Hochschule and, a few weeks later, to a professor at the Moscow Conservatory. The former took offense to my straight-backed posture (meaning threat), describing how it stiffened my sound, that Chopin's music shouldn't be stiff, and that stiff-backed Russian pianists should not be used as examples (backfire), whereas the later argued that my (now adopted) round-backed, fluid posture (meaning threat) took away from the fullness of my tone, took away from the nobility of the music, and that Viennese pianists had no say about the performance of Slavic music (backfire).

In reading this book about pianism, you will constantly participate in the process of meaning threat and backfire, selectively accepting and rejecting many of this book's claims—like this one—to augment or diminish the size of the belief and reality spaces of your pianism (recall figure 1.1). You do the same thing when you have a piano lesson, receive criticism about your playing in a masterclass, or read the review of your concert in the newspaper.

The psychological game of "assumed veracity vs. meaning threats" is constantly being played out inside your mind, accepting what it likes and rejecting what it doesn't. Your ability to assess the value of both and be open to embracing the benefits of new and useful information matters a lot to the success of your pianism. It is what will allow you to implement the *best information* on *all aspects* of pianism, from mechanical advice to sound organization, from practicing to interpretation, and toward the imaginative risk-taking required of being an original artist.

"Meaning Threat": To Accept or Reject?

The following common (though fictitious) scenario shows the inner thoughts of a student being criticized in a piano masterclass. They are typical responses of a belief system under threat.

- Belief system attack:

   "In the masterclass, the teacher found fault with my keystroke and said that it was affecting my technique. I didn't agree." [criticism threatens the student's belief system about finger technique]

- Belief system defense:

   "What would he know anyway: he doesn't have a big career, he is not a famous teacher, and I didn't even like his playing. [rejecting and discrediting threatening information] *And besides, the audience said they loved my playing, I thought I played well, and nobody has ever told me before that my keystroke has problems."* [accepting and re-affirming current belief]

- Outcome for the student:

   In this example, there may or may not be a problem with this student's keystroke, but who is to know, and by whose authority? More importantly, how is *this* student going to know, and who should they consult to clear up their confusion? Another teacher? Another piano guide?

Unless we learn to use our minds better, our primitive responses to meaning threats will persist, keeping us feeling confident in our own thoughts yet blind to its risks and deaf to the opportunities that the new context is trying to share with us. Keeping our minds alert to the quality of the information that it accepts and rejects is part of the process of optimizing our pianism. Though, sadly, it is usually not until our belief system receives an unavoidable confrontation with reality that it becomes aware of its mistaken assumptions: like an injury, criticism from a new teacher, a disastrous performance, or a sustained run of unmet professional expectations.

I CAN!—REFRAMING BELIEFS

Functionally, then, our thoughts arise from a cognitive system that doubles as an information filter: trapping information in and trapping information out depending largely on what it has previously been trained to authorize. As pianists we want our belief system to *include* the most useful information possible and *exclude* the information that is not useful, as the endorsed information is what we will be putting into practice to shape our future pianism. Being flexible with our beliefs is, obviously, the only way to proceed here, as it acknowledges that *a better way of doing things probably exists* even if it is not yet known to us.

Thankfully, changing our beliefs is ridiculously easy to do—if we allow it. Beliefs have formed within our brains because of the lottery of the circumstances and context in which they arose, and so they can just as easily be replaced by different ones: but, this time, from circumstances of our choosing. Psychologically, our minds will try to scare us into thinking that making changes to our beliefs is more difficult than it is, but this is just its modus operandi trick of trying to maintain its modus operandi.

There is no need to be a puppet of our old mind's operation system. Our job is to be the leader of a new one, an ideal one, that combines the most courageous fictions of artistic imagination with the best tools that reality can offer to deliver them.

Upgrade Your Pianistic Beliefs—Create Your Own "Ideal Belief Bubble"

What if it were *only* your beliefs—not your talent nor your commitment to practicing—that were preventing you from excelling? Wouldn't those beliefs be worth recognising and upgrading *prior* to embarking on your career, or the next few thousand hours of practice? Compare the following two belief systems ("belief bubbles"). Which of them do you think is more likely to lead to excellence in pianism?

Belief Bubble #1

- Small-scale vision of the artistic experience and career:
  → *"If I get through the concert, perhaps they'll invite me back again."*
- Unclear musical ideas:
  → *"I really don't understand this piece. Hopefully if I just play the notes right the piece will sound ok."*
- Wrong mechanical information:
  → *"I keep trying to play with arm weight, as my teacher recommends, but my playing is getting worse. It's lumpy and inaccurate."*
- Unhelpful mental processes:
  → *"I had memory lapses again—I am not a good memoriser."*

Belief Bubble #2

- Large-scale vision of the artistic experience and career potential:
  → *"I have prepared a unique programme for my audience. I will engage with them in a way that they have never experienced before that will leave them wanting more."*
- Creative ideas:
  → *"My interpretations are novel, I know it—I've experimented with the elements of the music to find new effects and emotions."*
- Useful mechanical information:
  → *"For every passage, I have solved the motor-mechanical problems—I feel in control of my playing and am ready to play on any instrument in any scenario."*
- Strategic mental processes:
  → *"Three weeks before the concert, I divided up my practice time and systematically worked through a priority list of problems to be solved, enhancing my physical practice with memory strategies to ensure maximal learning effectiveness."*

Here, the contents of Belief Bubble #1 are unhelpful. They are infused with negativity and feelings of disempowerment. Each time its beliefs are put into practice, they interact with reality in a suboptimal way. The full potential of this person's pianism is denied before it has had the chance to excel. By contrast, Belief Bubble #2 is full of positivity, striving to push the limits of their artistry further and using the full range of resources available to them. It does not mean that they will succeed, but if they think bigger and act better, they are massively increasing their chances of excelling.

Building New Belief Bubbles

Exercise 1.
One simple way of creating an improved belief system is . . . to create an improved belief system. Imagine removing yourself from your current system of thoughts and placing yourself into a new one—an *ideal* one—that you have created just for you (e.g., like replacing the thoughts of Bubble #1 with those of Bubble #2). Inside your new Belief Bubble, you may include anything you want. Believe that everything is possible. You may even ignore logic, science and evidence—that's what belief systems do. Create your ultimate pianism: one that you really, *really* want to exist, technically and artistically. Be courageous and generous with yourself, because whatever you put into this "pianistic self-image" will define the limits of your future pianism. You will not be able to outperform this self-image.

Exercise 2.
As an alternative exercise, imagine what it might feel like to be inside your favorite pianist's Belief Bubble. For example, knowing what you know of Liszt, how do you think his beliefs shaped the 3 Ms of his piano playing? If you jumped into his bubble and made it yours, how would you think and play? What if you chose Cortot, Tureck or De Pachmann? Equally, if somebody else chose to be inside your belief bubble, what would they say? How would they end up playing? Existentially, looking from the outside, *what would you say to yourself* about your pianistic beliefs and your approach to playing?

I'M RIGHT BECAUSE . . . —COGNITIVE BIASES

Cognitive biases are "automatic patterns of thought that sometimes distort thinking and potentially lead to errors."[12] There are over two hundred known biases ready to strike into action when we judge information[13] and it is worth considering how they affect our decision-making about our pianism. We may not think they are important, but these biases, like beliefs, influence everything from our global attitude toward our pianism down to the hundreds of second-by-second decisions that we make about it in the practice room. Their accumulative effect is, therefore, significant.

If our subconscious biases are already helping us to be the pianist that we want, then, like beliefs, there is no strong reason to interrogate them. Some (lucky) pianists, whose biases unconsciously provide them with the right set of pianistic conditions in which to thrive, may not feel any need to know why their playing works. Other pianists may have biases that, while doing no apparent harm, do not allow for maximal improvement. Occasionally, biases may cause us to engage in actions that violate the laws of physics and physiology—like when subjecting muscles and joints to physically impossible tasks. These biases are dangerous because they are so obtusely detached from reality that they are likely to cause physical injury, if not immediately, years down the track, when the consequences for having habituated the wrong information are finally realized.

10 Believable Beliefs about Pianism: True or False, and Why?

Read the following pedagogical statements. Choose a response. What beliefs and biases underlie your responses?

1. *It is better to play with flatter fingers than curved fingers.*
2. *Your sitting position influences the quality of your sound.*
3. *Rachmaninoff practiced scales and Hanon, and so should you.*
4. *Playing deeply into the key helps to project the tone.*
5. *Good posture improves your pianism.*
6. *Use arm weight to produce a full, singing tone.*
7. *Neuhaus was a great teacher as he produced so many great players.*
8. *An expert pianist can produce better piano-tone quality than an amateur.*
9. *Strengthening the muscles in your hand will give you more control.*
10. *One shouldn't use the pedals when playing Bach or Mozart.*

Whatever response you chose, imagine, now, that you believe in an *alternative* or *opposite* statement. How would this change the way that you practice? Would it allow you to let go of certain ways of playing or practicing?

Note the following list of common cognitive biases and how they can affect our pianism:

- Confirmation bias—where information in your environment is selectively interpreted in your favor to reinforce your current beliefs.

    e.g., *I press deeply into the key to produce an espressivo sound, and so did Beethoven.*

    e.g., *I sit high at the keyboard, as both my teacher and Arthur Rubinstein also did.*

    → *... therefore it must be right.*

In humans, much of the belief-affirming, reality-filtration processes carried out by the mind are examples of *confirmation bias*. In the world of piano playing, this bias is responsible for perpetuating many of piano pedagogy's biggest lies. Rightly, confirmation bias has been called "the mother of all misconceptions."[14]

- Authority bias—accepting information because it comes from an authority.

    e.g., *Liszt said to practice that way.*
    e.g., *My famous teacher from conservatory XYZ recommended it.*
    → ... *therefore it must be right.*

- Social Proof—accepting information because everybody else is doing it.

    e.g., *Everybody practices Hanon in my class.*
    e.g., *All the other pianists I've seen at my school are playing like that.*
    → ... *therefore it must be ok.*

- Contrast Effect—downgrading information because it is not dramatic or obvious.

    e.g., *I've been practicing like that for years and have never had any problems.*
    e.g., *The advice was so easy to implement that I did not value it very highly.*
    → ... *therefore I continue doing what I am doing.*

- Availability bias—believing information that is easily available or memorable to the mind.

    e.g., *I practice octaves that way because the book on my shelf recommended it.*
    e.g., *I learned from the best pianists in my town.*
    → ... *therefore that must be the way to play.*

Like beliefs, our biases are important to recognize because they can provide us with reassurances about our playing despite there being flaws within it. When it comes to optimizing our practice, *quality* information is what we need to put into practice: information that allows us to play mechanically, mentally and musically optimally. Quality information has nothing to do with being popular, arising from an authority or being expensive.

Reasons to Caution What You Believe In (and Why)

- Expert pianists disagree on many aspects of piano pedagogy (i.e., there is no consensus of opinion. See Part II.)
- What an expert pianist says may not correlate with what they *do*, what *else* they do, or what they have *previously* done. (Missing information and confounding factors invalidate links of causality.)
- An association between two events does not prove causality. For example, just because Rachmaninoff practiced Hanon[15] *and* was an expert pianist, does not mean that practicing Hanon *made* him an expert pianist. (Again, missing information and confounding factors invalidate the links of causality.)
- What works for one pianist may not work for you. (Case studies and anecdotes of success do not prove their universality.[16])
- Some pedagogical methods serve a social, self-interested or commercial goal, not a pianistic one (i.e., there is a conflict of interest regarding the information that they share).[17]
- Suboptimal performance and injuries are rarely included in the outcomes of the piano methods being promoted (i.e., conclusions are being made from incomplete data sets).[18]

NOTES

1. Donovan, Sandy. *Hypatia : Mathematician, Inventor, and Philosopher*. Minneapolis: Compass Point Books, 2008, 42.

2. Rankin, Catharine H., Thomas Abrams, Robert J. Barry, Seema Bhatnagar, David F. Clayton, John Colombo, Gianluca Coppola, et al. "Habituation Revisited: An Updated and Revised Description of the Behavioral Characteristics of Habituation." *Neurobiology of Learning and Memory* 92, no. 2 (September 2009): 135–38. doi:https://doi.org/10.1016/j.nlm.2008.09.012.

3. Connors, Michael H., and Peter W. Halligan. "A Cognitive Account of Belief: A Tentative Road Map." *Frontiers in Psychology* 5 (February 13, 2015). doi:https://doi.org/10.3389/fpsyg.2014.01588.

4. Jones, Josh. "Igor Stravinsky Remembers the 'Riotous' Premiere of His Rite of Spring in 1913: 'They Were Very Shocked. They Were Naive and Stupid People.'" *Open Culture*, 2018. https://www.openculture.com/2018/04/igor-stravinsky-remembers-the-riotous-premiere-of-his-rite-of-spring.html.

5. Alford, Robert R., and Andras Szanto. "Orpheus Wounded: The Experience of Pain in the Professional Worlds of the Piano." *Theory and Society* 25, no. 1 (February 1996): 1–44. doi:https://doi.org/10.1007/bf00140757, 35.

6. Harari, Yuval Noah. *Sapiens: A Brief History of Humankind*. New York: HarperPerennial, 2015, 236.

7. Stephens, G. Lynn, and George Graham. "Reconceiving Delusion." *International Review of Psychiatry* 16, no. 3 (August 2004): 236–41. doi:https://doi.org/10.1080/09540260400003982.

8. Leach, Stefan, and Mario Weick. "Can People Judge the Veracity of Their Intuitions?" *Social Psychological and Personality Science* 9, no. 1 (July 31, 2017): 40–49. doi:https://doi.org/10.1177/1948550617706732.

9. Personal account, from pianist Darryl Cremasco. darrylspiano."Sonata Deformed: An Injured Musician's Chronicle Pt.1." *Darryl's Piano*, March 5, 2018. https://darrylspiano.com/2018/03/04/sonata-deformed-an-injured-musicians-chronicle-pt-1/.

10. Information that conflicts with an established belief system is called a *meaning threat*. Tullett, Alexa M, Mike S Prentice, Rimma Teper, Kyle A Nash, Michael Inzlicht, and Ian McGregor. "Neural and Motivational Mechanics of Meaning and Threat." *American Psychological Association EBooks*, January 1, 2013, 401–19. doi:https://doi.org/10.1037/14040-020.

11. Lewandowsky, Stephan, Ullrich K. H. Ecker, Colleen M. Seifert, Norbert Schwarz, and John Cook. "Misinformation and Its Correction: Continued Influence and Successful Debiasing." *Psychological Science in the Public Interest* 13, no. 3 (September 17, 2012): 106–31. doi:https://doi.org/10.1177/1529100612451018; Dossey, Larry. "Compasses, Craziness, and the Thieves of Reason: How Thinking Goes Wrong." *EXPLORE* 12, no. 5 (September 2016): 295–301. doi:https://doi.org/10.1016/j.explore.2016.06.007.

12. Howard, Jonathan. *Cognitive Errors and Diagnostic Mistakes*. Cham, Switzerland: Springer International Publishing, 2019. doi:https://doi.org/10.1007/978-3-319-93224-8, 4.

13. Howard, Jonathan. *Cognitive Errors and Diagnostic Mistakes*. Cham, Switzerland: Springer International Publishing, 2019. doi:https://doi.org/10.1007/978-3-319-93224-8, 4.

14. Dobelli's book is a very readable introduction to understanding how our minds are susceptible to unconscious biases. Dobelli, Rolf. *The Art of Thinking Clearly*. London: Sceptre, 2014.

15. Cooke, James Francis. *Great Pianists on Piano Playing: Godowsky, Hofmann, Lhévinne, Paderewski, and 24 Other Legendary Performers*. Mineola, NY: Dover Publications, 1999, 210–211.

16. In terms of scientific quality of evidence, anecdotes and expert opinion rank the lowest. Oxford Centre for Evidence-Based Medicine. "Oxford Centre for Evidence-Based Medicine: Levels of Evidence (March 2009)—Centre for Evidence-Based Medicine, University of Oxford." *Www.cebm.ox.ac.uk*, 2009. https://www.cebm.ox.ac.uk/resources/levels-of-evidence/oxford-centre-for-evidence-based-medicine-levels-of-evidence-march-2009.

17. For example, Hanon's *The Virtuoso Pianist* was written for the benefit of teaching poor, homeless children in a northern village of France, and Kalkbrenner promoted his hand-rail device (and its associated finger-touch method) for his own

personal and financial gain. Adams, Andrew, and Bradley Martin. "The Man behind the Virtuoso Pianist: Charles-Louis Hanon's Life and Works." *Hanon-Online*, 2014. https://www.hanon-online.com/the-man-behind-the-virtuoso-pianist-charles-louis-hanon-s-life-and-works-p1/. Weitzmann, Karl Friedrich, Otto Lessmann, and Theodore Baker. 1893. *A History of Pianoforte-Playing and Pianoforte-Literature*. From the 2d augm. and rev. German ed., by Dr. Th. Baker. New York: G. Schirmer.

18. Certainly, if the narratives of all the injured pianists were taken into account, certain methods of practice may not be viewed so favorably. (Read Alford and Szanto, *Orpheus Wounded: The Experience of Pain in the Professional Worlds of the Piano*).

Chapter 2

Mind Traps and Mental Shortcuts

"Neither the quantity nor the quality of the evidence counts for much in subjective confidence"[1]—Daniel Kahneman

Many of the reasons for the decision-making mistakes that we make in pianism—and in life—are a result of the mind's tendency to believe in the assumptions that it generates. Nobel Prize winner, Daniel Kahneman, in his book, *Thinking, Fast and Slow*,[2] makes a comprehensive study of this, and this section looks at how we, as pianists, may be able to benefit from his research.

Kahneman argues that over millions of years, the brain has evolved to be able to make quick decisions about its environment (based on learned assumptions and associations) and deliberate decisions (based on reasoning). He categorizes these mental algorithms as System 1 and System 2, respectively. As pianists, we benefit from both these processes, but it is the mental shortcuts of System 1 that usually lead us to errors of judgment.

As Kahneman points out, when assumptions are repeated regularly and made more familiar to us (like with political propaganda, marketing campaigns—or weekly piano lessons), they more easily turn into beliefs. But as popular as any idea might be, *familiar* does not mean *factual*—familiar just means it has been habituated.[3] The mistakes that humans create for themselves by confusing feelings with facts are as common as they are comical. In life, they lead to real-world behaviors like believing that the Sun revolves around the Earth (it *appears* that way), saying a prayer to your god before sleeping at night (*feeling* the need for protection), or drinking excess amounts of water to "cleanse the body" (logically, "clean is good," right?)[4] They *feel* right, *feel* logical and *feel* true—having also been endorsed by those who *feel* the same belief—but are no more influential on objective outcomes than doing nothing, saying hello to a frog or hugging a tree.

Regarding piano methods and traditions, much the same can be said, where we engage in practices that *feel* right, *feel* logical and *feel* true—and are endorsed by many—but are no better at improving our pianism than not engaging in them at all. Believing that sitting low and playing with flat fingers, hoping that it will make our sound more like Horowitz, is a classic example of a corner-cutting assumption that our mind's System 1 tries to sell us. The assumption is association-based and data-limited—not to mention, data erroneous. Committing to the assumption won't help us one bit. Here, should we really want to embrace System 1's proposal, in addition to sitting low and playing with flat fingers, we might also learn to speak Russian, place a scrunched-up handkerchief on our piano and change our surname to start with the letter "H."[5]

True-or-False? Comparing Thinking System 1 with Thinking System 2

Assumption: "Flat-finger techniques are better than curled-finger techniques."

System 1's (fast, associative) response says, "Yes" because:

- *"I see many great pianists playing with flat fingers, like Horowitz."*
- *"My (famous) teacher and other colleagues talk about the benefits of flat-finger playing."*
- *"I've heard that flat-finger playing is better for injury prevention."*
- *"Playing with flat fingers helps to get the fleshy part of the fingertip to push into the key, which helps it achieve a singing quality."*
- *"I've always used flat fingers and I'm happy with my playing."*

but . . .

System 2's (slow, interrogative) response might be critical and say "No" because:

- *"I've seen just as many great pianists use normally curved fingers, and in fact, I've noticed that Horowitz plays with curled fingers lots of the time too."*
- *"My current teacher, and many others I know, do not see any particular benefit from curled or flat-finger techniques, and nor do my colleagues."*
- *"Injuries are caused by many factors, and many pianists get injured for reasons that have nothing to do with the degree of finger curl."*

> In fact, routinely playing with flat fingers can create other problems that curled fingers would avoid."
> - "I've not seen any evidence that playing with the fleshy part of the finger makes a more singing tone quality, whatever that may be."
> - "I've never needed to deliberately try to use flat fingers, and I'm very happy with my playing."

Kahneman proposes that (mistaken) beliefs about causality are made when the information about them is *associatively coherent*.[6] He writes, "the measure of success for System 1 is the coherence of the story it manages to create. The amount and quality of the data on which the story is based are largely irrelevant."[7] This is exactly what the above examples show. They ooze with confirmation bias, appealing to what we want to believe in with their emotional appeal and coherent stories but, ultimately, remaining void of facts.

Unless System 1's assumptions receive System 2's critical check, System 1's ideas will pervade the decisions that you make about your pianism.

REALITY EVASION #1—THE *I'M RIGHT* PIANIST

Adding to the pianist's fact-finding problem, is that the success of the associative system is enhanced by the laziness of the rational mind (System 2) to exert effort to challenge it. Kahneman writes, "errors of intuitive thought are often difficult to prevent. Biases cannot always be avoided, because System 2 may have no clue to the error."[8] Thus, like other beliefs, any self-generated assumption about piano playing that *appears* to work, will automatically become a self-certified winner (especially if it can be propagated through a group of like-minded pianists).

To demonstrate the point, suppose that a pianist wants to adopt a flat-finger technique for their playing (whatever that should mean), and that a flat-finger technique is supported by their teacher, their institution and everybody else within their pianistic context. This pianist would have every reason to believe in flat-fingered playing and no reason to doubt it. The pianist's belief about flat-fingered playing would maintain perfect associative coherence and, like all the other participants who share in the flat-fingered idea, will conclude that they are right to adopt it.

Flat-fingered playing may help some pianists solve some pianistic problems but for those for whom it doesn't, we might ask: why make the technical change in the first place? Why join System 1's speculative narrative of flat-fingered playing if the source of the pianistic problem lies elsewhere, like with poor sound organization, poor imagination or poor listening skills? And, to throw more reality at the belief, flat-fingered playing is not without its own physical and physiological problems too (see Part III). Has this been considered?

The matter of concern here, and elsewhere in pedagogy, is *not* that "flat-fingered playing" is good or bad, *nor* that "curved-fingered playing" is good or bad, but *the insistence in the belief* that one is better than the other when there is little or no supporting evidence.

The concept of associative coherence can go a long way to explaining how the belief systems of piano pedagogy are constructed and perpetuated. Take, for example, the following sequence of assumptions that surround the production of "a long, *cantabile* piano sound":

1. The mind makes up a coherent story to explain a certain pianistic phenomena:

    "A long cantabile sound is produced by playing deeply with sustained pressure into the key."

    ↓

2. What-you-see-is-all-there-is (WYSIATI)[9] arguments that do not rely on facts substantiate the story:

    "A deep, sustained pressure with the finger feels like it helps to sustain the tone."

    ↓

3. The validity of the story goes unchallenged because the story appears to be plausible, and System 2 is never activated (because it has never become aware of the assumptions being made):

    "I have no reason to think otherwise, the deep sustained pressure helps to produce a long cantabile sound."

    ↓

4. The story—self-fulfilling before it was ever challenged—fits seamlessly into the pianist's belief system, serving to reinforce it for next time.

"My approach to producing a long cantabile sound works. I have no reason to think otherwise and it agrees with what others say about it. I will share this information with my students and colleagues."

In piano pedagogy, "I'm right" arguments flourish despite them having no objective proof. Thankfully, however—by sheer luck (as we will see in Parts II and III)—most pianists avoid the dire consequences of their cognitive biases because most of the time, what they think is happening, isn't, and what they don't think is happening, is.

REALITY EVASION #2—THE *I COULD'VE IF I'D WANTED TO* PIANIST

The last category of thought errors that will be discussed arise from *cognitive dissonance*—the engine room of the *I-could've-if-I'd-wanted-to* pianist. Here, pianists, in spite of being aware of important information, shy away from it and choose to follow a substandard pathway of action. There is a conflict between what the mind *wants* to be true and what *is* true (in reality), and the mind escapes from the discomfort by seeking "conflict reduction and preference change"[10], by looking for excuses, belittling facts and rationalizing alternative (easier) solutions. It is analogous to the backfire rejection responses to a meaning threat, as described earlier.

Consider the list of excuses made by pianists (see the textbox below). Each scenario hints at a real pianistic problem that needs solving but which the pianist circumnavigates with an excuse—to minimize the cognitive dissonance. Suboptimal pianistic outcomes are the long-term result.

Common Excuses Made by Pianists

- "Nobody will notice that it isn't perfect."
  → This might be true, but who are you kidding? Something is not working. You need to fix it. Your playing is not optimized.
- "This information doesn't apply to me because I'm a successful player."
  → Yes, it does. All players are subject to the same physical laws and the processes of physiology. Perhaps you could be even better if you acted upon all the information available to you.
- "I know that my left wrist often gets too stiff, but I can still play most things OK."

> - → No, the stiff wrist is a sign of a coordination problem. It will limit your technical options, if not now, later.
> - "I don't need to worry; the problem should go away by itself."
>   - → No, there is a problem. It has got there for some reason and there is no reason why it should miraculously just go away.
> - "I could have played it better if I'd wanted to."
>   - → No, admit that you can't play it. If you could reliably play it well, you would have.
> - "My memory is usually good; I'm just having some bad days."
>   - → No, your memory has become unreliable. You need to find out why and work to secure it.
> - "I don't like Chopin etudes."
>   - → Actually, no, you haven't yet worked out how to play them (whereupon you might like them).

By contrast, the attitudes and behaviors (and lack of cognitive dissonance) of the following well-known keyboard players is noteworthy:

"Ceaseless work, analysis, reflection, writing much, endless self-correction, that is my secret."—J. S. Bach

"Nothing is more intolerable than to have to admit to yourself your own errors."—Beethoven

"I should think myself at the apex of my career; yet I know how much I still lack, to reach perfection."—Chopin

Filling in the Gap: "Minding" the Information Gap

Along with System 1's predilection for making quick assumptions about the touch-tone relationship based on limited information, there is a further reason why our understanding of the tone-touch relationship can become so lost from reality: it is because the key-lever-hammer-string interaction is *hidden from our view*, thereby removing much of the important reality-based information that the brain needs in order to make better hypotheses.

With feelings mobilized during piano playing, System 1 remains the master storyteller, not the fact detective, and happily fills in the information gap to maintain the upkeep of the operator's belief system. As Kahneman says, "The gap [in knowledge] is filled in by a guess that fits one's emotional response"[11] and the guess is taken as truth. This cognitive muddle, so frequently seen in piano pedagogy, is the driving force behind the information that feeds into an unfathomable number of piano methods, teaching studios and our private practice sessions. Collectively, they create the confusion that leaves us unable to know what actually matters when we learn technique, and unable to fix problems when things don't work.

Oddly, compared to other instrumentalists, the pianists' problem of needing to guess how tone quality is "produced" is rather unique, for it is a problem that stems from the fact that the pianist's touch *indirectly* produces its sound (via a series of hidden levers and a free-flying hammer hitting a string). Other instrumentalists, who can *directly* manipulate the sound at the moment of sound production, (e.g., via a bow touching a string, or the embouchure on a mouthpiece) do not need to guess as much, as the mind has less missing information to fill in as to the chain of events that link one's touch to one's tone. One might even say that it is a credit to the leading piano makers that we, as pianists, who cannot directly participate in the touch-tone interaction (the hammer, not the finger, hits the string) are so readily convinced that the qualities of our touch are transferred into the qualities of our tone.

PIANISTIC IMPLICATIONS OF YOUR BELIEFS

Evidently, much of piano pedagogy is based on speculative beliefs that may or may not correlate with reality, may or may not lead to optimal pianistic outcomes, and may or may not cause harm. It is not a very convincing panorama. Nevertheless, the point of the book is not to criticize pianists, teachers, and institutions, nor discredit the formidable wealth of material—and enjoyment—that can be used as we play the piano. The purpose is to highlight that if we are 100 percent committed to excellence, we need to be *much* more selective about the information that we put into practice. An Olympic sportsperson would do no less, nor expect any less from their sports-science team.

Although most of our beliefs and biases operate without any conscious thought, the following textbox reminds us that the outcomes they cause are, nevertheless, very real. So much of what we do—and become—is an outcome of them. The examples may seem obvious (in hindsight) but this is because, most of the time, our day-to-day pianism is working well enough in its current environment that we have no reason to seek out the assumptions that are driving it. Our thoughts and habits are molded to our environment. "The mind is not merely embodied, but embodied in such a way that our conceptual systems draw largely upon the commonalities of our bodies and of the environments we live in."[12] Habituation is at work, shielding us from the realities that lie beyond the comforts of its walls.

Pianistic Implications of Your Beliefs

- Sound. Your beliefs about touch and tone will influence the type of movements that you use and, subsequently, the types of sounds that you produce.
  - → e.g., if you think that a rich sound requires a slow movement of weight into the key, you will adopt such a movement, acquire the habit of using that movement, and be stuck with the type of sound that that movement provides.
- Posture and Positions. Your beliefs about touch and tone will influence what positions you choose for your fingers, hand, wrist and sitting position.
  - → e.g., if you think that Gould's playing was better because he sat low and played with flat fingers, and you choose to do the same, be prepared for the physical and pianistic changes that this will bring.
- Technical. Your beliefs about the mechanics of touch will influence the choices that you make about your movements and how to practice them.
  - → e.g., if you think that playing fast and evenly requires you to practice Hanon using an isolated finger stroke, then this is what you will end up doing.
- Musical imagination. Your beliefs about the limits of the touch-tone interaction will affect what you think is musically possible.
  - → e.g., if you think that you need to learn how to touch the key in a specific way to produce a certain sound, then you may be limiting yourself to the sound worlds that that touch offers. Whereas, if your imagination guides your touch, you may find new ways of touching the key that you had not previously thought of.

- Psychological. Your beliefs about pianism and your role as a pianist will be reflected in your playing on stage and through the sounds you make.
  - → e.g., if you think that your goal as a pianist is to play all the notes on the page as written, and you fail to do so, will you consider this a failure as your role as a pianist?
- Practice. Your beliefs about how touch and sounds are learned will affect the amount and the way that you practice.
  - → e.g., if you think that you have to learn specific movements to produce certain sounds, then this will occupy your practice time.
- Injury. Your beliefs about tone causality and motor-skills learning may lead you to practice in ways that disrespect physiological limits and lead to injury.
  - → e.g., if you think that playing strongly into the key bed is good for your keystroke, then expect the consequences of doing so.
- Audience. Your beliefs about the purpose of gestures during performance will influence the musical meaning that you provide to your listeners.
  - → e.g., if you think that the only function of your movements is to control sound, then accept that this may limit the experience that your performances provide to your listeners.
- Pedagogical. Your beliefs about how pianism "works" will affect how you assess pianism in yourself and in others.
  - → e.g., if you think that the best way of playing is the way that you know, then your playing will be shaped by that knowledge.

This list raises many questions about the central importance that our touch-tone beliefs have in guiding our practice (and teaching) habits. Certainly, given the way that our mind plays tricks on us, it suggests that, before anything, we ought to be upgrading our levels of awareness and checking that what we endorse in our practice room is in our long-term interest. Until we have a better understanding of "what causes what" in piano playing, we should not be blindly praising any pedagogical method any more than we should be criticizing it.

While we are quick to praise the pedagogical methods that lead to "successful" pianism, why is it that we do not enquire about the lives and practice habits of the "failed" pianists who never achieved their potential or got injured along the way? Why are the negative consequences of certain pedagogical methods never challenged or held to account? And how is it that teachers and institutions can continue to justify their teaching methods when these failed pianists were products of the same teaching methods in which others succeeded? Is it because these pianists were following recommended pedagogical traditions and failed, or is it because they were not following recommended traditions and failed? Why do we not seek to clarify what the critical factors are that allow virtuosic pianism to work and what the main factors are that put it at risk of going wrong? Would this not save us all from a lot of unnecessary misadventure?

NOTES

1. Kahneman, Daniel. *Thinking, Fast and Slow*. London: Penguin, 2011, 87.
2. Kahneman, Daniel. *Thinking, Fast and Slow*. London: Penguin, 2011.
3. Hassan, Aumyo, and Sarah J. Barber. "The Effects of Repetition Frequency on the Illusory Truth Effect." *Cognitive Research: Principles and Implications* 6, no. 1 (May 13, 2021). doi:https://doi.org/10.1186/s41235-021-00301-5; Swire, Briony, Ullrich K. H. Ecker, and Stephan Lewandowsky. "The Role of Familiarity in Correcting Inaccurate Information." *Journal of Experimental Psychology: Learning, Memory, and Cognition* 43, no. 12 (December 2017): 1948–61. doi:https://doi.org/10.1037/xlm0000422.
4. Drinking too much water will only make you urinate more as the body tries to remove the excess water and avoid the potential life-threating effects of electrolyte dilution.
5. Which, adding more folly to the argument, in Russian, starts with a "G," not an "H."
6. Kahneman, Daniel. *Thinking, Fast and Slow*. London: Penguin, 2011, 51.
7. Kahneman, Daniel. *Thinking, Fast and Slow*. London: Penguin, 2011, 85.
8. Kahneman, Daniel. *Thinking, Fast and Slow*. London: Penguin, 2011, 28.
9. Kahneman, Daniel. *Thinking, Fast and Slow*. London: Penguin, 2011, 86.
10. Colosio, Marco, Anna Shestakova, Vadim V. Nikulin, Evgeny Blagovechtchenski, and Vasily Klucharev. "Neural Mechanisms of Cognitive Dissonance (Revised): An EEG Study." *The Journal of Neuroscience* 37, no. 20 (April 24, 2017): 5074–83. doi:https://doi.org/10.1523/jneurosci.3209-16.2017.
11. Kahneman, Daniel. *Thinking, Fast and Slow*. London: Penguin, 2011, 82.
12. Lakoff, George, and Mark Johnson. *Philosophy in the Flesh: The Embodied Mind and Its Challenge to Western Thought*. New York: Basic Books, 1999.

Part II

TOUCH BELIEFS AND REALITIES

"Art is a lie that makes us realize truth [...] The artist must know the manner whereby to convince others of the truthfulness of his lies."[1]
—Pablo Picasso

---

1. Picasso, Pablo. "Picasso Speaks: A Statement by the Artist." *The Arts: An Illustrated Monthly Magazine Covering All Phases of Ancient and Modern Art*, vol. 3, no. 5, January–June 1923, 315.

Chapter 3

The Touch-Tone Relationship—Performers' Perspectives

"The notion of illusion is bound up with the very principle of piano sound."[1]—Samuil Feinberg

The debate as to whether a pianist can cause changes in the quality of a piano tone quality (timbre) *independent of its quantity* by means of touch is long-standing. It has traditionally been considered a science-versus-art debate, where scientists describe tone production as a mechanico-acoustic event—where the intensity and harmonics of the produced tone are dependent on the speed at which the hammer hits the string—and where performers (artists) describe the interaction more subjectively, claiming that "a certain something" can be done to the key, and *needs* to be done, during the act of touch to alter its timbre independently of its volume.

Each viewpoint has different implications. The implication of the scientist's view is that any amateur pianist (or inanimate object) can produce a note of the same tonal quality as that of an experienced pianist. The implication of the artist's view is that pianists can (and need to) *acquire* the skill of playing notes with equal dynamics but different timbres. Each viewpoint necessarily influences how we practice, for if our touch *does not* alter tone quality independently of its volume, the role of touch can immediately be objectified and directed toward producing desired sounds with optimized keystroke biomechanics. Whereas, if different types of touch *do* vary tone quality, we will need to invest time in learning the different types of movements that produce such timbral changes and accept that those movements may introduce another layer of complexity into one's technique and movements that may not coincide with optimal biomechanics.

Given that there is more than two hundred years' worth of modern piano-playing pedagogy to draw from, we might expect agreement on the subject of how to press down the key and what to expect from it. But this is not the case—especially among experts. This should raise alarm bells as to the validity of any touch-tone relationship claim, and any piano method that is derived from it, as it suggests that there is something *substantively missing* in our understanding of how the touch-tone interaction functions.

This chapter categorizes the variety of opinions that pianists hold about how touch affects tone quality. Besides showing the disparity of these opinions, the intention is to show that depending on how we *think* about the function of the touch-tone interaction, it will influence our touch behaviors and, ultimately, lead us toward different pianistic endpoints. Following the presentation of these different opinions, the same topics will be discussed from the point of view of science. It is not a right-versus-wrong witch-hunt, but it does show that the mismatch between what pianists *think* happens and what *actually* happens when a note is played can be extreme.

TONE QUALITY—WHAT DETERMINES TONE QUALITY?

> **Checking Your Touch-Tone Assumptions**
>
> Choose a note on the piano and play it *mf* with a "bright" quality. Next, play it *mf* with a "dull" quality. Try to make the volume the same for each note. What aspects of your touch did you change in attempting to produce the two different sound qualities? Why? How do you know that the sound quality actually changed? Could other people detect the same change that you heard if they closed their eyes or listened to a recorded sound? What do you assume about the physical relationship between your touch and the tone quality? Does this assumption affect the way that you approach your keystrokes—or teach them?

The way in which tone quality is described—and thought to exist—gives us many clues as to what some of our touch-tone assumptions might be and why so many pedagogical theories about touch and technique are questionable. To begin the discussion of the touch-tone relationship, let us examine a large sample of expert opinions about how to produce a piano tone with a "singing" (*cantabile*) quality.

Josef Lhévinne, in his book, *Basic Principles in Pianoforte Playing*, devotes an entire chapter to "The Secret of a Beautiful Tone" and a further section to "The ringing, singing tone" where, using a variety of subjective concepts and adjectives, he defines it and outlines a technical approach to achieving it.[2] Understandably, the metaphorical link between "beautiful," "ringing," and "singing," encourages pianists to think in vocal (non-percussive) ways, but there is a flaw in his argument: who decides what is "ringing," "singing," and "beautiful"? Is the quality absolute or relative?

Lhévinne believed that "by hard work and experience in listening to pianists who do possess a beautiful tone, you may develop it."[3] Similarly, the famed Russian teacher, Heinrich Neuhaus wrote, "the first and main concern of every pianist should be to acquire a deep, full, rich tone."[4] Implicitly, Lhévinne and Neuhaus (both famed teacher-pianists of the Russian school) believed that tone quality *existed*, that there was something *absolute* about it, and that *it could be learned* by copying or by instruction.

By contrast, other pianists classify tone quality as a relative phenomenon. Percy Grainger, for example, believed that differences in tone quality were achieved "by contrasts of quantity, or different sound strengths."[5] Abby Whiteside categorically dismissed the existence of tone quality, stating, "one cannot "color" a piano tone [...] There is no such thing as a 'singing' tone with the piano."[6] And Samuil Feinberg, challenged that "we cannot distinguish whether the key is pressed down by a finger, by a wad of cotton wool, or—with the same intensity—by a piece of metal."[7] Implicitly, these pianists believed that neither the concept of absolute quality existed (for individual tones), nor was there any specific need to *learn* it.

That the act of tone production should have any formal pedagogical method attached to it *at all*, is bypassed by those who believe that tone quality is a relative phenomenon. Horowitz, for example, admitted that, "To be able to produce many varieties of sound, now that is what I call technique [...] I don't adhere to any methods,"[8] "the secret lies mainly in contrast."[9] Similarly, Gieseking argued that, "It is useless to look for the reason of the beautiful tone in some particular finger position or hand position [...] the only way to learn to produce beautiful tone is systematic ear training."[10] Also, Anton Rubinstein reportedly, "paid little attention to a theory of touch"[11] and achieved his beautiful sound "more by willing the tone rather than by touching the key in any particular way."[12] These pianists believed that no formal correlation needed to be made about the touch and its resultant tone quality. Simply, the keystroke was deemed correct if it fulfilled their musical needs.

USING THE BODY—FAT, SKINNY, CURLED, OR STRAIGHT FINGERS?

Quality Depends on Your Finger Shape and Position

Furthering the debate on whether different tone qualities can exist for notes of the same volume, are the opinions of pianists regarding how it is achieved. One area of belief is that the shape and anatomical position of the finger during its contact with the key makes a difference. For example, "flat-finger" playing is often recommended as a way to enhance the singing quality of a piano tone. As Leschetizky writes, "the elastic finger-tip gives a richer tone"[13] and as Horowitz stated, "You get a better sound that way [...] the entire ball of the finger, not merely the tip, is on the key."[14] Leon Fleisher deliberately instructed students to play the key with flat fingers to obtain a singing, "carrying" sound.[15]

By contrast, however, Hummel maintained that "extending the fingers flat on the keys [...] are altogether faulty positions"[16] and John Field's famous *cantabile* was apparently achieved "with fingers standing almost perpendicular to the keyboard."[17] Interestingly, Beethoven recommended that "the hand [be] contracted as much as possible"[18] when playing *cantabile*—an approach verified by Schindler, who observed Beethoven performing such passages with "tightly, curled fingers."[19] Such a curled-finger position also coincided with that of Brendel, who wrote that he used "rounded, hooked-under and, as it were, bony fingers to produce the oboe's singing tone."[20]

At other times, pianists claim that certain anatomical features of the hand are responsible for the different tonal outcomes. For example, Lhévinne stated how "[Anton] Rubinstein had a fat, pudgy hand, with fingers so broad at the fingertips [that] his glorious tone was in no small measure due to this."[21] And Leschetizky agreed, that "a well-trained piano hand is broad, flexible in the wrist, equipped with wide finger-tips, and muscular."[22]

Contradiction Alert: Mismatch between Claims and Outcomes?

If thick and wide fingertips are so important to a *cantabile* tone quality, what are we to make of the tone quality arising from Chopin's or Liszt's slender hands? Were they unable to produce a singing tone? What, too, are we to make of the often-observed finger-tip *cantabile* playing of pianistic virtuosi Ashkenazy, Pletnev, Iturbi, a multitude of others, and indeed Horowitz (who previously claimed that flat fingers were better)? And if a finger starts out flat but then immediately curls during its descent into the key, does this classify it as a flat finger or a curled finger? What about the thumb, playing on its side: does this exclude it from the possibility of being able to produce a *cantabile* tone?

Interrogating further, how does the piano know that you have played it with a fat, fleshy finger-tip or a skinny, bony finger-tip? Will its sound quality change halfway through the note if you change from flat finger to curled finger halfway through? And how does it know the feelings inside your body when you play it? What does it care? And further still, how are we supposed to judge the sound of a succession of notes played by different fingers that are each shaped differently and each curled by different amounts? Does the quality of the cantabile change with the degree of curvature of each finger, as many players are trying to claim? And if it does, how is it that these same pianists—the supposed experts at observing the finer nuances of the piano sound—accept the supposed tone quality irregularities that playing with differently curved fingers supposedly produces?

Bluntly, if neither the shape, the angle nor the finger-part alter the quality of the sound, why does any pianist (or teacher) insist *at all* about what part of the finger plays into the key? If the reason is for biomechanical reasons, this should be stated. If it is for psychological reasons, this too should be stated. Either reason may be completely valid for any given context, *but the presumption that one touch will necessarily fulfill both functions is misleading*—and wrong.

Quality Comes from Your Arm Weight

Arm-weight playing began to appear in piano technique during the nineteenth century. Initially, it served as a biomechanical aid to overcoming the increased key resistance, as Hummel remarked in 1829: "the touch [of the new Broadwood pianos] is much heavier, the key sinks much deeper."[23] Over time, however, arm-weight playing, and arm-weight pedagogy began to evolve toward being used not only *for* tone production (e.g., Breithaupt: "[the fingers] take turns in carrying and transmitting the weight[24]) but *as* tone quality (e.g., Lhévinne: "a touch without weight has no tone quality"[25]).

How pianists blur, merge or distinguish between the two functions of arm-weight playing should be noted. For example, Matthay believed that notes that are produced using muscular effort led to "harshness," whereas notes that are produced using arm weight are "full, round, sweet, [and have a] carrying quality."[26] Neuhaus maneuvered himself psychologically through the problem by encouraging the "fullest flexibility [with] relaxed weightiness."[27] Advocates of the Alexander technique insist that "quality of sound [...] is completely dependent upon freedom of the arm."[28] It is difficult to know with any degree of clarity what most of these descriptions are supposed to mean in physical-mechanical terms.

By contrast, the influential Stuttgart School of the late 1800s insisted on high finger-lifts and a fast finger attack to achieve "beautiful, rich tones."[29] Percy Grainger, for example, influenced by this school of pianism, asked for "stiff fingers, stiff wrist, stiff arm"[30] when projecting a melody line out from its surrounding accompaniment.

Contradiction Alert: Metaphors Exposed

Looking closer at arm-weight methods and the logic of the arguments that its ambassadors use, we might wish to seek a little more clarity as to how it works. We could start with some questions, like: what specific tone "quality" and what specific arm "freedom" are authors claiming to associate with arm-weight playing? Are we to believe that *more* arm weight and *more* arm freedom equate to *more* (or *better*) tone quality? And, by correlation, is *less* arm weight and *less* arm freedom equated to *less* (or *worse*) tone quality? And, if so, how is the supposedly tight, muscular *cantabile* playing of Grainger, Brendel, and Beethoven meant to be classified? Was the quality of their tone worse for playing with tighter muscles?

If only *some* amount of arm weight and arm freedom is needed to produce a tone of good quality, what amount is it? Is it in any way different to the amount required to just produce the necessary volume of the tone itself? And if it is different, what portion of the arm weight and/or freedom is supposed to be needed for the tone *quantity* and what portion is meant for the tone *quality*? How might the arm carry out such a division of roles?

Moreover, if a certain amount of weight is necessary to satisfy the requirements of a "sufficient" or "good" tone quality, would this amount be different for *ff* tones and *pp* tones, or Schubert tones or Scriabin tones? Do small children suffer a disadvantage for having lighter arms, or large adults have an advantage for having heavier arms? Existentially, how does the flying hammer inside the piano know how much muscular "freedom" or "tension" our muscles have? Again, what does it care? Has anybody stopped to consider that perhaps "arm-weight playing" has nothing to do with sound quality production but is, instead, a surrogate for some other physical or psychological factor that leads us to a specific feeling about sound quality?

In this example, in using (the belief of) arm-weight to produce good tone quality, it is clear that the *process* of producing the piano tone is being mixed up with the *goal* that the process strives for: i.e., the act of *full* weight is being equated to *full* tone. It is metaphorical. There is no proof of causality. It is the same logic used by rain dancers: to dance *vigorously* to promote a *vigorous* rainfall. No causality is demonstrated, just the feeling of one—a meaningful feeling, and perhaps an overwhelming one, but, nevertheless, a useless one, should rainfall be what needs to be produced. Piano pedagogy is full of such metaphors of understanding: and if your rain dance doesn't produce rain, it might be worth questioning the reason for the dance.

KEY CONTACT—POKE, PRESS, PULL, OR PUSH?

Understandably, the manner in which pianists touch and move the key is taken very seriously—it is *the* moment when the artist's ideas are converted into sound and music. The obsessive detail in which pianists describe the finger's *state* during the moment of touch gives us enormous insight into how we think about tone production, and, in turn, why touch-tone theories appear in such variety.

Quality Depends on the Key-Surface Contact

Clara Schumann's father (and teacher), Friedrich Wieck, advised that "the blow of the finger upon the key should never be audible, but only the music sound."[31] This view was also shared by John Field, who "most disliked [the] percussive attack on the keyboard itself"[32]—a claim verified by Glinka: "[He] did not actually strike the keys, but his fingers simply fell."[33] Chopin, too, carefully judged the finger-key impact, and asked that "the hand fall softly on the keys and feel the key rather than striking it!"[34] Similarly, Safonoff talked of "an elastic fall"[35] onto the keys.

Whether these pianists were trying to eliminate the contact noise or gain more mechanical control over the key, or both, is not clear, though it does appear that they were interested in *something* about the speed and weight of the fall of the finger, hand and arm onto the key. Somewhat uniquely, Gát openly expressed his interest in the relationship between touch, touch noise and sound quality. He neither encouraged nor discouraged touch noise, but saw it as a source of opportunity: "We should not renounce the tone-coloring effects attained by raising the fingers to [and dropping them from] different levels."[36] This parallels, in some way, to Leon Fleisher's pragmatic approach to the relationship between touch and tone, that "if you are trying to get a certain sound, you just experiment around to find the movement that will get this sound."[37]

Quality Depends on the Velocity of the Key's Descent

The speed of the descent of the finger into the key is also considered by some to be a factor in determining tone quality. For example, Matthay says that "If you want the sound to be beautiful in quality, you must set Key and String gradually into motion"[38] by increasing the key's "down-speed gradually—by acceleration."[39] Lhévinne also sought a smooth decent of the key, where there was "no spot, no place, no movement where the movement [of the key] seemed to stop on the way down."[40] Needless to say, this is the exact opposite of what the Stuttgart school was advocating, that a fast key descent is needed for a beautiful tone. We are left no closer to knowing which pathway is the best, the easiest or the most factual.

Quality Lies in the Keybed

In addition to the surface noises of touch, tone quality is also purported to be influenced by the noise made by the impact of the key on the keybed. For example, Mack Jost, a pupil of Ignaz Friedman, wrote: "weak tone quality [is] caused of course by not quite reaching the keybed."[41] Similarly, Levinskaya recommended that the fingers "Go deep into the keybeds"[42] and "[be] firmly held by the finger tip."[43] Alan Fraser goes one step further, claiming that tone quality is further influenced by remaining stuck to the keybed (obviously, after the hammer has hit the string), writing, "one must really dig in to the key and hold on heartily."[44]

But such keybed-promoting practices are certainly not universally accepted. Dorothy Taubman expressly advised never to "grip the keys"[45] and Matthay challenged that "it is wrong to squeeze the key upon the bed beneath"[46] on the grounds that "anything you do to the key after that moment cannot possibly help to make the sound in any way."[47] Interestingly, Boris Berman, like Jost, claimed that "every properly trained pianist is able to hear the difference between deep and shallow touch"[48] but advises that "the depth should not be exaggerated as it invites pressure, which in turn produces a forced, strangulated tone."[49]

> **Contradiction List: Where Tone Quality "Definitely" (!) Comes From**
>
> So far, from the survey of expert pianists and teachers we have looked at, we might conclude that the beautiful, singing *cantabile* piano tone is "definitely" due to any or all of the following:
>
> - *flat fingers* • *curved fingers* • *fat fingers* • *skinny fingers* • *key surface noise* • *no key surface noise* • *promotion of key-keybed impact* •

avoidance of key-keybed impact • fast key descent • slow key descent • relaxed muscles • tense muscles • arm weight • finger weight • gripping the keybed • not gripping the keybed • learning by watching and observing experts • not learning by watching or observing experts.

PIANOS, PIANO-TECHNICIANS AND ACOUSTICS—WHERE DOES THE QUALITY COME FROM?

Complicating touch-tone causality matters further, is the influence that the instrument itself has on determining each note's quality—a factor that is beyond the control of the pianist's touch. This further puts into question the degree of contribution that a pianist's touch has on tone quality.

The "special" tone qualities that we attribute to the touch of many distinguished pianists is made possible by the idiosyncrasies of the instrument that they play on, not because of the type of keystroke that the pianist uses. These tonal changes can be further altered by piano makers and piano technicians. Throughout history, there have always been a small number of top-flight performers who have had the luxury of traveling with their own instrument to use during performances. This is not a pretentious decision by the pianist but an artistic one, as it ensures that the touch-tone relationship remains constant and predictable for them on that piano.

More commonly, these days, modern professional pianists travel with their own piano technician, who can alter the instrument's sound (hammer voicing) and "feel" (action regulation) according to the performer's personal taste.[50] Horowitz, for example, in his later years, was entirely dependent on both his instrument and his technician, and refused to perform at all unless both were involved: "If my tuner does not come back, there will not be a second concert."[51] Franz Mohr, Horowitz's preferred technician for twenty-five years, recalls, "He [Horowitz] was always very, very conscious about acoustics. The acoustics had to be right, it had to be his own piano and his own piano tuner."[52]

Not surprisingly, when Horowitz's instrument was played by others, its tonal idiosyncrasies were immediately noted. David Wilde remembers "hammers so toned that the bass was gigantic; the descant always sang bel canto, and the extreme treble sparkled like Feux d'artifice."[53] And Claudette Sorel recalls, "The magic of its sound will never leave me and will never be duplicated."[54] This did not mean that the piano was any easier to play, or that it magically turned individual tones into musically interesting (combined) tones, but it did mean that independent of any mode of touch or artistry, Horowitz's piano provided him with a palette of tonal resources which was unique, and had an action that was fully customized to facilitate his biomechanical habits. Among celebrated performers, this is not an uncommon situation, and logically, we ought to be wary of drawing quick conclusions about how their touch affects the timbre of individual notes.

Adding further complexity to the difficulty in identifying the exact correlation between touch and tone quality, is that pianos sound different when played in different performance spaces. Pianists easily recognize this difference, as Brendel remarked, "anyone who has ever traveled with a piano knows that the same Steinway or Bösendorfer not only sounds different in different halls, but also seems to react differently in its mechanism."[55] Horowitz, too, in his attempts to control the controllable factors of sound production, obsessed that "the piano has to be properly centered on the stage, sometimes deeper or closer. But every acoustic is different."[56] Regarding studio-recorded sounds, the potential to artificially manipulate the sound is extreme and one should be very careful about making conclusions about the player's touch and the tone qualities that it produces. Watch Glenn Gould record Scriabin, for example.[57]

SOUND PERCEPTION—*I FEEL IT; DON'T YOU?*

Historically, one of the recurring sticking points in the debate between pianists and scientists is the argument by pianists that "something else" is occurring to the key (and/or the hammer) when a note is played. Although this "something" has proven difficult to validate from a mechanico-acoustic perspective, its importance to pianists suggests that, at the very least, it plays an important role in our perception of the touch-tone event and in the decisions we make about touch.

Quality Lies in the Metaphor

Not uncommonly, when pianists describe their experience of the touch event, physical and psychological domains merge. For example, Neuhaus writes that "to get a tender, warm, penetrating tone you have to press the keys very intensively, [and] deeply."[58] But here, one could interchange the position of any of the adjectives of the sentence and still maintain the same meaning of the sentence. Thalberg's description of *cantabile* touch, though highly figurative, also mixes the sensuality of the act of touch with its physical purpose: "For simple, tender, and graceful melodies one should knead the keys, so to speak, pressing and working them as with a boneless hand and fingers of velvet."[59] Adolph Marx also melts the boundaries that would otherwise delineate motor, sensory and emotional functions, writing that "each finger must be able to seize the emotional tone by itself [... and the key] must be seized with feeling."[60]

Brendel openly expresses his intention to fuse his musico-psychological concept with the physical act. He writes, "The sound of the oboe I achieve with rounded, hooked-under and, as it were, bony fingers [...] The pianist should play harp notes with round, tensed fingers."[61] Here, Brendel takes the physico-sonic attributes of the orchestral instruments and translates them into finger postures. His fingers *embody* the musical idea just as his mind embodies the ideas that his fingers give him.[62] Whether or not such finger postures translate into specific tonal differences is unclear, but regardless, Brendel *believes* that to allow embodiment to occur is, at a minimum, acceptable, probably useful, and perhaps essential to the process of achieving desired tonal outcomes. In keeping with this attitude, he recognizes the influence that the perceptual experience has on touch behaviors: "the resistance of the key, over and above the measurable mechanical aspect, is a psychological factor."[63] Coincidently, this explanation of the touch-tone event resonates exactly with how Schindler described Beethoven's playing, that the act of touch carries "double import: The physical or material, and the psychological."[64]

That pianists of the stature of Brendel and Beethoven not only accept, but pursue, touch forms that embody the emotional character of the music, indicates that pianists are often willing, and wanting, to sacrifice physical efficiency for the sake of musico-haptic fulfillment.[65]

But the use of metaphor and embodiment to explain tone quality causality extends further yet. Deppe, for example, postulated that "striking with force, stiffens the wrist, [and] cuts off the singing quality of the tone."[66] But to have tone "cut off," implies that it was in some way "flowing" through the body in the first place. How exactly is tone cut off by a stiff wrist? Claudio Arrau described something similar, emphasizing that "if you are stiff in any joint you impede the emotional physical current of what the music dictates to you. You don't let it go through to the keyboard."[67] By such logic, regardless of its acoustic outcome, a tone that is produced with a stiff wrist will be rejected as being of poor quality. This invites the question: At what point in the journey of the keystroke does the tone quality become poor? Is it poor *before* the arm has even touched the key?

Quality Lies in the Eye of the Beholder

Lastly, pianists also alter their touch, not to manipulate the sound, but to manipulate the audience's perception of the quality of it. Leschetizky writes, "it surely does no harm to influence the listener's ear through his eye, and make the former more receptive."⁶⁸ The same sentiment was echoed by Marguerite Long: "ugly to the eye, ugly to the ear,"⁶⁹ and also by Samuil Feinberg: "One of the most reliable means of achieving a singing quality in performance lies in the use of tangible expressive movements of the hand."⁷⁰ Without hesitation, these esteemed pianists and teachers were happy to encourage the use of visual maneuvers that had no link whatsoever to the mechanical process of sound production.

Metaphors Versus Reality or Metaphors In Reality?

The power of the metaphor in making our actions align in quality with the aesthetic goals that they seek is a masterstroke of cognitive trickery. Look at the following touch-tone associations (previously mentioned).

Desired TONE Quality	←→	Desired TOUCH Quality
penetrating tone	←→	*press the key intensively*
tender melody	←→	*knead the key with fingers of velvet*
emotional tone	←→	*finger seizing the key*
harp sound (plucked)	←→	*round, tense fingers*
strangulated tone	←→	*too much key pressure*
cuts off tone	←→	*stiff wrist*
impedes emotional current	←→	*stiff joint*

In these examples, notice how intuitively we seek specific tone qualities using movements that try to assimilate the same specific qualities. Furthermore, look at the physical effect that this has on our movements. The metaphor-seeking movements may be helpful to us or unhelpful, but we do not challenge their correctness because we are blinded by their emotional coherence of the metaphor that guides them.

In reality, although we use metaphors to convey causality, they are not causality. A "deep" tone does not need a "deep" touch, and, in the world of pedagogy, a "deep" touch does not need to be taught to produce a "deep" tone. Though it makes us feel good, the conceptual merging of our desires with our actions corrupts our ability to reason.

RE-DEFINING THE TOUCH-TONE DEBATE?

To fully understand the diversity of opinions surrounding tone quality causality and the touch-tone relationship, *both* the mechanics of touch *and* the psychology of touch need to be understood. Clearly, the psychology of one's touch, matters: expert pianists and teachers openly encourage movements, gestures, metaphors and ideas about the keystroke that are psychologically appealing, and often highly practical, yet highly fictional in their explanation of the physical processes that underlie them. Equally, the mechanics of one's touch matters too, for irrespective of any amount of psychological approval, unless one's keystrokes operate mechanically effectively to produce the sounds and music required of your musical conception, the psychology is of little value.

What is it, then, about the *impression* of one's movements, the *impression* of their feel and the *impression* of their sounds that makes them overwhelm our ability to sensibly separate their physical objectives from the subjective experience they serve to create? Alexander Goldenweiser posits:

> "The coordination between bodily movements and sensation and the sound that we strive to project is of such importance [that] this affects both the visual impression made on the listener and the physical sensations of the performer, as well as the actual sound produced by the instrument."[71]

And Abby Whiteside speculates:

> "One presses the keybed because of emotional feeling for the tone, and the listening becomes associated with the pressure—"touch." The tone has not been influenced by that pressure but the performer has expressed emotions with it, and thus he has been led to believe that the quality of the tone was changed by it."[72]

Such observations acknowledge the complexity of the touch-tone interaction and make a strong case for needing to interpret pedagogical theory within the context of a human mind that is prone to construct theories based on limited though emotionally plausible information, that readily substitutes metaphors for facts, and that interprets motor and sensory information using an individually tainted perception.

NOTES

1. Barnes, Christopher. *The Russian Piano School*. London: Kahn and Averill, 2008, 15.
2. Lhévinne, Josef. *Basic Principles in Pianoforte Playing*. New York: Dover Publications, 1972. Also, corroborated by his student, John Browning. See: pianopera. "Basic Principles in Piano Playing as Taught by Josef & Rosina Lhévinne, Explained by John Browning." YouTube, August 23, 2017. https://www.youtube.com/watch?v=Eru9FDvUfz4.
3. Lhévinne, Josef. *Basic Principles in Pianoforte Playing*. New York: Dover Publications, 1972, 17.
4. Neuhaus, Heinrich. *The Art of Piano Playing*. Translated by K. A. Leibovitch. London: Kahn & Averill, 1993, 67.
5. Cooke, James Francis. *Great Pianists on Piano Playing: Godowsky, Hofmann, Lhévinne, Paderewski, and 24 Other Legendary Performers*. Mineola, NY: Dover Publications, 1999, 369.
6. Whiteside, Abby. *Mastering the Chopin Etudes and Other Essays*. New York: C. Scribner's Sons, 1969, 153.
7. Barnes, Christopher. *The Russian Piano School*. London: Kahn and Averill, 2008, p. 4.
8. Mach, Elyse. *Great Contemporary Pianists Speak for Themselves*. New York: Dodd, Mead and Company, Inc, 1991, 117.
9. Holland, Bernard. "Vladimir Horowitz, Titan of the Piano, Dies." *Nytimes.com. The New York Times*, November 6, 1989. https://www.nytimes.com/1989/11/06/obituaries/vladimir-horowitz-titan-of-the-piano-dies.html.
10. Kochevitsky, George. *The Art of Piano Playing*. Summy-Birchard Music, 1967, 38.
11. Bowen, Catherine. *Free Artist*. New York: Random House, 1939, 344.
12. Bowen, Catherine. *Free Artist*. New York: Random House, 1939, 336.
13. Brée, Malwine, Arthur Elson, and Seymour Bernstein. *The Leschetizky Method: A Guide to Fine and Correct Piano Playing*. Mineola, NY: Dover, 1997, 5.
14. Schonberg, Harold C. *Horowitz: His Life and Music*. New York: Simon & Schuster, 1992, 296.
15. Music Academy of the West. "Leon Fleisher Solo Piano Masterclass July 13, 2015." *YouTube*, July 29, 2015. https://www.youtube.com/watch?v=EGRnYBxx2Y8.
16. Gerig, Reginald R. *Famous Pianists & Their Technique*. Robert B. Luce, 1974, 73.
17. According to a student of Field. See: Kochevitsky, George. *The Art of Piano Playing*. Summy-Birchard Music, 1967, 38.
18. As written in one of his notebooks. See: Gerig, Reginald R. *Famous Pianists & Their Technique*. Robert B. Luce, 1974, 93.
19. Schindler, Anton Felix. *Beethoven as I Knew Him. A Biography*. Translated by Constance S Jolly. 1860. Chapel Hill: University of North Carolina Press; London, 1966, 380.

20. Brendel, Alfred. *Musical Thoughts & Afterthoughts*. Robson Books Limited, 1976, 95.

21. Lhévinne, Josef. *Basic Principles in Pianoforte Playing*. New York: Dover Publications, 1972, 14.

22. Brée, Malwine, Arthur Elson, and Seymour Bernstein. *The Leschetizky Method: A Guide to Fine and Correct Piano Playing*. Mineola, NY: Dover, 1997, 5.

23. Gerig, Reginald R. *Famous Pianists & Their Technique*. Robert B. Luce, 1974, 78–79.

24. Gerig, Reginald R. *Famous Pianists & Their Technique*. Robert B. Luce, 1974, 343.

25. Lhévinne, Josef. *Basic Principles in Pianoforte Playing*. New York: Dover Publications, 1972, 7.

26. Williamson, Elsie B., Ronald Chamberlain, and N. Victor Edwards. "The Truth about Pianoforte Touch and Tone-Colour." *The Musical Times* 71, no. 1053 (November 1, 1930): 1021. doi:https://doi.org/10.2307/915441.

27. Neuhaus, Heinrich. *The Art of Piano Playing*. Translated by K. A. Leibovitch. London: Kahn & Averill, 1993, 66.

28. Adams, Debi. "An Introduction to the Alexander Technique for Pianists and Their Teachers." *Debi Adams, Alexander Technique*. Debi Adams, Alexander Technique, July 10, 2012. https://debiadamsat.com/about/an-introduction-to-the-alexander-technique-for-pianists-and-their-teachers/

29. Gerig, Reginald R. *Famous Pianists & Their Technique*. Robert B. Luce, 1974, 231.

30. Grainger, Percy. *The Man I Love. In a transcription for the piano by the composer* (orig. George Gershwin). New York: Harms. 1944, 5.

31. Palmieri, Robert. *The Piano*. New York: Routledge, 2003, 385.

32. Piggott, Patrick. *The Life and Music of John Field, 1782–1837, Creator of the Nocturne*. Berkeley: University of California Press, 1973, 105.

33. Piggott, Patrick. *The Life and Music of John Field, 1782–1837, Creator of the Nocturne*. Berkeley: University of California Press, 1973, 103.

34. Eigeldinger, Jean-Jacques. *Chopin: Pianist and Teacher as Seen by His Pupils*. Cambridge Cambridgeshire; New York: Cambridge University Press, 1986, 30–31.

35. Safonoff, Wassili. *New Formula for the Piano Teacher and Piano Student*. Brighton, Sussex: J. & W. Chester, 1916, 15.

36. Gát, József. *The Technique of Piano Playing*. 3rd ed. Budapest, Hungary: Corvina, 1968, 26.

37. Mach, Elyse. *Great Contemporary Pianists Speak for Themselves*. New York: Dodd, Mead And Company, Inc, 1991, 4.

38. Matthay, Tobias. *The First Principles of Pianoforte Playing*. London: Longmans, Green & Co, 1922, 2.

39. Matthay, Tobias. *The Visible and Invisible in Pianoforte Technique*. Oxford: Oxford University Press, 1932. Here, Matthay displays a complete lack of understanding of physics. He asks that the key increases in speed "gradually" but in the next sentence asks that "this acceleration during descent must be 'gradual' and at

an *increasing* rate of increase." If the acceleration itself were increasing, this would result in an exponentially fast increase in speed of the key, not gradual, as he insists. And, even if it did increase gradually, it is not what actually happens to the key's velocity profile when it is played (see chapter 4). That this most famed pedagogue should construct his theories on such basic errors of physics should remind us to caution every pedagogical theory, especially the ones that try to "use science" to prove their self-confirmation biases.

40. Lhévinne, Josef. *Basic Principles in Pianoforte Playing.* New York: Dover Publications, 1972, 22.

41. Jost, Mack. *Yet Another Guide to Piano Playing.* Armidale, NSW Australia: Allans Publishing, 1974, 79. Note, even though Jost writes about the importance of playing *to* the keybed to produce a full-bodied tone, he never once made a point of it during my 8 years of study with him. This further suggests that there are discrepancies between what pianists (and teachers) say, write, mean and do.

42. Levinskaya, Maria. *The Levinskaya System of Pianoforte Technique and Tone-Colour through Mental & Muscular Control.* London; Toronto: J.M. Dent and Sons, 1930, 183.

43. Levinskaya, Maria. *The Levinskaya System of Pianoforte Technique and Tone-Colour through Mental & Muscular Control.* London; Toronto : J.M. Dent and Sons, 1930, 188.

44. Fraser, Alan. *The Craft of Piano Playing: A New Approach to Piano Technique.* Lanham, MD: Scarecrow Press, 2003, 39.

45. Milanovic, Therese. "Learning and Teaching Healthy Piano Technique: Training as an Instructor in the Taubman Approach," 2011, 104.

46. Matthay, Tobias. *The First Principles of Pianoforte Playing.* London: Longmans, Green & Co, 1922, 2.

47. Matthay, Tobias. *The First Principles of Pianoforte Playing.* London: Longmans, Green & Co, 1922, 1.

48. Berman, Boris. *Notes from the Pianist's Bench.* New Haven, CT: Yale University Press, 2000, 12.

49. Berman, Boris. *Notes from the Pianist's Bench.* New Haven, CT: Yale University Press, 2000, 12.

50. Alfred Brendel gives a detailed account of the use, and importance, of piano technicians in his book chapter, "Coping With Pianos." Brendel, Alfred. *Musical Thoughts & Afterthoughts.* Robson Books Limited, 1976, 129-39.

51. Mohr, Franz, and Edith Schaeffer. *My Life with the Great Pianists.* Grand Rapids, MI: Ravens Ridge Books, 1992, 22.

52. Bruceduffie.com. "Piano Technician Franz Mohr," 1992. http://www.bruceduffie.com/mohr.html.

53. Dubal, David. *Reflections from the Keyboard.* New York: Summit Books, 1984, 322-323.

54. Dubal, David. *Reflections from the Keyboard.* New York: Summit Books, 1984, 313.

55. Brendel, Alfred. *Musical Thoughts & Afterthoughts.* Robson Books Limited, 1976, 130.

56. Dubal, David. *Reflections from the Keyboard.* New York: Summit Books, 1984, 207.

57. Erick Martinez. "Glenn Gould Scriabin Op. 57 Recording Sesion the Paths of Music." YouTube, November 7, 2017. https://www.youtube.com/watch?v=fMuZUC18gDs.

58. Neuhaus, Heinrich. *The Art of Piano Playing.* Translated by K. A. Leibovitch. London: Kahn & Averill, 1993, 72.

59. Kullak, Adolf. *The Aesthetics of Pianoforte-Playing.* Translated by T Baker. 5th ed. 1893. Reprint, New York: G. Schirmer, 1972, 90.

60. Kullak, Adolf. *The Aesthetics of Pianoforte-Playing.* Translated by T Baker. 5th ed. 1893. Reprint, New York: G. Schirmer, 1972, 85.

61. Brendel, Alfred. *Musical Thoughts & Afterthoughts.* Robson Books Limited, 1976, 95-96.

62. Embodiment, or Embodied Cognition, are concepts that recognize that our motor system influences our cognition, just as our cognition influences our motor system.

63. Brendel, Alfred. *Musical Thoughts & Afterthoughts.* Robson Books Limited, 1976, 130.

64. Schindler, Anton Felix. *Beethoven as I Knew Him. A Biography.* Translated by Constance S. Jolly. 1860. Reprint, Chapel Hill: University of North Carolina Press; London, 1966, 380.

65. This mechanical inefficiency has been demonstrated by professional pianists when playing *con espressione*, evidenced by a sustained excess of pressure in the keybed well after the onset of the tone. See: Tiedemann, J., D. Drescher, and E. Altenmüller. "Aus-Druck Beim Klavierspiel: Eine Untersuchung Zur Tastendruckdynamik." *Musikphysiologie Und Musikermedizin* 7 (2000): 13–21.

66. Fay, Amy. *Music-Study in Germany.* 1896. Reprint, New York: Macmillan Company, 1922, 288.

67. Bookspan, M. 1987. *Claudio Arrau – The 80th Birthday Recital.* Liner notes. West Long Beach, New Jersey: Kultur.

68. Brée, Malwine, Arthur Elson, and Seymour Bernstein. *The Leschetizky Method: A Guide to Fine and Correct Piano Playing.* Mineola, NY: Dover, 1997, 5.

69. Long, Marguerite. *Le Piano.* Paris: Éd. Salabert, 1959, XIII.

70. Barnes, Christopher. *The Russian Piano School.* London: Kahn and Averill, 2008, 15.

71. Barnes, Christopher. *The Russian Piano School.* London: Kahn and Averill, 2008, 56.

72. Whiteside, Abby. *Indispensables of Piano Playing.* 2nd ed. New York: Charles Scribner's Sons, 1961, 52.

Chapter 4

The Touch-Tone Relationship—Scientists' Perspectives

"We can easily forgive a child who is afraid of the dark; the real tragedy of life is when men are afraid of the light."—Plato (in *The Republic*, Book 7)

Although the traditional scientific position continues to be well-substantiated by physicists—that "there is no change of [tone] color without change of loudness"[1]—it does not bring to an end the touch-tone debate. Rather, it is a starting point, where mechanical physics must also share the scientific stage with that of neuroscience and psychology so that the issues of human perception are accounted for.

This section, therefore, examines the science of the touch-tone relationship from both physical and psychological perspectives. Though there are many facts that pedagogy gets wrong about the mechanics of touch, there are, notably, many feelings that pianists have about touch and tone that have an explainable, underlying cause.

THE PHYSICS OF TOUCH AND TONE QUALITY

The Hammer Head: Speed, Felt, Compression

Piano makers and physicists have long known that "the make of the hammer has an immense influence on the quality of tone"[2] and following over a century and a half of investigations, no study refutes the fact that the speed of the hammer (when it hits the string) correlates to the volume of the piano tone.[3]

The main mechanical function of the keystroke is to provide momentum to the key and, via the lever system of the piano action, to the hammer.

Often ignored, however, is the fact that the hammer speed affects volume and quality *simultaneously*. This is because a faster hammer will cause the hammer felt to compress more when it hits the string (effectively, becoming harder), resulting in a reduced hammer-string contact time and an increased production of higher-frequency harmonics. This increases the so-called brightness of the tone.[4]

The faster the hammer speed when it hits the string, the "brighter" the sound.
The slower the hammer speed when it hits the string, the "duller" the sound.
Louder sounds are brighter. Softer sounds are duller.

Additionally, the quick rebound of the hammer off the string prevents it from muffling the vibrations of the string. Timpanists experience the same principle when playing drums: soft sticks will muffle the vibrations traveling across the skin of the drum, but hard sticks will not—hence the brighter sounds when using the harder sticks. The difference between timpanists and pianists, however, is that timpanists can choose to play softly with hard sticks or loudly with soft (i.e., compressible) sticks, whereas pianists are stuck with only one set of "sticks"—sticks that will become harder when played loudly and become softer when played softly. We cannot physically make our sticks softer by playing louder. Should we desire a "loud & dull" tone or "soft & bright" tone, our only physical option is to ask a piano technician to alter the compressibility of the felt of the hammers.

Same Sound, Different Look

Whatever manner of touch, body contortion or soulful spirit you give to the note being played, for single tones, the hammer speed that you generate will be what defines the volume of the note *and* its correlative timbre. There is no escaping it: the hammer speed, the tone volume, and the tone quality all change together.

A major reason for the confusion surrounding this point, is that there are many ways of touching a key that, despite feeling and looking unique, nevertheless produce the same hammer speed (see Chapter 6: Mechanical Skills). This misunderstanding further contributes to piano pedagogy's diverse array of offerings of how one "ought to" touch the key to produce specific timbres.

Like all roads leading to Rome, all touches can lead to a specific tone quality. For example, Beethoven's contracted hand and tightly curled fingers, Horowitz's flat (and curled) fingers, John Field's perpendicular fingers, the Stuttgart School's fast finger attack, Lhévinne's smooth arm-weight drop, and Grainger's stiff wrist are all capable of producing the same *cantabile*-like sound quality. They may not all be biomechanically efficient, physiologically friendly or visually appealing, but in terms of being *effective*, they are equals. The different finger positions, wrist positions, degrees of joint firmness, arm weights, speeds of keystroke, and angles of attack, are just different mechanical surrogates for generating a specific hammer speed—and hence, a specific tone quality.

Given that hammer hardness and tonal brightness are physically linked, every note on the piano will have its own tonal limitations. For example, hammers in the lower registers are usually less compressed (like the hammers of a new, unplayed piano) and will tend to produce duller sounds. This is why one must accept to play them louder if one wants to create the impression of brightness out of them[5] (or within a musical context, to play such notes shorter, semi-detached or without pedal, to give the *illusion* of brightness—based on the greater relative peak-trough spread of sound intensity). Similarly, it is futile to fight against the high-frequency brightness of an overused piano (like those found in the practice rooms of conservatories) where the hammers have been beaten into a fixed state of compression. When hammers are already fully hardened, it becomes almost impossible to reduce their brightness, even when playing quietly.[6]

Ideally, each note of a well-regulated piano will have a mechanism that allows the pianist to transition *gradually* and *reliably* from slow key-descents causing soft/dull sounds up to fast key-descents causing loud/bright sounds. How gradual or sudden this transition occurs will be unique for each note on the instrument. On a poorly regulated instrument, a situation often arises where some notes will have abrupt transition points (or none at all) and the notes will "stick out" for being too bright (or too dull) however we try to play them. If the piano action cannot be altered, the pianist must adapt to the irregularities of this gradient and still try to make music out of it. Figure 4.1 shows the variability of the brightness response for hammers of different degrees of felt compressibility when played at different speeds.

Voicing of the hammers (by a piano technician) pre-defines the range of sound quality possibilities that each individual note can make. This can give pianists a head start in influencing the auditory sensations and emotions of their listeners.[7] Franz Mohr's description of preparing Horowitz's piano prior his concerts gives insight into its importance. He writes, "I built up the tone. I made it as brilliant as I could [...] I filed and lacquered the hammers."[8]

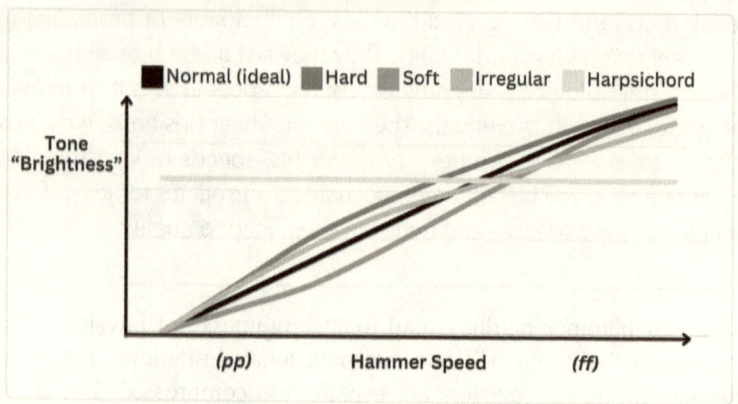

Figure 4.1. Tone Brightness vs Hammer Speed. Author created

> *Because the act of hammer voicing remains out of sight to its observers, we need to be wary of copying the touch styles of famous pianists with an expectation that the same tone qualities will be able to be produced by using the same keystrokes, if at all.*

Hard-Hammer-Bright-Tone Reality Meets Piano-Pedagogy Beliefs

Given the physical impossibility of playing softer and brighter, or louder and duller, pianists will typically find themselves caught in a psychic conflict between the *psychological desire* to produce a certain tone quality and the *physical impossibility* of achieving it. As the physics of the mechanics of touch cannot be altered, this requires pianists to resort to manipulating the *perception* of the quality of the tone by other means. This typically involves manipulating the context around which that tone sits—just as Horowitz hinted, "the secret lies mainly in contrast."[9]

The history of piano playing provides multiple examples of how to do this. In many respects, the art of perceptual manipulation, not just the literal reproduction of the written notes, is one of the skills that differentiates an average pianist from a great pianist. It is why playing the notes *as printed* will only get one so far in terms of being musically interesting—like an actor who just reads their words, or a chef who just mixes the prescribed ingredients.

The following textbox shows some common ways in which pianists create tonal illusions out of the otherwise banal piano tone.

Creating Tone-Quality Illusions

Sound context manipulation

Here, the underlying perceptual goal is "to increase contrast with the note to be emphasized."[10] Options here include: volume contrasts between phrases; volume contrasts between R.H. and L.H.; volume contrasts between notes of the same chord; altering duration of notes to alter perception of percussiveness; finding textural contrasts or layering sound into zones or voices; using asynchrony of notes; using silence abruptly before or after notes, and so on.

Music context manipulation (and agogics)

Here, the goal is to overcome the banality of the piano sound by manipulating the timing of the notes being played. This requires altering elements like rubato, phrase directionality, breath spaces, tempo, ornamentation, pedalling and other agogics, and so on. The importance of these types of manipulations should not be underestimated. Besides characterizing the playing of many distinguished pianists, they offer a solution to overcoming the limitations of the piano's tone—and the psychological "desire vs. reality" conflict that accompanies it.

Gestural manipulation:

Here, the intentions of the music can be conveyed to the audience (and to yourself) even if the objective sound goals are not met. Options include: finger and arm movements, facial movements, and other bodily contortions. Such movements are usually involuntary, though they don't have to be. The commonly seen "sinking and rounding" movement of the wrist during *cantabile* playing is an example.

Instrument manipulation (voicing of the hammers):

Strictly, this is a type of physical manipulation, but because it is out of the sight of the audience *and* it alters the physics of the touch-tone relationship, it could also be categorized as perceptual manipulation.

As a separate point of interest, it is worth reflecting on how performers of other instruments also use these four types of contextual manipulations to deal with the conflict between the technical difficulties (physical reality) of producing sound on their instrument and their artistic goals (psychological desires). Each instrumentalist tends to find a different idiosyncratic agogic solution to the problems they face:

- Harpsichord: use of ornaments, trills, and arpeggiation (to overcome weak sound and quick tonal decay)
- Flute: predilection for quicker tempos (to avoid losing pitch or running out of air at ends of longer phrases)
- Organ: use of different stop settings and registrations (to overcome the monotony of each tone's quality and lack of sound decay)
- Violin/cello: swelling of sound during long bow strokes (due to the shape of the bow and its increase of force upon the strings at its mid-point)

The Hammer Shaft: Flexing and Wobbling

Putting the microscope on the mechanics of touch further, a small number of studies have shown that different types of touch cause different vibration patterns in the hammer shaft and hammer head. Differences have been noted in the trajectory arc of the hammer head, likely due to differences in the degrees of flexing of the shaft, and in an oscillatory wobble pattern of the hammer head—see Figure 4.2.[11] It has also been shown that the point on the string where the hammer hits, changes slightly (fractions of a millimeter) when a strong percussive (*staccato*) touch is used.[12]

Given that the string is being hit by the hammer at a slightly different position with respect to the bridge, and that a slightly different part of the hammer

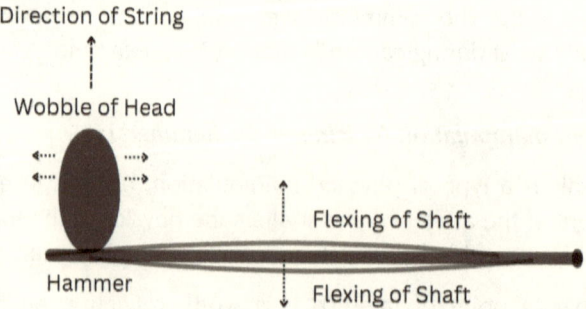

Figure 4.2. Hammer Shaft Flexing and Hammer Head Wobbling. Author created

felt is (likely to be) contacting the string (more *rubbing* on the string?) this provides a theoretical, physical explanation for how such a "percussive" touch (with noise made by the finger contacting the key) might cause tonal differences compared to a "pressed" touch (without noise made by the finger contacting the key) for a hammer of the same moving velocity.

Despite the attractiveness of the theory, however, there are formidable problems in translating it into practice. First, the magnitude of the physical changes of the "flex" and the "wobble" only becomes significant when artificial enhanced-flexibility hammer shafts are used. Second, only the percussive touch shows any reliability in increasing the flex of the shaft at louder volumes—but given that it is impossible to use a pressed touch to produce loud volumes, no relative benefit is attainable; all loud tones come from a percussive touch. Third, the shaft vibrations cannot be controlled by pianists.[13]

Nevertheless, knowing that the hammer shaft flexes *some* amount (compared to *no* amount) during the percussive touch does provide us with useful information: it helps us to better understand touch *behavior*. For example, for any given final hammer speed, the percussive touch causes the hammer to reach its maximum speed sooner than that of the pressed touch.[14] This implies that a slightly higher peak force will be required in producing the percussive touch (because the time period over which the maximum hammer speed is generated is less). This *may* make the keystroke feel different.

Because of the higher peak force used in the percussive touch (exceedingly small as it is), pianists may wish to give thought to the pianistic advantages and disadvantages associated with it. Theoretically, a pianist may be able to benefit from the percussive touch because of being able to play into the key and return back out of it quicker (and still produce the same tone quality)—like the high frequency pogostick-like movements of the hand during fast octave playing. But given that this would be the same movement that would be used to execute fast octaves anyway, no meaningful change to the timbre of the sound is possible.

On the negative side, using higher peak forces to produce tones would come at the cost of increased muscle work, fatigue, and may, potentially, contribute to injury risk, should those excess forces be too frequent or excessive. The noise arising from the contact between the finger and the key would also have to be considered and accepted as an unavoidable outcome of employing such a touch.

> *For all practical purposes, whether or not the flex and wobble of the hammer shaft contributes to changes in tone quality, is irrelevant. Its contribution is negligible, if at all, and neither variable can be reliably controlled by a pianist's touch.*

IMPACT NOISES: THE KEYBED AND THE "THUMP"

The act of touch also produces noises that do not arise from the hammer-string interaction. Historically, some scientists have dismissed the importance of touch noise: "It does not affect the tone itself"[15]—while others have affirmed it: "a very conspicuous element in the sound produced by any instrument or voice is not tone, as such, at all but noise, pure and simple—the noise of production of the tone."[16] There is no longer any need to debate the topic, as countless studies confirm that *noise* is inextricably enmeshed in the piano sound, and that it is the differences in the noise components of touch that are likely to be responsible for any differences in sound quality that associate with different touch forms.

A notable feature of tone-production noises is that, due to the interconnectedness of the instrument's parts, noises associated with our touch (from the key surface and the keybed) are readily transmitted throughout the instrument. As the piano-acoustic physicist, Askenfelt, explains, "the vibrations in the soundboard, originally excited via the strings, will soon spread to the rim and keybed and vice versa, and an exchange occurs."[17] Objectively, "[differences in tone quality] might be attributable to sounds associated with the mechanical components of the piano action."[18]

Given that the design and components of each piano are unique, it is to be expected that the vibrations transmitted through the instrument, in response to touch, will be different for different instruments. In turn, it ought to be expected that a pianist will sense a different response to their touch—i.e., a different touch-tone relationship—depending on the instrument that is being played or because of the acoustic setting in which it is being played. Such an observation corresponds exactly with Brendel's observation that pianos behave differently in different settings.[19]

> *Pedagogical rules about touch (and the mechanical habits that we acquire) that are derived from playing on one particular instrument may not necessarily apply to other instruments. What works for you on your familiar instrument at home may not work on the instrument that you use on stage.*

The Keybed

That "the recognized piano makers select the wood for the keybed with great care"[20] to achieve the right thump quality, is further evidence that the vibrations transmitted from the pianist's touch into the keybed will affect the quality of the piano tone. Notably, in experiments, when a piano is played with the keybed intentionally removed, its sound is described as being thin and hollow, and "resembles a plucked string."[21] The change in tone quality is easily observed by musicians.[22] This does not tell us how, or by how much, the key-keybed interaction can be manipulated by the pianist, but it does tell us that it *might* be an area of intervention that is touch-responsive.

Also interacting with the pianist's touch at the keybed level, are the felt washers. Primarily, these serve to cushion the blow of the key on the keybed, but they also serve a sonic role: "the stiffness of the felt washers under the keys can influence the attack sound noticeably."[23] Thus, because of the type (their compressibility) and condition (they wear out) of the felt washers, both the feel and the sound will be different when a note is played. Again, we observe how the quality of the feel of the touch on any given keyboard is *unavoidably* entangled with the quality of the sound it produces:

> *The collision of the key with the keybed will sound and feel different depending on the type of keybed, type of felt washers and the force of the impact. Given that each pianist will seek a different "feel of touch" when playing, it is predictable that pianists will diverge in their opinions about what the keybed interaction should feel like when playing, and will make quality judgements about the sound of the instrument based on that feel.*

The "Thump"

Romantic metaphors aside, the piano is a percussive instrument. Its sound is caused by the hitting of a hammer onto a string. The contact may be stronger or weaker (depending on the speed of the hammer impact), or longer or shorter (depending on the compressibility of the hammer's felt), but the hammer-string contact is nevertheless an abrupt percussive "hit" lasting between 1–4 ms and, thereafter, "the piano tone is condemned to decay and die"[24] irrespective of any attempt to massage the key with the finger. As pianist Garrick Ohlsson remarks, the piano is a "diminuendo box."[25]

Depending on the musical context, we might associate the percussive event of the pianists touch (which includes the finger-key contact, the key-keybed contact and the hammer-string contact) with negative connotations like "thumping," "banging," and "pounding," or with positive connotations like "well-accented," "sparkling," and "incisive." It should also go without saying, that if a pianist is musical, the percussiveness of the piano notes will fit appropriately into the musical-performance narrative. This is why unmusical pianists are more likely to be criticized for thumping. It is not that they are playing any louder than a great virtuoso does, it is that the volume and timing of their notes is poorly judged with respect to the context of the music. Horowitz's predilection for starting melodies with full volume, or grouping notes with loud volume together and then allowing the subsequent notes of the phrase to *fit in* to the natural decay of the sound, is an example of an agogic solution to the piano tone's percussive wave-form.[26]

Regardless of the qualities that we give to our piano tone "thumps" or the ways in which we wish to deny their existence, *the thump noise is intrinsic to the piano tone and cannot be eliminated from it*. Waveform analysis shows that the thump is comprised of two separate components: a "loud" and a "soft" component.[27] Understanding this is of major importance—should we wish to understand how a piano tone is produced.

There are several intriguing findings to comment on here. First, the soft component appears to be touch-sensitive. Second, although it appears to be touch-sensitive, it is *not* because of the interaction of the hammer with the string *nor* is it because of any personalized manipulation of the key that the pianist thinks has been transferred to the hammer. Third, "touch-sensitive" does not mean "touch-audible," and although some studies have found that the soft component is detectable on digital wave analysis, it has been shown to only be *occasionally* audible to *some* people during listening experiments, and invariably from a close listening range (or a closely recorded microphone) of approximately 10–50 cm.[29]

Notably, in these experiments, professional pianists did not perceive the differences in tone quality any better than non-pianists, thereby ruining the idea that pianists are any better at identifying, or agreeing upon, an "objective quality" of an isolated piano tone than anybody else. In fact, when pianists played single notes themselves (compared to only listening to them) they were more likely to be *worse* at discerning their qualitative tonal differences and more likely to assign them qualities which corresponded to the *feel* of their touch.[30] (The psychological reasons for this are discussed in the following chapter.)

The different percussive noises caused by the finger hitting the key surface and the key hitting the keybed—and the transmission of these noises through the action, soundboard, casing and strings—appear to be the most likely reasons for the different timbres that different keystrokes provide.

Table 4.1. Dissecting the Thump: Loud and Soft Components

"Loud" Component	"Soft" Component
• = the noise of the impact of the hammer with the string.	• = the noise of the finger-key collision and/or noises within the action that are transmitted through the instrument because of it.
• is louder if the hammer speed is faster.	• arises fractionally (microseconds) before the hammer-string impact.
• is only 10 dB softer than the vibration sound from the string that immediately follows it.	• is 35 dB softer than the string vibration sound.
• is not touch-sensitive.	• appears to be touch-sensitive.

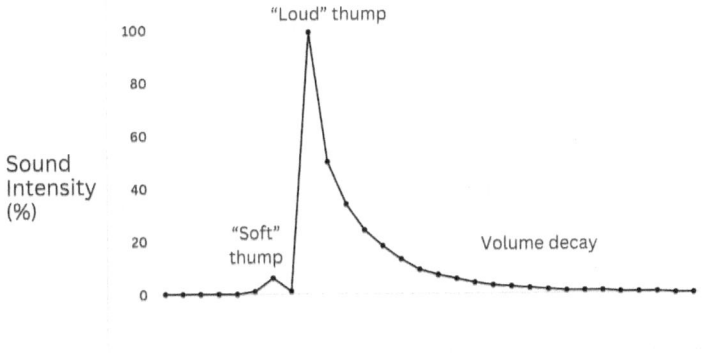

Figure 4.3. The Thump Components of the Piano Tone. Author created.[28]

Given that the percussive noises of one's touch vibrate throughout the instrument, it is plausible that during normal playing, when multiple notes are played at the same time, or held down by the sustain pedal, and more strings are allowed to vibrate, any noises that arise from the finger-key contact will *more likely* be captured by those resonating strings and, in turn, become perceptible. Such an explanation would (rightly) give support to pianists' claims that different touches alter tone quality *within a normal playing context* but less so, if at all, in a sterile, single-played-note context. It would also explain why pianists may continue to use a variety of different touches when the sustain pedal is held down, as this is when the percussive touch noises have the best chance of being "captured" and affect sound quality.[31]

Altering the Soft:Loud Thump Ratio—Is It Worth the Effort?

If the soft component is touch-sensitive and causes an audible difference, we would have objective reasons to experiment with different keystrokes to try and enhance or decrease the soft-component of the thump relative to the loud-component. But as optimistic as we might wish to be about this touch-tone link, its implications need to be put into perspective.

There are distinct advantages and disadvantages of trying to alter the soft thump component independently of the loud thump component. From an artistic point of view, the obvious advantage is that if the touch can cause audible changes to the tone's timbre, the pianist has an acoustically justified reason to pursue them physically. On the other hand, if the acoustic differences are inaudible, or inconsistently audible, we might question whether altering our techniques to pursue them is worth our effort. Simply, is it worth changing your technique from a more curved-finger technique to a less-curved-finger technique, or sitting higher or lower, or using more or less arm weight, changing teachers or practicing hour after hour convincing yourself that you are "acquiring the necessary skills" of producing different tone qualities when there is no discernible acoustic change?

Also, given that the soft component of the thump is overwhelmed in volume by the almost instantaneously appearing loud component thereafter, it would suggest that we should also be focusing on trying to manipulate the louder component of the thump to alter the difference between the two component noises and, in turn, alter the quality of the sound. This, despite any gestural attempts, is physically impossible to achieve: the loud component of the thump sound *is* the sound of the impact of the hammer hitting the string: it will increase or decrease in volume in proportion to how fast or slow the hammer hits the string.

As disappointing as these facts are for keystroke romantics, the romance would not have lasted very long anyway. Even if we could alter the thump of the hammer against the string, what would we do about it? Would we try to increase it: resulting in a more loud and full sound (good) but at the expense of it being more percussive (bad); or try to decrease it: resulting in a less percussive sound (good) but at the expense of it sounding softer and thinner (bad)?

> **Producing a piano sound is either a "win, lose" scenario (richer sound, more percussive) or a "lose, win" (less rich sound, less percussive) scenario. A "win, win" (rich sound, less percussive) scenario does not exist, despite all our collective physical attempts, beliefs, biases, pedagogical claims and parochial backslapping. A piano hammer cannot hit a string both quickly and slowly simultaneously any more than one can punch a wall quickly and slowly simultaneously. The noise and the sound of a single piano tone are coupled.**

In trying to adapt to the limitations of the instrument's sound, pianists (as musicians) have continually sought ways to make the piano tone *appear* to be less "thump-y" (by avoiding *verticalization* of sound), and more "singing" (by trying to stretch sound more *horizontally*). From an artistic point of view, this is the right way of thinking (should note *length* be your goal), but being physically, mechanically and acoustically impossible to achieve (for a single piano note), it creates one of the core existential problems that pianists face: of wanting notes to sound singing-like but having no physical means of achieving it.

Aside from replacing the piano or re-voicing the hammers, a pianist can only increase the singing-ness of a note in two ways. They are the same ways that the pianist uses to try to overcome the "louder equals brighter" problem of the hammer-stringer collision. The first, is to deceive oneself by upholding one's self-confirmation beliefs that it is possible. The second, is to accept the reality of the percussive piano tone and make efforts to alter the *impression* of it—namely, to alter the listener's *perception* of it. Expert pianists have found countless ways of doing both. The following textbox shows some of them.

Overcoming the Sound vs. Noise Paradox—Thump-Minimisation Techniques

The following list shows some of the practical ways that pianists try promoting the illusion of the horizontal "sound" while minimizing its vertical "noise":

- by using *tenuto* (to increase the temporal length of selected notes and give them the impression of being more singing relative to the notes surrounding it).[32]
- by playing accompaniments more softly (to be able to hear the long decay of the singing notes more easily) and smoothly (so that one's attention is not drawn to them).
- by applying crescendo and decrescendo to the accompaniment (to create the illusion of breath speed in the singing voice).
- by (trying to) minimize the finger-key collision noise (thereby reducing the percussive profile of the sound).
- by cleverly using the sustain pedal (to homogenize the textures of the notes being played and making them relatively less percussive. Adding pedal will also help to prolong the duration of any held note, making it appear more singing-like).
- by avoiding synchronicity of the R.H. with the L.H. (synchronicity does two things: it superimposes the sound waves which amplifies the percussive spike; and it makes it harder to hear the melody note, hence by using asynchrony, the melody note does not have to be played as loudly to be heard, and being less loud, will have a reduced thump)

- by promoting the spreading and arpeggiating of chords (as before, to avoid the superimposition of the thumps of simultaneous notes).[33]
- to use *rubato* (to direct one's attention away from vertical sound and more toward its horizontal line).
- to adopt "slow, deep, long, and rounded" gestures (to visually, and psychologically "round out" the percussive thump).[34]
- to voice the hammers (to alter their hardness and change their tone quality).
- to tune the piano (this tends to prolong the decay of each note).

THE PSYCHOLOGY OF TOUCH AND TONE QUALITY

For both the pianist and the listener, the experience of tone quality is more than just a mechanico-acoustic event. Pianists instinctively transfer their feelings for the music into their movements—an act that ensures that movements are flavored by psychological factors, not just mechanical goals. Yet, the act of listening, too, is shaped by sensory inputs other than just auditory ones, and this too, distorts our ability to objectify the touch-tone interaction.

It is the integration of multiple sensory and motor inputs that shape our experience of piano tone quality and also our attempts to explain its causality.[35] The cognitive process that underlies this is called *cross-modal interference*[36]—or *cross-modal integration*.[37] It provides us with "the best estimate of the external property [being observed]"[38]—how touch affects tone quality—and produces "a unified perceptual experience of multisensory events."[39]

Embodiment and the Feel of the Gesture

Previously, it was shown how pianists tend to interchange the quality of the feeling of their movements with the quality of the sounds that they strive to produce. For example, a "caressing" movement might be used to try to enhance the "caressing" quality of the sound (and music), and vice versa, music that evokes "caressing" feelings may encourage the use of "caressing" movements. Here, the mixed sensory experience of the keystroke, the feel of its movements (haptics and kinaesthetics), the sound it produces, and the emotions it engages with, blend together. There is *crossover* of the domains of the mind in an attempt to *unify the experience*. This is cross-modal integration.

The fusion of our ideas and feelings with our movements and actions is an example of embodiment—where our ideas and feelings are represented physically, and vice versa. Musicians constantly use embodiment.[40] Arguably, embodiment is what artists *do*: infusing their physical medium with their feelings and ideas and, in equal measure, responding to it, like painters with their brushstrokes, sculptures with their hands and dancers with their bodies.

But other professionals demonstrate embodiment too, revealing that cross-modal integration is constantly at work in our brains, shaping our actions in ways that align with the mental ideas that underlie them. For example:

- golfers use *soft* and *gentle* hands when trying to achieve a *soft* and *gentle* outcome for the ball from their golf stroke;
- anesthetists use a *floating gently* manual technique when inserting central venous catheters that need to *float gently* inside the vessel;[41]
- humans adopt postures of kneeling and bowing (*lower, reduced body size*) as we feel submission (*lower, reduced body size*) toward a god, authority figure or idol;
- chiropractors highlight joint *alignment* as being important for physical and psychological health *alignment*.
- dancers (the quintessential examples of embodiment in art) allow their bodies to become one in feeling and action with the metaphor and physical space in which it participates.[42]

As pianists, it is worth thinking about how the processes of cross-modal integration and embodiment shape our perception of touch. In a controlled experiment involving professional pianists, Galembo examined the interplay between our different senses during the process of evaluating touch quality. Crucially, he showed that the physical aspects of our touch (tactile and proprioceptive senses) interfered with our perception of the quality of the sound produced (audition). Professional pianists, for example, could easily agree upon the qualities of a range of tones on a range of different pianos when playing *and* listening to them but not when *only* listening to them. That is, *playing* the instrument caused the pianist to have a different perception of the instrument's sound quality. From this, he makes several observations:[43]

- "the performer's judgment of the tone is affected by some touch-sensitive information which is not available to the listener [and] includes all possible audible touch-dependent attack elements, as well as the mechanical feedback from the action via the key";
- "pianists unconsciously include the kinesthetic feedback when they evaluate timbre";
- "performers' judgments of the tone quality were "infected" by the impression of the mechanical response."

Galembo's experiment shows cross-modal interference occurring in a touch-to-audition direction. This phenomenon is known to neuroscientists: "the human motor system plays a functional role in auditory perception."[44]

But cross-modal interference can occur in an audition-to-touch direction too, where one's perception of the quality of one's touch is influenced by what one hears. For example, in experiments where different sounds are provided to listeners who participate in a specific touch task, "audition significantly modulated tactile perception when [different] stimuli were presented simultaneously."[45] Also, "participants typically tend to weight tactile cues more heavily when combined audio-tactile information is available."[46]

Knowing that one's perception of an event is based on nothing more (or less) than the mind's best guess assumption using the information available to it, we can better understand why some pianists will attribute the "soft"-ness of their cantabile playing to the "soft" pads of their fingertips, and, oppositely, when they use the "soft" pads of their fingertips, may be led to believe that their cantabile sound will possess more "soft"-ness.

That we become puppets of our own perceptual fancies, is exactly what pianist Whiteside was trying to describe: "one presses the keybed because of emotional feeling for the tone, and the listening becomes associated with the pressure [... and we are then] led to believe that the quality of the tone was changed by it."[47] Scientifically, it is also how the musicologist Richard Parncutt described it: "the perception of a motoric goal cannot be separated from proprioception [... and the] pianists' perception of timbre cannot be separated from their perception of the gestures used to achieve it."[48]

Gesture, Pleasure, and Meaning

Understanding the multi-modal nature of the tone-touch relationship also provides us with insight into why our gestures provide us with feelings of pleasure and meaning. Neuhaus's description of his own playing during peak states of performance suggests an almost zen-like experience of auditory-tactile integration. He writes, "I am acutely aware of the pleasure I derive from the physical process of playing, the joy I feel not only in my 'soul,' my ear, but in my fingers from their contact with the keyboard."[49] Here, we appreciate a function of touch that goes beyond its mechanico-acoustic role, as it seeks, and seeks to find pleasure in, a unified musico-haptic experience.

Famed teacher Dorothy Taubman openly encouraged the unification (and optimization) of the auditory-haptic experience, saying that playing the piano "should become something loving to you," "the feeling of playing the piano should feel absolutely delicious."[50] Here, we note how the experience of pleasure is considered to be a *requirement*, a *goal* and a *reward* of an optimized touch—the experience of pleasure and the fulfillment of motor goals are intertwined. This represents a clear departure away from a mechanico-acoustic model of understanding the touch-tone relationship.

But the pleasure (or displeasure) that we get from our movements and gestures and the role that they play in altering our perception of our touch—*affective proprioception*[51]—is not simply a matter of "feels good, *is* good" or "feels bad, *is* bad." What is important, from a pedagogical point of view, is what "feels good" tells us about our touch-tone thinking: that "pleasure in movement may depend not on feedback but also on harmony between intention and action."[52]

Fleisher's advice to a student in a 2015 masterclass exemplifies the use—and misuse—of affective proprioception in pedagogy.[53] On many occasions, when discussing touch and sound quality, he encourages a student to align their musical intentions with their touch actions. It is standard pedagogical rhetoric. In teaching the opening bars of Beethoven's Op. 110, he advises:

- to use the pads of the fingers (soft pads align with *soft, floating, ethereal* tone and sentiment);
- to play with flatter fingers (*flat* fingers align with *flat* keys and a metaphorical unification with the instrument. Quote: "the keyboard is an extension of your fingers . . . you and it are one");
- to play the key with a "horizontal and upward" gesture (!) (*horizontal and upward* movements align metaphorically with *horizontal and upward* tones traveling further horizontally through time. Quote: "listen how it carries through the air").

Noteworthy too, during the class, was Fleisher's failure to notice that when he demonstrated using flat fingers with a horizontal-and-upward motion, the volume of the sound reduced (due to loss of effective momentum—see chapter 6: Mechanical Skills). His approach, agreed, makes the tone quality softer but also at the expense of it being quantitatively softer, which means the tone's duration will be shorter too, *not* longer, as he asserts. The situation exemplifies the influence that cross-modal interference has on our ability to objectify the touch-tone event—and our ability to teach it.[54]

Our sense of feeling "good" and "right" about our movements *when they carry out what we have conceptualized* for them, rather than what is *objectively needed* of them, needs to be checked. If what we have conceptualized is not useful to us in reality, then feeling good about it will not be useful to us either. (Here, we may recall figure 1.3 from chapter 1 about the goal of increasing the amount belief-reality alignment.) Olympic athletes would never fall for the trap. Track athletes would never "run on all fours like a cheetah" (because cheetahs are fast), "move their arms straight along the lines of the track" (because straight lines equate to the most direct path) or "bend their tongue when turning around a bend" (to help become "at one" with the bend-iness of the track) if it didn't improve their actual performance, safely or efficiently. Why, then, would we submit to aligning our actions to equivalent, emotionally appealing percepts—like pressing deeply for a deep sound, playing with padded fingers for a padded sound, or using a heavy arm for a heavy sound—if it didn't improve our actual performance, safely or efficiently?

The value that we give *to the accomplishment of our movement goals* distorts our ability to be objective about them. In piano playing, we must remind ourselves that "previous exposure to a "grammar" of movement is a factor in determining the relative aesthetic value."[55] This movement grammar is what our various teachers (and piano methods) teach us over years of training, and it is what we learn to judge our and others' movements by—irrespective of whether or not they are the *best* movements for the job. Again, unawares, "the actions of others are perceived through the lens of the self."[56]

Consequently, "haptic success" (literally, the pleasure derived from the sensations of our movements) may not equate with "sonic success," and, possibly, it might make the latter even harder to achieve, because when haptic goals are prioritized in favor of sonic outcomes (or any other musical goal), sonic outcomes risk being neglected. Worse, sonic outcomes may be objectively poor (e.g., poor dynamic control, execution errors etc.) yet still be perceived as being successful because of the cross-modal interference and perceptual dominance of the performer's "successful" haptic experience. Here are some more examples of how affective proprioception influences our piano-playing behaviors:

- "I felt the pleasure of being "at one" with my instrument during the performance... but later, listening to the recording, I realized how untidy much of my playing was."
- "The pianist played with calm, relaxed movements . . . but their playing lacked vitality and was poorly articulated."
- "My teacher was so happy with my improved physical postures and tension-free movements . . . but I still couldn't play the difficult passages well."
- "I played with lots of arm-weight during the *ff* sections to make a full, round sound . . . but many people said it sounded like I was bashing."

Depending on the circumstances, we—as students, teachers, performers or listeners—may benefit *or* suffer from the perceptual distortion that our haptics have over our ability to listen to sound objectively. Any one of us could be trained to feel good about sitting straight, or flattening out the hand, or using weighty arms, but none of them will *necessarily* improve our pianism. Pleasing our affective proprioception neurons is not the primary goal of piano playing, though it may be a beneficial accompanying goal.

Levinskaya's account of hearing Breithaupt play (the famed German pedagogue) serves as an excellent reminder of the pianistic problems that can occur when one loses the ability to distinguish between haptic success and sonic success: "On hearing his version of correct passage playing [...] at once I decided to study with Godowsky [...] In playing he [Breithaupt] evidently tried to follow his own precepts, and avoid all precise finger articulation."[57]

But to suggest that it is an easy task to overcome the perceptual dominance that our movements' feelings have over our ability to assess their pianistic utility, would be untrue. The skill of being able to objectify our own movements and sounds when being fully caught up in their feelings and emotions of playing is an acquired skill of experts, and even then, still a challenge, as the interface between what we want to hear and what we think we hear remains hazy.

Haptic Success, Sonic Failure

The "haptic success, sonic failure" scenario (i.e., "feels good, sounds bad") is a predictable outcome for those who are unaware of the influence that their haptics have over their ability to objectify the touch-tone event. The problem commonly feeds into pedagogical doctrines that prioritize "how to move" at the expense of focusing on "how to listen". Mistaken pedagogical beliefs that arise from being a slave to haptic influences rather than sonic ones might include the following:

- believing that your pianism will necessarily improve because of having adopted a specific hand position, sitting position, posture or gestural movement.
- believing that the haptic qualities of your movements will automatically transfer themselves into mechanical or musical qualities.
- that by successfully aligning your movements with an established movement-focused strategy (e.g., Alexander technique, Feldenkreis, etc.), that your pianism will improve.[58]

Given the widespread frequency of the above beliefs, for many pianists, optimized piano playing will remain an impossibility. This is because it is far easier in practice to participate in haptic pleasures and pedagogical theories that align with self-confirmation biases than deal with the daily nitty-gritty tasks of achieving the mechanico-expressive perfection required of elite-performance music making.

Metaphors, Reality, and the Single Mental Representation

It should becoming apparent that attempting to attribute our perception of piano tone quality to any single cause is futile because of the multi-modal web of neural connections that contribute to it. The brain likes to *integrate* not separate its functions. The guessing that we make in piano pedagogy can be more easily removed when the neuroscience that underlies it is better understood. Here are some examples of how the brain integrates its many functions to *accomplish* the act of touch when playing music:[59]

- areas of the brain that are involved in gestural movements are shared with areas that are involved in speech production and language syntax;
- the same areas involved in gestures and speech overlap with areas that link action recognition and action production;
- these areas are also involved in auditory-sensorimotor integration;
- and all these areas share connections with the supplementary motor and premotor areas, which are responsible for movement planning and, ultimately, movement execution.

Given the extent of these connections, it is easy to see why metaphors and gestures are such powerful drivers of musical communication and touch-tone beliefs. On a physiological level, emotions, ideas, gestures, sound, motor actions and sensory feedback all interconnect, and the mind creates metaphors to unify these disparate processes into a singular, simple, workable and shareable idea.[60] Metaphors provide a singularity where "both actions and percepts depend on a single underlying mental representation."[61]

And it is because of this single mental representation, that we feel *natural*—literally, neuro-biologically—when we "'breathe with the wrist" (Chopin)[62] or "play harp notes with round, tensed fingers" (Brendel).[63] Wrists don't breathe, but the physical release of the wrist off from the keyboard at the end of a musical phrase to *portray* a musical breath, does; just as harp-like fingers don't pluck the strings, but if they act harp-like, the pianist and the audience might be more convinced of the harp-like-ness of the sounds they make.

If we extend the application of the concept of the single mental representation to other areas of tone-touch pedagogy, many of its pseudo-scientific and metaphor-based theories become exposed. For example, it is understandable that advocates of arm-weight methods will believe that using the arms, shoulders and back are essential for producing a "full, sonorous and round"[64] sound, and that using solely a finger touch will produce a "thin, wooden, sharp sound."[65] Here, the mental representation of "weight" is shared with "fullness"—a quality that a "heavy" arm could provide but a "thin" finger never could.

Failing to understand the limits of metaphors tends to facilitate the spread of misinformation throughout the piano-pedagogical literature. As we have seen in the previous section, just because a percept and its action are aligned doesn't mean that either the percept or the action are useful to us. Any coherently matched percept-action pair could happily exist in its own abstract utopia while remaining entirely oblivious to the real-world outcomes that it produces.

This psychological blind-spot is not always obvious to us though, which is why so many pedagogical ideas about touch, tone and technique can lead us down the wrong paths: where we engage musically with a metaphor, align it with a touch metaphor, proceed to use a keystroke that aligns (metaphorically and physically) in some way with it, be convinced of its utility (affective proprioception and self-confirmation biases) yet remain entirely unaware that what we have invested our time in, may not be musically or mechanically useful, let alone, optimal, to our pianistic goals.

> ***Should we wish to excel in our pianism, we must take time out to identify our psychological blind-spots so as not to become puppets to "great in theory, bad in practice" scenarios, and be ready to replace them with "great in practice, great in theory" scenarios.***

Virtuosic pianism *might* arise from such a method—by coincidence of its alignment with what needs to happen in reality—but the alignment of the metaphorical percept with the metaphorical action will *not* be the reason why. Plucking the keys does not ensure a harp sound. Sitting proud and straight does not ensure a *maestoso* sound. Agitating your muscles will not ensure an *agitato* musical expression.

Percept-Action Alignment—Feeling "Right"

When there is alignment between the percept and the action, like playing an "intense" tenuto with an "intense" fingertip pressure, we tend to feel right and do not seek further proof of the rightness of the activity. Percept-action agreement is enough to convince our minds of the verity of the event. If there is conflict, however, i.e., if the action violates the percept, like producing a *cantabile* using "a piece of metal," feelings of repulsion, of being "unnatural" and other forms of criticism are likely to arise.

The following examples indicate how far-reaching, and damaging, the effects of some percept-action couplings can be for pianists. Many couplings, though respected by some, may be rejected by others (depending on their degree of habituation). They remind us why we should not blindly believe all that we are taught, nor all that we feel is right:

- using your thumb on the black keys;
- passing your thumb *over* the hand, not under;
- using the sustain pedal when playing Bach;[66]
- playing ornaments before the beat;
- playing with flat fingers;
- adding or removing notes from the score when performing;
- not practicing *hard*;
- arpeggiating chords;
- using science rather than traditions to advise on matters of pianism;
- wearing a tuxedo and black tie when performing;
- including electronic music in your concerts.

In the Eye of the Beholder

In addition to the influence that touch and gesture have on the perception of sound quality, is the influence of visual information.[67] Its importance should not be underestimated. As piano-physicist Ortmann observed, "so many qualities are read into the piano tone by the eye [that] it is very difficult for even an experienced listener to dissociate the two sense-impressions."[68] Pianists are constantly using sleight-of-hand tricks to manipulate the audience into believing something about the meaning of the touch that isn't acoustically there. Such tricks exploit the ambiguity that exists in the mind as it attempts to make best-guess predictions about the meaning of combined visual-auditory information.[69]

The Marimba Tone Illusion

Experimentally, it has been shown that when subjects observe the visual-audio playback of marimba players, they are lead to believe that tones are longer in duration when performers play them with "long" physical gestures, even when tones have the same temporal length.[70] Also, when notes of different duration are artificially superimposed upon different images, subjects are more likely to adjust and correlate their perception of the lengths of those notes with their visual representation. Such findings explain why pianists might use "long," "broad," and "rounded" gestures when playing *tenuto* or *cantabile* phrases: the visual length of the note convinces the listener (and the performer) of its acoustic length and, by correlation, of its singing-ness.

Compared to listening-only experiences, listening to *and* watching a performance can enhance the viewer's understanding of its expressive intention.[71] Why else would audiences rush to fill the seats of the auditorium where they can see the hands of the performer? Gestures add meaning, and possibly, to an audience ignorant of the finer points of the music being played, *provide* the meaning.

Certainly, it is rare *not* to find a player who exploits the visual effects of their gestures to some degree. It is a natural practice (musical percepts align with musical actions) and one that can easily be brought into one's practice.[72] The powerful visual effect of the movements of the playing of Grigory Sokolov—whether intentional or not—is a modern example of how a pianist's gestures can provide an additional layer of expression to their touch that takes it beyond its mechanico-acoustic function. As described in a concert review, "His [Sokolov's] hands often fly up after a particularly telling note, providing an idiosyncratic balletic correlate to the sound. His performance makes perfect sense on CD, but seeing it adds further meaning."[73]

As Davidson demonstrated in her study of the gesturally-rich pianist, Lang Lang, vision not only carries musical meaning, but can be *more* informative than sound in forming an observer's understanding of the performer's expressive intentions.[74] Somewhat perversely, it has also been shown that major international piano competition winners can be accurately predicted by watching short visual snippets of their performances with the sound removed.[75] Evidently, the "listeners' musical mind can readily be accessed [and influenced by pianists] through body movement"[76] in the absence of sound.

But to put things in perspective, a well-considered use of gesture isn't always needed to make piano playing great, nor do gestures need to be flamboyant for them to be meaningful. When gestures are incongruent with their expected musical meaning, and the expected percept-action unity becomes violated, watching the music might not be preferred to listening only, if the visual information is disliked. On the other hand, gestures offer us "a wonderful window into unspoken thoughts"[77] and may clarify meaning in situations where the meaning is unclear or ambiguous—as in the case of an inanimate piano tone—or to enhance meaning in situations where the basic meaning is already implied—like a *cantabile* passage.

> *Gestures may enhance or diminish musical meaning depending on how well they align with the observer's expectation of their function. Thus, gesturally generous playing may help to provide meaning to an audience that needs, or enjoys, a visual guide to the musical narrative, whereas gesturally economical playing may be sufficient to fulfill the needs of other types of listeners who can, or prefer, to follow the musical narrative through sound alone.*

Mirror Neurons: Learning Meaning

The role that *mirror neurons* play in our learning of the musical meaning of movements provides another route to understanding why we each treat the touch-tone relationship differently. Mirror neurons (located at the back of the frontal lobe) have been identified as being responsible for *the learning of the meaning* of others' actions. For example, object-related actions that are normally identified by a specific sound (e.g., the ripping of a piece of paper, the scraping of fingernails on a blackboard, or the sound that appears from a piano when a pianist plays a note) are known to activate the same mirror neurons in the observer as the performer.[78]

This reciprocal activation in the observer occurs regardless of whether the action is performed with or without sound. The feat is neurologically possible because the mirror neuron cells have "trimodal (motor, visual, and auditory) properties."[79] "The sound alone, the vision alone or the motor intention alone could then evoke [...] firing in such neurons even if the sound or the vision originate from someone else's movements."[80] Thus, mirror neurons allow the meaning of an action to be transmitted between a pianist and an observer without the pianist needing to include all the sensory information (e.g., sounds) that would normally accompany it.

Predictably, once mirror neurons have learned to associate a meaning to an action, that same association will be used to give meaning to it (and judge it) in the future. The ability of mirror neurons to *learn meaning* is another reason why distinctive (and conflicting) pedagogical schools of thought exist about the touch-tone relationship: each school correlates the visio-auditory-motor aspects of *their* keystrokes to *their* unique meaning—which is then propagated throughout its disciple members.

To be expected, schools that indoctrinate vast numbers of students are the ones that are more likely to have their touch-tone beliefs spread far and wide. Within specific regions of the world, where such beliefs are transmitted from generation to generation, these beliefs may dominate pedagogical trends—not because their beliefs about touch are any more useful than any other schools', but because, statistically, their particular learned meaning lives in the mirror neurons of more pianists—who then pass it on . . .

Understandably, because there are so many different ways of learning meaning about the touch-tone relationship, disagreements about the nature of the touch-tone relationship will arise whenever two different pianists from two different belief systems meet—which, as history shows, is most of the time.

> *The diversity of opinions about the effect of touch on tone quality is, in part, a consequence of the meaning that each person's mirror neurons have learned to attach to it. If one's touch only served a mechanical function, such diversity of opinion would not exist, because objectively there would be a best mechanical way of touching the key, which would then very quickly be known and adopted by all pianists.*

The combining of (objective) physical movements of tone production with (subjective) gestural movements is something that is forged into a pianist's technique from the earliest years of training where we are taught to produce a "basic" piano tone with a downward drop of the arm—"to sing"—and an upward movement of the wrist—"to breathe." The metaphor of the gesture is, of course, not inappropriate, but the use of metaphor to explain *the causality* of the sound quality is.[81] Neither historic nor modern pedagogy authorities seem to care for the difference. The London College of Music, in their handbook for pianists preparing for their Grade 3 piano examinations, states: "The melody is marked *cantabile* (in a singing style)—to produce a full, rich sound (like that of a singer), relax your wrist and harness the weight from your arm, allowing your fingers to explore the depth of each key; this will help attain a beautiful singing tone."[82]

This soup of metaphors and subjective associations—mixing *cantabile, singing, full, rich, relax, harness, weight, arm, explore, depth, attain,* and *beautiful*—adds subjective meaning to a keystroke that is otherwise mechanically, acoustically and objectively banal—and not to mention, simple. It is motor-sensory-auditory-visual-haptic indoctrination at its best, and the mirror neurons love it: as they attempt to join the dots of these multiple inputs and create a singular, unified musical meaning out of them: "[As] the development of the ability to play an instrument builds up, in the performer's motor system, a vocabulary of (musical-directed) motor acts that allow the agent to understand the actions, emotions, and intentions behind the musical signal."[83]

Thus, in addition to their mechanical role in producing sounds, motor actions learn to embody musical meaning and convey it motorically. What meaning the movements learn depends on what meaning they are taught—which takes us back to our learning years: if a certain arm-drop movement has been taught to you as one that produces a "*dolce* sound quality," and that's the movement that you use, and that's the movement that coincides with what your audience has learned, then a "*dolce* experience" will be the outcome for both you and the audience. You have provided the motor-sensory cues that will trigger a *dolce* experience in the mirror neurons of *that* audience. If, however, the *dolce* experience of your audience is triggered by a different set of motor-sensory cues, you can expect your audience to be both disappointed with the experience and critical of your movements that failed to produce the *dolce* sound that they expected. And the same might be said for other movement-generated music-quality experiences, like *espressivo, legato, marcato, maestoso, appassionato, tenuto, pesante*, and so on.

In a broader sense, the motor-sensory information provided by a pianist to an audience has to operate within a context in which the motor-sensory cues being exchanged are already (to enough of a degree) known. Otherwise, some transfer of meaning will be lost. This is why the musical meaning of a keystroke can be obvious to an observer within a performing context in which they have already been indoctrinated with the same rules, and why meaning can be so illusive outside of those rules, e.g., within a scientific, laboratory context where the usual contextual cues are removed. As the neuroscientist Chatterjee observed, "context has a profound influence on how we experience most objects and, importantly, how we experience pleasure."[84]

When a context provides a *group* of people with the right cues to trigger their emotions of pleasure, the sense of euphoria that is created may make it difficult—if not impossible—for alternative opinions to be respected. For example, in the post-concert audience euphoria of a famous pianist's recital, try convincing someone that the cause of the tone qualities of the individual notes that the performer played had nothing to do with their finger, hand or body movements, and everything to do with the way that they created illusions of tone quality *by manipulating the context* of each and every piano tone, be it by sound-based manipulations (contrasts of volume and texture), tempo and rhythm-based manipulations (rubato and agogics), instrument manipulations (by having the piano technician voice the hammers) or other multi-modal means.

Certainly, expressing an individual opinion that opposes a consensus opinion is an uphill battle in any discipline where indoctrinated belief systems prevail. And in the world of touch-tone piano pedagogy, it is no different, as the exasperated Lhévinne exclaimed, "the whole world has gone mad over the idea of relaxation [...] there must be hand-firmness, [... and] there must be finger-firmness also, or there is no accuracy."[85] Irrespective of the quality of his advice, Lhévinne, in this situation, was experiencing the driving power of pedagogical tribalism, where: "[the] perception of an object or scene is not determined solely by the empirical sensory information, but rather is subject to top–down processes and expectations."[86]

That we should arrive at such a conclusion—that our experience of tone quality is shaped by the meaning that we give to *motor actions*—repeat, *motor actions*, not sounds—demands that we be more critical of the touch-tone claims that we, and others, make. Furthermore, given that the processes of associative learning shape the values that we ascribe to sound quality, the opinions of teachers, institutions and other schools of pianism may need to be more critically evaluated, or, at least, contextualized, for the way in which a pianist *offers* a particular tone quality experience—let alone a musical experience—in one context may be rejected within another for no other reason except that the rules that govern each observer's tone-quality belief system are different.

The End of Touch-Tone Uncertainty?

Where, then, does this leave us? If our touch doesn't do what we think it does, and our opinions about how it influences sound are biased toward subjective criteria like what we *feel* is happening, what we *want to believe* is happening and what we've been *taught to believe* is happening, who and what should we actually believe about the touch-tone relationship? Does it matter?

Yes, it matters—in many ways. Recognizing that we each operate inside our own personalized belief system, puts us at a huge advantage. Importantly, it protects us from wasting time implementing beliefs that are neither useful to us, nor possible. But chiefly, it gives us permission to be free to pursue alternative beliefs that *are* useful, *are* possible, and *can be adapted* to suit the requirements of our pianistic ambitions.

When it comes to touch, knowing that the act of touch participates in two functions—*sound production* (objective and mechanical) and *meaning transmission* (subjective and emotional)—is a big prize of useful information. It prevents us from being duped by pedagogical theories that only value one function at the expense of the other. It prevents us from mistaking our perceptions for truths. It prevents us from deluding ourselves that our approach to pianism is better than it actually is. It prevents us from presuming that "musical talent" will automatically translate into "mechanical talent." And, above all, it provides us with a clear-thinking space upon which *we can choose and construct our own, optimized pianism* that integrates both its objective needs and subjective goals.

NOTES

1. White, William B. "The Human Element in Piano Tone Production." *The Journal of the Acoustical Society of America* 1, no. 3A (1930): 357–65. doi:https://doi.org/10.1121/1.1915190, 362.

2. Von Helmholtz, Hermann. *On the Sensations of Tone as a Physiological Basis for the Theory of Music*. Translated by Alexander Ellis. 1875. Reprint, London: Longmans, Green, And Co., 1895, 77.

3. Hart, Harry C, Melville W Fuller, and Walter S Lusby. "A Precision Study of Piano Touch and Tone." *The Journal of the Acoustical Society of America* 6, no. 2 (October 1, 1934): 80–94. doi:https://doi.org/10.1121/1.1915706; Culver, Charles A. *Musical Acoustics*. Philadelphia: Blakiston Company, 1947; Askenfelt, Anders, ed. *Five Lectures on the Acoustics of the Piano*. Stockholm: Royal Swedish Academy of Music, 1990; Conklin, Harold A. "Design and Tone in the Mechanoacoustic Piano. Part I. Piano Hammers and Tonal Effects." *Journal of the Acoustical Society of America* 99, no. 6 (June 1, 1996): 3286–96. doi:https://doi.org/10.1121/1.414947; Goebl, Werner, Roberto Bresin, and Alexander Galembo. "Once Again: The Perception of Piano Touch and Tone. Can Touch Audibly Change Piano Sound Independently of Intensity?" *Proceedings of the International Symposium on Musical Acoustics, Nara, Japan, March 31 to April 3.*, 2004, 332–35.

4. Von Helmholtz, Hermann. *On the Sensations of Tone as a Physiological Basis for the Theory of Music*. Translated by Alexander Ellis. 1875. Reprint, London: Longmans, Green, And Co., 1895; Suzuki, Hideo. "Spectrum Analysis and Tone Quality Evaluation of Piano Sounds with Hard and Soft Touches." *Acoustical Science and Technology* 28, no. 1 (2007): 1–6. doi:https://doi.org/10.1250/ast.28.1; Askenfelt, Anders, and Erik V Jansson. "From Touch to String Vibrations. II: The Motion of the Key and Hammer." *Journal of the Acoustical Society of America* 90, no. 5 (November 1, 1991): 2383–93. doi:https://doi.org/10.1121/1.402043; Conklin, Harold A. "Design and Tone in the Mechanoacoustic Piano. Part I. Piano Hammers and Tonal Effects." *Journal of the Acoustical Society of America* 99, no. 6 (June 1, 1996): 3286–96. doi:https://doi.org/10.1121/1.414947.

5. Suzuki, Hideo. "Spectrum Analysis and Tone Quality Evaluation of Piano Sounds with Hard and Soft Touches." *Acoustical Science and Technology* 28, no. 1 (2007): 1–6. doi:https://doi.org/10.1250/ast.28.1; Conklin, Harold A. "Design and Tone in the Mechanoacoustic Piano. Part I. Piano Hammers and Tonal Effects." *Journal of the Acoustical Society of America* 99, no. 6 (June 1, 1996): 3286–96. doi:https://doi.org/10.1121/1.414947; Askenfelt, Anders, ed. *Five Lectures on the Acoustics of the Piano*. Stockholm: Royal Swedish Academy of Music, 1990, Lecture 3 by Donald Hall.

6. Actually, this feature is exploited by Horowitz, whose hammers produced clear, bright tones, even when hitting the strings quietly.

7. Timbre independently affects the perception of emotions in music. See: Hailstone, Julia C., Rohani Omar, Susie M. D. Henley, Chris Frost, Michael G. Kenward, and Jason D. Warren. "It's Not What You Play, It's How You

Play It: Timbre Affects Perception of Emotion in Music." *Quarterly Journal of Experimental Psychology* 62, no. 11 (November 2009): 2141–55. doi:https://doi.org/10.1080/17470210902765957, 2142.

8. Mohr, Franz, and Edith Schaeffer. *My Life with the Great Pianists*. Grand Rapids, MI: Ravens Ridge Books, 1992, 127.

9. Holland, Bernard. "Vladimir Horowitz, Titan of the Piano, Dies." *Nytimes. com. The New York Times*, November 6, 1989. https://www.nytimes.com/1989/11/06/obituaries/vladimir-horowitz-titan-of-the-piano-dies.html.

10. Altenmüller, Eckart, Jürg Kesselring, and Mario Wiesendanger. *Music, Motor Control and the Brain*. Oxford: Oxford University Press, 2006, 85.

11. Diagrammatic representation based on those in Askenfelt, Anders, and Erik V Jansson. "From Touch to String Vibrations. II: The Motion of the Key and Hammer." *Journal of the Acoustical Society of America* 90, no. 5 (November 1, 1991): 2383–93. doi:https://doi.org/10.1121/1.402043.

12. If more flexible hammer shafts are used, this may increase to 0.4 mm. See: Askenfelt, Anders, and Erik V Jansson. "From Touch to String Vibrations. II: The Motion of the Key and Hammer." *Journal of the Acoustical Society of America* 90, no. 5 (November 1, 1991): 2383–93. doi:https://doi.org/10.1121/1.402043.

13. Askenfelt, Anders. "Measuring the motion of the piano hammer during string contact." *Department for Speech, Music and Hearing KTH Sweden: Quarterly Progress and Status Report* (1991), 33.

14. Askenfelt, Anders, Alexander Galembo, and Lola L Cuddy. "On the Acoustics and Psychology of Piano Touch and Tone." *Journal of the Acoustical Society of America* 103, no. 5 Supplement (May 1, 1998): 2873–73. doi:https://doi.org/10.1121/1.421527, 2873.

15. Ortmann, Otto. *The Physiological Mechanics of Piano Technique*. New York: Dutton, 1962, 340.

16. Hill, William G. "Noise in Piano Tone." *The Musical Times* 81, no. 1173 (November 1940): 458. doi:https://doi.org/10.2307/923870, 248.

17. Askenfelt, Anders. "Observations on the transient components of the piano tone." *Speech Transmission Laboratory – Quarterly Progress and Status Report* 90, no. 4 (July 28, 1993): 15–22, 15.

18. Goebl, Werner, Roberto Bresin, and Ichiro Fujinaga. "Perception of Touch Quality in Piano Tones." *The Journal of the Acoustical Society of America* 136, no. 5 (November 2014): 2839–50. doi:https://doi.org/10.1121/1.4896461, 2839.

19. Brendel, Alfred. *Musical Thoughts & Afterthoughts*. Robson Books Limited, 1976, 130.

20. Askenfelt, Anders. "Observations on the transient components of the piano tone." *Speech Transmission Laboratory – Quarterly Progress and Status Report* 90, no. 4 (July 28, 1993): 15–22, 21.

21. Askenfelt, Anders, and Erik V Jansson. "From Touch to String Vibrations. II: The Motion of the Key and Hammer." *Journal of the Acoustical Society of America* 90, no. 5 (November 1, 1991): 2383–93. doi:https://doi.org/10.1121/1.402043.

22. Goebl, Werner, Roberto Bresin, and Ichiro Fujinaga. "Perception of Touch Quality in Piano Tones." *The Journal of the Acoustical Society of America* 136, no. 5 (November 2014): 2839–50. doi:https://doi.org/10.1121/1.4896461.

23. Askenfelt, Anders. "Observations on the transient components of the piano tone." *Speech Transmission Laboratory – Quarterly Progress and Status Report* 90, no. 4 (July 28, 1993): 15–22.

24. Askenfelt, Anders, ed. *Five Lectures on the Acoustics of the Piano*. Stockholm: Royal Swedish Academy of Music, 1990.

25. tonebase Piano. "Ten Piano Technique Tips from Garrick Ohlsson." *YouTube*, August 12, 2024. https://www.youtube.com/watch?v=FWGZUHJQMrc.

26. For example, listen to: "Rachmaninoff: Études-Tableaux Op. 33, No. 2 (in C) [Horowitz 1967]" https://www.youtube.com/watch?v=q5OPvxVDYfA; or the 2nd subject, 1st movement in: "Horowitz Rachmaninoff 3rd Concerto Mehta NYPO 1978" – https://www.youtube.com/watch?v=D5mxU_7BTRA

27. Askenfelt, Anders. "Observations on the transient components of the piano tone." *Speech Transmission Laboratory – Quarterly Progress and Status Report* 90, no. 4 (July 28, 1993): 15–22; Goebl, Werner, Roberto Bresin, and Alexander Galembo. "Once Again: The Perception of Piano Touch and Tone. Can Touch Audibly Change Piano Sound Independently of Intensity?" *Proceedings of the International Symposium on Musical Acoustics, Nara, Japan, March 31 to April 3.*, 2004, 332–35; Koornhof, G., & Walt, A. "The influence of touch on piano sound." *Proceedings of the Stockholm Music Acoustics Conference (SMAC'93)* 79 (1994): 297–301; Suzuki, Hideo. "Spectrum Analysis and Tone Quality Evaluation of Piano Sounds with Hard and Soft Touches." *Acoustical Science and Technology* 28, no. 1 (2007): 1–6. doi:https://doi.org/10.1250/ast.28.1; Goebl, Werner, Roberto Bresin, and Ichiro Fujinaga. "Perception of Touch Quality in Piano Tones." *The Journal of the Acoustical Society of America* 136, no. 5 (November 2014): 2839–50. doi:https://doi.org/10.1121/1.4896461.

28. Diagrammatic representation derived from multiple sources, previously mentioned in text body.

29. Goebl, Werner, Roberto Bresin, and Ichiro Fujinaga. "Perception of Touch Quality in Piano Tones." *The Journal of the Acoustical Society of America* 136, no. 5 (November 2014): 2839–50. doi:https://doi.org/10.1121/1.4896461; Goebl, Werner, Roberto Bresin, and Alexander Galembo. "Once Again: The Perception of Piano Touch and Tone. Can Touch Audibly Change Piano Sound Independently of Intensity?" *Proceedings of the International Symposium on Musical Acoustics, Nara, Japan, March 31 to April 3*, 2004, 332–35; Suzuki, Hideo. "Spectrum Analysis and Tone Quality Evaluation of Piano Sounds with Hard and Soft Touches." *Acoustical Science and Technology* 28, no. 1 (2007): 1–6. doi:https://doi.org/10.1250/ast.28.1.

30. Galembo, Alexander, and Anders Askenfelt. "Perception of Musical Instrument by Performer and Listener (with Application to the Piano)." *Proceedings of the International Workshop on Human Supervision and Control in Engineering and Music*, (September 21–24, 2001) 257–66. http://www.engineeringandmusic.de/individu/galealex/Galambo-Paper.html.

31. In fact, it is very easy to demonstrate that touch surface noises resonate throughout the instrument: depress the sustain pedal of the piano and then tap on the key surface (without allowing the hammer to hit the string)—a significant amount of touch noise is captured by the free-to-resonate strings.

32. This technique is so common that it barely needs mentioning—though for want of some examples, listen to the playing of some of the early twentieth-century pianists (e.g., Pachmann, Hofmann, Rachmaninoff, Godowsky, Schnabel, Friedman).

33. Again, this is a standard feature of nineteenth-century and early twentieth-century piano playing, probably indicative of their strong commitment to making music "sing."

34. Predictably, these gestures are more commonly witnessed during loud *cantabile* playing, where pianists desire a more rounded attack to the sound, not a direct attack. It is especially used by pianists when playing loudly in the high treble R.H. registers of the piano (where the keybed thump may be heard relatively more compared to the sound of the vibrating strings). An example of this occurs in the final minutes of Rachmaninoff's 3rd Concerto, where the climax of the theme is played very loudly in chords in the high register of the piano (with the orchestra also very loud).

35. Zatorre, Robert J., Joyce L. Chen, and Virginia B. Penhune. "When the Brain Plays Music: Auditory–Motor Interactions in Music Perception and Production." *Nature Reviews Neuroscience* 8, no. 7 (July 2007): 547–58. doi:https://doi.org/10.1038/nrn2152; MacRitchie, Jennifer. "The Art and Science behind Piano Touch: A Review Connecting Multi-Disciplinary Literature." *Musicae Scientiae* 19, no. 2 (March 13, 2015): 171–90. doi:https://doi.org/10.1177/1029864915572813; Driver, Jon, and Charles Spence. "Multisensory Perception: Beyond Modularity and Convergence." *Current Biology* 10, no. 20 (October 2000): R731–35. doi:https://doi.org/10.1016/s0960-9822(00)00740-5.

36. Parncutt, Richard. "Piano Touch, Timbre, Ecological Psychology, and Cross-Modal Interference." *International Symposium on Performance Science.*, January 1, 2013. http://iwk.mdw.ac.at/lit_db_iwk/download.php?id=22058.

37. Driver, Jon, and Charles Spence. "Multisensory Perception: Beyond Modularity and Convergence." *Current Biology* 10, no. 20 (October 2000): R731–35. doi:https://doi.org/10.1016/s0960-9822(00)00740-5.

38. Driver, Jon, and Charles Spence. "Multisensory Perception: Beyond Modularity and Convergence." *Current Biology* 10, no. 20 (October 2000): R731–35. doi:https://doi.org/10.1016/s0960-9822(00)00740-5, 731.

39. Talsma, Durk, Daniel Senkowski, Salvador Soto-Faraco, and Marty G. Woldorff. "The Multifaceted Interplay between Attention and Multisensory Integration." *Trends in Cognitive Sciences* 14, no. 9 (September 2010): 400–410. doi:https://doi.org/10.1016/j.tics.2010.06.008, 401.

40. Maes, Pieter-Jan, Marc Leman, Caroline Palmer, and Marcelo M. Wanderley. "Action-Based Effects on Music Perception." *Frontiers in Psychology* 4 (2014). doi:https://doi.org/10.3389/fpsyg.2013.01008, 1.

41. Personal experience from working in Cardiac Intensive Care departments in the UK.

42. For example, observe the traditional dances of indigenous peoples like the Aboriginal Australians.

43. Galembo, Alexander. "Perception of Musical Instrument by Performer and Listener (with Application to the Piano)." *Proceedings of the International Workshop on Human Supervision and Control in Engineering and Music*, (September 21–24, 2001) 257–66. http://www.engineeringandmusic.de/individu/galealex/Galambo-Paper.html.

44. Maes, Pieter-Jan, Marc Leman, Caroline Palmer, and Marcelo M. Wanderley. "Action-Based Effects on Music Perception." *Frontiers in Psychology* 4 (2014). doi:https://doi.org/10.3389/fpsyg.2013.01008, 1.

45. Bresciani, Jean-Pierre, Marc O. Ernst, Knut Drewing, Guillaume Bouyer, Vincent Maury, and Abderrahmane Kheddar. "Feeling What You Hear: Auditory Signals Can Modulate Tactile Tap Perception." *Experimental Brain Research* 162, no. 2 (December 10, 2004): 172–80. doi:https://doi.org/10.1007/s00221-004-2128-2, 172.

46. Guest, Steve, Caroline Catmur, Donna Lloyd, and Charles Spence. "Audiotactile Interactions in Roughness Perception." *Experimental Brain Research* 146, no. 2 (September 1, 2002): 161–71. doi:https://doi.org/10.1007/s00221-002-1164-z.

47. Whiteside, Abby. *Indispensables of Piano Playing*. 2nd ed. New York: Charles Scribner's Sons, 1961, 52.

48. Parncutt, Richard. "Piano Touch, Timbre, Ecological Psychology, and Cross-Modal Interference." *International Symposium on Performance Science.*, January 1, 2013. http://iwk.mdw.ac.at/lit_db_iwk/download.php?id=22058, 2.

49. Neuhaus, Heinrich. *The Art of Piano Playing*. Translated by K. A. Leibovitch. London: Kahn & Averill, 1993, 152.

50. Del Pico-Taylor, Maria, and S. Tammam. "The Wisdom of Dorothy Taubman." *Clavier*, 2005, 19.

51. Cole, Jonathan, and Barbara Montero. "Affective Proprioception." *Janus Head* 9, no. 2 (2007): 299–317. doi:https://doi.org/10.5840/jh2006922.

52. Cole, Jonathan, and Barbara Montero. "Affective Proprioception." *Janus Head* 9, no. 2 (2007): 299–317. doi:https://doi.org/10.5840/jh2006922, 299.

53. Music Academy of the West. "Leon Fleisher Solo Piano Masterclass July 13, 2015." *YouTube*, July 29, 2015. https://www.youtube.com/watch?v=EGRnYBxx2Y8.

54. Just for the record, I love Fleisher's playing, his teachings and his musings. I am not judging his artistry. I know many people who studied with him and I too feel privileged to have witnessed him teach and play (Mozart, K. 414) when I was a student at the 1995 Tanglewood Music Festival.

55. Paterson, Mark. "Movement for Movement's Sake? On the Relationship between Kinaesthesia and Aesthetics." *Essays in Philosophy* 13, no. 2 (2012): 471–97. doi:https://doi.org/10.7710/1526-0569.1433, 471.

56. McElvery, Raleigh. "How the Brain Links Gestures, Perception and Meaning." *Quanta Magazine*, March 25, 2019. https://www.quantamagazine.org/how-the-brain-links-gestures-perception-and-meaning-20190325/.

57. Levinskaya, Maria. *The Levinskaya System of Pianoforte Technique and Tone-Colour through Mental & Muscular Control*. London; Toronto: J.M. Dent and Sons, 1930, 57.

58. In this regard, there are too many books to mention, though books like those of Arnold Schultz (*The Riddle of the Pianist's Finger*), Alan Fraser (*The Craft of Piano Playing*) and Thomas Mark (*What Every Pianist Needs to Know About the Body*) are, in my opinion, representative of the pedagogical mistake of focusing too much on haptic issues and affective proprioception (e.g., insisting on specific joint positions, degrees of muscle tension and/or levels of awareness of them) at the expense of pursuing the musical goals for which they serve. One could engage, or not engage, in such tasks and be no closer to acquiring the skills needed to be a virtuosic pianist (and quite possibly, might direct us further from it).

59. To paraphrase: Rizzolatti, Giacomo, and Michael A. Arbib. "Language within Our Grasp." *Trends in Neurosciences* 21, no. 5 (May 1998): 188–94. doi:https://doi.org/10.1016/s0166-2236(98)01260-0; Zatorre, Robert J., Joyce L. Chen, and Virginia B. Penhune. "When the Brain Plays Music: Auditory–Motor Interactions in Music Perception and Production." *Nature Reviews Neuroscience* 8, no. 7 (July 2007): 547–58. doi:https://doi.org/10.1038/nrn2152; Bangert, Marc, Thomas Peschel, Gottfried Schlaug, Michael Rotte, Dieter Drescher, Hermann Hinrichs, Hans-Jochen Heinze, and Eckart Altenmüller. "Shared Networks for Auditory and Motor Processing in Professional Pianists: Evidence from FMRI Conjunction." *NeuroImage* 30, no. 3 (April 2006): 917–26. doi:https://doi.org/10.1016/j.neuroimage.2005.10.044.

60. Taylor, Cynthia, and Bryan M. Dewsbury. "On the Problem and Promise of Metaphor Use in Science and Science Communication." *Journal of Microbiology & Biology Education* 19, no. 1 (January 26, 2018). doi:https://doi.org/10.1128/jmbe.v19i1.1538.

61. Zatorre, Robert J., Joyce L. Chen, and Virginia B. Penhune. "When the Brain Plays Music: Auditory–Motor Interactions in Music Perception and Production." *Nature Reviews Neuroscience* 8, no. 7 (July 2007): 547–58. doi:https://doi.org/10.1038/nrn2152, 550.

62. Eigeldinger, Jean-Jacques. *Chopin: Pianist and Teacher as Seen by His Pupils*. Cambridge, Cambridgeshire; New York: Cambridge University Press, 1986, 45.

63. Brendel, Alfred. *Musical Thoughts & Afterthoughts*. Robson Books Limited, 1976, 95-96.

64. Breithaupt, Rudolf Maria . *Natural Piano-Technic. Vol. II. School of Weight-Touch ... Preliminary to Intermediate Grade ... Translation by John Bernhoff*. Translated by John Bernhoff. Leipzig: C. F. Kahnt Nachfolger, 1909, 56.

65. Breithaupt, Rudolf Maria . *Natural Piano-Technic. Vol. II. School of Weight-Touch ... Preliminary to Intermediate Grade ... Translation by John Bernhoff*. Translated by John Bernhoff. Leipzig: C. F. Kahnt Nachfolger, 1909, 56.

66. Playing Bach *at all* on the piano, is still considered by many to be a (percept-action) violation.

67. Davidson, Jane W. "Visual Perception of Performance Manner in the Movements of Solo Musicians." *Psychology of Music* 21, no. 2 (April 1993): 103–13. doi:https://doi.org/10.1177/030573569302100201; Spence, Charles. "Audiovisual Multisensory Integration." *Acoustical Science and Technology* 28, no. 2 (2007): 61–70.

doi:https://doi.org/10.1250/ast.28.61; Cook, Nicholas. "Beyond the Notes." *Nature* 453, no. 7199 (June 2008): 1186–87. doi:https://doi.org/10.1038/4531186a; Behne, Klaus-Ernst, and Clemens Wöllner. "Seeing or Hearing the Pianists? A Synopsis of an Early Audiovisual Perception Experiment and a Replication." *Musicae Scientiae* 15, no. 3 (August 15, 2011): 324–42. doi:https://doi.org/10.1177/1029864911410955; Platz, Friedrich, and Reinhard Kopiez. "When the Eye Listens: A Meta-Analysis of How Audio-Visual Presentation Enhances the Appreciation of Music Performance." *Music Perception: An Interdisciplinary Journal* 30, no. 1 (September 2012): 71–83. doi:https://doi.org/10.1525/mp.2012.30.1.71.

68. Ortmann, Otto. *The Physiological Mechanics of Piano Technique*. New York: Dutton, 1962, 341.

69. These tricks are no different to the techniques used by ventriloquists, who use the Ventriloquism effect and the McGurk effect to exploit the ambiguity that lies behind the perception of meaning in speech. See: Broughton, Mary C., and Catherine J. Stevens. "Analyzing Expressive Qualities in Movement and Stillness: Effort-Shape Analyses of Solo Marimbists' Bodily Expression." *Music Perception: An Interdisciplinary Journal* 29, no. 4 (April 1, 2012): 339–57. doi:https://doi.org/10.1525/mp.2012.29.4.339.

70. Schutz, Michael, and Scott Lipscomb. "Hearing Gestures, Seeing Music: Vision Influences Perceived Tone Duration." *Perception* 36, no. 6 (June 2007): 888–97. doi:https://doi.org/10.1068/p5635.

71. Broughton, Mary C., and Catherine J. Stevens. "Analyzing Expressive Qualities in Movement and Stillness: Effort-Shape Analyses of Solo Marimbists' Bodily Expression." *Music Perception: An Interdisciplinary Journal* 29, no. 4 (April 1, 2012): 339–57. doi:https://doi.org/10.1525/mp.2012.29.4.339.

72. Parncutt, Richard, and Malcolm Troup. "Piano." In *The Science and Psychology of Music Performance: Creative Strategies for Teaching and Learning*, edited by Gary McPherson, 285–302. Oxford: Oxford University Press, 2002.

73. Cook, Nicholas. "Beyond the Notes." *Nature* 453, no. 7199 (June 2008): 1186–87. doi:https://doi.org/10.1038/4531186a, 1187.

74. Davidson, Jane W. "Bodily Movement and Facial Actions in Expressive Musical Performance by Solo and Duo Instrumentalists: Two Distinctive Case Studies." *Psychology of Music* 40, no. 5 (August 20, 2012): 595–633. doi:https://doi.org/10.1177/0305735612449896.

75. Tsay, Chia-Jung. "Sight over Sound in the Judgment of Music Performance." *Proceedings of the National Academy of Sciences* 110, no. 36 (August 19, 2013): 14580–85. doi:https://doi.org/10.1073/pnas.1221454110.

76. Maes, Pieter-Jan, Marc Leman, Caroline Palmer, and Marcelo M. Wanderley. "Action-Based Effects on Music Perception." *Frontiers in Psychology* 4 (2014). doi:https://doi.org/10.3389/fpsyg.2013.01008, 1.

77. Says neuroscientist, S. Golden-Meadow in: McElvery, Raleigh. "How the Brain Links Gestures, Perception and Meaning." *Quanta Magazine*, March 25, 2019. https://www.quantamagazine.org/how-the-brain-links-gestures-perception-and-meaning-20190325/.

78. Kohler, Evelyne, Christian Keysers, M. Alessandra Umiltà, Leonardo Fogassi, Vittorio Gallese, and Giacomo Rizzolatti. "Hearing Sounds, Understanding Actions: Action Representation in Mirror Neurons." *Science* 297, no. 5582 (August 2, 2002): 846–48. doi:https://doi.org/10.1126/science.1070311.

79. D'Ausilio, Alessandro. "Mirror-like Mechanisms and Music." *The Scientific World JOURNAL* 9, no. 9 (2009): 1415–22. doi:https://doi.org/10.1100/tsw.2009.160, 1417.

80. Keysers, Christian, Evelyne Kohler, M. Alessandra Umiltà, Luca Nanetti, Leonardo Fogassi, and Vittorio Gallese. "Audiovisual mirror neurons and action recognition." *Experimental brain research* 153 (2003): 628-636, 635. This feat is neurologically possible because the mirror neuron cells have "trimodal (motor, visual, and auditory) properties" See: D'Ausilio, Alessandro. "Mirror-like Mechanisms and Music." *The Scientific World JOURNAL* 9, no. 9 (2009): 1415–22. doi:https://doi.org/10.1100/tsw.2009.160, 1417.

81. To paraphrase Altenmüller and Furuya, the pianists' movements have become "acculturated emotional gestures." In: Altenmüller, Eckart, and Shinichi Furuya. "Apollos Gift and Curse: Making Music as a Model for Adaptive and Maladaptive Plasticity." *E-Neuroforum* 23, no. 2 (January 24, 2017). doi:https://doi.org/10.1515/nf-2016-a054.

82. London College of Music. *Piano: Grade 3. Piano 2018-2020*. University of West London, LCM publications. (2017), p. 20.

83. Schiavio, Andrea, Damiano Menin, and Jakub Matyja. "Music in the Flesh: Embodied Simulation in Musical Understanding." *Psychomusicology: Music, Mind, and Brain* 24, no. 4 (December 2014): 340–43. doi:https://doi.org/10.1037/pmu0000052, 341.

84. Chatterjee, Anjan. *The Aesthetic Brain: How We Evolved to Desire Beauty and Enjoy Art*. New York: Oxford University Press, 2015, 9.

85. Lhévinne, Josef. "Good Tone Is Born in the Player's Mind." *The Musician* 28, no. 7 (1923), 7.

86. Connors, Michael H., and Peter W. Halligan. "A Cognitive Account of Belief: A Tentative Road Map." *Frontiers in Psychology* 5 (February 13, 2015). doi:https://doi.org/10.3389/fpsyg.2014.01588, 3.

Part III

OPTIMIZING PIANISM

"We cannot solve our problems with the same thinking we used to create them."[1] – (attr.) Albert Einstein

---

1. https://hsm.stackexchange.com/questions/7751/did-einstein-say-we-cannot-solve-our-problems-with-the-same-thinking-we-used-to

Chapter 5

Pursuing Excellence

Beliefs, 3 Ms, and Process

"Would you tell me, please, which way I ought to go from here?"
"That depends a good deal on where you want to get to," said the Cat.—Lewis Carroll (in *Alice's Adventures in Wonderland*, chapter 6.)

Up until now, we have examined a large amount of touch-tone information. Specifically, we have looked at how our understanding of the touch-tone interaction affects the decisions that we make about our pianism, and that this understanding is influenced by cognitive forces that we are largely unaware of, including: previously endorsed beliefs, unchecked biases, mental short-cuts, cross-modal interference, assumptions about causality, single mental representations, and the action meanings of mirror-neurons. We have observed, also, that facts about pianism are often only sought, selectively, to self-confirm our beliefs or, as a last resort, when our beliefs fail to work in the real world.

The purpose for understanding the pitfalls and limitations of human perception is not to become an academic or a psychologist but to realize that the pedagogical information that we use on a daily basis is riddled with assumptions and that implementing it may not be any more useful than not implementing it at all. If excellence in pianism is our goal, and the music that we wish to share with the world depends on it, it makes no sense to be practicing using information of such variable quality.

We've addressed the topic of the relative nature of our beliefs. Now we must take advantage of that relativity and upgrade the information that we put into practice. What might this look like: what is it that we need to get right to excel? *What matters*?

Firstly, as discussed, our *Beliefs* about pianism need to be framed in a way that allows optimal pianism to occur. Even if our beliefs about pianism are factually incorrect, our beliefs must, at least, not be so distorted that they prevent our pianism from functioning well in the real world.

Secondly, we need to optimize our skills in the areas of pianism that objectively matter: our *Mechanical* skills, our *Mental* skills, and our *Musical* skills. The complexity of pianism cannot be reduced to a simpler form: a brain (*mental*) must function to move muscles to move keys (*mechanical*) to make meaningful sounds that contribute to the musical experience (*musical*). Without a brain, muscles and sounds, music cannot be made on the piano. With a well-trained brain, well-coordinated movements and well-organized sounds (and a sprinkle of creativity), great music can be made.

Thirdly, we need a *Process* of practicing that ensures that our skills improve quickly, reliably and safely.

All these aspects of pianism are represented below, conceptually, in the 3M Triangle.

3M TRIANGLE OF PIANISM

The 3M Triangle Explained

Note, firstly, in the 3M Triangle, the centrality of our Beliefs (our combined thoughts, feelings and understanding about pianism) and the influence that they exert on the way that we practice the Mechanical, Mental, and Musical aspects of our pianism.

Next, note that although our beliefs influence our actions, ultimately, *it is the reality of the function of our 3 Ms* that defines our pianism, not our beliefs

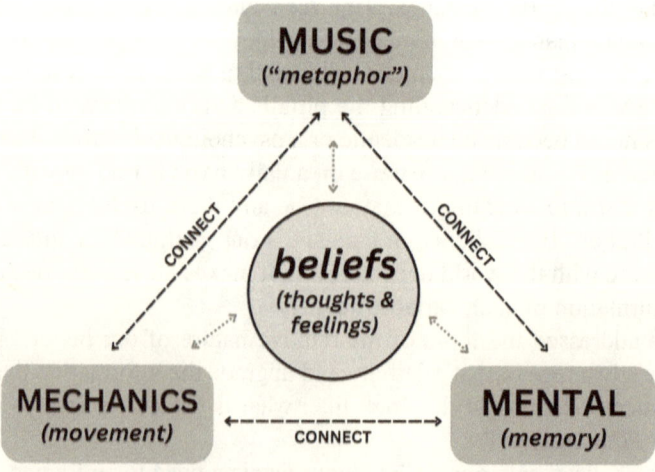

Figure 5.1. The 3M Triangle. Author created

about them. (Again, recall figure 1.3 from chapter 1.) That is, we might *think* that we are being expressive, that the movements of our fingers are correct, or that our method of practice is productive, but if none of it is true, *what we think* about them ought to be questioned and/or rejected and/or improved. Only beliefs that are useful should be held.

Furthermore, note how there is no limit to how much any "M" can develop. One can never have too much Musical skill, Mechanical skill or Mental skill, and it should not be taken for granted that our skills in any of our 3 Ms will ever fully be maximized. Our musical ideas can always reach further, the mechanics of our touch can always be more efficient and our ability to learn, recall, and execute music can always be more effective.

But at the same time, exceptional skills in one area of pianism will not necessarily solve the problems of the other areas. Pianists with excellent mechanics may still be boring to listen to and have memory lapses; pianists with the highest levels of musicality may still have messy passagework or take forever to learn repertoire; and pianists that can learn and memorize music quickly may still have nothing interesting to offer, musically or technically.

For pianism to really work, not only must each M function at a high level, but each M must learn how to connect with the other Ms. Acknowledging this interrelationship is indispensable. As developed as any single M might be in isolation, until it functions in partnership with the other Ms, it is not, *in reality*, particularly useful. This point is particularly evident (often painfully so), when it is exposed under performance conditions, where:

- Good musical ideas are only as good as their being able to be remembered and expressed via touch during performance; and
- Having good touch mechanics in the practice room is useless unless your movements are also capable of transmitting ideas through them; and
- Having an encyclopedic memory is irrelevant if your pianism is of poor quality and the ideas transmitted through it are mundane.

In short, each M and each of the connections between them needs to be optimized for optimized pianism to occur. Almost certainly, if your pianism is not thriving, one (or more) of your beliefs, your mechanics, your mental skills, your musical skills, or your process of practicing, will be limiting you. It is your job to find the sources of your problems and fix them.

To state the obvious, *improving* your pianism will require:

- adopting useful Beliefs about your pianism
- *better* Mechanics of touch

- *better* Mental skills
- *better* Musical ideas
- *better* Processes of practicing

Not improving your pianism, will require:

- rejecting useless Beliefs about your pianism
- *worse* Mechanics of touch
- *worse* Mental skills
- *worse* Musical ideas
- *worse* Processes of practicing

The 3M model is designed to show the links of causality that lie within your piano playing. It can be used to expose strengths and weaknesses. Both pianists and teachers can use it to diagnose *specific* pianistic problems and prescribe *tailored* practice solutions. It removes the guesswork from the practice room and the indiscriminate implementation of speculative pedagogical advice. It ensures excellence and efficiency of learning.

Curiously, when pianists begin to engage more deliberately in the process of assessing and improving their 3Ms, several realizations usually occur:

- that none of your Ms are fully optimized;
- that many of your Ms have small, yet easily correctable problems;
- that the connections between your Ms may be underdeveloped;
- that a single, small problem may be causing a disproportionately large negative effect on your overall performance;
- that the strengths of your playing may be covering over its weaknesses;
- that your practice routines habitually neglect specific aspects of your 3M Triangle; and
- that when you directly improve your Ms, your previously held beliefs about your pianism may no longer appear true or relevant.

Finger Exercises, the 3 Ms and Seeing through the Notes

Case study: the "Hanon" pianist

Besides its role in helping you to identify strengths and weaknesses in your playing, by giving more focus to your 3 Ms, you can ensure that your practice efforts remain useful whatever you practice. As an example, consider a pianist who devotes daily practice time to Hanon exercises (or anything similar)—a musically void but, nevertheless, commonly prescribed task. Imagine, also, that this pianist learns to play these exercises with great speed and dexterity. On first impression, this may seem commendable, but let us reflect upon what it *does not* tell us about what this pianist has learned:

Mechanically:
- it says nothing about which fingers of this pianist work better or worse, in which combinations, what their level of accuracy is, whether the momentum transfer of the touch is efficient, whether the wrist is locked or tight, whether they feel comfortable when playing the instrument, or whether it causes pain or injury.

Mentally:
- although it suggests an ability to learn different finger sequences, it says nothing about the pianist's ability to make music at the same time as playing those sequences, the efficiency of their learning, their ability to memorize music, whether the same finger dexterity could have been obtained (or improved) by playing proper music, whether practicing the exercises in one's head would have lead to the same improvement, or whether there is enjoyment (or stress) associated with the task.

Musically:
- importantly, it does not tell us whether the pianist has any artistic vision, is able to think musically or creatively, is able to play other types of piano music (with different touches, speeds and dynamics), or whether the pianist has any ability whatsoever to interpret or communicate ideas through sound.

In reality, to be able to play Hanon well, or any other finger exercise, tells us very little about anything useful—i.e., it does not tell us about the function of the 3 Ms *under musical conditions*. The only thing that it tells us, and worryingly so, is that the pianist has chosen to spend their precious practice time on cultivating a mono-dimensional finger-stroke at the expense of extending their musical imagination, optimizing their biomechanics or challenging their mental skills.

Without deliberately focusing on a specific M, or the connections between the Ms, it is difficult to recommend such mono-dimensional activities. And even should the Hanon be used to improve one of the 3 Ms, a tough question still needs to be answered: given the amount of good music available to improve such skills, why choose the exercises of Hanon at all? Why not just use scales or make up your own exercise? Or play a study, like Czerny, or, better, Cramer, Moszkowsky, Chopin or Liszt? I am still yet to attend a Hanon recital.

Chapter 6

Mechanical Skills

"[Do] whatever goes straight to the point and smoothes the technical side of the art"[1]—Frédéric Chopin

This section outlines the principles of the mechanics of touch. By knowing these principles, it is possible to work out the best mechanical solution to any pianistic problem *and* stay away from self-inflicted injury. The mechanical principles that underlie successful pianism are not complicated. They are knowable, easy to learn and optimisable. Guessing solutions to technical problems is no longer required. (Many videos showing how to apply theory to practice can be found at www.cameronroberts.com.au.)

Playing with good mechanics allows us to perform efficiently, effectively and comfortably within physiological limits. As the laws of motion are universal, these principles apply to everybody. They do not change between pianists, teachers, institutions, across borders or across generations. Knowing the rules allows us to cut through the noise of pedagogy and solve the mechanical problems of technique independently. It prevents us from wasting time learning hundreds of types of keystrokes that draw our attention away from what is a simple mechanico-acoustic process.[2]

As our pianism reflects the combined output of our 3 Ms, ensuring that the mechanics of our touch are kept optimized needs to be one of the constant points of practice focus. Like a painter's brushstroke, a golfer's swing or a dancer's body, our movements are an unavoidable physical reality through which our creative ideas must pass. If our movements limit us, so too will they limit our pianism.

Our touch has no other function than to facilitate the expression of our ideas. If we have no ideas, there is no point "practicing" touch, and if we have ideas, we need our touch to facilitate those ideas as reliably as possible.

For some pianists, effective and efficient ways of playing are nurtured early in their development. They will have little need to think about the mechanics of their playing. Others, however, will have acquired bad mechanical habits that will prevent them from playing virtuosic repertoire. These errors may be subtle, hidden from the pianist's awareness, though, nevertheless, simple to fix.

To be clear, despite the need to play with a high level of mechanical efficiency for many types of passageworks, our biomechanics do not *always* need to be perfect in order to play well most of the time. On many occasions, there are good reasons for our touch *not* to be mechanically efficient (explained later). Understanding when efficiency matters and when it doesn't is important so as not to spend any more time on mechanical issues than is absolutely necessary.

THE PIANO ACTION

Understanding the piano action gives us a head start in understanding how to optimize the mechanics of our keystrokes.

- The Lever Action

The piano key acts as a lever. The sequence of events within the piano action are as follows: pressing down the key pushes up the wippen, which pushes up the jack, which pushes up on the knuckle of the hammer shaft, which moves the shaft upwards, which then separates from the jack ("escapement") and flies upwards until the head of the hammer hits the string.

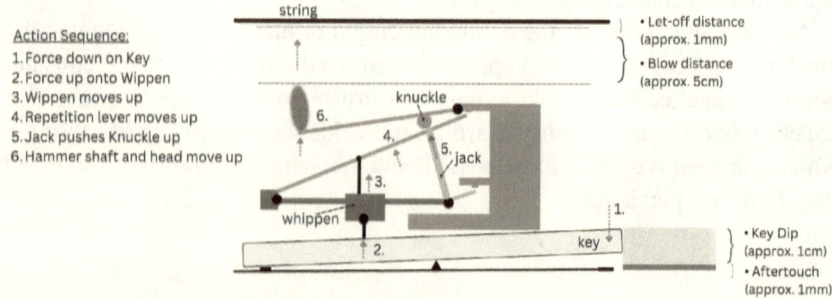

Figure 6.1. The Piano Action. Author created

The key, being a lever, is mechanically easiest to push down at the edge of the key—the point furthest away from its fulcrum (called the *balance rail*). This point may not always be the easiest to use from a practical point of view, but there will be many times when playing nearer to the edge (than we otherwise might have) will make the touch stroke feel easier (less force required).

- The Key Dip

The key dip is the distance that the key moves down before it hits the keybed. In a typical, late eighteenth-century Viennese piano, the key dip was around 5 mm. In an early nineteenth-century English piano, it was around 7.5 mm.[3] The heavier touch of the English piano was due to this increased key dip—a necessary consequence of requiring more key leverage to generate speed in the heavier hammers.[4] In the modern piano, the key dip is around 9–12 mm (3/8ths–4/10ths of an inch) and the minimum amount of mass required to make a sound, if it is placed onto the key surface—the *drop weight*—is approximately 50 g.[5]

> *In the 17th and 18th centuries, keys were much shorter in length. For practical reasons, curled-fingered techniques were required. However, because of the extra leverage required of the actions of the early 19th century pianos, the length of the keys and the distance of the key dip had to increase. Although this allowed for less-curled fingers to be used, their use was not immediately adopted by pianists who had grown up with the earlier instruments (like Beethoven). Not until Chopin and Liszt were these more relaxed hand positions used, with fingers less curled—an observation that needs to be remembered when addressing the technical problems of the repertoire of this transitional period (the early 1800s).*

- Escapement, Let-off and Aftertouch

Escapement (let-off) is the moment when the jack slides off the knuckle of the hammer shaft and leaves the hammer flying unaided toward the string—i.e., the hammer *escapes* and *lets off* from the key's influence. When a key is pressed, the moment of escapement occurs when the hammer head is approximately 1–3 mm away from the string.[6] This is called the *let-off distance*. The let-off moment typically occurs when the key is approximately 96–98 percent of its way into its key-dip journey.[7]

> *Because of the proximity of the hammer to the string and the proximity of the key to the keybed at the moment of let-off, our minds are given the (false) impression that our touch is controlling the hammer all the way up*

to, and including, the point of impact with the string (and, for some, including the key-keybed interaction too). This perceptual mis-interpretation of the mechanics of the touch-tone event infiltrates many of the pedagogical misunderstandings about the touch-tone relationship.*

Let-off distances that are extremely small may provide the pianist with fractionally more control over the hammer (because it extends the time that the key—and the finger that moves it—is in contact with the hammer)[8] but making the distance *too* small comes at the cost of creating a technical problem in the action as it risks that the hammer double-hits the string (as it overcorrects in the direction of the string after having already rebounded off it).[9] The distance that the key moves after let-off is called the *aftertouch*. Piano technicians point out that although pianists have no control over the hammer during the aftertouch, the aftertouch is "THE most important thing to the artist, even though they may not know exactly what it is."[10]

When the aftertouch is larger, there will be a bigger mismatch between the timing of the hammer-string collision and the key-keybed collision. Pianists may perceive this as a loss of key control or responsiveness.

- Action Leverage

Generally, the leverage provided by the piano action is around 5:1—i.e., for every 1 mm the key moves, the hammer moves 5 mm. This is called the *action ratio*. Given that the kep dip is approximately 1 cm, the distance that the hammer travels before it hits the string (the *blow distance*) will be approximately 5 cm.[11] Obviously, the exact amount of leverage that each key has may differ slightly between instruments. It may also differ within the same instrument depending on how the instrument is regulated.

Given the differences in leverage between different pianos, pianists should anticipate that their habitual keystrokes will result in subtly different mechanical and acoustic outcomes when playing them.

Failing to notice these differences and adapt to them can be a fault of amateur pianists who might instinctively *impose* their habitual technique upon an unfamiliar piano and expect mechanico-acoustic outcomes from it which it is incapable of delivering. Doing so may contribute to the use of inappropriate keystroke forces, inappropriate means of producing those forces or inappropriate acoustic outcomes.

When playing on an unfamiliar instrument, the importance of "the warmup" should not be underestimated. Besides warming up the muscles (and your concentration) it provides you with vital mechanical and tonal information about that instrument. To be thorough, a warmup should include music that involves different keystrokes in different registers and dynamics. Given that the full process can take several hours, it seems unjust that pianists are continually being assessed in conservatories and concert halls around the world where insufficient time is allowed to make such important mechanico-acoustic adaptations.

THE WINDOW OF OPPORTUNITY

Up until the moment of escapement, the key, the jack, the knuckle and the hammer are all in contact with each other, and the force that the pianist gives to the key can be directly transmitted to the hammer. Thus, the period represents a *window of opportunity* for the pianist to move the hammer.

The timeframe of this window of opportunity will depend on the speed of the key depression and the type of keystroke used. For example, the time taken to complete a full key dip varies between approximately 0.02 s (*forte*) and 0.16 s (*pianissimo*)[12] though given that escapement occurs at a point approximately 97 percent through the key dip, the actual duration of the window of opportunity will be approximately 3 percent less than these durations. Notably, the time frame would be reduced fractionally more if the touch is *very staccato* and the force from the finger is completely withdrawn from the key prior to the commencement of escapement.

During the keystroke, the pianist has approximately 0.02–0.16 s to generate the hammer velocity. This is not much time for romance. 0.03 s is the delay time of a knee-jerk reflex[13] (which is only fractionally slower than the contact time of hitting a golf ball[14]). 0.16 s is the approximate duration of a blink of an eye.[15]

Furthermore, as the key descent time is so short, there is no physiological possibility that the human body can meaningfully correct for any errors of key descent speed once the key is in motion. The fastest neuro-motor reaction time to an auditory stimulus is approximately 0.14–0.16 s, and to a touch stimulus, approximately 0.15 s.[16] Both these durations are too brief for the body to make adaptive corrections, especially given that the brain would need even longer than this to make a higher-level decision based on the integration of *all* motor-sensory inputs *plus* musical and aesthetic considerations.

The brevity of the time period of the key descent emphasizes (and proves) how important it is to have a goal for the sound before the keystroke begins.

Nothing can be done to correct for errors in the speed of the key descent once the key has begun its key descent.[17]

Provocatively, even *if* our brain could perform these neuro-motor tasks fast enough (which it can't), how would it even know that the key is being depressed too quickly or too slowly, given that it has not yet even received the auditory feedback of the sound wave from the string's vibration? Such a question is directed at the center of the mishmash that is touch-tone pedagogy: are we supposing that pianists evaluate tone quality based on the sound or the feel of the instrument when played? The truth, as Galembo and other researchers have demonstrated, is that we pianists respond to, and are influenced by, the feel of our touch much more than we are aware.

The Window of Opportunity and Attentional Shifts

Besides its mechanical implications, the brevity of the window of opportunity has important perceptual implications. Because the window of opportunity is so brief for each single piano note, the brain will not have enough time to attribute different percept qualities to each individual note when a group of notes are played in quick succession.

To overcome the perception problem, the brain, as usual, takes a short cut and makes a "best guess" about the quality of each individual note based on the quality that it assigns to the larger group as a whole. Strictly, this is not a cognitive error, it is just multimodal *integration* at work, where "sensory inputs are combined together to yield a unified perceptual experience."[18]

As useful (and energy efficient) as this cognitive process is, however, it comes at the cost of not being able to immediately attend to—or be aware of—*all* the important sensory information available to us. This makes us susceptible to interpreting events incorrectly, missing specific details and assigning certain qualities to one modality because of the overriding influence of another modality. As recognized, "attentional shifts in one modality can affect orienting in other modalities."[19]

In the world of piano playing, these perceptual shortcuts can lead to some fantastic errors of judgment about what is actually occurring, like:

- presuming that *all* your fingers are playing physical legato because the passage appears to sound legato;

- presuming that *all* your fingers need to play physically legato to make the passage sound legato;
- presuming that the biomechanics of *all* your fingers are working well because the passage that they are playing sounds OK;
- presuming that you are giving arm weight to *all* your fingers during a passage because you feel that arm weight is being given to your fingers;
- presuming that because you are feeling the emotions of the music in your body that those emotions are being transmitted through the sounds that you make.

As a consequence of multimodal integration, pianists will find it difficult to assess the full quality of their sound when giving full attention to the quality of the feel of their touch, and conversely, will find it difficult to assess the full quality of the feel of their touch when they are giving full attention to the quality of their sound.

This perceptual illusion caused by cross-modal interference has many implications for how we practice. It shows us how easily our attention can be drawn to toward one biased point of interest at the expense of another. We might even argue that the ability to overcome this bias (by using Kahneman's System 2) and learn to separate the touch qualities from the tone qualities, is an acquired learned skill of expert pianists—to avoid being perceptually deceived that the sounds that are being produced are optimal just because their physical *feel* is ideal or, vice versa, that the mechanics of their keystroke are optimized just because the music being produced *sounds* optimized.

Our minds are constantly shifting attention between the sensory clues available to it to heighten or diminish the experience that it chooses to focus on. Probably, it is for these reasons that pianists who are intensely focused on listening to and controlling the finest minutiae of their piano sounds (e.g., Horowitz) are largely unconcerned about the contradictory things they say about the mechanics of producing it (e.g., Horowitz). Similarly, it is probably why pianists who are focused on the theory and feel of their touch (e.g., Breithaupt) may be completely unaware of the inconsistencies of sound and the poverty of musical interest that their playing provides (e.g., Breithaupt).

> From the point of view of practicing, these findings ought to remind us that if we want to ensure that any single aspect of our pianism becomes optimized, we will need to pass it through *some period of exclusive attention*—to be able to objectify its features as much as possible and improve them without our evaluation of them being influenced by the other motor-sensory events occurring simultaneously. For example, in the simplest of terms, should a phrase of music be chosen for practicing, *one* of the Ms should be chosen per repetition to ensure that it gets the most concentrated form of attention that our brains are able to offer it.

PRESSED VERSUS PERCUSSIVE NOTES

Depending on whether a note is played with a *pressed* touch (finger pushes down from the key surface) or a *percussive* touch (finger drops onto the key surface from above it), there will be subtle differences in hammer behavior (recall chapter 4). During a pressed touch, there is a *direct, linear* correlation between the key speed and the hammer speed up until the point of let-off.[20]

Given the linear correlation of the pressed touch, it might reasonably be considered to be the preferred touch for controlling hammer velocity—and hence, tone quality. However, there are two practical limitations to consider here. Firstly, it is difficult to produce loud tone volumes (e.g., louder than *mf-f*) using the pressed touch because the finger has less distance over which to generate its speed (because it has been denied its backswing and "run up" into the key). And secondly, for the same reason, it is extremely impractical—if not impossible—to play *most* piano passages with a pressed-touch-only technique. Pianists do not realize that most piano notes are played with fingers that land *onto* the key (from positions above the key) even when one *thinks* they are pressing the key without any percussive noise.[21]

> *Although a pressed touch should, theoretically, provide more control over the hammer speed, it comes with several significant practical limitations which counterbalance this potential benefit.*

When a percussive touch is used, the correlation between the key movement and the hammer movement is different. Firstly, the initial burst in key velocity does *not* correlate to a burst in hammer velocity: there is a brief lag time before the hammer starts to move. This indicates that the energy from the initial key movement is transferred into potential energy somewhere within the physical components of the action (due to the compressibility and flexibility of its parts, like the shaft of the hammer).

When the hammer does start to move, its velocity increases rapidly (and more rapidly than the pressed touch). Paradoxically, almost immediately after this initial burst of acceleration, *the key then comes to a temporary and almost complete standstill.* Following this pause, when the key does start to move again, it contributes very little more to the increase in hammer velocity.[22] This reinforces, again, the importance of having a sound goal in the mind *prior* to playing the note, as the majority of the energy transfer into the hammer is during the *early* moments of the key descent, not the latter.

Given that the percussive touch is the predominant touch form used in piano playing (not to be confused with the type of sound that the pianist might seek from it), we may assume that for the majority of notes played by pianists, the final hammer velocity is the result of the initial impulse that the pianist gives to the key—the "breaking of the ice," so to speak, of the key's initial descent to the keybed.

SLIDING OFF THE KNUCKLE

As a small aside, we play the piano assuming that for any given note, the leverage ratio is fixed. For example, when the key descends, it pushes up on the jack, which pushes up on the knuckle until the point of let-off, whereupon there is *no* further contact of the jack with the knuckle. It is presumed that this is a binary event—of *full* jack-knuckle contact up until when there is *no* jack-knuckle contact. However, there are other possible (non-binary) outcomes of the keystroke that have touch-tone relationship implications:

- where the jack pushes up on the knuckle without ever sliding off it (as happens in a very short, *staccato* touch when the finger stops its descent into the key before the key hits the keybed);
- where the jack pushes up on the knuckle but, *during* its sliding off from it, continues to push up on it in reducing amounts (as is the case with most keystrokes, and more so in those that depress the key slowly).

Because of the different amounts of contact time and degrees of force transmitted between the jack and the knuckle for different types of keystroke, pianists could theoretically produce notes of the same volume but with different key velocity profiles.

TO HIT, OR NOT TO HIT, THE KEYBED

As discussed in chapter 4, the key-keybed impact provides an important sonic contribution to the piano tone. Irrespective of whether we think the contribution is desirable or not (or in what registers, or at what volumes), it is worth thinking about what the realistic possibilities of altering it independently of the already-in-motion hammer are.

As we know, during a pressed touch, the key and the hammer both increase in velocity smoothly up until the moment of escapement (at approximately 97 percent of the way during the key's descent). After escapement, the pianist has no meaningful opportunity to abort from the keystroke or reduce the speed of the key prior to its impact with the keybed. Hence, we can assume that the speed of the key at the moment of escapement is effectively the same as that when it hits the keybed. This implies that the keybed impact noise will be proportional to the hammer speed at the moment of escapement, which, during a pressed touch, will also be proportional to the initial speed of the key descent.

During the pressed touch, it is physically impossible to reduce the keybed noise without also reducing the hammer speed.[23]

With the percussive touch, however, there *may* be an opportunity to achieve a certain hammer speed while independently minimizing the key-keybed impact. This possibility arises because of two specific mechanical differences caused by the percussive touch: (i.) that the maximum hammer speed is reached earlier during the key's descent (about halfway down); and (ii.) at the point of maximum hammer speed, the key comes to a temporary standstill.

The momentary standstill of the key during the percussive stroke provides us with an opportunity to abort the keystroke early and reduce the amount of follow through of the finger into the keybed. Although the timeframes for doing this are exceedingly brief, it is not improbable that one could anticipate it and produce a keystroke that stops the key from accelerating at an earlier point in its descent. Doing this would reduce the momentum of the impact of the key with the keybed (while still giving the same impulse to the key and producing the same final hammer velocity).

Coincidentally, two examples of such a keystroke already exist: a *staccato* stroke where the finger attempts to stop moving into the key *immediately* after it makes contact with the key; and the "flicking finger" *staccato* technique, where the fingertip initiates the key descent (and makes a percussive noise with the key surface) but then angles across the key during its descent to such a degree that it barely, if at all, follows through onto the keybed (reducing its key-keybed noise). Most curiously, the latter keystroke is used abundantly in *leggiero* playing, and this explanation may explain why.

Mechanically, the percussive touch offers pianists an opportunity to alter the volume of the keybed noise independently of the hammer velocity. It is in the different degrees of percussiveness (on the key surface and the keybed) that pianists may find a way to alter tone quality independently of hammer velocity.

Like the pressed touch, the percussive touch also has limitations. Functionally, its window of opportunity is briefer than that of a pressed touch. Also, the correlation between the key speed and the hammer speed is non-linear. Both these factors make hammer-speed control more difficult. On the other hand, the percussive touch is much more practical in terms of its playability as the fingers don't need to be resting on the key surfaces before playing them. This provides pianists with more freedom for movement and gesture when playing.

An "Ideal" Combined Pressed-Percussive Touch?

The reason for the predilection that many great pianists have for *"falling" "gently onto"* the key and *"controlling the key's descent"* with *"the full sensation of the fingertip,"* should now be clear:

- the "falling" is biomechanically easy, allows for gestural freedom, provides for a variety of finger-key surface noises, can easily produce any variety of initial key-descent speeds, and can potentially help to alter the key-keybed noise;
- the "gently" helps to minimize the volatility of any of the above features, which makes the fine-tuning of them easier;
- the "control of the key's descent" encourages the pianist to give attention to this most important mechanical feature of the keystroke, and in doing so, enhances key control and one's ability to respond to any idiosyncratic differences of the piano action;
- the "full sensation of the fingertip" allows one to experience as fully as possible the motor-sensory feedback of the keystroke.

Importantly, even if the above advice offers only marginal benefits, if we were to do the opposite—to "press" "abruptly" "from the surface of the key" "without trying to control the key's descent" and "without trying to feel it"—we would be putting ourselves in a position of mechanical disadvantage and denying ourselves the possible advantages that the science suggests we might otherwise receive.

From both a mechanical and psychological point of view, a combined pressed-percussive touch provides us with the best *balanced* solution to managing, optimizing and rapidly adjusting to *any* or *all* of the competing needs of the keystroke, which include:

- to be mechanically efficient (i.e., to minimize wasted energy on unnecessary body movements or key-keybed collisions)
- to be mechanically effective (i.e., to maintain optimal hammer control)

- to produce any range of dynamics
- to alter the finger-key contact noise
- to alter the key-keybed impact noises
- to easily alter the speed of the initial phase of the key's descent (which will alter the feel of the keystroke)
- to alter the duration of the key-keybed time
- to achieve different tone qualities for notes of similar quantity
- to be practical (in respect to playability)
- to be gesturally free (and perceptually free to enjoy your preferred touch experience)

Should the combined percussive-pressed touch do what the theory suggests it could, its popularity (as a generic keystroke) would be justified. It encourages pianists to direct their utmost care and attention to the moment of finger-key contact and the initial speed of the key's descent—the moment when one's touch has the greatest mechanical chance of succeeding in its goals of varying and controlling different tone qualities and quantities with ease.

OPTIMIZING THE BODY'S MOVEMENTS

One of the secrets to the mechanical success of piano playing is coordination. It requires moving the right part of our body, the right amount at the right time. As Dorothy Taubman rightly says, "it is correct motion, not muscular development, that makes great technique."[24] When it is done well, playing is easy. When it is done poorly, playing is difficult.

In the previous section, it was shown that we only have a brief moment of time—the window of opportunity—to alter the tonal outcome of a note. In order to be mechanically efficient, therefore, we must ensure that our keystroke (which involves the finger, the hand, the forearm and the arm) is coordinated in a way *so that it exerts its desired amount of force into the key during this time*. This, in sport, is called "timing the swing," and in piano playing it could be considered the same. If we fail to time our swing properly—or better, *swings*—especially when mechanical efficiency is required of us, like during virtuosic passagework requiring extreme speeds, volume, leaps or stamina, our pianism will struggle.

Good timing of your finger into the key is a core ingredient of mechanical efficiency. It implies that physical efforts have been well spent, contributing to the production of sound, or the control of it, during the window of opportunity.

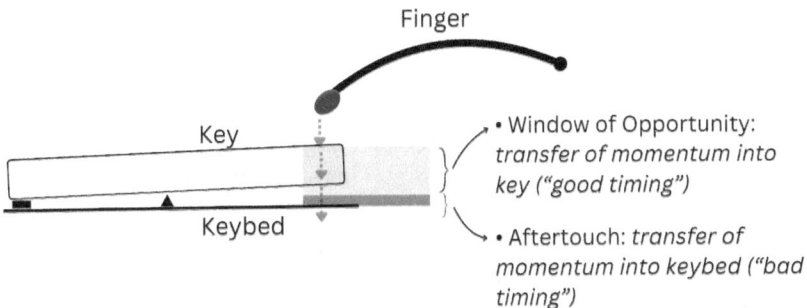

Figure 6.2. Good Timing. Bad Timing. Author created

MASS BRIDGING, PARTIAL BRIDGING AND EFFECTIVE MASS

As our mechanical goal is to move the right body parts at the right time, let's understand what those parts are and how they relate to each other.

Firstly, definitions. All objects have a mass (m), measured in kilograms (kg). In the piano literature, the word *weight* is usually used to mean *mass*. Scientifically, this is incorrect,[25] but as it is the common colloquial use of the word, there is no reasonable reason not to use it, so long as it refers to the *mass* of an object and not something else, like *momentum* (= mass x velocity), for which it is often mistaken. The average masses of the different parts of an adult body are, approximately:[26] finger, 0.1 kg; hand, 0.5 kg; forearm, 1.5 kg; arm, 2 kg.

During the piano stroke, these body parts *act together* in varying degrees[27] forming "specific functional muscle-joint linkages."[28] Functionally, therefore, the separate masses *join together* as the "groups of muscles or joints temporarily assemble into coherent units to achieve specific task goals, such as hitting a ball or performing a dive [... or hitting a piano key]."[29] Understandably, to maximize efficiency, different movement tasks benefit from *different* amounts of bridging across different joints.

For the sake of explanation, the joining of masses between different sections of the upper limb (finger, hand, forearm, arm) we shall call, *mass bridging*. If there is complete rigidity in a joint during impact, there is *complete* bridging and the *effective mass* of the keystroke will be the sum of its parts. If there is laxity, "give" or "breaking" in the joint during impact, there will be *partial* bridging, and in such circumstances, the *effective mass* of the keystroke will be less than the sum of its parts.

> *The degree of joint bridging during finger-key impact—determined by the joint position and/or the tightness of the muscles and soft tissues around the*

joint—is exceedingly important, as this will have an enormous effect on what the overall effective mass of the keystroke will be.

Evidently, there are an unlimited number of ways to bridge the separate masses of the upper limb together during any movement task—and especially during the tasks of piano playing. This is known as *degrees of freedom*—a feature of animal motor systems, where a given motor task can be accomplished by using any number of different joint positions and movements. In piano playing, most of the time, piano strokes only require small amounts of muscle effort to fulfill its bridging tasks and maintain a state of comfort and ease while playing.[30] When it comes to matters of coordination, the body has already learned how to solve the degrees of freedom problem over millions of years of evolution. Therefore, beyond giving it a musical goal and some basic postures within which to operate, it generally does not need to be told what to do. Would you presume to tell your body how to walk?

The factors that contribute to the bridging (and support) at the joints are:

- the bony joint structure;
- the muscles that operate across the joint;
- the ligaments that surround and support the joints.

How the workload of our touch is distributed across these structures will determine how easy our movements feel and how likely they are to become fatigued or injured. Predictably, there are better ways and worse ways of moving, which is why some pianists find piano playing relatively effortless, despite its technical difficulties, and others find it relatively effortful, dealing with constant problems of tightness, fatigue and pain, even when the technical difficulties are relatively minimal.

During the impact of our finger with the key, depending on the tightness of the bridging of the joints throughout our arm, a different effective mass will be delivered into the key. If the joints are all *fully* (tightly) bridged, the effective mass of a typical forearm stroke (i.e., with the hinge of the stroke at the elbow joint) will be:[31]

$$(5 \times 0.1) + 0.5 + 1.5 = 2.5 \text{ kg}$$

And for a whole-arm stroke (i.e., with the hinge of the stroke at the shoulder joint) it will be:

$$(5 \times 0.1) + 0.5 + 1.5 + 2 = 4.5 \text{ kg}$$

About 4.5 kg of effective mass is an exceptionally large (and inappropriate) amount of mass to be using to play the piano (as we will see shortly). This should reassure everybody: that *having a large physique is not required* to produce loud sounds on the instrument. Actually, half this mass (e.g., that used by a child or small adult) would also be beyond most pianistic needs. Muscle power is not a limitation either for most people—even children can grip very strongly if needed.

This immediately tells us something else important: that for the overwhelming majority of the sounds produced during piano playing, only *small degrees* of *partial bridging* across the joints of the arm will be required; that *small changes* in these small degrees is enough to change the effective mass considerably (and, hence the sound quantity);[32] and that *good timing and coordination* are far more important to piano playing than muscle power and brute force.

The concept of partial bridging helps to explain why the mechanical claims of arm-weight pedagogy are so erroneous yet so plausible: the full weight of the arm is rarely ever transmitted into the key. Yes, the mass components of the arm move, but during key impact, knuckles "collapse," the wrist "sinks" and the "relaxed" arm of the pianist contribute to there being significant partial bridging between those mass units, and hence, an effective mass that is much less than the presumed 4.5 kg of arm weight.

If the full mass of the arm were to be used during piano playing, and all of it were transmitted into the key, movements would be very slow and cumbersome, because:

- moving 4.5 kg vertically and horizontally for each keystroke would make fast playing and fast leaps impossible (unless one had very large shoulder muscles—like an elephant);
- precise movements would be more difficult (because one would need very large shoulder muscles to quickly correct and control the movements of the heavy mass);
- the speed of the keystroke would *necessarily* have to be slower, otherwise too much momentum would be given to the key and the keybed.

Depending on the musical context, the mechanical inefficiency of partial bridging can be either helpful or unhelpful. Contrary to the belief that "efficient = good," most piano playing will work best when small degrees of inefficiency are built into it. For example, having some slack in the bridging system may be useful to help prevent "bashing" during loud playing (to reduce the excessive momentum of a keystroke that an overly tight wrist might cause) or to improve kinaesthetic feeling during key descent.

On the other hand, mechanical inefficiencies will be unhelpful when a responsive (immediate) tone is sought from the keystroke—e.g., during extended, fast or loud passagework—where no key-descent time and no muscle energy can afford to be lost.

Pedagogical Myths Revisited

Ironically, any benefits that using an arm-weight approach to touch might provide will be due to factors that have nothing to do with what arm-weight methods claim is happening: one's keystroke may involve "loose *heavy* arms" or "tight *weight-less* arms" and produce exactly the same tone—as neither assertion actually correlates to the mechanical reality.

Notably, to observe a pianist's movements and make a prediction about the amount of arm-weight that they are putting into the key, is extremely risky, as watching someone's movements tells us little about the degree of bridging between the joints *at the moment of impact*—a crucial piece of information missing from our analysis of their touch mechanics. In reality, even in "arm-weight playing," the fingers and wrist joints become increasingly bridged as they begin to strike the keys.[33] Again, pedagogical belief and physical reality are different.

To be fair, the purpose of this analysis is not to attack arm-weight methods. They need not be criticized (or praised) any more than any other method which attempts to make up a theory based on feelings of understanding—because in reality, and especially mechanically, *no piano method does what it thinks it does*. Advocates of the "finger-only" methods are just as mistaken if they believe that only the mass of the finger is being transmitted into the key when playing loudly. Here, too, there is muscular bridging of the joints of the finger to the hand, and of the hand to the forearm, and an increase in the total effective mass of the keystroke ensues.

Amusingly, it is quite possible that in playing certain passages, for example, fast, loud semi-quavers, believing in either method would generate the same biomechanical profile. Given that the "arm-weight players" would not be able to move their large arm masses up and down fast enough to play at speed, they would, unavoidably, need to rely on their fingers to move up and down quickly. The "finger-only players," on the other hand, with their small-mass fingers would, unavoidably, need to rely on the bridging of their fingers to the larger masses of the forearm and arm to increase the momentum of the keystroke to play loudly (and without fatigue).

> *Predictably, problems arise in piano playing from dogmatically over-subscribing to either approach and interfering too much with the body's natural ability to deal with complex motor tasks: with poor finger articulation, slow speeds and inaccurate leaps being the rewards for "arm-weight" enthusiasts, versus fatigue of the hand and forearm muscles (and stiff wrists) being the rewards for "finger-only" enthusiasts.*

If such performance-limiting outcomes weren't so tragic, the role of formalized pedagogical theories in advising on matters of piano technique should be seen as a comedy, as it points out that most of the time, pianists would be better off following their own instincts, pursuing their own musical-sound goals, and experimenting with touch (while allowing the body to solve its degrees-of-freedom and motor-coordination issues). At least this would provide an opportunity for pianists *to work out what works best for them* and make improvements by trial and error. Here, pianist Shura Cherkassky's naivety strikes gold:

> *"Teach? Never! Not for a million dollars [...] because while I can teach myself, if I would try to teach the same things to another person it could be rather harmful to them because it probably wouldn't suit their personality. In fact I believe to copy somebody actually does harm. Anyway, how can I tell someone how to do it when I don't know myself how I do it?"*[34]

INERTIA AND "THE INERTIA PROBLEM"

If a mass needs to be moved—be it a finger or a key—it will require an external force applied to it. In piano playing, this force either comes from gravity (no muscular work required for the hand to fall) or from muscle contractions (work required to move our fingers up and down). Piano playing uses both.

By definition, the larger the mass of an object, the more force will be required to change its speed (Newton's 2nd law). Similarly, the smaller the mass of an object, the less force will be required to change its speed. The resistance of any object to change speed (or direction) is called *inertia*. Managing the inertia problems of piano playing lies at the core of mechanical success. The following paragraphs show how Newton's laws can be applied to piano playing to make the mechanics of playing easier.

- *Where fast changes in movement are required, use a smaller mass.*

Thankfully, fast, virtuosic playing rarely requires the quick shifting of large masses, and when fast changes in movement are required, the parts of our body that need to move fast, are already well-adapted to the task (i.e., fingers and hands weigh very little). These smaller masses should not be denied their role of moving fast when our pianism most needs it.

- *Do not use masses that are so small that they need to be moved excessively fast in order to achieve enough volume.*

Making small muscles work to their physical limits (or beyond them) leads to earlier onset fatigue and increases injury risk. To increase volume, therefore, in such situations, one should increase the effective mass of the keystroke by improving its bridging, involving larger muscle groups or, wherever possible, using gravity to play some of the notes.

Note, also, how using a mass that is too small can create a different type of problem when playing *pp*—that it may become more difficult to control the speed of the key descent. This problem is especially noticed when playing on poorly regulated pianos (where the key resistance is irregular) or when the key resistance is more than what one is expecting (e.g., when playing on an unfamiliar piano)—the result being that the key either falls too fast or not fast enough (because the variability of the resistance is relatively high compared to the momentum of the keystroke being used).

- *Try to minimize the number of changes in direction of any mass unit, especially if it is heavy or the changes in direction are abrupt.*

Muscles do most of their work when starting and stopping movements (to overcome the inertia). Newton's 2nd law of motion explains why. $F = m \times a$ (where F is the force given to a mass (m) to get it to accelerate (a). The more mass an object has, the more force will be required to change its speed (or direction). Similarly, the more quickly we wish to change the speed of an object, the more force will be required.

As muscles will be the main provider of the force to move masses up and down quickly, they will fatigue significantly faster if they are required to do this more often (think, repetitive octaves) or when playing louder (more key speed needed, hence more force needed). For these reasons, the movement of smaller masses is generally required for fast playing. But if fast *and* loud playing is required, increased effective mass, improved angles of key attack and a clever use of gravity will also need to be used to increase the force into the keys.

What needs to move fast should not be heavy but what needs to be loud should not be light—and therein, a balance must be found. Generally, it makes no mechanical sense to be excessively moving around a large arm mass when only a small fraction of its mass is going to be needed for the keystroke, nor does it make sense to be excessively raising small finger masses up and down at excessive speeds when large volumes are required.

And so, in playing fast trills, fast octaves or fast repeated chords, small movements of the finger and hand should, in general, be chosen in preference to large movements of the forearm and upper arm. Additionally, keystrokes only need to depress the key *enough* to propel the hammer toward the string at the desired speed and withdrawn from the key *enough* so that the key can then be replayed. Reducing the mass and the range of our movements when fast movements are required helps to overcome the inertia problems that moving about large masses creates. This might come at the expense of volume—as Rachmaninoff (purportedly) said, "the faster you play, the lighter you play"— but the loss of volume is of no consequence should other agogics be used to create the illusions of volume intensity—e.g., accents, crescendo, rubato, and pedal effects (as previously mentioned in the following textbox).[35]

Smooth Circular Movements vs Jerky Square Movements

When larger masses (e.g., forearms and arms) are moved during playing, one way of conserving muscle energy is to encourage movements that are curved ("circular") rather than side-to-side ("square"). Curved pianistic movements *gradually* change the direction of the moving body part while making use of the kinetic energy that it already has. Curved movements also help to distribute the workload more equally across different muscle groups rather than just a few—a strategy that helps to prevent fatigue and injuries.

This smooth, continuous flow of more circular movements is (rightly) alluded to in many pedagogical methods, some choice examples being those of Chopin, with his observed constant movement of the wrist,[36] Taubmann with her "shaping"[37] and Peter Feuchtwanger: "there must always be a small movement present [...] so that the playing organism doesn't get stiff."[38]

> ***Stop-start, square movements represent the mechanical death of piano playing—they limit speed, they expend more muscular energy, they waste more kinetic energy, they increase the volatility of the momentum of the touch (making key control more difficult), they create more tension across joints, and the increased muscle tension impacts upon our psychology too, altering our perception of events.***

Simple ways of promoting smooth, continuous, circular pianistic movements include:

- applying small amounts of *forearm rotation* to notes that are in sequence and in the same direction as the rotation;
- using the *same* drop of the hand into the key to play several different notes at a time (especially useful during fast passagework);
- using some *rotational* forearm movement when playing leaps (i.e., use "arcs" not "straight lines" to get from one hand position to another).
- avoiding the side-to-side, stop-start movements that are caused by "trying to get over the next note before playing it"—a well-intended strategy to promote accuracy, but one that comes at the cost of speed[39] and muscle fatigue when repeated fast leaps are involved. By necessity, this means that virtuosic playing which involves leaps, requires taking some risks regarding accuracy.[40]
- avoid thumb "under the hand" playing during fast passagework if it limits the ability of the forearm to rotate or if it prevents the hand from smoothly continuing onto the next hand position.[41]

The principle of keeping the hand in motion rather than stopping and starting it for every change in hand position is epitomized by Chopin. His reported predilection for idly glissando-ing a finger up and down the keyboard—to keep a *smooth, constant flow* of the hand and forearm[42]—is a big clue as to how he approached scale-like and arpeggiated-like figures, for example, like those found in his Études Op. 10, Nos. 1, 2, 5, 8, 12, or similarly, in the use of smooth circular motions, in his Études Op.10, Nos. 9 (L.H.) and 11, and Op.25, Nos. 1 and 3 (L.H.). Such pieces become physically difficult to execute (if not, impossible) when the movement of the hand (or forearm) stops in its tracks or adopts jerky, stop-start, zig-zag movements. With great interest, we should recall how Chopin exasperated stiffness, found fault with stiff wrists and advocated suppleness[43]—muscular states that promote smooth, continuous movements and avoid the jerky, poorly-coordinated movements which stifle virtuosic playing.

VELOCITY AND MOMENTUM

Next, let us look at how we can optimize the momentum of the keystroke.

Key and Hammer Facts

- Objects that move have a *velocity* (*v*), colloquially known as speed.
- During a keystroke, the key velocity generally ranges between 0.02 m/s (*pp*) and 1 m/s (*ff*). Such key velocities correspond to hammer velocities in the range of 0.1-0.2 m/s (*ppp*) to 5-10 m/s (*fff*).[44]
- Given that the leverage of the action is approximately 5:1, the time that the hammer takes to arrive at the string will be in the range of 0.02 s (*fff*) - 0.5 s (*ppp*)[45]—not long to inject your passion into the note.

Momentum and Vectors

Much more important than the velocity of an object, however, is its *momentum* (*p*), the product of its mass (*m*) and its velocity (*v*):

$$p = m \cdot v$$

For example, a 1 kg object (e.g., a finger-hand-forearm unit) that hits a key at 0.1 m/s will deliver the same momentum as a 0.1 kg (e.g., a finger) traveling at 1 m/s.

During collisions, it is the momentum of the object (not its individual mass or velocity) that determines the movement of that object, and any other object that it collides with. Crucially, the *direction* in which an object travels, matters just as much, as this will determine the direction of the transfer of the momentum of that object into any object that it hits.

All moving objects are defined by their mass, velocity and direction (i.e., they are vectors). It is meaningless to talk about the impact of one object (e.g., your hand) on another object (e.g., the key) without taking into account ALL THREE variables of the vector.

The "Momentum Chain" of Touch

Vectors are added together when they act together. Accordingly, the momentum of a pianist's touch (p_{touch}) can be thought of as the total of all the *p* components that participate in the keystroke. Mathematically, this can be approximated by the following "momentum chain" equation:

$$p_{touch} = (m_{finger} \cdot v_{finger}) + (m_{hand} \cdot v_{hand}) + (m_{forearm} \cdot v_{forearm}) + (m_{arm} \cdot v_{arm})$$

This means that if the movements of our finger, hand, forearm and arm all move in the same direction at the same time—and are all locked (bridged) together—their individual momentums can be added together. It is this *combined* momentum that influences the total momentum of the keystroke.

Touch Angle and Momentum Transfer

Depending on the direction of a moving object, profoundly different outcomes can result from its collision with another object—like landing a plane at a 4-degree angle (causing a small bump) versus a 40 degree angle (causing a crash). The difference in outcomes is because the vertical component of the vector downwards is different—very small in the former, but very large in the latter).

> *The keystroke of pianists is the same as landing a plane. The angle at which we "land our touch" onto the key determines the amount of momentum that gets delivered into the key, and subsequently, alters the volume and quality of the sound.*

The most efficient transfer of momentum into the key is when the effective mass moves into the key in a straight-down direction—i.e., in the direction of gravity. This we shall define as being a touch angle of 0°. Most of the time, however, when a finger plays a note, the finger is not directed straight down but is slanted slightly across it. Thus, even though the key moves down—because it has no other option—it only fools us into believing that all the momentum from the touch has been transferred into it, which it most certainly has not.[46]

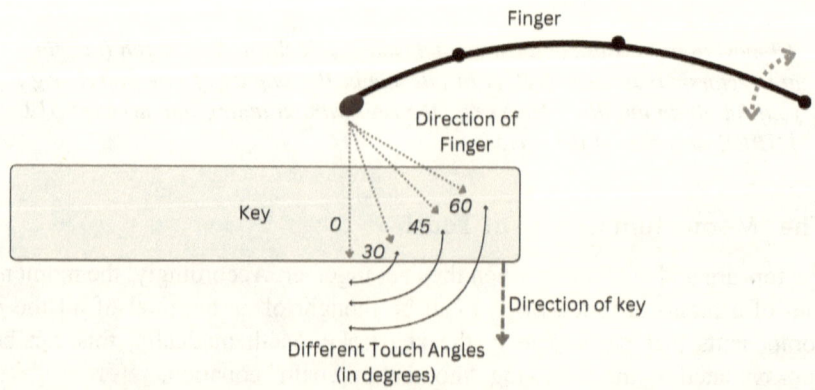

Figure 6.3. Touch Angles. Author created

Ignoring the importance of the touch angle in piano playing is inexcusable, and its omission from pedagogical literature is concerning. Commonly, surrogates for different touch angles are alluded to, like using a dropping motion, gripping with the fingertips, or using a (horizontal) caressing movement on the key, but such advice does not explain the reason why they might work. The touch angle plays just as important a role in piano technique (sound control, mechanical efficiency and injury prevention etc.) as does its mass and velocity.

Touch Angles and Mechanical Efficiency

The following table shows how much of the touch momentum is actually transferred into the key depending on the touch angle.

Touch Angle	Transfer of Momentum[47]
0°	100%
30°	87%
45°	**71%**
60°	50%
90°	0%

Notice how a touch angle of 45° transfers only 71 percent of its momentum into the key. For the pianist, this means a 29 percent loss of mechanical efficiency with a 29 percent loss of momentum in the downward direction of the key, which will correlate to a 29 percent loss of key speed and a corresponding loss of volume in the slower-flying hammer. This also corresponds to a change in tone quality—more *dull*, less *bright*.

Obviously, the goal of piano playing is not to generate fast key speeds (quite often it is to avoid them) but it *should* be our duty to know what a maximally efficiency keystroke looks like, feels like, and be able to use, should we want to, for it is precisely this efficiency that is required of us when playing at extreme speeds and/or in preventing muscles from fatiguing when playing over prolonged periods—like playing a book of Chopin or Liszt etudes, which is "easy" to pianists who have learned to play mechanically efficiently but insurmountably difficult for those who haven't.

Unless something mechanical is done to make up for the inefficiencies caused by a highly slanting touch angle, any combination of tone volume, speed of passagework or muscle endurance are going to be compromised. This will then oblige us to resort to other musical-agogic solutions to cover up for such technical weaknesses—or abandon certain repertoire entirely.

Mechanically, there are only four solutions available to us to increase the speed of the key descent, and hence the hammer speed:

- increase v—i.e., by using the same movement but making the finger move faster. This will require a stronger muscle contraction or a higher finger lift (to create more distance for the finger to build up speed prior to it contacting the key). Both these options increase muscle fatigue. It is rarely the best option to choose.
- increase m—i.e., by using the same movement but increasing the bridging of the joints to increase the effective mass. This is what the natural finger-hand arch provides (requiring little muscular effort), or, in less skilled pianists, what the stiff wrist provides (requiring more muscular effort).
- improve the touch *angle*—i.e., by making small adjustments to the curvature of the fingers, the position of the wrist, or the pathway that the finger and hand take as they play into the key, the touch angle can be converted into a more straight-down-into-the-key direction.[48] Such adjustments are simple, effective and physiologically-friendly solutions.
- improve the *timing* (coordination) of your swing—i.e., ensuring that the keystroke shares its desired momentum with the key during the window of opportunity and not before or after it.

Benefits of Mechanical Inefficiency

While promoting the benefits of mechanical efficiency, it is important to keep theory in perspective: mechanical efficiency is *not* the goal of pianism, just as it is *not* always required to deliver excellent pianism. It is a tool to be used, sometimes more and sometimes less, to help us solve the problems of pianism. Following are some reasons why inefficiencies in touch mechanics may be accepted or even preferred:

- No need. For example, in playing relatively easy, non-virtuosic music, so long as the right sounds are being made, there is very little mechanical or physiological demand that *requires* needing to play mechanically efficiently. For this reason, most amateur pianists can get away with using

suboptimal mechanics during their childhood (and most teachers can get away without teaching them anything about mechanics) but will struggle latter when music becomes more technically demanding.
- Depending on the demands of the task, small inefficiencies in the angle of touch may have no practical consequences whatsoever. For example, a touch angle of 80° is already very efficient, and improving it from 80° to 85° is not going to make any practical difference, whereas improving a touch angle from 30 to 80 percent during periods of sustained virtuosity could be the deciding factor in whether or not those passages can be played *at all*, or whether one's muscles will have the stamina to get through the whole piece (or recital).
- Often, an inefficient touch angle provides specific mechanical benefits which help with artistic goals. For example, during soft playing, a large touch angle will ensure that less momentum will be transferred into the key, even if the mass or the velocity of the keystroke are high. A fingertip "massaging the key" (e.g., typical of soft L.H. accompaniments) is an example of this, so is a quick flick of the fingertip diagonally across the surface of the key to produce a *leggiero* staccato sound, as it limits the key's downward momentum.
- When our emotional feelings for a musical gesture override any mechanical objectives. This has been discussed at length in Part II.

It is almost certain that experienced pianists learn to achieve incredibly high levels of key control using idiosyncratic and variable degrees of imperceptible "fingertip-angled-across-the-key-surface" techniques. The touch angles being used may not be maximally efficient (because they don't need to be), but they might be maximally effective.

The Blessed Curse of Mechanical Inefficiencies

Being able to play the piano with mechanical inefficiencies—and get away with it—can be both a benefit and a risk of being a pianist. The fact that most repertoire can be played without needing to be particularly efficient explains many curiosities related to the culture of piano playing that could never exist when playing other instruments:
- it is why amateurs can get immediate enjoyment from the piano sound with little training—because the same tone qualities are

available to them, and can be made by them, just like any other expert pianist. No extra skill is required to create key velocity.
- it is why anyone can feel like their opinion is correct about how to produce a note with a certain tone quality—because there are an infinite number of biomechanical ways (both efficient and inefficient) to produce any type of tone. If a certain keystroke produces the desired sound, it will *appear* to be a good way of doing it.
- it is why one can be nervous and play with trembling hands during a performance and still manage to play well enough that nobody notices—because so long as one hits the right notes with the right sound at the right time, nobody can *hear* our muscles shaking. Unlike that of a violinist's bowing arm, or a horn player's flow of breath, our shaking muscles don't cause a shaky sound.
- it is why copying the techniques of great pianists is not necessarily transferable to *your* own playing—because their playing will contain varying degrees of mechanical inefficiency to meet their musical needs which will be invisible to you.
- it is why some pianists can manage some types of technical difficulties very well but will struggle with others—because the inefficiencies of their playing will only become problematic when challenged by virtuosic passagework.

MOMENTUM TRANSFER DURING DIFFERENT TYPES OF COLLISION

The following section contains the mathematics behind why some keystrokes will be mechanically better to use than others in certain situations. If you don't like math, just skip over the equations and read the text. If you really hate math, just skip to the conclusions.

When objects collide, the total momentum of the objects prior to collision is the same as the total momentum of the objects after the collision. This is called *the conservation of momentum*, where:

$$p_{in} = p_{out}$$

When playing the piano, the momentum put into the key comes from our touch:

$$p_{in} = p_{touch}$$
$$= m_{touch} \cdot v_{touch}$$

The momentum of the hammer is a direct result of the momentum of the key. Therefore:

The combined m, the v, and the touch angle of the pianist's touch, are the factors that affect the momentum of the hammer.[49]

Immediately following the collision of our finger with the key, the speed of the pianist's finger and the speed of the key will change (the key will speed up; the finger will slow down). However, although the momentum is being transferred from the finger to the key, the *combined* momentum (of the finger and the key) remain the same:

$$p_{out} = p_{touch} + p_{key}$$
$$= (m_{touch} \cdot v_{touch}) + (m_{key} \cdot v_{key})^{50}$$

The velocity of the descending key (v_{key}) *is what correlates to the hammer velocity, which, due to the 5:1 ratio of the lever system, will move approximately 5 times faster than the key.*

Case Study No.1—Playing mf with different touch masses (see Appendix 1)

- When a note is played with a large effective mass of 2 kg, v_{touch} will drop only minimally from 0.5 m/s to 0.475 m/s during this time. This demonstrates that:

The inertia of a large touch mass (e.g., 2 kg) is barely affected by its interaction with the key. In practice, the slow touch velocity will correlate with the pianist's feeling of a slow, smooth drop into the key. It might also give the pianist the impression of improved key control, given that the finger speed at escapement (0.475 m/s) is very closely matched to that of the initial touch speed (0.5 m/s).

- When a note is played with a small effective mass of 0.1 kg, in order to produce the same *mf* volume, the pianist's finger will initially need to be traveling at 10 m/s. It will then drop to 9.5 m/s by the end of the keystroke. Note that this is a bigger reduction in velocity (0.5 m/s compared to 0.025 m/s).

The keystroke that uses a smaller mass is slowed down more by its impact with the key. This increased variation in velocity may be recognized by pianists as decreased controllability of the speed of the key's descent. It becomes a practical problem when playing softly, and especially so during fast leggiero passages, where there is very little margin for error for getting the key's velocity wrong. Because of these difficulties, we understand why pianists often choose to adopt a "safe" approach to playing such passages, choosing a slightly heavier touch (i.e., a keystroke with a higher effective mass) to ensure that all the notes have more chance of sounding, though this would come at the expense of being louder, less leggiero, and less artistically interesting.

Inertia and Pedagogy

Already, understanding the physics of touch leads us to several practical conclusions:

The arguments of arm-weight methods and finger-only methods can both be right and wrong.

A high-inertia, slow-to-move arm-weight touch (impractical) may make louder sounds and key-descent speeds easier to control (practically useful), whereas a small-inertia, fast-to-move finger touch (practically useful) may make softer sounds and key-descent speeds more difficult to control (impractical). This is the scientific basis that underlies the arguments for and against arm-weight playing *and* for and against finger-only playing.

The right touch depends on the goal of that touch.

There is no such thing as a "this-is-how-you-should-play" way of playing the piano. This is because the best mechanical option *depends* on the musical and mechanical needs of the touch. There cannot be a "best" mechanical solution until there is a musical, physiological or psychological goal at which to aim. Opinions will *always* differ about how to play a certain passage—because depending on each player's musical goals, their mechanical approach to achieving them will differ.

Generally, avoiding extremes of mass, speed and touch angle will solve—or at least, avoid—most major pianistic problems.

Although there is no *single* mechanical solution for every pianistic problem, there is usually a best *zone of operation* (see later) that allows us to play with the best trade-off between touch speed (light mass) and key control (heavy mass).

Coordinated and Uncoordinated Movements

When movements are well coordinated, it implies that they produce the desired musical outcomes with the least amount of mechanical effort. In piano playing, it implies excellence in the *timing* and *sequencing* of one's movements such that the fingers, hand, forearm and arm act to supply the desired momentum of the keystroke *during the key descent*—i.e., during the window of opportunity. This definition is no different to that used by a golfer or a tennis player who coordinate the timing and movements of their swing to be maximally effective at the moment of impact.

Again, the goal of piano playing is *not* perfect coordination, and, as with mechanical inefficiency, there are many acceptable situations where perfect coordination is not essential: e.g., where *control* of sound is more important, where *enough* coordination is already enough for the task, or when the preparation of the *following notes* need to be prioritized. However, *if* the passagework is highly technically challenging, involving sustained periods of speed, volume, wide intervals or leaps, then excellent coordination will be required, or problems will arise.

Playing with coordinated movements will feel easy because each muscle group is acting at the right time, in the right proportion, with the least effort, and moving comfortably within its physiological range.

How does one go about improving the coordination of one's touch? Firstly, by teaching it movements that are compatible with human physiology and universal physical laws, and secondly, once taught, to let it coordinate itself as it seeks to realize the musical goals that you have set it.

If the coordination of your movements is poor, either you, your muscles or your pianism are likely to complain. Pianistic outcomes will be substandard and, because some muscles will be forced to work harder than they usually would to compensate for the loss of momentum that the uncoordinated movement caused, there will be early-onset fatigue and/or less muscle control. A common example of poor coordination is when forearm muscles are forced to work harder to move the fingers up and down to compensate for poor touch angles and/or poor timing of the hand drop into the key. Another example is the involuntary tightening of the wrist (to increase the effective mass of a keystroke) to compensate for a lack of finger momentum into the key.

In practice, in trying to keep the value of p_{touch} propped up by using suboptimal mechanical solutions (mechanical "band-aids"), we invite unwanted compensation errors into our pianism. These equate to "high-risk (more energy expended), low-reward (limited effectiveness)" actions—see Process Optimization in chapter 7. In the long term, it will have negative consequences.

> *Poor coordination compromises virtuosity: firstly, because it is mechanically substandard; secondly, because compensating muscles are less adept at carrying out the desired pianistic tasks; and thirdly, because of this extra burden of work, they will fatigue quicker and be less agile. If your muscles tire quickly or the joints of your arm appear to be tight, you are likely to have a coordination problem. Solve it by improving the quality of your mechanics not the quantity of your practice.*

Elastic and Inelastic Collisions

Another factor to be aware of when discussing the physics of touch, is the difference between elastic and inelastic collisions. Theoretically, in the *elastic* collision, the finger that plays the key would hit the key and bounce off it instantaneously (like two billiard balls colliding). In piano playing, it is impossible to replicate a fully elastic collision. The closest approximation is to play with an exceedingly small contact time—the type of touch often used by pianists during *staccatissimo* passagework, where the key surface is tapped very quickly with a minimally-compressible part of the finger (e.g., at a point near its very tip, or even, with very curved fingers, with the fingernail).

Given, however, that it is impractical to be stopping the finger from moving further into the key immediately after touching it, for almost all keystrokes played on the piano, the finger will *stay in contact with the key during its descent* for some period of time (usually to the keybed), and the collision will be classified as *inelastic*.

On a practical level, it is not important to know how inelastic your touch is. On a theoretical level, however, it provides insight into why some types of touch are going to be more suited to some tasks than others, or why notes of exactly the same volume can be produced using different looking keystrokes. Pianists can vary, by the smallest of fractions, the degree of inelasticity of their touch.

With these thoughts in mind, let us examine the momentum transfer of touch, comparing two different touch masses (2 kg and 0.1 kg) during elastic and inelastic collisions while giving them each the same momentum ($p_{in} = 1$). Again, the maths is in Appendix B, so go there if it interests you.

- *If* a note were played with a large effective mass of 2 kg in an elastic collision, the key would descend at 10 m/s. (This is equivalent to the maximum

Mechanical Skills

speed of a boxer's punch.)[51] And given the 5:1 leverage ratio of the piano action, then this would mean that the hammer speed would be around 50 m/s. This is impossible. It has never been recorded this fast, and, in any case, is far beyond the needs of piano playing (maximal forte generally occurs at hammer speeds of 5-7 m/s).[52]

If a pianist were to use an elastic, or a near-elastic, collision, very fast hammer speeds can be created with very little touch mass. If a 1-2 kg mass were used, this would generate hammer speeds that far exceed the limits of the instrument. This is, probably, why stiff-wristed playing sounds so inappropriately loud and percussive, and also why it probably breaks more strings.

- In a fully inelastic collision using a 2 kg touch mass to produce a *mf* volume, the final key velocity (0.476 m/s) is *extremely similar* to that of the initial touch velocity (0.5 m/s). This makes perfect sense, and it is similar to the situation described earlier, where the velocity of a large mass moving into the key is largely unaffected by the low inertia of the key.
- In a fully inelastic collision using a 0.1 kg touch mass to produce a *mf* volume, however, the initial fast-moving finger slows down significantly (from 10 m/s to 5 m/s) after it meets with the key. Although the final key velocity of 5 m/s is still likely to be unrealistically high (using these values), the equation proves the concept that an object with small inertia (the finger) will slow down more significantly when met with a force against it.

The point of interest here is that, despite both inelastic touches starting with the same amount of momentum, the touch using the lighter mass will produce a faster final key speed. This is because, compared to the heavier touch, relatively more of its momentum will have been transmitted to the key (rather than transmitted into the keybed—evidenced by its significant drop in velocity prior to keybed collision). If a fully inelastic collision were to occur during the window of opportunity, the lighter touch will be more efficient (though be it, potentially harder to control) because less of its momentum will have been transmitted into the keybed.

Minimal Volatility—an Ideal Playing Zone?

Bringing more applications to our understanding of inelastic collisions, consider the data in table 6.1. It shows how a *mf* tone ($v_{touch+key}$ = 0.5 m/s) can be produced using different combinations of touch mass and velocity.[53]

What do these numbers tell us? Besides the obvious—that a smaller mass will need to be moved faster to achieve a given tone quantity—they tell us that *if* the pianist's touch is represented by an inelastic collision (and m_{touch}

Table 6.1 Playing *mf* Using Different *m-v* Pairs (Inelastic Collisions)

if m_{touch} = 2.0	v_{touch} = 0.52	(p_{in} = 1.05)
if m_{touch} = 1.5	v_{touch} = 0.53	(p_{in} = 0.80)
if m_{touch} = 1.0	v_{touch} = 0.55	(p_{in} = 0.55)
if m_{touch} = 0.5	v_{touch} = 0.60	(p_{in} = 0.30)
if m_{touch} = 0.25	**v_{touch} = 0.70**	**(p_{in} = 0.18)**
if m_{touch} = 0.1	v_{touch} = 1.00	(p_{in} = 0.10)
if m_{touch} = 0.05	v_{touch} = 1.50	(p_{in} = 0.10)

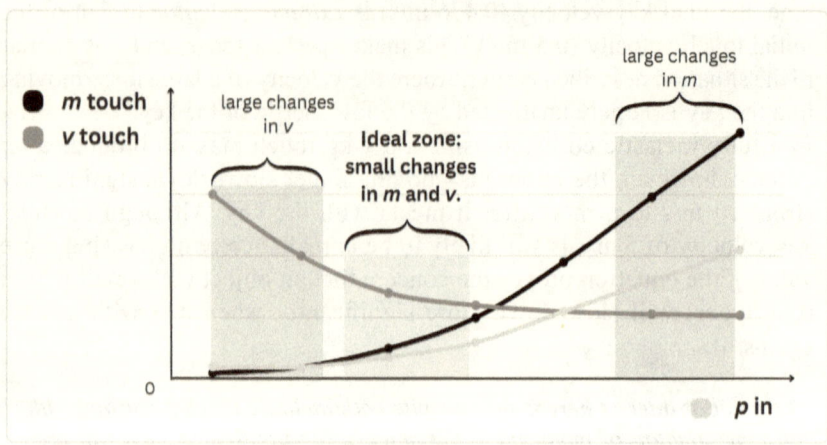

Figure 6.4. *m-v* Pairs (*mf* Tone). Author created

remains constant during the keystroke), *there exists a zone where small changes in m_{touch} are proportionally matched by small changes in v_{touch}*. The center of this zone is highlighted in the table and corresponds to a touch mass of 0.25 kg. On the graph (figure 6.4) it is the area where extreme quantitative changes in *m* or *v* are avoided.

> In practice, the "ideal zone" indicates where pianists can find a compromise between using too much mass too slowly and too little mass too quickly. It is the point where the pianist's touch optimally balances the competing goals of key control and key responsiveness.

For the *mf* sound, the touch mass where changes in m_{touch} and v_{touch} are best correlated, is around 0.25 kg (highlighted in bold font). We should take note of this mass, and the values closely surrounding it, for if we, as pianists, are looking for an appropriate mass to use to produce a *mf* sound, it represents a theoretically ideal place to start.

We should also note that for this *mf* sound, the ideal mass (0.25 kg) corresponds to a weight that is slightly heavier than a finger but slightly lighter than a hand. When playing the piano, such an effective mass is very easy to produce. It requires only the slightest amount of bridging across the joints of the finger and wrist and has the added benefit of causing no practical problems related to its inertia, as it is neither too large nor too small.

If the same equation is used to find the ideal touch mass for producing a *ff* tone ($v_{touch+key}$ = 2.5 m/s), the ideal *m-v* zone surrounds a touch mass of approximately 0.5 kg. For producing a *pp* tone, the ideal *m-v* zone surrounds a touch mass of approximately 0.1 kg. (See Appendix C for the maths).

Worthy of extra special comment here is the fact that, although the ideal touch mass was more to produce a *ff* tone (0.5 kg)—no surprise—and less to produce a *pp* tone (0.1 kg)—again, no surprise—neither of these masses were *much* different to the 0.25 kg mass that produced the *mf* tone with ideal *m-v* pairing. Thus, regardless of the accuracy of the absolute numbers used in these calculations:

pianists need to make only relatively small changes to the mass of the keystroke to stay close to the ideal m-v zones for most dynamic ranges of piano playing.

Ideal *m-v* Combination Zones: The Holy Grail of Touch Mechanics?

Putting together the findings from the inelastic touch collision equations, we may conclude:

- For a note of any chosen volume, there exists an "ideal" *m-v* pair where the variability of the touch mass and touch velocity are *both* reduced—i.e., where a *small-ish* change in one will be accompanied by an equivalently *small-ish* change in the other. Practically, this means that the competing interests of effectiveness and efficiency are optimally balanced: where the practical problems of

extreme key responsiveness (where control becomes difficult) and extreme control (where key responsiveness becomes compromised) are avoided yet *both* still remain easily attainable.[54]
- Because the most ideal *m-v* pair sits within a zone of almost-ideal pairs, deviating slightly away from the most ideal pair (e.g., because of using slightly more or less *m*), will result in very little disruption to the ideal balance between responsiveness and control.
- Note that the ideal *m-v* zone lies comfortably *in between* the extremes of the *m*'s and *v*'s, indicating that extreme m-v pairs are rarely, if ever, needed in piano playing.
- Given that the ideal *m-v* pair ranges between 0.1 kg–0.5 kg for note volumes between *pp-ff*, it suggests that a well-coordinated finger-hand-forearm stroke that can provide various degrees of partial bridging (with ease) will be able to satisfy most pianistic needs. Whether this is achieved under the guise of a finger-weight method, an arm-weight method, or any other name, is completely irrelevant. The science doesn't change. Chopin's advice to *"Laissez tomber les mains* [Let your hands fall]..."[55] will prove eternal.
- Given that piano playing often involves playing groups of notes that require a similar type of sound, it makes sense to identify what the ideal zone of *m-v* combinations would be for *that* group of notes, and to try to stay within it.
- The smooth, controlled and seemingly effortless movements of the great players suggests that they deviate very little from the ideal *m-v* zones and that the volatility of their *m-v* combinations is kept very low. Obviously, notes that require sudden changes of sound, or leaps, will require abrupt changes in momentum, but, even then, *m*'s outside of the 0.1–0.5 kg range should be thought of as exceptions (e.g., for loud chordal playing or accents) and, generally speaking, rarely required.

FORCE AND REBOUND FORCE

Understanding the forces of touch is a complicated theme and, in my opinion, not required to understand how to optimize pianism.[56] Two pedagogical claims will be examined, however, as they often appear without evidence in discussions. The first of these, is that a loud sound can be produced easily without needing lots of force if a "slow-and-weighty-keystroke" is used; and second, that the reactive force to the keystroke can be reduced by keeping the body more relaxed.

Firstly, back to Newton and his laws: an object will only change speed when a force is applied to it (Newton's 1st law) and the change of speed of that object (acceleration or deceleration) will be more when *more force* is applied to it (Newton's 2nd law):

$$F = m \cdot a$$

(F = force; m = mass; a = acceleration)

Which can be expanded to:

$$F = m \cdot \Delta v / \Delta t$$

(Δv = the change in velocity; Δt = the change in time)

Given a fixed m, if our finger acts on the key with more force (due to muscular force or gravitational force), the key will accelerate more. Also, given a fixed m, if our finger applies its force over a longer period of time,[57] the key will have more time over which to accelerate, and its final velocity will be increased.

Thus, should we wish to reduce the force of our touch and still produce a note of the same volume, the only way this could occur is if the force of our touch were distributed over a *longer* period of time—as claimed by the slow-but-weighty-keystroke. However, if a longer period of time is used to push the key down, the velocity of the key at the moment of let-off will be *less* (not more). This will produce a hammer with less speed and, hence, less volume—the opposite to what is being claimed.

Theoretically, by using a slow-but-weighty-keystroke, the force might be able to be distributed more evenly during key descent—compared to a quick *staccato* touch (which delivers more of its force at the beginning of the keystroke)—but given the brevity of this time frame (approximately 0.02 s for a *forte* touch), providing any meaningful redistribution of the force into the key ought to be dismissed as improbable.

The perception that less force is being given to the key to make the loud sound is illusory, and it is probably based on the fact that there is a longer time period of force distribution *into the keybed* after the hammer has already let off, which gives the sensation that less force has been used.

The idea that we can produce a louder sound with a slower descent of the key is fictitious. The use of arm-weight might make producing loud sounds feel physically easier, but if a louder sound is required, the key speed will need to be faster, by definition.

The other claim, that the rebound force back into our body can be reduced by maintaining a relaxed body, is also erroneous. Newton's 3rd law states that "whenever one object exerts a force on a second object, the second object exerts an equal and opposite force on the first."[58] Therefore, whatever magnitude of force is being put into the key via your finger, the force returned to your body via that finger will be *the same*. Furthermore, the force in and the force out occur *simultaneously*. There's no delay. The forces *are* the interaction. Whatever muscles are active at the moment of impact are the same muscles that are active . . . at the moment of impact. Any idea that the rebound forces can be avoided by having "relaxed muscles" or "loose wrists" is fictitious. If the rebound force is being avoided, it means there was never any incident force in the first place.

COMBINING ANATOMY WITH PHYSICS

This section looks at anatomically efficient ways to provide momentum (by delivering force) into the key. In general, it explores how to use the body in ways that are more compatible with its natural, evolved, function.

Arches and Domes

The Roman arch is a simple physical structure that can withstand heavy loads (large forces) while requiring minimal effort to maintain stability. It is able to do this because: (i.) the forces are transmitted through multiple smaller units under compression (rather than tension) and (ii.) the shape and positioning of the blocks in the arch allow the force to be more equally distributed throughout the structure—which reduces the peak force that any single component of the arch will need to withstand. Both mechanical engineers and nature itself have benefited from the physics of the arch structure. Free to use and already built into the human hand (like the foot), the arch also happens to be very useful to pianists.

The natural, resting position of the hand contains three anatomical arches—the *proximal transverse arch*, the *distal transverse arch*, and the *longitudinal arch*. They provide structure and function to the hand and are created by the positioning of the bones, muscles, tendons, ligaments and aponeuroses (a thick connective tissue under the palm). Their function is to

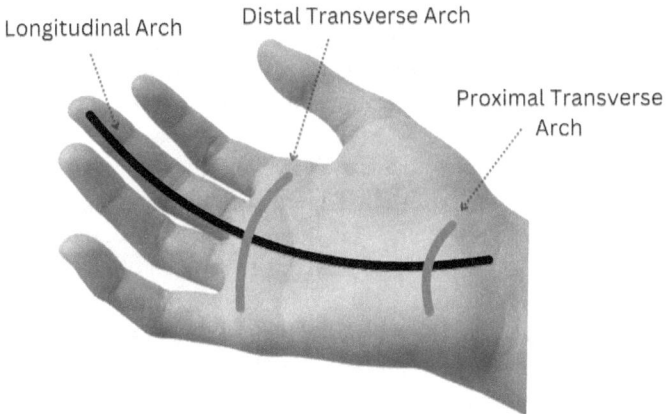

Figure 6.5. Arches of the Hand. Author created

"provide a balance between stability and mobility for grasping"[59]—again, functions that pianists rely on.

The proximal transverse arch is found at the base of the hand near the wrist. It is of the least interest to pianists because it is *fixed* in position by the bones and ligaments that form it. The other two arches, however, are *mobile*, and their shape can be altered to the advantage (or disadvantage) of the pianist during playing.

The distal transverse arch approximates to a line that runs *under the row of knuckles* (thus running parallel to the proximal arch). The longitudinal arch runs perpendicular to these arches and is represented by a curved line that runs *from the fingertips along the curve of the fingers up to the knuckles and then down again to the base of the wrist joint.*

> *Combined, the three arches of the hand create a dome shape, which is fundamental to the stability of the hand during piano playing and the equal distribution of forces throughout it.*

Not coincidentally, the commonly taught hand position in piano pedagogy—the "hold-an-apple-in-your-hand position"—maintains the integrity of these arches (i.e., with partially-curled fingers, mildly-raised knuckles and a neutral wrist position). The position also corresponds closely to the natural resting position of the hand (as it would if hanging by your side). Both positions approximate the *functional position* of the hand (the position used by doctors to rest the hand when it is recovering from a fracture or tendon injury—because it is the position where the muscles and tendons are least strained).

A dome shape, created by the arches of the hand and the gentle curve of the fingers, is an intrinsically strong structure and requires the least amount of muscular effort to maintain.[60] It is a physiologically appropriate default position to adopt (and try to maintain) when playing the piano.

The predilection of some pianists, however, to eliminate these natural arches by choosing to play with flat fingers with no angle at the knuckles,[61] is mechanically counterproductive—it flattens the arches and renders them less effective. Thus, instead of easily having the forces of the keystroke distributed through these intrinsic arches, other muscles that are less suited to the task, like the small muscles of the hand and the muscles of the forearm, must take up the work. Along with fatiguing these muscles unnecessarily, the added tension in the forearm muscles has the secondary effect of tightening the wrist, which in turn, restricts the mobility of the hand and increases the effective mass of the keystroke—something that may not be wished for by the pianist. Thus, by intentionally abolishing the natural arches of the hand, a self-inflicted mechanical inefficiency is introduced. No professional runner would ever intentionally abolish the natural arches of the foot.

If the hand arches are weakened, flattened or broken, the distribution of forces throughout the hand will be passed on to alternative, less suitable anatomical structures within the hand, wrist and forearm. These structures may be able to withstand this increased demand to some extent, but why should they have to? It only makes the mechanics of piano playing harder and increases the risk of fatigue and injury.

Small-handed pianists suffer unfairly regarding receiving the full benefit from the hand arches because so much of the piano repertoire demands that their hands and fingers are more stretched out relative to their size, causing flatter arches. "Double-jointed" pianists—or those with joint hypermobility problems—may also have difficulty maintaining the natural arches. These pianists need to find creative solutions, both physically and musically, to compensate for the mechanical loss of the missing arch.

The fatigue (and injury) of the muscles of the hand that may occur when playing the music of Rachmaninoff, or other music where wide stretches are frequently required (e.g., Chopin etudes), is exacerbated by the loss of the arches of the hand and the extra work that the smaller muscles must carry out in order to compensate.

In addition to the natural arches of the hand, pianists can create other types of arches, both small and large, to optimize the mechanics of different types of keystrokes:

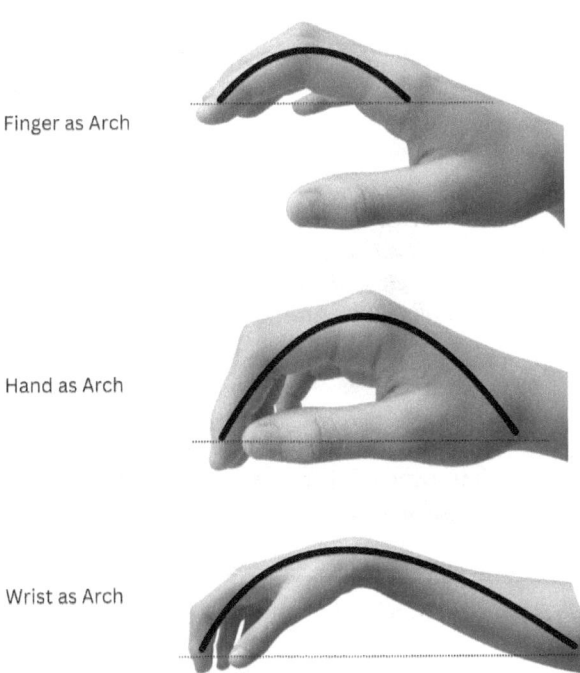

Figure 6.6. Three Longitudinal Arches. Author created

- small arch: a small longitudinal arch can be made using a simple, curved finger: where the fingertip serves as one of its bases and the hand knuckle, the other base. Playing with this arch requires a slightly lower wrist position but it is also an exceedingly efficient (and common) biomechanical position to use (Horowitz did), should it be used.
- large arch: on other occasions, a longer longitudinal arch might be preferred, where the wrist serves as the highpoint of the arch and the fingertips and the elbow make the bases of the arch. Note how, in both scenarios, hand arches are still maintained. With good reason, this higher (but not high) wrist position also features commonly in piano playing and pedagogy.[62] It is well-suited to solving many types of passagework, especially those that involve slightly wider finger spacings, wide-spaced chords or, most obviously, with an even higher wrist positions, in loud and fast octave passages (watch Horowitz, Lang Lang, Cziffra and Argerich, amongst others) where the pillars of the arches (i.e., the fingers) are aligned in a more vertical direction, making the transfer of momentum into the key direct and efficient.

Hammers and High-Knuckle Positions

Another mechanically strong structure that can be replicated by the hand, is the hammer. If a finger stands up straight upon the key, and its knuckle is positioned above it, a hammer structure is created. The high-wrist octave-playing position (just mentioned), because of its very high arch, almost approximates a hammer structure because the top of the arch is almost directly above the contact point of the finger on the key.

Forces can be effortlessly transmitted into the key using hammer-like positions because the forces are easily transmitted through bones that are aligned end-on-end (like our vertebral column). Further, the right-angled hammer-like joint position is relatively effortlessly kept in position by the bony joint structure and its surrounding ligaments, tendons and skin.

As efficient as it may be to play the piano with a standing-up finger position, it is, of course, absurd to argue that such a position makes for a good *default* piano playing position. Its obvious problem is that the fingertips will be angled *across* the keys when they move—scratching and skimming across the surface of the key instead of moving down into it.

Better Arches—Better Mechanics

Extreme arches (causing hammer positions) are not the solution to piano playing any more than no arches (flat finger with flat hand positions) are, but an *improvement* in your arch positions—e.g., from a "no arch" position to a "some arch" position, or the choosing of one type of arch over another, may provide effortless mechanical (and health) benefits to your playing. Examples here could include:

- playing loud chords or repeated octaves. Minimal finger movement and minimal forearm muscle tension is required if the hand drops onto the key with fingers "standing up taller" (rather than "lying down flat") with the wrist higher.
- projecting out a melodic voice or any individual voice within a chord. Intuitively, many pianists do this when playing melodies with the 5th finger (e.g., watch Cortot, Barenboim, Volodos or Sokolov).
- playing an outstretched 5th finger. Here, any attempt to improve the "knuckle-over-the-contact-point" position will spare the 5th finger's muscles from stretching and fatiguing.

Notice how the higher the arch, the less flexion movement is needed by the finger and the more hand-forearm drop downwards onto the key is required. Thus, there is a three-way relationship—and a balance to be found—between the type of arch, the touch angle and the amount of hand drop. Finger movement is only one part of any mechanical solution, which is why deliberately isolating their movements should generally be avoided. Some hand drop with some degree of hand arch is almost always mechanically beneficial to any keystroke.

Gravity

Because of its muscle-work-sparing benefits, the proper use of gravity ought to be considered an important feature of an optimized technique. Using gravity in piano playing is not essential—the body has enough muscles to direct the arm, hand and fingers down into the key without needing it—but given that gravity is a force provided to us for free, it makes sense to use it whenever possible to reduce the burden of work on the muscles.

When the force of gravity acts upon a mass, the mass will accelerate, and its velocity will increase. When a pianist's hand drops onto a key from higher above it, gravity will have more time to act and the final speed of the hand when it hits the key will be more. Table 6.2 shows these differences in speed.

From this table, we can make several conclusions:

- Suitable touch speeds can easily be generated by dropping onto the key from very short distances above it.
- If these drop heights are accompanied with large effective masses, very (very) large touch momentums can be achieved very easily.
- However, should we allow our hand to fall onto the key from a high height above it, we must also accept that we will have to wait longer for it to fall to the key. This extra amount of time may not always be musically affordable.
- Clearly, if fast, repetitive keystrokes are required (e.g., any semiquaver passage), the idea of "using gravity" is absurd. Here, muscular action will have to dominate the keystroke.

Table 6.2. Gravity and Free Fall Speeds

Height Above Key before Hand Drop	Time Duration of Free Fall	Speed of Hand at the Key Surface
1 cm	0.05 s	0.44 m/s
2 cm	0.06 s	0.63 m/s
3 cm	0.08 s	0.77 m/s
4 cm	0.09 s	0.89 m/s
5 cm	0.10 s	0.99 m/s
10 cm	0.14 s	1.40 m/s

- Notwithstanding the time delay of larger free falls, there is still usually some time to be found between most note groups of most musical phrases, which will allow us to use gravity, or some gravity, in the keystroke.

Optimizing Mechanical Efficiency: The "Triple-Stroke"

Pianists can choose to alter any of the variables shown in the textbox below to improve or alter the mechanical efficiency of their keystrokes.

How to Improve the Mechanical Efficiency of the Keystroke

Extreme arches (causing hammer positions) are not the solution to piano playing any more than no arches (flat finger with flat hand positions) are, but an *improvement* in your arch positions—e.g., from a "no arch" position to a "some arch" position, or the choosing of one type of arch over another, may provide effortless mechanical (and health) benefits to your playing, at no cost. Examples here could include:

- playing loud chords or repeated octaves. Minimal finger movement and minimal forearm muscle tension is required if the hand drops onto the key with fingers "standing up taller" (rather than "lying down flat") with the wrist higher.
- projecting out a melodic voice or any individual voice within a chord. Intuitively, many pianists do this when playing melodies with the 5th finger (e.g., watch Cortot, Barenboim, Volodos or Sokolov).
- playing an outstretched 5th finger. Here, any attempt to improve the "knuckle-over-the-contact-point" position will spare the 5th finger's muscles from stretching and fatiguing.

Notice how the higher the arch, the less flexion movement is needed by the finger and the more hand-forearm drop downwards onto the key is required. Thus, there is a three-way relationship—and a balance to be found—between the type of arch, the touch angle and the amount of hand drop. Finger movement is only one part of any mechanical solution, which is why deliberately isolating their movements should generally be avoided. Some hand drop with some degree of hand arch is almost always mechanically beneficial to any keystroke.

Despite the complexity of all the theory, the keystroke that allows all this to happen—a "triple-stroke"—is ridiculously simple to learn and apply. It asks for "a little bit" of finger, "a little bit" of hand and "a little bit" of forearm to *all* be directed into the key *at the same time*. Every single musical passage will need a little bit more or a little bit less of a contribution from each component, but by adopting a triple-stroke, the mechanical problems of piano playing will always be solvable. There is always an ideal *m-v* pair.

The following examples suggest what might be the best body parts to use to arrive at an ideal *m-v* pair for different types of musical passagework. It considers the momentum requirements of the keystroke and the inertia problems of moving the fingers, hand and arm during those passages:

- *Finger* → Mozart: Sonata K.331, 3rd movement—*Alla Turca*. (R.H. semi-quavers)
- *Finger-hand* → Chopin: Étude in A flat. Op.10, No.10. (R.H.)
- *Hand* → Scriabin: Etude in D# minor. Op.8, No.12. (R.H. octave gestures)
- *Hand-forearm* → Rachmaninoff: Prelude in E minor. Op.32, No. 4. (Climax)
- *Forearm* → Beethoven Piano Concerto No.5, 1st Movement. (Climax *ff* octaves)
- *Forearm-Arm* → Rachmaninoff: Prelude in C# minor. Op.3, No.2. (Climax loud chords)

> *Should a default keystroke ever be wished for in piano playing, the most effective, efficient and physically healthy stroke to use is the triple-stroke, where finger, hand and forearm all contribute to the keystroke using a combination of muscle movement and gravity, and while operating close to mid-range joint positions. This triple-stroke is, ironically, what the body would probably learn to do itself if it weren't actively taught to do the wrong thing by speculative pedagogical theories.*
>
> *Biomechanically, what goes wrong in piano playing, when it goes wrong, is that some, or many, of the above conditions are not met. The story is always the same: that pianists choose to isolate finger, hand and forearm movements instead of coordinating them, that touch angles are inefficient, that gravity is underused, or that notes are played when joints are at the extremes of their ranges.*

There are many thousands of professional pianists in the world using well-coordinated triple-stroke keystrokes all the time. Many of these pianists may never be famous (musical or mental skills might lack) but their techniques could all be recommended as good reference points as far as the mechanics of piano playing are concerned. For want of some famous-pianist examples, one could observe the biomechanical movements of Rubinstein, Schiff, Zimmerman, Michelangeli, Horowitz (the younger), Cziffra, Argerich, Richter,

Pletnev, Hough, Sokolov or Volodos, amongst many others—although one shouldn't expect to *see* anything unusual when observing them.[63] Coordinated movements do not tend to attract attention.

Finger Dependence, Interdependence and Independence

Forearm Muscles

Two groups of muscles move our fingers: forearm muscles and hand muscles. There are *no* intrinsic finger muscles. (Hence, to "strengthen the fingers" is factually erroneous). Forearm muscles attach to the bones in our forearm and arm (near to the elbow joint). They cross over our hand and attach to the bones of our fingers to allow them to flex (e.g., finger stroke) and extend (e.g., finger lift). They also stabilise the joints in position (bridging) during the impact of the keystroke.

Forearm muscles are larger than the muscles of the hand, and so it is logical that they take on the greater burden of the work. Also, the flexor muscles of the forearm are larger than the extensor muscles of the forearm (because we have evolved to grasp strongly, rather than un-grasp strongly) thus, giving finger flexion more strength than finger extension.

> *Because of their size, the flexor muscles of the forearm should carry out the bulk of any muscular work of piano playing. The muscles of the hand and the extensor muscles of the forearm should be used more sparingly. This implies that flat fingers, wide stretches between the fingers, and high finger-lifting should be kept to a minimum.*

This said, there are problems associated with only relying on forearm muscles to play the piano too. The main problem being that when forearm muscles are excessively contracted and relaxed (e.g., during sustained, rapid passagework)—like those found in Chopin etudes—the wrist unavoidably becomes tighter, because of the *constant* movement of the tendons forward and backward across the top and bottom of the wrist.

Although to some degree this increased wrist tightness is unavoidable, it is made much worse if the fingers are stretched out wide when playing.[64] As a consequence, in such passages, efforts need to be made to keep the fingers and hand as close to their anatomically neutral positions as possible—just as Chopin's pupil reminds us: "The object of which [i.e., Chopin's fingering] is to keep the hand in its proper position."[65] It is a challenge that needs to be solved, as it will help to restore the arches of the hand, which will, in turn, require less muscular force from the muscles. It will also oblige the hand to contribute to the momentum of the keystroke by dropping (or rotating) fractionally more into the key—all factors which will improve the mechanical efficiency of the touch.

Hand Muscles

The second group of muscles that move our fingers are our hand muscles. These muscles have evolved to provide the hand with improved finger independence, improved fine motor control, and to fine tune the cruder grasping movements of the forearm muscles: "fine control of finger movements [is] superimposed on these simpler [grasping] patterns."[66]

In order to provide this finger independence, the intrinsic muscles are confined to the hand itself (hence, "intrinsic" muscles of the hand), attaching *between the hand and the finger* (not between the forearm and the finger). There are four groups: the *thenar* (helps thumb movements), *hypothenar* (helps 5th-finger movements), *interossei* (help sideways finger movements) and the *lumbricals*.

> **If the intrinsic hand muscles didn't exist, all movements of the fingers would be limited to collective, grasping, movements. The intrinsic muscles help to overcome this evolutionary primitive collective movement by enhancing finger independence.**

Worthy of special comment are the lumbrical muscles. For piano players, they are uniquely helpful. Compared to other muscles, they are packed full of *muscle spindles*—specialized sensory receptors that allow the body to rapidly fine tune its movements.[67] Notably, "the deep flexor muscles [of the forearm] are strong but slow, and exhibit low independence between the fingers, while the lumbricals are the opposite: weak, fast, and independent."[68] This is a built-in function of the body that pianists would be crazy not to exploit.[69]

Lumbricals do not attach to bone but directly to the flexor and extensor tendons. This feature allows them to perform the special function of allowing the finger to flex at the knuckle joint *while* extending at the two finger joints (i.e., to "poke"). It allows more independence to each individual finger: "pianists may avoid extensive use of the extrinsic muscles [of the forearm] that are known to exhibit strong biomechanical coupling, by generating movements from the lumbrical muscles that are known to be fairly independent."[70]

> **The "poking" movement into the key afforded by the lumbricals is especially useful for pianists as it allows the finger to straighten itself out from its otherwise curved (grasping) trajectory around the axis of its knuckle. Thus, the straightening, or partial straightening, can be used to improve the touch angle and improve the efficiency of the transfer of momentum from the finger into the key. This reduces the amount of work done by the forearm muscles and reduces the tension in the tendons across the wrist. It also aids the mobility of the wrist and allows for individuation of each finger's movement, improving key control. These are important benefits to piano playing.**

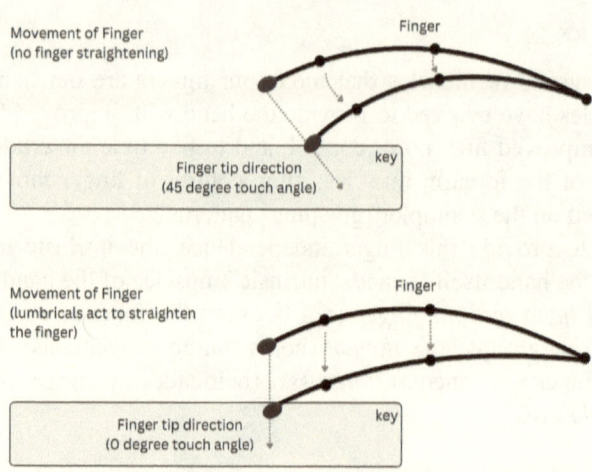

Figure 6.7. Lumbricals Can Improve the Touch Angle. Author created

Juncturae Tendinum

Regarding hand anatomy, another particular mechanical challenge that the pianist must learn to overcome (that is not self-inflicted) is the restricted ability of the 4th finger to independently extend at the knuckle joint. This limitation exists because the extensor tendons of fingers 3, 4, and 5 are each partially bound to each other by bands of connective tissue—*juncturae tendinum*[71]—on the back of the hand. The function of these inter-tendinous bands is to *help distribute the forces across the hand* when involved in gripping and holding movements.

> *The juncturae tendinum account for why, when the 3rd finger is flexed (and to a lesser extent, the 5th), it will be more difficult to extend the 4th finger. Equally, if the 4th finger is extended, it will naturally cause some extension in the neighboring fingers. This is often noticed when the 4th finger extends itself in preparation to play a note and the 5th finger extends itself in company. As these finger couplings are anatomical—and useful to force transmission and distribution—technical exercises that presume to know better and try to stop such movements from happening should be disregarded.*

The less independent 4th finger (and to some extent the 3rd) is also limited by the fact that it does not have its own muscle or group of muscles to help it, as is the case with the thumb (*thenar* muscles), the index finger (*extensor indicis*) and the 5th finger (*hypothenar* muscles).

> *With freedom of movement compromised, the 4th finger may need extra biomechanical support in order to maintain the same level of function as the other fingers. This means improving the mechanics of its momentum transfer.*

Note, however, that because of the restrictive anatomy of the 4th finger, trying to increase its finger lift is not the best or most viable solution.

The Hand as a Functioning Unit

Unavoidably, in playing the piano, we must learn to individuate our finger movements—to train our fingers *not* to move dependently. And, undeniably, we can do this to achieve very sophisticated (and quite perverse) levels of finger independence. However, although independence is a skill that human fingers *can* do, it is not necessarily what they *want* to do. Coordinated movements are still what the mammalian motor systems does best.

Motor programming and muscle training are required to overcome our fingers' primitive wish to operate dependently. Examples of this are the instinctual fisted grabbing movements of infants, the lack of finger independence demonstrated by beginner pianists who have not yet "learned" to play the piano, the inherent awkwardness of 3–4 or 4–5 trills, or even the flailing grabbing-like movement that our fingers resort to when our muscles are over-fatigued at the end of a long, demanding recital.

The difficulty that the body has in achieving full independence of the fingers is known as *enslavement*, where it is recognized that "the major constraint that governs finger movements is that it is virtually impossible to restrict motion to a single finger."[72] As we have seen, enslavement can be anatomical, due to the *juncturae tendinum*, the shapes of joints, or the positions of muscle insertions, or it can be neurological, where the brain automatically activates the movements of adjacents fingers to benefit from force optimization and task fulfillment.[73] Either way, we cannot fight the physiology that underlies enslavement—that fingers *want* to function together as a group, not separately, both in mechanics and in gesture.

> **Extreme, repetitive and deliberate finger-individuating exercises are physiologically unnatural, and accordingly, they will be charged with additional physiological risk to our health—the major risks being tendonitis injuries (because of their overuse with over-force) and focal dystonia (because of the overly-enlarged and overly-overlapping representation of each finger in the motor cortex). Plainly, it would be more sensible to view finger independence as a "physiological bonus" that allows us to play the piano, or as an adaptive "bi-product" of playing it, rather than something to actively aim for.**

Joint Positions and Muscle Strength

Generally, muscles contract best when they act within a (close) range of their anatomically neutral joint positions.[74] Power generation is easier because the contraction is stronger, synergy with other muscle groups is enhanced, and the onset of muscle fatigue is delayed.[75] Doing the opposite, playing using extreme joint positions, is disadvantageous for the same reasons: that maximal contractile force will be less, that more muscles and more collective muscle work will be needed to deliver any given force, and that the onset of muscle fatigue will be earlier.

Logically, muscles that are subjected to prolonged episodes of high work load and/or operate in non-neutral joint positions and/or have smaller muscle bellies, are the ones that are going to fatigue earlier.[76] This is why muscle fatigue is so common when playing works like Chopin's etudes, where there are extended sequences of fast, repetitive notes requiring the use of hand and forearm muscles (with limited opportunity to use gravity as a force supplement) *and* often in stretched-out hand positions.

> ***Thankfully, during piano playing, pushing our muscles to the point of maximum force or maximum fatigue is rarely required. Certainly, it need never be sought. There is always a mechanical solution that makes difficult technical situations easy.***

If we wish to optimize the contractility of our muscles, we also need to know what the neutral joint positions are, across which they contract. The neutral (mid-range) position for the joints in the arm below the elbow are, approximately:

- Wrist: $20°$ extended
- Knuckles: $45°$ flexed
- Large (proximal) finger joint: $35°$ flexed
- Small (distal) finger joint: $10°$ flexed

As mentioned earlier, these joint positions approximate to the "relaxed hand" position or, as used in piano pedagogy, a "holding an apple in the hand" position.

Sitting Postures

An "ideal" sitting position is one that allows us to deliver our m's and v's while using joint positions that stay comfortably within their normal ranges. This is not a complicated task; it does not need to be overthought, as Chopin reminds us: "Position yourself so as to be able to reach both ends of the keyboard without leaning to either side"[77] and "one needs only to study a certain positioning of the hand in relation to the keys to obtain with ease the most beautiful quality of sound."[78]

Despite pedagogical claims that one can more easily deliver more arm weight to the key by sitting higher (or lower?) or that this will make the quality of the sound better (or worse?) and that this will help your overall pianism (or not?) we have shown how factless such claims are. Most piano playing doesn't *need* much arm weight, and most of the time it doesn't *want* much arm weight either (because of the inertia problems that it creates). Further, as shown, the sound that any touch makes is not determined by the arm weight but the *momentum of the keystroke* which is dependent on the mass, the velocity and the touch angle of the keystroke.

Regardless of the sitting position, there will always be a compromise between what is most *comfortable* for our body and what is most *useful* for our pianism. No sitting position exists that can keep *all* the joints of the arm in neutral positions *all* the time *and* still play the piano. Even when adopting a typically "normal" sitting position, if we tried to maintain mid-range joint positions in the elbow and the shoulder also, it would cause a nonsensical playing position for the hand: involving a forearm partially extended in front of the body but with the palm of the hand facing sideways (!)—a position suited to shaking someone's hand, but not for playing the piano.

Turning Natural Positions into Piano-Playing Positions

In order to get the hand into a practical piano-playing position with the palm facing down and the knuckles of the hand running roughly parallel to the keys, one or more of the following adjustments must occur:

- the forearm pronates (i.e., it rotates the hand into a palm-down position);
- the elbows move outwards to the sides of the body (this rotates the shoulder so that the palm can face down without requiring as much forearm pronation);
- the upper-arms extend out in front of the body (this rotates the shoulder so that the palm can be more face down without the elbows needing to be out to the sides as much);
- when either hand plays in the middle register of the piano (or its opposite register), the right hand will have to "twist" to some degree to the right (called "ulnar deviation") or, if it is the left hand, to the left, in order to keep the knuckles (roughly) parallel with the keyboard.

These are the biomechanical adjustments that every pianist makes when playing the piano, though because every pianist plays using a slightly different combination of the above adjustments, we observe a huge variety of *different looking* but *completely acceptable* piano playing postures.[79]

Our choice of posture at the piano should not be driven by any assumption that it will affect our sound quality. It should be driven, like everything else in technique, by how it will contribute to the musical experience, our playability, and our physical health long term.

Practically, should we wish to concern ourselves with the issue, we need to decide how high/low and how near/far to sit to the keyboard. They are both connected, as they both have an impact on how we will deal with the problems of momentum transfer into the key, body inertia, and joint neutrality. Generally, pedagogy is preoccupied with how high or low we sit, but this misses the point. We should be just as concerned about how near or far from the keyboard we sit, as this will impact just as much, if not more, on the issues just described.

For example, to sit too close to the keyboard will compromise joint neutrality, as it will require either extreme ulnar deviation of the hand at the wrist or significantly more internal rotation at the shoulder (causing chicken-wing elbows out the side of our body) *but* by bringing the axis of the torso closer to the keyboard it will make moving our forearms over the keyboard easier (because the stronger muscles arising from our trunk and shoulders can exert their forces on mass units in the arm which are nearer to them). When Horowitz plays virtuoso music (e.g., watch his performance of his Carmen Variations transcription[80]) his torso tends to tilt slightly in toward the instrument, and his forearms move in very close ranges in front of him. With almost no upper arm movement, he minimizes the inertia problems that fast, changing, horizontal movements across the keyboard create. Conversely, sitting too far away may lead to the opposite situation where overall joint neutrality for the limb is improved *but*, because of the longer distance of the hands away from the trunk, and the increased inertia of the arm in front of the body, problems with leaping agility may arise.

Sitting at the piano requires finding a balance between what is most natural for our body's muscles and joints, and what is most practical for dealing with the momentum and inertia needs of the keystroke.

Famous Pianists' Sitting Positions

Classifying the sitting positions of some of history's great pianists is one way of pointing out the folly of trying to correlate sitting positions with tone-quality, tone quantity, or even, pianism outcomes. Although some of the above sitting positions may capture one's attention as being extreme, they are still *workable* positions that allow the mechanics of piano playing to succeed.

- High-sitting: Rubinstein, Barenboim, Brendel, Kissin, Cherkassky
- Low-sitting: Backhaus, Cziffra, Michelangeli, Schiff, Horowitz, Gould
- Near-sitting: Kissin, Horowitz, Gould
- Far-sitting: Cziffra, Michelangeli, Schiff
- Variable/Free-moving: Kissin, Lang Lang, Uchida, Liszt (reportedly)
- Somewhere "in between" sitting: The majority of pianists

Because of its iconic nature, however, the sitting position of Gould deserves special comment. His very low sitting position was certainly unusual, and it required several of the previously mentioned biomechanical adjustments to make it workable. These included, most notably: the exaggerated flexion at the wrist; the exaggerated ulnar deviation at the wrist; and the elbows being held out the sides of his body. These adjustments allowed his hand (and fingers) to assume completely normal positions at the keyboard and provide the necessary m-v combinations and angles. Nevertheless, although workable, such extreme joint angles could never be recommended to other pianists on the physiological grounds that they unnecessarily stretch ligaments and tendons, put undue strain through some joints and make many muscles of the upper limb work in suboptimal positions. These most certainly contributed to the injuries and pain that Gould suffered during his life.

Personally, I suspect Gould enjoyed sitting low and playing with a hand that hovered over the keys for the following reasons: (i.) that it helped him to reduce the effective mass of his touch (the extreme flexion at the wrist necessitated that it be very loosely bridged otherwise muscle fatigue and mobility limitations would have resulted). This allowed him, and required him, to control each key using a finger-predominant touch, which, in turn, demanded that the action of his instrument was very precisely regulated and hyper touch sensitive—which it was; (ii.) it allowed his brain to get closer to his fingers, literally, physically, facilitating the intense psychological bond of embodiment that he had between his mind and his fingers; and (iii.) it is what he was accustomed to doing, habitually, physically and psychologically.

THE FIVE FINGERS—STRENGTHS AND WEAKNESSES

"As each finger is differently formed, it's better not to attempt to destroy the particular charm of each one's touch but on the contrary to develop it."[81]
—Frédéric Chopin

1st finger (the thumb)
The most obvious feature of the thumb is its mobility. Functionally, this is both a strength and a weakness. Although the thumb is reasonably strong during flexion and opposition (when moving across the palm toward the tips of the other fingers) these are not the directions in which the thumb typically depresses the keys—or if they are, they shouldn't be.

To be useful in piano playing, the thumb must be taught to move up and down (like its neighboring fingers) so that it plays vertically down into the key. This downward movement into the key (palmar abduction), although not as strong as flexion, makes up for it with its highly efficient momentum transfer into the key (with an easily achievable 0^0 touch angle).

The other solution to overcoming the thumb's abduction weakness is to take advantage of its position at the end of the row of fingers—where forearm rotational movements can be used to supplement the thumb's momentum into the key (because of bridging) without the thumb itself needing to move much at all. This is the science behind Taubman's advice that "the forearm plays the thumb."[82] The thumb movements of Martha Argerich (or indeed any other of her pianistic movements) may be considered excellent examples of mechanical efficiency.

2nd finger (index finger)
The 2nd finger is both strong and independent with a good range of movement. It receives strong muscles from the forearm, including a pair of muscles *solely* for it, and, like other fingers, it has intrinsic muscles arising from within the hand to control finger movement. Mechanical problems should not occur with this finger, though they might if the finger becomes too curled or too straight, both of which will restrict movement at the wrist (because of the pull of the tendons).

3rd finger (middle finger)
This finger offers a variety of basic functions. Its movement profile represents a mixture of the characteristics of the 2nd and 4th fingers: operating predominantly in a flexion-extension direction with some scope for sideways movements but ultimately moving with less independence than the 2nd finger because it has fewer individual muscles to help it and because it has the *juncturae tendinum* binding it to the 4th finger. Its main mechanical problem is not its independence but its length, which must be managed to ensure that its contact point with the key is not too far away from its overlying knuckle (which flattens the hand arch).

4th finger (ring finger)
As already discussed, the feature of this finger is that its extensor tendons are wrapped by bands of connective tissue in the hand, the *juncturae tendinum*. These bands connect to the tendons of the 3rd, 4th, and 5th fingers to varying

degrees and help to distribute the forces across the hand during grasping movements. These bands limit independence but promote interdependence. Accordingly, extension movements of any of these fingers will be more difficult when any of its companion fingers move in the opposite direction. Note, however, that the 4th finger has no difficulty extending at the knuckle joint if its neighboring fingers also accompany it in extension.

The solution to overcoming any functional limitation of 4th finger extension, is unequivocally *not* to try to force it to extend in isolation but to coordinate its movement with its adjacent fingers. Given that the connective tissue bands support interdependence of the fingers, this feature should be facilitated, not restricted. For example, when playing a sequence of notes, when the 3rd finger is being lifted, the 4th finger should not be denied the opportunity of lifting with it. Or similarly, if the 4th finger is being lifted, the 5th finger should not be denied the opportunity of lifting with it—the adjacent fingers *want* to move together.

Also, similar to the 3rd finger, it is long and runs the risk that its contact point with the key will be far away from its overlying knuckle causing flattening of the hand arches and a compensatory stiffer wrist to make up for its loss of momentum transfer. Given that the 4th finger may be restricted in its extension movement because of the flexion movements of its neighboring fingers, its limited backswing may further limit its maximum achievable velocity during its downswing into the key. Finding ways to optimize its mechanical efficiency is therefore needed. There are many options here (as discussed earlier).

5th finger (pinky)
The movement of the 5th finger deserves special attention. Like flat hands, a poorly angled thumb, an overly curled 2nd finger, or too-straight 3rd or 4th fingers, poor mechanics of our 5th finger can have negative consequences for

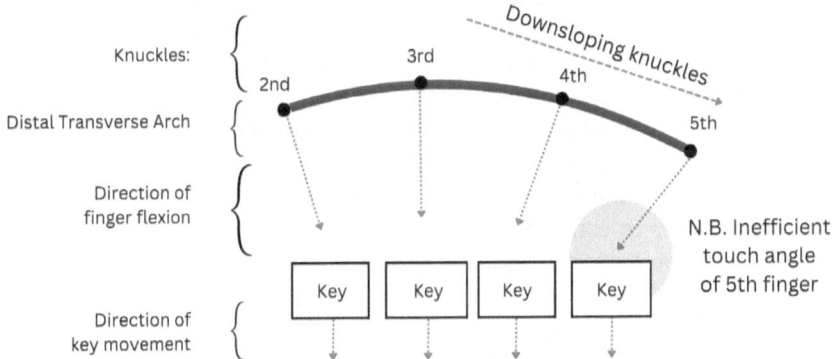

Figure 6.8. 5th Finger Touch Angles: Good and Bad. Author created

the overall functioning of our pianism. With the 5th finger, all our skills in optimizing mechanics and physiology are put to the test—which is perhaps why it is so easily fatigued and injured.

The 5th finger receives shared muscles (as tendons) from the forearm (like all the other fingers) *plus* another couple of muscles of its own (also from the forearm) to help with flexion and extension (similar to the index finger) *plus* a double set of intrinsic small hand muscles to allow for the poke movement and to give it extra strength when spreading outwards or grabbing. The net result is that although the 5th finger is relatively mobile and independent, despite its additional muscles, it still remains relatively weak.

As we know, if the 5th finger plays notes while being outstretched and tries to support too much weight from the arm, its small muscles will fatigue quicker. Not surprisingly, a common cause of pain in pianists is due to the (over-)stretching of the 5th finger muscles when playing octaves and chords[83]—a problem that is only worsened by the musical need for the 5th finger to play louder than the other notes when balancing a chord or projecting out a melody).

As with other mechanical problems, the solution to the mechanical problems of the 5th finger lies with optimizing the momentum of its keystroke—its P_{in} equation. Along with improving the coordination of its swing into the key, special attention should be given to improving its touch angle. This is because, at the piano, it operates at an anatomical disadvantage. When a hand rests on the keyboard in a "normal" playing position, the touch angle of the 5th finger tends to be at a *slant* across the key. As we know, this means that less of its momentum will be transferred into the *downward* direction of the key—the direction of maximal efficiency.

There are two anatomical reasons which contribute to this unfavorable slant. First, the most anatomically neutral position for the arm to be in when we sit at the piano is a "shaking someone's hand" position, not a palm-down hand position. Thus, our body will have a natural tendency to want to return to this joint-neutral position, which will exacerbate the 5th finger's diagonal slant across the key. Secondly, the natural direction of flexion of the 5th finger is *diagonally across* the palm toward the scaphoid bone (in the center of the wrist near the base of the thumb), not straight downwards along the edge of the palm.

If both these normal anatomical factors are ignored, the slant of the 5th finger across the key can easily reach 30^0–45^0 or more (see Figure 6.8), causing significant mechanical inefficiency to the finger that can least afford it. Thus, in order to compensate for the momentum loss, the 5th finger will either have to strike faster (more *v*) or recruit more mass from the forearm (more bridging). But asking the small muscles of the 5th finger to strike faster fatigues them more quickly and bridging more mass from the forearm tightens the wrist, which limits finger independence. Additionally, transmitting heavy weights (forces) across the small joints of the 5th finger subjects them to levels of mechanical stress that they are not built for. The bony bumps (*osteophytes*) often seen around the small joints of the pianist's 5th finger represent the body's adaptive response to these stresses.[84]

Slope the Hand Up Toward the 5th Finger Knuckle

A better solution to overcoming the poor touch angle of the 5th finger, is to pronate the forearm a little more and/or allow the elbow to move slightly more out to the side of the body. This creates a more *horizontal* line (imaginary) between the knuckles on the back of the hand—rather than a line that slopes downwards toward the 5th finger. The slightly higher knuckle position helps to improve the 5th finger's touch angle.

To fully counterbalance the natural slant of the 5th finger across the palm, furthermore pronation/elbow-out movement will be required—so that the imaginary line running through your knuckles now *slopes up* toward the 5th finger. This position may feel unusual to most pianists (never habituated), but when used, it improves the touch angle of the 5th finger significantly, and in so doing, spares the small muscles of the hand of unnecessary work while also sparing the finger's small joints of inappropriately large cross-slanting forces. This spares them of fatigue and injury, respectively. The hand position does not have to be used all the time, but in passages that involve constant use of the 5th (or 4th) finger, the improved angle of attack may transform the ease of the movement.

Additionally, with a higher 5th finger knuckle, it will improve the knuckle-over-key-contact point. This, as mentioned previously, allows mechanical forces to be transmitted *through the line of compression* of these small bones and joints—as they prefer—rather than across them. The straighter, more standing up positions of the 5th fingers of Cortot, Volodos, Michelangeli, Sokolov, and Barenboim are examples of them exploiting this efficiency, especially useful in passages requiring high volume, where larger forces can be transmitted with less effort and less risk to injury.

Finally, to further help the mechanics of the 5th finger, its stroke into the key should collaborate with some degree of forearm rotation. Like the thumb stroke, this is easy to do, given that the 5th finger is at the end of the row of fingers. Doing this increases the effective mass of the stroke without needing to increase the work done by the small muscles of the hand.

Combining any or all of the above actions will help to convert a mechanically very inefficient 5th finger keystroke into an extremely efficient one.

MUSCLES, PAIN, AND INJURIES

Muscles consist of a central belly (which contracts) which merges into a tendon at each end that attaches to the bone. Tendons can be easily felt (and seen) on the underside of our wrists and along the top of our hands. Tendons do not contract and do not stretch—they are tight and strong, like ropes. Like ropes, too, if they rub on a (rough) surface for extended periods of time, friction will injure their fibers and this will result in *inflammation*. Inflammation is the physiological process where the body responds to, and tries to repair, cellular and tissue injury. It results in heat, swelling, redness and pain due to the added blood supply and the activation of a cascade of cellular and chemical pathways involved in the repair process.

Pain is part of the inflammatory process and is your body's way of telling your brain that something is wrong and needs to rest to repair the injury.

If a tendon is forced to stretch more than it should, for example if it lifts too-heavy weights, lifts them too often or is forced to stretch around the corners of joints in extreme positions, it is more likely to become injured. The most common pathology for a pianist is *tenosynovitis* (inflammation of the tendon sheath—the surrounding layer of the tendon that allows it to slide across other tissues) and the most common touch that causes it is playing octaves and chords.[85]

As there is no obvious evolutionary need for fingers to move up and down rapidly and forcefully for extended periods of time (as in piano playing), it should be expected that the tendons of pianists will constantly be at an increased risk of injury.

Muscles have the ability to adapt to new demands (as do nerves and bones)—which is why we improve with practice—but adaptive changes to tissues take time and they will not cope if demands are too sudden or beyond their adaptable range. This is a reason why injuries to muscles and tendons are so common in pianists who *suddenly* increase their amounts of practice following periods of inactivity.[86]

Muscles try to grow and adapt to the tasks that are asked of them but pushing beyond their point of fatigue to see if they can survive is not something to strive for. The better solution, and the one that proves that your biomechanics are working properly, is to learn to play such that fatigue never occurs in the first place.

Inflammation that persists for many weeks or months may be called *chronic* inflammation (compared with *acute* that lasts only a few days or weeks) and it results in scarring of the tissues involved. Scarred tissue (like a scar on the skin) does not function as well as the original tissue and, unfortunately, is more prone to repeated injury. The ability of youthful tissue (up until young adulthood) to adapt, repair and withstand extreme physiological demands is impressive and far surpasses that of older persons' tissue.

The adaptability and quick recovery of function of soft tissues in young people is a reason why young pianists can get away with high-risk playing habits, poor mechanics (and their associated micro-injuries) for years without knowing that they are gradually injuring themselves in the background.

Preventing Injury

The solution to avoiding pain and injury is obvious—minimize your risk of causing tissue damage. To do this, you need to minimize the *frequency* and *degree* of the straining and stretching of the muscles, tendons and ligaments, and the transmission of large forces across small joints. This requires improving the mechanical efficiency of your playing: improved *m-v* combinations, touch angles, arch positions, joint positions, and a better coordination of the elements of the p_{in} momentum equation—*the very same elements that contribute to optimized playing*.

The other way to prevent physical injury is to minimize the total amount of physical work performed practicing.[87] This can be done by improving your scheduling of practice sessions (more frequent, less long), the quality of your learning (more concentration, more intention), the content of your learning (more variety, more targeted) or by shifting a greater proportion of your learning to mental practice. These issues are addressed in the next chapter.

Out-of-the-blue injuries that have no obvious cause are rare in piano playing. Usually, injuries can be traced back to poor decisions that have permitted actions that have pushed the body beyond its physiologically adaptable limits. Poor decisions stem from not caring (your choice), not knowing (read the book) or not knowing that you don't know (re-read chapter 1). Poor decisions that negatively affect our health commonly include:[88]

- Playing using extreme anatomical positions or postures.
- Playing excessively fast and loud for sustained periods of time.
- Playing fast and loud without warming up your muscles.
- Giving small muscles of the hand lots of work to do.
- Transmitting large forces *across* small joints.
- Performing any singular action repeatedly, without allowing time for your cells to adapt to it.
- practicing through pain or injury.
- practicing too much, suddenly, after a period of no activity (e.g., a holiday)[89]
- practicing with a negative mental state.

The focus of this book is not playing-related injuries but no pedagogical approach to piano playing is being true to itself if it does not acknowledge the risks of its methods. After all, what prize does an injured pianist win? Unpredictably, some pianists will get injured for having done very little wrong to their bodies while others will not get injured for doing much that is. We each have different thresholds and genetic risks for becoming injured. But as none of us know where our threshold point for injury lies, common sense suggests that we ought to avoid going near to that point of injury in the first place by avoiding high-risk practices and heeding warning signs of injury early.

Repetitive Motion Disorder, Focal Dystonia, and Chronic Pain.

Repetitive Motion Disorders (also called Repetitive Strain Injuries, Performance-Related Musculoskeletal Disorders, and similar names) are common playing-related injuries.[90] Colloquially, they are "overuse" injuries and result from having practiced too hard or too much. They are characterized by "pain, tingling, numbness, visible swelling or redness of the affected area, and the loss of flexibility and strength."[91] These symptoms reflect the inflammation of the injured tissues. Usually, there is an obvious mechanical reason to explain such injuries.

A dystonia is a type of movement disorder affecting coordination. Focal dystonias affect pianists by causing involuntary loss of muscle control (typically, unwanted muscle spasms involving cramping, twisting, curling, straightening of the small muscles of the hand and forearm) while performing specific tasks at the instrument.[92] There is no single cause of the problem although several risk factors have been identified, including: the repeated execution of motor tasks that are complex or require extreme precision, especially those that involve small muscles, excessive workloads, and those that have "a consequence" attached to their success or failure (like missed puts in golf, or missed notes in piano recitals)—all factors that a pianist can make adjustments to minimize.

Chronic Pain is pain that persists beyond the normal healing time of an injury. Sometimes, the event that caused the initial tissue damage will be obvious, but other times, it will not. In either case, the nerve signals that transmit the pain remain active, causing the pain to persist for months or years. Typically, the experience of chronic pain feels *different* (i.e., burning, tingling, aching, stabbing, dull or fatiguing in nature), and is *disproportionate* to the amount of stimulus that is causing it. Also, it is often accompanied with a psychological overlay of negative emotions. Thus, "unpacking" the contributing factors of the pain is the first step to understanding how to treat it. These will be physical, physiological, and psychological—all that can be improved with targeted physical and cognitive training.

NOTES

1. Eigeldinger, Jean-Jacques. *Chopin: Pianist and Teacher as Seen by His Pupils.* Cambridge, Cambridgeshire; New York: Cambridge University Press, 1986, 23.

2. For example, Seymour Fink's suggested movements in *Mastering Piano Technique* could hardly be more useless: "The pushing arm staccato, which always starts from the surface of the keys with straightened fingers, uses large, forward, spirited, upper-arm and shoulder-girdle cycles to produce sharp (long with pedal), accurate, moderately paced sounds."

Fink, Seymour. *Mastering Piano Technique: A Guide for Students, Teachers, and Performers.* Portland: Amadeus, 1999, 86.

3. Igrec, Mario. *Pianos inside out: A Comprehensive Guide to Piano Tuning, Repairing, and Rebuilding.* Mandeville, La.: In Tune Press, 2013.

4. Igrec, Mario. *Pianos inside out: A Comprehensive Guide to Piano Tuning, Repairing, and Rebuilding.* Mandeville, La.: In Tune Press, 2013.

5. Igrec, Mario. *Pianos inside out: A Comprehensive Guide to Piano Tuning, Repairing, and Rebuilding.* Mandeville, La.: In Tune Press, 2013.

6. Askenfelt, Anders, ed. *Five Lectures on the Acoustics of the Piano.* Stockholm: Royal Swedish Academy of Music, 1990.

7. $0.0625 \div 1.875 = 0.0333 \approx 3.3\%$.

8. Steinway technician, Franz Mohr commenting on Gould's and Horowitz's pianos. See: Mohr, Franz, and Edith Schaeffer. *My Life with the Great Pianists.* Ravens Ridge Books, 1992. Also, it has been observed that shorter travel times of the hammer are often preferred by pianists. See: Goebl, Werner, Roberto Bresin, and Alexander Galembo. "Once Again: The Perception of Piano Touch and Tone. Can Touch Audibly Change Piano Sound Independently of Intensity?" *Proceedings of the*

International Symposium on Musical Acoustics, Nara, Japan, March 31 to April 3, 2004, 332–35.

9. Occasionally, this is noticeable when performing on, or listening to performers playing on instruments with very small let-off distances.

10. Busby, Jim. *Grand Piano Regulation.* Piano Technician Tutorials. Apple Books, 2016. https://books.apple.com/us/book/grand-piano-regulation/id1135106813.

11. It is typically set between 45–50 mm. Igrec, Mario. *Pianos inside out: A Comprehensive Guide to Piano Tuning, Repairing, and Rebuilding.* Mandeville, La.: In Tune Press, 2013.

12. Goebl, Werner, Roberto Bresin, and Alexander Galembo. "Once Again: The Perception of Piano Touch and Tone. Can Touch Audibly Change Piano Sound Independently of Intensity?" *Proceedings of the International Symposium on Musical Acoustics, Nara, Japan, March 31 to April 3,* 2004, 332–35.

13. Mamizuka, Naotaka, Masataka Sakane, Koji Kaneoka, Noriyuki Hori, and Naoyuki Ochiai. "Kinematic quantitation of the patellar tendon reflex using a tri-axial accelerometer." *Journal of Biomechanics* 40, no. 9 (2007): 2107–2111.

14. Roberts, Jonathan R., Roy Jones, and S. J. Rothberg. "Measurement of contact time in short duration sports ball impacts: an experimental method and correlation with the perceptions of elite golfers." *Sports Engineering* 4, no. 4 (2001): 191–203.

15. Schiffman, Harvey Richard. *Sensation and Perception.* 6th ed. Hoboken, NJ: John Wiley & Sons, 2012.

16. BIO10NUMB3R5. "Reaction Times to Sound, Light and Touch – Human Homo Sapiens – BNID 110800," 2012. https://bionumbers.hms.harvard.edu/bionumber.aspx?s=n&v=4&id=110800.

17. Actually, there is evidence showing that when there is going to be an error of precision in a motor task, it is already "known" to the brain (and can be detected) *before* the physical movement has even commenced *and* that the brain can make adjustments to it. This doubly reinforces the importance of having a clear picture about what we are aiming for musically and mechanically. It strongly supports the role of mental practice. See: Ruiz, María Herrojo, Hans-Christian Jabusch, and Eckart Altenmüller. "Detecting wrong notes in advance: neuronal correlates of error monitoring in pianists." *Cerebral cortex* 19, no. 11 (2009): 2625–2639; Gabitov, Ella, Ovidiu Lungu, Geneviève Albouy, and Julien Doyon. "Movement Errors during Skilled Motor Performance Engage Distinct Prediction Error Mechanisms." *Communications Biology* 3, no. 1 (December 2020). doi:https://doi.org/10.1038/s42003-020-01465-4.

18. Talsma, Durk, Daniel Senkowski, Salvador Soto-Faraco, and Marty G. Woldorff. "The Multifaceted Interplay between Attention and Multisensory Integration." *Trends in Cognitive Sciences* 14, no. 9 (September 2010): 400–410. doi:https://doi.org/10.1016/j.tics.2010.06.008.

19. Talsma, Durk, Daniel Senkowski, Salvador Soto-Faraco, and Marty G. Woldorff. "The Multifaceted Interplay between Attention and Multisensory Integration." *Trends in Cognitive Sciences* 14, no. 9 (September 2010): 400–410. doi:https://doi.org/10.1016/j.tics.2010.06.008.

20. Note that the maximum achievable hammer velocity using a pressed touch is approximately 4 m/s, compared to 6–10 m/s using a percussive touch. See: Goebl,

Werner, Roberto Bresin, and Alexander Galembo. "Once Again: The Perception of Piano Touch and Tone. Can Touch Audibly Change Piano Sound Independently of Intensity?" *Proceedings of the International Symposium on Musical Acoustics, Nara, Japan, March 31 to April 3*, 2004, 332–35; Askenfelt, Anders, and Erik V. Jansson. "From Touch to String Vibrations. II: The Motion of the Key and Hammer." *Journal of the Acoustical Society of America* 90, no. 5 (November 1, 1991): 2383–93. doi:https://doi.org/10.1121/1.402043.

21. Record and watch yourself playing in slow motion if you have any doubts.

22. Goebl, Werner, Roberto Bresin, and Alexander Galembo. "Once Again: The Perception of Piano Touch and Tone. Can Touch Audibly Change Piano Sound Independently of Intensity?" *Proceedings of the International Symposium on Musical Acoustics, Nara, Japan, March 31 to April 3*, 2004, 332–35.

23. At extreme *pp* volumes, there may, theoretically, be time for a pianist to change the speed of the keystroke after escapement, but given that such slow key velocities are used in a *pp* touch, this is unlikely to result in any significant change to the noise of the key-keybed impact, as it is already negligible.

24. Milanovic, Therese. "The Taubman Approach to Piano Technique." *The Piano Teacher*, May 6, 2014. http://thepianoteacher.com.au/articles/the-taubman-approach-to-piano-technique/.

25. By definition, *weight* is a force (measured in Newtons, N). On Earth, the force of gravity on an object is approximately 10 N/kg. Thus, a 2 kg arm will always have a mass of 2 kg, but its weight *on Earth* will be 20 N.

26. Plagenhoef, Stanley, F. Gaynor Evans, and Thomas Abdelnour. "Anatomical Data for Analyzing Human Motion." *Research Quarterly for Exercise and Sport* 54, no. 2 (June 1983): 169–78. doi:https://doi.org/10.1080/02701367.1983.10605290; Leva, Paulo de. "Adjustments to Zatsiorsky-Seluyanov's Segment Inertia Parameters." *Journal of Biomechanics* 29, no. 9 (1996): 1223–30. doi:https://doi.org/10.1016/0021-9290(95)00178-6.

27. Dounskaia, Natalia. "Control of Human Limb Movements: The Leading Joint Hypothesis and Its Practical Applications." *Exercise and Sport Sciences Reviews* 38, no. 4 (October 2010): 201–8. doi:https://doi.org/10.1097/jes.0b013e3181f45194.

28. Barris, Coralie Sian. "An examination of learning design in elite springboard diving." PhD diss., Queensland University of Technology, 2013, 18.

29. Barris, Coralie Sian. "An examination of learning design in elite springboard diving." PhD diss., Queensland University of Technology, 2013, 18.

30. Dounskaia, Natalia. "Control of Human Limb Movements: The Leading Joint Hypothesis and Its Practical Applications." *Exercise and Sport Sciences Reviews* 38, no. 4 (October 2010): 201–8. doi:https://doi.org/10.1097/jes.0b013e3181f45194. Recall, also, it only requires around 50 g to move the key down.

31. These numbers are approximations given for the sake of explaining the concept. Accept that they simplify a more complex and dynamic synergy of interaction between the joints of the limb.

32. This explains why the pianist Gyorgy Sandor felt that "the quality of the sound [...] depends on the degree to which the joints have been fixed"—the degree of bridging alters the effective mass of the keystroke. Sándor, György. *On Piano Playing*. Schirmer Books, 1981, 42.

33. Complex coordinated movements of the body are currently explained, scientifically, by the Leading Joint Hypothesis, where it is shown that most movement tasks have one dynamic foundation for the motion of the entire limb (the "leading" joint) and other subordinate joints (the "trailing" joints), of which the latter may take on more importance near the end of the movement to fine tune the movement to accomplish the task, at which point the initial leading joint may have finished its contribution to the task. See: Dounskaia, Natalia. "Control of Human Limb Movements: The Leading Joint Hypothesis and Its Practical Applications." *Exercise and Sport Sciences Reviews* 38, no. 4 (October 2010): 201–8. doi:https://doi.org/10.1097/jes.0b013e3181f45194.

34. Carr, Elizabeth. *Shura Cherkassky*. Lanham, MD: Scarecrow Press, 2006, 42.

35. When listening to Rachmaninoff's playing, for example, in his transcription of *A Midsummer Night's Dream* (Mendelssohn), Liszt's *Gnomenreigen* or the exposition of his *3rd Concerto*, it can be observed that his fast semi-quaver passagework is generally played *leggiero*, and that the illusion of energy and volume is achieved using agogics like incisive accents, rhythmic energy and rapid swells of volume (with the help of rubato, stretto and the sustain pedal).

36. Multiple citations in: Eigeldinger, Jean-Jacques. *Chopin: Pianist and Teacher as Seen by His Pupils*. Cambridge, Cambridgeshire; New York: Cambridge University Press, 1986.

37. Milanovic, Therese. "The Taubman Approach to Piano Technique." *The Piano Teacher*, May 6, 2014. http://thepianoteacher.com.au/articles/the-taubman-approach-to-piano-technique/., p.121.

38. Blido, Stefan. "Stefan Blido: Zen in the Art of Playing the Piano." *Peter-Feuchtwanger.de*. Accessed September 27, 2024. http://www.peter-feuchtwanger.de/english-version/texts/stefan-blido-zen-in-the-art-of-playing-the-piano/index.html.

39. Like in baseball, slalom skiing and F-1 sportscar racing, "anticipating" and "rounding" corners by taking a slightly wider arc results in faster times than changing directions abruptly in straight lines. It results in less wear-and-tear of the machine too. Piano playing is the same.

40. Paradoxically, the risk of missing notes when using an arc trajectory is not nearly as much as one fears (if it exists at all), as the trajectory of the arc movement is *more* predictable than the more volatile stop-start zig-zag movement. When playing very fast leaping passages, this risk must be accepted as there is not enough time to get to each note and "check" before playing it.

41. Lipatti: "it has been at least ten years since I last crossed my thumb under the third finger." See: Rosen, Charles. *Piano Notes: The World of the Pianist*. New York: Free Press, 2002, 1.

42. Quite possibly, the upper arm of Chopin moved very little, as evidenced by his advice to keep the elbows by the side of the body, unless following the movement of the hands. Eigeldinger, Jean-Jacques. *Chopin: Pianist and Teacher as Seen by His Pupils*. Cambridge, Cambridgeshire; New York: Cambridge University Press, 1986, 30.

43. Eigeldinger, Jean-Jacques. *Chopin: Pianist and Teacher as Seen by His Pupils*. Cambridge, Cambridgeshire; New York: Cambridge University Press, 1986, 29–30.

44. As previously mentioned, if a pressed touch is used, the maximum hammer speed achievable, approximately 4 m/s, is much less than that of a percussive touch, approximately 6–10 m/s, depending on the set-up of the instrument. This ruins claims that one can produce large volumes of sound without any percussive element. See: Goebl, Werner, Roberto Bresin, and Alexander Galembo. "Once Again: The Perception of Piano Touch and Tone. Can Touch Audibly Change Piano Sound Independently of Intensity?" *Proceedings of the International Symposium on Musical Acoustics, Nara, Japan, March 31 to April 3.*, 2004, 332–35; Askenfelt, Anders, and Erik V Jansson. "From Touch to String Vibrations. II: The Motion of the Key and Hammer." *Journal of the Acoustical Society of America* 90, no. 5 (November 1, 1991): 2383–93. doi:https://doi.org/10.1121/1.402043.

45. Goebl, Werner, Roberto Bresin, and Alexander Galembo. "Once Again: The Perception of Piano Touch and Tone. Can Touch Audibly Change Piano Sound Independently of Intensity?" *Proceedings of the International Symposium on Musical Acoustics, Nara, Japan, March 31 to April 3*, 2004, 332–35.

46. In fact, the only occasion where *all* the momentum of a keystroke is given to a key, is when the pianist's finger finalizes its descent into the key *before* escapement – a rare scenario indeed, though one that does exist during an extreme *staccato* touch when the touch angle nears 90^0.

47. These figures are probably slightly generous as they assume that the finger continues to travel at the same speed and in the same direction throughout its key dip.

48. Note here the absurdity of pedagogical arguments that claim that sitting postures are important in the "generation" of tone quality. Given the infinite number of ways of delivering any touch-angle (using different finger, knuckle and wrist joint angles), one could sit perfectly—by any definition—and then proceed to waste that (perceived) good work by playing with inefficient touch angles and loose bridging. And vice versa, one could sit with a terrible posture—by any definition—but touch the keys with a well-aligned, coordinated keystroke involving finger, hand and forearm.

49. Note, although all the momentum of the hammer comes from the touch, not all of the momentum of the touch goes into the hammer. Significant amounts of the touch momentum are transferred into other parts of the action, including the keybed, the key stop rail, and the damper leaver system (the mechanism that raises the dampers).

50. The effective mass of the damper mechanism is taken into account in the mass of the key.

51. Kimm, Dennis, and David V. Thiel. "Hand Speed Measurements in Boxing." *Procedia Engineering* 112 (2015): 502–6. doi:https://doi.org/10.1016/j.proeng.2015.07.232.

52. Goebl, Werner, Roberto Bresin, and Alexander Galembo. "Once Again: The Perception of Piano Touch and Tone. Can Touch Audibly Change Piano Sound Independently of Intensity?" *Proceedings of the International Symposium on Musical Acoustics, Nara, Japan, March 31 to April 3*, 2004, 332–35; Russell, Daniel Allen, and T. Rossing. "Testing the Nonlinearity of Piano Hammers Using Residual Shock Spectra." *Acustica* 84, no. 5 (September 1, 1998): 967–75; Askenfelt, Anders, and Erik V. Jansson. "From Touch to String Vibrations. II: The Motion of the Key

and Hammer." *Journal of the Acoustical Society of America* 90, no. 5 (November 1, 1991): 2383–93. doi:https://doi.org/10.1121/1.402043.

53. Using the same inelastic collision equation as before: $m_{touch} \cdot v_{touch} = (m_{touch} + m_{key}) \cdot v_{touch+key}$

54. If there is a holy grail of the mechanics of touch, then this is it: it indicates, free of charge, where "playability" is, generally, best—where the mechanics of effectiveness and efficiency overlap—and where the efforts of one's touch are best rewarded. If pianists remained aware of making the right sound with the easiest movements, they would probably also find themselves closely aligned to this zone most of the time.

55. Eigeldinger, Jean-Jacques. *Chopin: Pianist and Teacher as Seen by His Pupils.* Cambridge, Cambridgeshire; New York: Cambridge University Press, 1986, 30.

56. Personally, I believe that thinking about the mechanics of touch in terms of forces is unhelpful. Should one need to think about mechanical issues, it is more practical to think about the components of momentum (mass, velocity and direction) which are more readily visible and tangible.

57. This is called *impulse*. (*Impulse* = F . *t*)

58. https://www1.grc.nasa.gov/beginners-guide-to-aeronautics/newtons-laws-of-motion/

59. Norkin, Cynthia C, and Pamela K. Levangie. *Joint Structure & Function a Comprehensive Analysis.* Philadelphia: F.A. Davis, 1992.

60. Indeed, the theoretical benefits of maintaining the arch during piano playing have been confirmed in several experiments, showing that a curved finger position with a large flexion angle at the knuckle joint reduces tension in the flexor tendons, minimizes the force in the small joints of the finger, and improved force transfer. Again, no surprise, given the human's evolution from quadruped life, where the natural arches of our hands (previously our front feet) had to support our body weight. See: Harding, David C., K.D. Brandt, and B.M. Hillberry. "Finger Joint Force Minimization in Pianists Using Optimization Techniques." *Journal of Biomechanics* 26, no. 12 (December 1993): 1403–12. doi:https://doi.org/10.1016/0021-9290(93)90091-r; Wolf, F. Gregory, Martha S. Keane, Kenneth D. Brandt, and Ben M. Hiliberry. "An investigation of finger joint and tendon forces in experienced pianists." *Medical Problems of Performing Artists* 8, no. 3 (1993): 84–95.

61. Feuchtwanger apparently encouraged this. See:Blido, Stefan. "Texts." *Peter-Feuchtwanger.de*, 2024. http://www.peter-feuchtwanger.de/english-version/texts/.

62. I believe Chopin had a natural tendency toward this slightly-higher wrist position. Curiously, there are also several sketches by artists of him sitting at the piano using such a position.

63. Although imperceptible to the eye, if one watches slow motion videos of these pianists playing, one can see that some (small) amount of their hand or forearm invariably falls into the keys at the same moment as their fingers play into the keys.

64. Although wide stretches are a common reason for a stiff wrist, a more common reason is an inefficient finger-stroke, i.e., one that does not provide enough momentum to the key itself or one that does not coordinate itself with the hand or forearm.

In these cases, the stiff wrist serves to mass-bridge the finger to the larger masses of the forearm.

65. Eigeldinger, Jean-Jacques. *Chopin: Pianist and Teacher as Seen by His Pupils.* Cambridge, Cambridgeshire; New York: Cambridge University Press, 1986, 39.

66. Altenmüller, Eckart, Jürg Kesselring, and Mario Wiesendanger. *Music, Motor Control and the Brain.* Oxford University Press, 2006, 82.

67. Wang, Keming, Evan P. McGlinn, and Kevin C. Chung. "A Biomechanical and Evolutionary Perspective on the Function of the Lumbrical Muscle." *Journal of Hand Surgery* 39, no. 1 (January 1, 2014): 149–55. doi:https://doi.org/10.1016/j.jhsa.2013.06.029.

68. Goebl, Werner, and Caroline Palmer. "Temporal Control and Hand Movement Efficiency in Skilled Music Performance." Edited by Ramesh Balasubramaniam. *PLoS ONE* 8, no. 1 (January 3, 2013): e50901. doi:https://doi.org/10.1371/journal.pone.0050901.

69. Actually, this feature of lumbrical muscles makes them ideally suited to clavichord playing, where extreme key control and finger independence (at soft volumes) is needed by the player.

70. Goebl, Werner, and Caroline Palmer. "Temporal Control and Hand Movement Efficiency in Skilled Music Performance." Edited by Ramesh Balasubramaniam. *PLoS ONE* 8, no. 1 (January 3, 2013): e50901. doi:https://doi.org/10.1371/journal.pone.0050901.

71. Levangie, Pamela K, and Cynthia C Norkin. *Joint Structure and Function: A Comprehensive Analysis.* Philadelpha: F.A. Davis, 2001.

72. Altenmüller, Eckart, Jürg Kesselring, and Mario Wiesendanger. *Music, Motor Control and the Brain.* Oxford: Oxford University Press, 2006, 80.

73. Li, Zong-Ming, Shouchen Dun, Daniel A. Harkness, and Teresa L. Brininger. "Motion Enslaving among Multiple Fingers of the Human Hand." *Motor Control* 8, no. 1 (January 2004): 1–15. doi:https://doi.org/10.1123/mcj.8.1.1; Abolins, Valters, Alex Stremoukhov, Caroline Walter, and Mark L Latash. "On the Origin of Finger Enslaving: Control with Referent Coordinates and Effects of Visual Feedback." *Journal of Neurophysiology* 124, no. 6 (December 1, 2020): 1625–36. doi:https://doi.org/10.1152/jn.00322.2020.

74. The force-length relationship of muscle contraction is optimized when the muscle is neither under nor over-stretched.

75. Muscle fatigue results in a decline in maximal force and power. It is associated with "diminished motor drive from the CNS and/or changes of metabolites, electrolytes or ultrastructural damage within muscle." See: Cairns, Simeon P. "Lactic Acid and Exercise Performance." *Sports Medicine* 36, no. 4 (2006): 279–91. doi:https://doi.org/10.2165/00007256-200636040-00001, 280.

76. For an overview of muscle function and fatigue, see: Williams, Craig A., and Sebastien Ratel. *Human Muscle Fatigue.* London; New York: Routledge, 2009.

77. Eigeldinger, Jean-Jacques. *Chopin: Pianist and Teacher as Seen by His Pupils.* Cambridge, Cambridgeshire; New York: Cambridge University Press, 1986, 28.

78. Eigeldinger, Jean-Jacques. *Chopin: Pianist and Teacher as Seen by His Pupils.* Cambridge, Cambridgeshire; New York: Cambridge University Press, 1986, 16.

79. This vast range of positions available to us to carry out any motor task are called "degrees of freedom." See: Bernstein, Nikolai. *Coordinate and Regulation of Movements.* Pergamon Press, 1967.

80. thepolonaise. "Vladimir Horowitz – Variation on a Theme of Bizet's – Carmen." *YouTube*, November 29, 2006. https://www.youtube.com/watch?v=WV_Nh884PKg.

81. Eigeldinger, Jean-Jacques. *Chopin: Pianist and Teacher as Seen by His Pupils.* Cambridge, Cambridgeshire; New York: Cambridge University Press, 1986, 32.

82. Milanovic, Therese. "Learning and Teaching Healthy Piano Technique: Training as an Instructor in the Taubman Approach," 2011, 206.

83. Williamon, Aaron. *Musical Excellence: Strategies and Techniques to Enhance Performance.* Oxford: Oxford University Press, 2004, 51.

84. Menkes, C-J., and N.E. Lane. "Are Osteophytes Good or Bad?" *Osteoarthritis and Cartilage* 12 (2004): 53–54. doi:https://doi.org/10.1016/j.joca.2003.09.003.

85. Williamon, Aaron. *Musical Excellence: Strategies and Techniques to Enhance Performance.* Oxford: Oxford University Press, 2004, 43 and 51.

86. Ackermann, Bronwen J. "How Much Training Is Too Much?" *Medical Problems of Performing Artists* 32, no. 1 (March 1, 2017): 61–62. doi:https://doi.org/10.21091/mppa.2017.1011. See also: Cruder, Cinzia, Marco Barbero, Pelagia Koufaki, Emiliano Soldini, and Nigel Gleeson. "Prevalence and Associated Factors of Playing-Related Musculoskeletal Disorders among Music Students in Europe. Baseline Findings from the Risk of Music Students (RISMUS) Longitudinal Multicentre Study." Edited by Feng Pan. *PLOS ONE* 15, no. 12 (December 9, 2020): e0242660. doi:https://doi.org/10.1371/journal.pone.0242660.

87. "The work:rest ratio and the acute:chronic workload ratio are considered critical [to injury causation]." Ackermann, Bronwen J. "How Much Training Is Too Much?" *Medical Problems of Performing Artists* 32, no. 1 (March 1, 2017): 61–62. doi:https://doi.org/10.21091/mppa.2017.1011.

88. Kenny, Dianna T., and Bronwen Ackermann. "Optimizing physical and psychological health in performing musicians." *The Oxford Handbook of Music Psychology* 1 (2009): 390–400.

89. This is the most common cause of performance-related injuries. Ioannou, Christos I, Julia Hafer, André Lee, and Eckart Altenmuller. "Epidemiology, Treatment Efficacy, and Anxiety Aspects of Music Students Affected by Playing-Related Pain: A Retrospective Evaluation with Follow-Up." *Medical Problems of Performing Artists* 33, no. 1 (March 1, 2018): 26–38. doi:https://doi.org/10.21091/mppa.2018.1006.

90. Bragge, Peter, Andrea Bialocerkowski, and Joan McMeeken. "A Systematic Review of Prevalence and Risk Factors Associated with Playing-Related Musculoskeletal Disorders in Pianists." *Occupational Medicine* 56, no. 1 (November 7, 2005): 28–38. doi:https://doi.org/10.1093/occmed/kqi177.

91. National Institute of Neurological Disorders and Stroke. "Repetitive Motion Disorders Information Page | National Institute of Neurological Disorders and Stroke." *Nih.gov*, July 19, 2024. https://www.ninds.nih.gov/Disorders/All-Disorders/Repetitive-Motion-Disorders-Information-Page.

92. Prof. Dr. Eckart Altenmüller, neurologist and specialist in musician's dystonias, proposes that dystonia is a neurological disorder involving maladaptive plasticity, and that "when there is excessive, near simultaneous repetitive movements, the topographical representation of the hand is degraded and the digits overlap with adjacent digits." See: Altenmüller, Eckart, Jürg Kesselring, and Mario Wiesendanger. *Music, Motor Control and the Brain*. Oxford: Oxford University Press, 2006, 295; Also: Altenmüller, Eckart. "Focal Dystonia: Advances in Brain Imaging and Understanding of Fine Motor Control in Musicians." *Hand Clinics* 19, no. 3 (August 2003): 523–38. doi:https://doi.org/10.1016/s0749-0712(03)00043-x.; Altenmüller, Eckart, and Shinichi Furuya. "Apollos Gift and Curse: Making Music as a Model for Adaptive and Maladaptive Plasticity." *E-Neuroforum* 23, no. 2 (January 24, 2017). doi:https://doi.org/10.1515/nf-2016-a054.

Chapter 7

Mental Skills

"The main thing that sets experts apart from the rest of us is that their years of practice have changed the neural circuitry in their brains to produce highly specialized mental representations"[1]—Ericsson

In chapters 3 and 4, it was explained how body movements consist of a physical (mechanical) component and a mental (motor organizational) component.[2] These are, of course, artificial segregations of a highly-integrated biological system, but nevertheless, it serves to point out that although we see the physical aspect of our touch (i.e., the fingers moving), there is a more complex web of interactions working behind the scenes in the brain that affect our motor performance—interactions involving musical imagery, movement planning, memory, dynamic motor-sensory information, and the integration of our movements with language systems, gestures and emotions.

How our pianism is *wired*, matters, and the way in which we wire our pianism will affect its outcomes tremendously. As the 3M Triangle indicates, no amount of *Mechanical* excellence nor *Musical* inspiration can make our pianism succeed unless we also have high functioning *Mental* pathways to connect our ideas to our fingers. In many respects, the development of the mental skills of piano playing is the forgotten topic of piano pedagogy, hidden from our view and presumed to either function well (or not) by some miracle of nature (or not).

But Mental skills can be systematically taught and improved just like any other pianistic skill and when they are well developed, one of the major limiting factors of playing virtuosically will be overcome: the speed at which our brains can learn, store, recall, and respond to changes in musical information inputs in real time.

MENTAL PRACTICE

Glenn Gould summarizes some of the features of mental practice nicely:

> *Ultimately, you play the piano not with your fingers but with your head. I know that sounds terribly simple and obvious cliché, but it's the truth. When you've a perfectly clear idea of what you want to do, there's not the slightest reason to reinforce that idea by practicing. If you don't have it, not all the Czerny studies and all the Hanon finger exercises in the world will be able to help you [...] In addition—needless to say—there were the dozens of occasions when I went through the [Brahms] Ballades in my head, during lengthy car journeys or in my apartment, where I in any case do most of my "work."*[3]

Mental practice (practicing in your mind) provides a pathway to improving pianism without needing to physically play the instrument or subject our bodies to its mechanical stresses. It is routinely used by professional sportspeople and it should be used routinely by professional musicians too. It works: facilitating learning when used alone, and significantly improving learning outcomes when combined with physical practice.[4] Walter Gieseking considered it a necessary step to achieving mastery: "[mental practice] is the only way in which really good and astonishing results can be obtained."[5]

Such findings should not come as a surprise, knowing that our music-making physical movements represent just the visible tip of the iceberg of a complex, multi-modal network of nerve connections operating in our brain, hidden from our view. Practicing in our head allows us to tap into the same neural networks that practicing with our fingers does:[6]

- Pre-motor areas of the brain are activated in the same way whether during musical imagery or execution.[7]
- "both motor and auditory cortical areas are active during musical thought processes."[8]
- "expressing and empathizing feelings in [musical] real time [...] is connected to an intense mental imagery process."[9]
- "Multimodal forward models of upcoming sounds and actions support motor preparation, facilitate error detection and correction, and guide perception."[10]

Visualization

Broadly, mental practice is any type of piano practice that occurs in the mind. This can involve learning the details, structure and patterns in the score (of which Walter Gieseking describes in his book[11]) or involve visual, auditory or movement imagery, like those described by the pianist Misha Dichter: "I consciously recreate in the room, as close as I can, the mental impulses that will be going on [...] during the concert."[12]

It does not matter what we choose to visualize—any of the 3 Ms of pianism can be improved. What does matter, is that the mental blueprint of what we want to have happen, is targeted with intense clarity. Movements can be rehearsed, errors detected and, remarkably, improvement of muscle strength can all occur with action imagery.[13] Stories of musicians practicing and learning large amounts of repertoire while away from the piano are not uncommon, and nor should they be considered in any way special. If anything, the opportunity to practice without a piano should be normalized.

Professionals from other disciplines use mental practice and visualization techniques to practice skills, rehearse sequences and test out different scenarios in their head prior to using them in the real world. Here is a typical example of the use of imagery in mental rehearsal by the famous swimmer Michael Phelps (as described by his coach, Bob Bowman):

"For months before a race Michael gets into a relaxed state. He mentally rehearses for two hours a day [!] He sees himself winning. He smells the air, tastes the water, hears the sounds [...] He sees himself overcoming obstacles, too. [...] Phelps practices all potential scenarios [...]"—"the most strongly held mental picture is where you'll be [...] your brain will immediately find ways to get you there"[14]

Creating an *ideal scenario* in our minds is one way of benefitting from the process, and the more vivid the details of our participation in the scenario, the better the outcomes. Musical psychologist Williamon suggests using all the senses to heighten our awareness of ourselves in the task.[15] Helding encourages to "take yourself to the edge of your imagination."[16] Dinu Lipatti's advice to a student deserves full quotation:

"I think above all of playing "mentally," as the work would be played by the most perfect of interpreters. Having lodged in one's mind an impression of perfect beauty given by this imaginary interpretation — an impression constantly renewed and revivified by repetition of the performance in the silence of the night — we can go on to actual technical work..."[17]

All aspects of music can be practiced mentally—and, arguably, should be practiced mentally—not just to improve the mental blueprint of our musical intentions but to expose how ill-prepared, mundane and fragile our blueprints actually are in the absence of the physical motor-sensory feedback received from playing. Hanon enthusiasts, be warned: "virtuoso performance in fact pertains to the cognitive domain—the domain of imagery and attention—rather than the mechanical."[18]

ANTICIPATORY IMAGES

Along with using general mental imagery skills, one of the specific mental skills that expert performers develop is that of *anticipatory imagery*. This is the the brain's ability to see (program) motor actions ahead of time, and, in doing so, improve the accuracy of their execution.[19] They are the internal images that secure the chain of motor events that we use when playing the piano. Anticipatory imagery is recognized as a key feature of virtuosity.[20] It "facilitates the planning and execution of musical actions."[21] It is "one of the hallmarks of memory for performance."[22] And it is shown to improve motor control, accuracy and speed.[23]

Further, because "learning sound sequences recruits similar brain structures as motor sequence learning"[24] our ability to recall musical sequences during playing can be triggered by either our anticipated sound images and/or our motor images. This is why some musicians feel that giving attention to motor sequence patterns drives their motor memory while others feel that listening *for* the sound sequences does. Most pianists likely possess both skills, though to differing extents.

Practice routines which deliberately nurture both sound and motor imagery are likely to be highly profitable in improving the reliability of our motor action recall and accuracy. A simple activity to check that you have defined both sound and motor anticipatory images for the music that you intend to perform is: (i.) can you sing the entire piece through without playing it on the instrument? (ii.) can you play the entire piece through without any sonic feedback, e.g., on a silent keyboard, a table, or in your head?

In piano playing, the problem is not that we don't use anticipatory imagery—our motor systems can't operate without it—but that we don't exploit its potential during our learning as much as we could. Mentally, we tend to leave a lot of the musical and movement details unattended to—hoping for excellence to occur, rather than ensuring that it does. This is not to deny the opportunity for spontaneity and freedom during performance—but, on the contrary, to give it more chance of happening. We tend to feel more comfortable taking musical risks playing repertoire, which is well known to us, or in the case of jazz musicians, to improvise with greater freedom, when the underlying musical sequences of the piece are well ingrained.

By investing time in defining our musical and mechanical targets better, the detail of our anticipatory images improves. Practically, we forge stronger links between our abstract ideas and the motor pathways that carry them out.[25] We cultivate the conditions that allow virtuosity to occur. How do we improve our mind's anticipatory images? For sure, by practicing, but a special type of practice is what is needed. Consider the following hypothetical scenario of a pianist practicing a certain phrase of music. Each scenario shows the pianist improving a specific detail of the music step by step. Says this pianist:

1. "As written, I plan to play the first 3 notes *ff* and *staccato*."
2. "Based on my interpretation, I plan to play the first 3 notes increasing from *f* to *ff*, and giving them a *mezzo staccato*."
3. "Based on my interpretation, I plan to play the first 3 notes increasing from *f* to *ff*, taking a little time before the third note, and giving them a *mezzo staccato* with increasing amounts of pedal."
4. "Based on my interpretation, I plan to play the first 3 notes increasing from *f* to *ff*, taking a little time before the third note but not us much time as the previous time it appeared in the piece, and giving them a *mezzo staccato* with increasing amounts of pedal with an exaggeration of length and volume given to the L.H. upper voice."
5. "Based on my interpretation, I plan to play the first 3 notes increasing from *f* to *ff*, taking a little time before the third note but not us much time as the previous time it appeared in the piece though mindful that all the dynamics and pedaling may need to be different when performing in a different acoustic, and giving them a *mezzo staccato* with increasing amounts of pedal with a preference of length and volume given to the L.H. upper voice though accepting that the balance to the R.H. will create a more *espressivo* effect if that's the way I choose to feel it during the performance."

Such details do not need to occupy your mind when performing on stage, and nor should they. They pertain to your interpretative experiments done in the practice room where increased refinement of the task brings increased definition to your anticipatory images, and, because of it, is built into your motor pathways.[26] Knowing your target helps you hit it, as Gould insinuated, as did the legendary golfer Jack Nicklaus also, who describes his process: "I think about the kind of drive I want to hit [including defining where the ball should land] and try to get my mind to make my body hit that kind of shot."[27]

The method is not complicated, nor novel, and involves the same cognitive processes used by gymnasts,[28] Formula 1 race car drivers ("racing drivers visually 'anticipate' upcoming bends"[29]) and other sports professionals[30] who repeatedly rehearse target-hitting using different cognitive domains to strengthen their mind's anticipatory images. In truth, from a motor skills point of view, the cognitive processes of Formula 1 drivers and virtuoso pianists is astonishingly similar, as both performers continuously visualize and hit different internal and external targets in rapid succession. For example, drivers need to continuously and rapidly "feel" the road (the music) while "feeling" the feedback from the car (the piano) combining previously learned and real-time multimodal skills to navigate a track full of different types of curves (the musical phrases). And they must do so at "high speeds" which requires a rapid sequencing of chunked blocks of information where each chunk is activated by a specifically sought-after auditory-visual stimulus along the track (e.g., a particular harmony, or accent, or rhythm, etc.). As Lappi writes:

> "The determinants of performance that limit a driver's speed are mostly information processing limits of the brain, not physical limits of the body."— "chunking of the scene in terms of familiar (sub)patterns of reference points overlaid on a scene layout [...] is the core of perceptual cognitive expertise of the racing driver."[31]

The following textbox shows that when it comes to improving anticipatory imagery using multimodal inputs, pianists are no different—only that our sequences are, presumably, more numerous when playing a recital of music, and include an emotional, expressive element to the actions.

Anticipatory Imagery and Virtuosity:
"Look, Listen and Feel Before You Leap"

As pianists, we can improve our brain's anticipatory images by participating in any of the following steps:

- "Hear it, play it"—i.e., hear exactly the sounds in your head before you play them. This has long been a guiding principle of how to practice effectively. The neuroscientific support for it is overwhelming, so much so that it has been proposed that "the only limit of movement accuracy and speed is the temporal and spatial resolution of the auditory [!] system."
- "See it, play it"—i.e., look exactly at where you want to leap to before you leap. Anticipating visual goals improves speed and accuracy of motor actions. "When your eyes provide the data, your motor system just knows what to do [...] Your brain is like a GPS system. It detects target, speed, intensity, and distance [...] locking onto the relevant stimulus during the relevant time frame greatly improves your chances of success."
- "Feel it, play it"—i.e., feel exactly the emotions (of the music) that you want before you play. Knowing the character and emotional

state of the music prior to playing it will prime your motor system to find ways of expressing such emotions through touch and other musical agogics.
- "Sense it, play it"—i.e., sense exactly the feeling you want to have in your muscles and body before you move. By anticipating ideal kinaesthetics, it can help to overcome maladaptive movements.

In practice, it takes a lot of discipline to *only* play the notes of the music when we have a purpose for them, but it is this type of discipline that defines *excellent* practice—and nurtures *excellent* results.[32] It ensures that the top-down commands to our fingers are optimized, requiring only excellent bottom-up feedback through our senses to check that they are doing what they are being told (see next sections).

If the premotor phase of our movements weren't important, any non-musician could easily learn to play virtuosically too, for they too can wiggle their fingers quickly up and down. But the movements of musicians' fingers are different: they move to fulfill musical tasks, not just mechanical tasks, and the skills that serve these tasks are built into the premotor neural circuitry over many years of musical training.

Our motor skills are shaped by the musical, sonic, mechanical, gestural, kinaesthetic, emotional and other abstract goals that we demand of them. This is because, prior to any touch movement being activated in the primary motor cortex, all these different, competing goals have to pass through premotor integration centers in the brain. These areas include the secondary motor areas—Supplemental Motor Area (SMA) for sequencing complex movements, the Pre-Motor Area (PMA) for movement planning, and the Cingulate Motor Area (CMA) for integrating movements with emotions—along with sensory, auditory and visual areas which connect to them.

What we "load" into our motor system, therefore, is of the utmost importance in determining how it will later function. If we teach it to connect to musical targets (e.g., sound, rhythm, textures etc.), it will learn how to deliver them. If we teach it to connect to emotional targets (e.g., different musical expressions), it will learn how to deliver them. If we teach it to connect to conceptually abstract targets (e.g., "energy flowing through your body") it will learn how to deliver them. And, if we teach it to connect to pain, stress and tension, it will learn how to deliver them too. The motor system provides for much more than just mechanics.

The importance of being aware of the beliefs that shape our practice-room actions must, therefore, again, be emphasized because what we think our movements are *for* or *capable of* will shape what they become good at. To succeed in pianism, we must take seriously what we feed into our motor systems. Consider what multimodal inputs might have been loaded into the premotor circuitry of the following pianists: J.S. Bach, Beethoven, Chopin, Liszt, Josef Hofmann, Artur Rubinstein, Michelangeli, Gould, Tureck, Lang Lang, Art Tatum, Bill Evans, or *you*? What were the specific goals that their motor systems were trained to achieve?

LEARNING AND NEUROPLASTICITY

Aside from enjoyment, professional musicians practice to learn. And in learning, we engage with the physiological process of *neuroplasticity*—where "the brain changes physically as we learn."[33] Understanding neuroplasticity (plasticity) helps us to understand how, how much (and how little) we can, should or need to practice. Biologically, neuroplasticity (plasticity) is the innate capacity of the nervous system to physically change in response to its environment. It is the inbuilt feature of our bodies that we most need to exploit if we seek super-performance, says Anders Ericsson:

> *"the clear message from decades of research is that no matter what role innate genetic endowment may play in the achievements of "gifted" people, the main gift that these people have is the same one we all have—the adaptability of the human brain and body, which they have taken advantage of more than the rest of us."*[34]

Principally, plasticity involves two aspects: "structural neuroplasticity," where nerves build *more connections* to other nerves (i.e., more axon-dendrite connections); and "functional neuroplasticity," where nerves build *stronger connections* to other nerves (stronger neurotransmitter-receptor responses between nerves).[35] Thus, the link between learning and nerve connections is not a mystery; it is physical and objectifiable. Skills are built. Talent is built. The science reminds us:

> *"Increased signalling by cortical neurons generates the growth of more branches, which increases the density of cellular material and enhances their ability to connect with other neurons—to form more synapses. These changes occur only in the parts of the brain that are used. They result from repeated firing of the specific neurons engaged in learning experiences, as well as from the presence of emotion chemicals around those neurons."*[36]

and

> "region- and pathway-specific plasticity sculpts the circuits involved in the performance of the skill as it becomes automatized."[37]

and

> "Neurons that fire together wire together."[38]

Taking Advantage of Neuroplasticity When Practicing

Given that *practicing* is the pianist's tool for causing adaptive changes in the brain, we can already make some conclusions about what we should try to do when we practice:

- increase the frequency of useful actions (to promote the growth of useful nerve connections).
- decrease the frequency of useless actions (to limit the growth of unhelpful nerve connections).
- find a balance between stimulating your cells enough (so that they grow) versus too much (so that the stimulus doesn't overwhelm their ability to process it). Like muscle cells, there is only so much stimulus any nerve cell can cope with before it becomes exhausted or it starts to function counterproductively. With respect to learning and metaplasticity, over-practicing may not always be advantageous.[39]
- give your brain cells enough time to rest between doses of practice (so that they have time to adapt). Cells need time to grow. They need time to build neurotransmitter molecules, cell receptors, protein structures and grow their axons and dendrites (the finger-like projections that connect to other cells).[40]
- practice regularly and give your attention to the specific tasks that you wish to improve (so that the number and strength of those specific nerve connections is increased).
- practice "learnable" material, i.e., material that is not too hard (so that "the to-be-remembered information is mapped to something that is familiar."[41])
- when learning something new, practice frequently over consecutive days (to remind the mind that the new information is important and needs to be remembered—so that new nerve connections will be built). Note that "forgetting" is also a natural function of the mind.

Forgetting is, in part, an "importance" filter for the mind, so that the brain does not waste energy building nerve connections for every single motor-sensory event that it encounters—nor has a need for. Our minds would be a complete jumble of information chaos if we didn't filter information and forget what is unimportant.

- the more learning you do, the more success your future learning is likely to have. (This is the concept of *metaplasticity*—where new skills become easier to learn when prior skills exist.[42])
- Engage emotionally during the learning process (to increase the strength of the nerve connections)[43] and, as far as possible, avoid practicing when negative emotions are involved.[44] "Neuro-active hormones, such as adrenalin (arousal), endorphins (pleasure), dopamine (rewarding experience) and stress hormones (fear of failure) support neuroplastic adaptations."[45]
- Bring variety to your learning with activities that challenge different parts of your brain in different ways. This ensures that you develop a wide range of nerve connections across multiple cognitive domains and a wider net of neuronal scaffolding upon which you can *retrieve* information (memory), *add* new information (learn) and *create* new ideas (creativity comes from new combinations).[46]

Nerve cells involved in learning need to be stimulated enough (to learn)—but not too much (to become overwhelmed)—yet rested enough (to consolidate what is being learned)—but not too rested (to have time to forget). The question of how much to practice is, therefore, necessarily bound to the question of how often.

Associations, Learning and Memorising

Finding ways of practicing that create *multiple* associations across *multiple* cognitive domains is key to learning and memory success. In musicians, these include (at least) motor, sensory, visual, auditory, proprioceptive, kinaesthetic and emotional domains.[47] Multiple associations help to create a larger network of cross-linked neurons upon which to add new information. Multiple associations also helps to reduce the risk of memory failure should several associations fail to activate during playing (as happens when performing live on stage).

"Goal-directed practice, multi-sensory-motor integration, high arousal, and emotional and social rewards contribute to these plasticity-induced brain adaptations"[48]

The following quotes show how mindful professional pianists are of practicing, learning and memorizing—all the same thing—in a variety of ways so that multiple senses and multiple parts of their brains are cross-linked:

- Vladimir Ashkenazy—"[Memory involves] everything, mind, vision, aural, everything."[49]
- Alicia de Larrocha—"memory is complex. You must have all kinds [of memory]."[50]
- Leon Fleisher—"[Memory involves] some combination of aural, visual and tactile [elements] ... try to understand [...] all its elements as much as possible."[51]
- Josef Hofmann—"[Memory involves] the acoustic picture, the optical picture, and the acquired habit of musical sequences."[52]
- Percy Grainger—"to approach memorization from several angles ... The physical memory 'tides one over" when the mind "becomes a blank.'"[53]
- John Browning—"you insure, you over-prepare, so that if you are distracted during a concert [...] you have so much backlog of preparation that it will carry you through automatically."[54]
- Alfred Cortot—"get at the principal—the heart of the thing you want to conquer [...] Make new material for technique practice out of them."[55]
- Misha Dichter—"I try to never remove musical meaning from what I'm going over."[56]
- Stephen Hough—"the brain is trained to use all of the senses [and so, when practicing] if you remove one of those senses, you make the other one develop more strongly, because it has to overcompensate."[57]

Categorically, memorizing musical material is not something that should be "added on" when you approach the end of learning a piece. Practicing IS Memorizing IS learning, and it should start on day 1 of learning a new piece.

During piano playing, the brain has countless opportunities to associate information across different cognitive domains and expand its nerve networks. Obviously, the task of practicing is to make associations that contribute to the type of pianism that we *seek*, not just associations *that happen to be present* at the time of practicing, or worse still, the ones that we have habituated without reason. Making this distinction matters, as the examples in the following textbox show.

Learned Associations

- "I play better at home than on stage."
  Why?... because your piano-playing nerve connections are accustomed to playing at home under home conditions (different instrument, different mechanical, visual and acoustic cues, with no audience, in calm emotional states, with different learning intentions), not on stage under stage conditions.
- "I felt uncomfortable and played badly sitting on the higher stool."
  Why?... because you always sit low when you practice.
- "My left hand forgets the notes if my right hand forgets its notes."
  Why?... because the movements of your left hand have become dependent on the movements of your right hand rather than their own musical sequences.
- "I push deeper into the keybed when I play espressivo."
  Why?... because your emotions have influenced your movements and now they have associated a pushing-deeply-into-the-keys movement with espressivo.
- "My face, neck and shoulders tense up more when there is more emotional tension in the music."
  Why?... because my body has learned to associate the musical tension with physical tension.
- "My wrist rises up at the ends of phrases."
  Why?... because you have learned to associate the idea of musical breathing at phrase ends with wrist rising.
- "If I look away from the keys, I am more likely to forget my place."
  Why?... because your memory has become too dependent on visual cues.
- "When the music becomes *pp*, my left foot automatically wants to press the *una corda* pedal"
  Why?... because you allow it to happen when practicing

Consider the following practice strategies and how they could be used to help with the learning or re-learning of more useful associations. Note how common these strategies are in piano pedagogy—because they work. Each strategy focuses on building either the *desired* connections directly or *alternative pathway* connections that amplify the skill set (neuronal web) of the pianist.

- practicing with attention to detail so that the correct musical details are associated with your movements.
- practicing using different types of dynamics, touch, register, rhythm and tempo.
- doing the opposite to what is asked—e.g., opposite touch, tempo, expression, character etc. (to become aware of your habitual associations and be made more aware of other associative possibilities).
- practicing each hand separately (to increase your awareness of each hand and to avoid either hand becoming overly dependent on the other).
- practicing away from the piano (to become more aware of your memory weaknesses and dependencies).
- practicing with your eyes closed (to make your pianism less dependent on your visual sense and more reliant on your listening and proprioceptive senses).
- singing the R.H. while playing the L.H.—or vice versa (to remove the influence that your idiosyncratic physical habits have on your melody shaping).
- playing the piece transposed into another key (to prove to yourself that you can think in terms of notes within a harmony, not just notes on the keyboard).
- practicing on different instruments, in different venues and with different audiences prior to an important performance (to be comfortable performing in scenarios that are not habitual).

Emotionalized Movements

Just as our movements seek to communicate emotions *via sound* (by making music), they are also hardwired to convey emotions *via gesture*. Knowing that there is a difference can help our pianism, for depending on how we train ourselves to express our emotions, either our sounds will be the beneficiary of our emotions (preferred) or our gestures will (may not be preferred). Certainly, if our emotions interfere with the mechanics of our gestures too much, there can be problems. The problems may include technical limitations, injuries and predictable, expressive gestures. Collectively, they can castrate our pianism. Overly emotionalized movements are the maladaptive gestures of the "caged bird" that Barbara Lister-Sink so correctly talks about in her "Freeing the Caged Bird" video series.[58]

As pianists, our emotions will constantly be affecting our movements, and it is one of our primary tasks to learn how to transmit emotions through sound (with appropriate gestures) without those emotions negatively affecting the precision or control of the movements that produce those sounds.[59]

One of the most important skills to develop as a pianist, therefore, is the ability to *combine* musical expression with optimal mechanics. It is an obvious skill to acquire, but not a simple one to master. Experts will know the problem. Firstly, the skill requires an awareness that when we engage fully in a task of musical expression, our attention may be drawn away from its mechanical needs, and, similarly, when we engage fully in a task of mechanical optimization, our attention may be drawn away from its musical needs.

Playing musically well doesn't make our mechanics excellent, and playing mechanically well doesn't make our music excellent.

The natural response of the human body—to embody feelings and concepts into movements—does not ensure efficiency nor efficacy regarding our *pianistic* movements. For example, to play an *agitato* passage with agitato-like movements or a *molto appassionato* passage with *molto appassionato*–like keystrokes could spell disaster for the speed, accuracy, and ease of our movements. Yet, to play with a sole focus on mechanical perfection comes at a risk too, as it may deny our pianism of the intuitive movements that emotionalized movements provide—and the pleasure that often accompanies them.

As mentioned previously, when trying to understand touch problems, we must acknowledge that *two* types of movement functions coexist: *mechanical* (objective, physical) and *meaning* (subjective, psychological). Body language experts know the importance of the latter in communication.[60] Depending on the type of musical passage being played, or the priorities of the pianist playing it, one of the two functions might get prioritized at the expense of the other.

We should be mindful of this dual function when we practice, otherwise playing exercises like Hanon, mechanically efficiently but devoid of musical meaning, might be no more helpful to our long-term pianism than playing a set of Chopin etudes emotionally well yet with poor biomechanics. Neither scenario helps because the sparkling finger-strokes of the Hanon player are not wired to express emotions through them, and the emotionally inspired movements of the Chopin player will, almost certainly, be cursed with biomechanical inefficiencies and other technical limitations.

Ideally, the emotions and mechanics of our playing are seamlessly integrated such that we put our emotions into the sounds, not our muscles, and that we play with biomechanical efficiency without denying ourselves emotional expression and gestural freedom.

We can train ourselves to play with full emotional expression and full mechanical excellence *if* we maintain cognizant that, despite any attempts to practice the two pathways separately, it is how well they combine as a mechanical-expressive event that proves that you have practiced well.

Knowing that our emotions affect our motor control helps to explain why our motor performance will behave differently under different performance conditions (e.g., during a recording, in an exam, in a lesson, at home, in a concert, etc.). To increase the chances that our touch movements will behave in the same way on stage as they do in the practice room, the strategies in the textbox below may be tried:

Combining Mechanics and Meaning in Touch

- to practice under a *wide variety* of musical-emotional conditions so that our motor system has multiple pathways with which to deal with the variety of emotional states that live performing might generate.
- to learn how to maintain the *same* musical-emotional states on stage as in the practice room. This can be done either by heating up or dampening down our musical emotions in the practice room (to match what we expect them to be on stage), or by heating up or dampening down our emotions on stage (to match what we did in the practice room).
- to do mental practice using visualization techniques that anticipate different emotional scenarios and rehearse them (this accesses the same neural pathways).
- to eliminate the distinction between *practicing* the piano and *playing* the piano so that maximum emotional intention and maximal mechanical efficiency is taught to every note, whether in the practice room or on stage. Pianist Harold Bauer appeared to strive for such: "think music, and nothing but music, all the time, down to the smallest detail even in technic."[61]
- by identifying what tends to go wrong with our motor skills when performing and to "exaggerate the solution" to those problems when practicing. For example, if our movements have a habit of becoming "rigid and jerky" on stage, we should exaggerate "relaxed smoothness" when practicing; or, should our fingers tend to "curl

> and claw" the keyboard, exaggerating their "non-curling, non-clawing" movements will solve the problem. Practicing the opposite of whatever goes wrong on stage is a highly effective practice strategy for practicing *any* pianistic problem as it builds more of the neuromotor pathways that lack and reinforces less of the pathways that are unwanted.

Body Language

Our emotions also affect our motor control via neurological pathways that are directly involved with communication: body language and gestures. When playing the piano, such communicative movements are usually spontaneous, automatic and musically intuitively as they seek to communicate meaning within the music.

> **In piano playing, giving full freedom to our gestures is a double-edged sword: they may help us to feel the music, feel the right movements and feel the right sounds, but they may also interfere with its mechanics, our perception of sound and the control of our movements.**

Consider how useful, or useless, the following gestural movements are, all commonly used by performing pianists.

Body Movements

- facial movements (jaw clenching, jaw dropping, pressed lips, pursed lips, eyebrow raising, eyebrow lowering, eyelid falling, smiling, frowning).
- head movements (head shaking, head nodding, ceiling staring).
- truncal movements (body swaying, body crouching, body extending).
- leg, feet, and toe movements (feet positioning changes, feet sliding, feet tapping, toe raising).
- vocalizations (grunts, sniffs, snorts and other audible breathing patterns).

Gestural Movements

- clawing and squeezing of the keys and keybed (that might accompany *molto espressivo* playing—recall Beethoven's tightly curled fingers).
- the forcing or overpressuring of the keys when emotionally stressed.
- "wrist locking" (that might accompany strong or forceful musical emotions).
- strange idiosyncratic gestures of the fingers, especially of the index finger.[62]

- posturing (e.g., back straight, head up, chest out, during loud majestic playing).
- gestures of the hand, wrist or arm (that choreograph the emotions of the sound without causing any change to the sound).

"Learned" Emotionalized Movements

- learning to use unusually flat fingers, or curled fingers, or any other specific finger posture, when specific expressive outcomes are sought.
- the (unintentional) use of the *una corda* pedal when playing *pp*.
- the deliberate learning to raise the wrist after playing a musical couplet or at the end of a phrase.
- the intuitive movements learned by the body to express certain emotions. For example, when playing your right hand melodies with your left hand (or vice versa, if you are left-handed), or using your left foot to operate the sostenuto pedal, you will notice subtle differences—that emotionalized movements have been built into your pianism over many years.

What you do about your emotionalized movements is a personal choice, and it will depend on how useful or harmful they are to your pianism. If they are a problem, then either your emotions need to be cooled or the connections between your emotions and your movements need to be re-wired—a task that requires discipline and patience.[63]

The problems that emotionalized movements can create for our playing highlights the importance of practicing properly: of wiring emotions to sounds, not muscles, and, ideally, doing so with perfect mechanics.

Mood and Movements and Expression and Pain

Our mood is another factor that may need to be taken into consideration when optimizing our pianism. It is rarely discussed in piano pedagogy, but it has a place. As psychiatrists know, besides affecting our thought patterns and decision-making ability, mood also affects our posture and the speed, precision and quality of our movements.[64]

Collectively, such factors may affect our touch, the decisions we make about touch, as well as our perception of it. Here are two examples:

- *Mental State #1: Confident, Dominant and Proud*
  Posture: confident, dominant and proud (e.g., high-sitting, straight-backed, chin-up, chest-out positions).

→ Keystroke: full-bodied (arm-weight dominant rather than finger-speed dominant approach), confident dropping of the arm into the keys, possibly more likely to play with larger forces into the keys and produce larger volumes.
- *Mental State #2: Withdrawn, Shy and Reflective*
Posture: shy, withdrawn or reflective (e.g., low-sitting, slouched or closed-body positions).
    → Keystroke: lighter-weight (finger-speed dominant rather than arm-weight dominant approach), keystrokes that "feel" rather than "hit" the key, and possibly more likely to play with softer volumes.

The above examples are observations, not rules, but the fact that our mental state affects our movements and that our movements affect our mental state, means that we ought to think about the influence that each might be having on our pianism. The following textbox shows more examples why.

Touching Moods and Moody Touches

To learn how to better recognize the connections between your mental state, postures, gestures, music thoughts and touch, you may wish to try the following experiments:

1. Find several different passages of music to play, each representing a different type of musical emotion. Next, play them using different types of sitting positions, postures and gestures. Sit very high. Sit very low. Sit leaning forward. Sit leaning backward. Play with liberal gestures, then play with no gestures. Imagine you are Rubinstein, then imagine you are Glenn Gould. Imagine you are Liszt or your idol. Note how each type of sitting position subtly affects your musical attitude, the nature of your touch, the style of your playing, your articulation and, ultimately, the sound world of your pianism.
2. Try to play sad music with a happy face, or happy music with a sad face. Note how the incongruity between the emotion and the gesture (e.g., sad music, happy face) makes this difficult to do. Ask: what type of "face" do you habitually bring to the piano? How does it affect your pianism? Does it give the same flavor (emotionally, conceptually, and mechanically) to everything you play? Is this what you want? What if learning how to use a "different face," selectively, allowed you to meet the challenges of different repertoire, different passagework and different styles?

To be aware of the two-way interaction between mental states and physical behaviors is important as it can provide you with clues as to why you adopt certain touch habits, why you sit and address the keyboard in the way that you do, and, importantly, why you might paint all your music with the same emotional color.

Unfortunately, negative subjective experiences, like pain, may also become wired into our pianistic movements. It tends to occur when there is some initial physical cause for the pain, but because of either the persistence of the injury or the persistence of the psychological stress associated with the injury, the pain experience becomes permanent.[65] Accordingly, irrespective of whether the initial injury has healed, the physical movements that were initially linked to the pain will continue to trigger a painful experience. This is *pain memory*.

Because of the complexity of the nerve connections, like with unwanted emotionalized movements, pain associated with playing can also be challenging to treat. New neuro-motor pathways have to be built. This requires time. Though this is not the book for the topic, understanding the principles of causality can help us to avoid the pianistic behaviors that may cause it. Logically, these include:

- don't get injured in the first place (play within physiological limits, play with proper biomechanics, do less physical practice and learn more efficiently using more mental practice);[66]
- don't play when injured (demanding full function out of tissue that is not fully functioning will perpetuate injury, cause longer healing times, longer pain signaling times, and lead to suboptimal long-term function);
- don't negatively emotionalise the pain experience (allow healing and give time for retraining and therapies to work without the overlay of negative psychology).

OPTIMIZING PRACTICING: IMPROVING NERVE CONNECTIONS

Empowered Learning. Deliberate Practice. Growth Mindset.

Besides the enjoyment of playing music, most of our time spent at the piano involves *learning*—learning notes, learning sounds and learning movements etc. Given the vast quantity of this learning, we might think to ask: could it be done more effectively?

"Practicing mechanically is a waste of time. It's not what intelligent humans should do. They should practice a little less, and think a little more."[67]—*András Schiff*

Unsurprisingly, professionals who excel in what they do tend to exhibit similar learning traits, the most common of which may be described by the concept of *empowered learning*—where there is an underlying desire, belief and commitment to do what it takes to succeed.[68] Our good friend J.S. Bach appeared to have the hallmarks of an empowered learner. Could we perhaps learn from his example: of *setting challenges*, taking *ownership and responsibility* for learning, and *taking an active role* in it?[69]

"Everything must be possible" ["Es muss alles möglich zu machen sein"] ...
"I was obliged to be industrious; whoever is equally industrious will succeed equally well."[70]—*J.S. Bach*

Learning experts might also say that Bach engages in *deliberate practice*—the type of practice characteristically shown by champions[71]—where "practice [is] motivated by increased standards,"[72] where "desirable difficulties"[73] are set and overcome, and where there is a "rage to master."[74]

"Physical motor or sensory exercises alone do not drive cortical changes; learning is required [...] learning also depends on levels of attention and motivation."[75]

Whatever Bach's personal motivations were, his constant efforts *to solve the problems that needed solving* exemplified optimized learning. Objectively, physiologically, Bach's learning behaviors could hardly be improved: *repetitively improving current skills* with *increasingly difficult challenges*.[76]

In a similar vein, the twenty-one-year-old Liszt's attitude toward practicing might also be recognized: "I study them [Beethoven, Bach, Hummel, Mozart, Weber], I meditate on them, I devour them with fury; besides this, I practice four to five hours of exercises [...] Provided I don't go mad you will find in me an artist!"[77] And here is Neuhaus' observation of Richter practicing: "the art of working, of learning compositions is characterized by an unwavering determination and an ability not to waste time."[78]

In addition to the benefits of keeping learning active and interesting, our learning receives a further boost when we *believe* in it. The catch-phrases of the entrepreneur Henry Ford—"whether you believe you can do a thing or not, you are right"[79]—and that of the famed author on motivation, D.

Schwartz—"look at things . . . as they can be"[80]—is no different to that of Bach ("everything must be possible").

In fact, scientifically, one of the main factors that has been shown to make people bother to give effort *at all* to any learning task, is whether they think there is going to be benefit gained from it.[81] Flooding (young) students with difficult, *non-desirable* technical exercises which foster *can't-do* beliefs may not be as useful to their learning as their ambitious teachers might think—"we stop doing what we do not do well and feel unrewarded for."[82]

Positive thinking also overlaps with the learning concepts of *Growth Mindset*, where "intelligence [is seen as] a malleable quality"[83] and the *O.P.T.I.M.A.L.* theory of motor learning, which creates conditions "that *enhance expectancies* for future performance success."[84] Their embrace of positive psychology also aligns with *deliberate play* strategies (as opposed to *deliberate practice*) which have also shown to deliver high achieving results in motivated individuals.[85]

Unquestionably, pianists and teachers could both help themselves tremendously by creating such positive learning conditions and instilling attitudes of "can do" and self-belief rather than ones of negative criticism and self-doubt, irrespective of the number of faults in their playing. As the pianist Stephen Hough encourages, "[work] hard with fun and with joy, and with a sense of achievement [...] If we begin from a spring-board of encouragement, then our best potential can come through."[86]

Unfaltering motivation may not be the attitude that we always bring into the practice room, but it can be a game changer when it is. Certainly, if our levels of interest in what we are practicing are low, the science would suggest that we are better not to practice at all, as productivity will be low and bad habits will be nurtured.

Quality Practice

On a physiological level, quality piano practice equates to the building of nerve connections that are useful to your pianism. On a practical level, says Ericsson, "deliberate practice remains the gold standard for anyone in any field who wishes to take advantage of the gift of adaptability in order to build new skills and abilities."[87] This is why "can-do" mindsets are so commonly associated with those that achieve outstanding results—they create *favorable conditions* for such nerve connections to occur. (Note, every topic discussed in this book seeks to create favorable conditions for optimizing motor-skills learning, musicianship and health.) The following textbox summarizes them.

Favorable Learning Conditions

- Participating in beliefs and activities that are going to *help* your pianism;
- Pursuing your *ideal* artistic ideas;
- *Optimizing* the mechanical, mental and musical aspects of your playing;
- Visualizing and mentally practicing *ideal* musical and mechanical outcomes;
- Being open to *exploring* the elements of your pianistic medium and finding ways to *extract more* expression from them;
- Learning with *purpose* and *an expectation* of skill development;
- Learning with a *positive emotional state*;
- Repeating "what you want to learn" while setting *challenging yet achievable* goals;[88]
- Practicing in a *variety* of ways that involve different cognitive modalities;
- Working within *sensible, healthy* physiological limits.

Music psychologist Williamon asserts that quality outcomes are a result of planned-out, motivated, goal-driven behaviors that are constantly being refined. He identifies five practice-trait categories associated with enhanced outcomes. His findings corroborate the cognitive and physiological principles presented throughout this book (given in square parentheses):[89]

1. Concentration [improves neuroplastic changes]
2. Goal setting [involves visualization of ideal musical outcomes]
3. Self-evaluation [involves assessing beliefs, strengths and weaknesses]
4. Strategies [exploit the maths of process optimization, the physics of mechanics, the physiology of neuro-motor learning and the neuroscience of improving artistic skills]
5. Knowing the Big Picture [contextualizing your artistic vision and knowing how to relate it to your audience]

Effort and Quantity

Visualising ideal musical outcomes and doing mental practice is certainly a step in the right direction to extract more from one's physical skills, but the importance of physical practice cannot be outright ignored. We cannot build the full web of neuro-motor pathways just by thinking about them. As Goethe realized, "Knowing is not enough; we must apply. Willing is not enough; we must do."[90]

Ericsson's finding of needing to accumulate "10,000 hours of practice over 10 years" to achieve professional competency is often quoted as a quantity that correlates with professional levels of expertise.[91] It is a general figure, vaguely defined, but it does give a useful reference point upon which to discuss the topic of practice amounts.

As Ericsson and others acknowledge, there is more to skills acquisition than just time spent practicing. *How* and *when* we practice, also matter. Studies have shown that far fewer accumulated hours can lead to the same results, especially when practice hours are accumulated during childhood (ideally before the age of 8), when innate "ability" exists, and when specific personality, opportunity, genetic and environmental factors are favorable.[92] Also, those that have more skills tend to become increasingly efficient at acquiring further skills—more begets more—(due to metaplasticity) which suggests that the speed of learning will be different for different people.

In addressing the problem of the optimization of learning, what constitutes "an hour of practice" needs to be described in much more detail. It is this "hour" that will be repeated for tens of thousands of hours throughout our piano-playing lives. Distinctions—*and choices*—need to be made regarding physical and mental practice, styles of learning, numbers of repetitions, time spent observing, listening to, and pondering over music, and the degrees of motivation and attention applied during learning sessions.

Practice, Purpose, Time, and the Hourglass

Given the importance of using time productively, the obvious question to ask is: *what is the best use of an hour of practice time?* This, logically, depends on what you are trying to achieve. Which is what? Is it learning a bunch of pieces quickly to pass your exam? Is it preparing next season's repertoire? Is it working toward improving your memory problems? Is it dealing with your L.H. mechanical problem? Is it striving for a *liquid* legato or a *sfumato* approach to pedaling? Are you improving your interpretative skills at all or just repeating what you usually do? Are you dreaming big? Are you growing as a pianist?

The question of *how to spend an hour* may expose a lack of clarity about what your pianistic purpose actually is. If this is the case, some targeted questions need to be asked:

- What is your practice being used for?
- What outcomes matter to you?
- Is your practice directed toward short- or long-term goals?
- Is more practice always useful? Could less practice or more targeted practice be more useful? Have you thought about which is more productive: 10 hrs/day for 2 days? 4 hrs/day for 5 days? 1 hr distributed 20 times throughout the week?
- Do you ensure high levels of learning effectiveness while practicing?
- Do you take into account injury risk when you practice?

Using your time properly will increase your chances of reaching your goals. If the so-called 10,000 hours (or any other number) could be reduced by 10 percent by exerting no extra effort and still maintaining the same outcomes, 1000 hours of time will have been saved. That's a lot of time saved, or reinvested . . . or spent on leisure.

The question of *how*, *how much* and *how often* to practice is the subject of much neuroscientific research, and although there are no neatly packaged answers to such questions, there are many facts that we can apply to our practice to make it more productive. Many suggestions are provided in the following paragraphs. Note how they all promote *physical nerves making better*

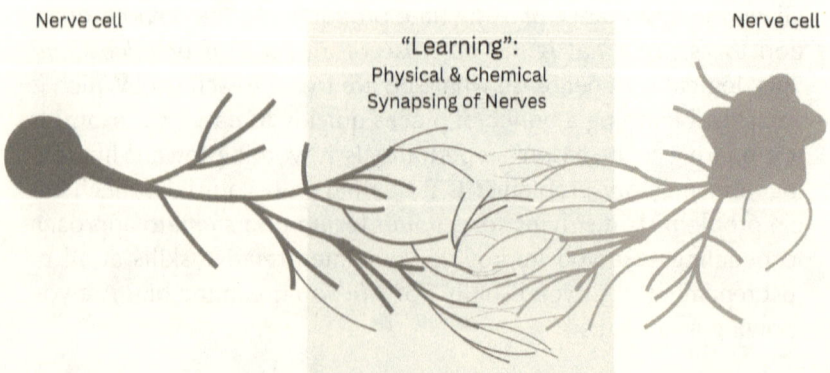

Figure 7.1. Connecting Nerves. Author created

connections, where the extent and strength of these connections is dependent on the *amount*, *frequency* and *type* of stimulus they receive. There is no magic to the process. It is objective.

- *Learn the right thing at the right time*

Because different neuro-motor skills develop across different cognitive domains and across different time frames, different skills will benefit from different types and amounts of practice.[93] Neuroscientifically, our learning occurs in 5 stages[94] (summarized below). Knowing these stages can help us to target the right learning task at the right time.

5 Learning Stages—What to Do, When?

1. *Encoding*—when we first learn to translate the notes on the page into hand positions, finger movements and an initial mental representation.
   → Encoding groups of notes into simple chunks of information that are logically connected will make later recall much easier and faster.[95]
   → Look for all the patterns that connect the notes: harmonic, rhythmic, structural, dynamic, etc.
2. *Consolidation*—when we continue to practice in a variety of ways, the loosely-remembered encoded material becomes more permanently remembered.
   → Use practice as a tool to convert short-term memory fragments into consolidated long-term memories. What gets remembered (stored) will depend *entirely* on what you choose to focus your attention on during this consolidation phase.
   → Don't be lazy with your focus, or else errors (wrong notes, wrong sounds, wrong movements etc.) will be made permanent.
3. *Storage*—the two main types of memory—*declarative* (e.g., the details of the score) and *procedural* (e.g., one's movements)—are stored in different parts of the brain. They are independent of each other, and they are improved in different ways. *Declarative* memory benefits from the identification of details (and their patterns) and repeated cognitive attempts to remember them. This repetition is commonly called *rote learning*. *Procedural* memory

benefits from physical repetition (without any need for cognitive understanding or emotional motivation).
→ Understanding these two types of memories explains why one's (intellectual) knowledge of music may not translate into one's ability to (physically) execute it, and vice versa, why one's ability to execute difficult passagework has nothing to do with one's ability to (intellectually) understand it.
→ When practicing, we should optimize both memory pathways in our playing. If we have a movement problem (biomechanical, speed, accuracy, coordination, etc.), we need to practice *physical repetitions*. This improves procedural memory. If we have a memory problem, we need to have a *clearer cognitive plan* for the sequencing of the music. This improves declarative memory.

4. *Retrieval*—like storage, our ability to retrieve memories is related to how well they have been encoded and consolidated in the first place.[96] Retrieval will involve many different domains of the brain (e.g., auditory, visual, proprioceptive, motor, sensory, emotional etc.) which reinforces why multiple domains should be used during practice.
→ When our memory fails during a performance, it is almost always because of a lack of consolidation of the necessary retrieval clues within the declarative memory, not the procedural memory.[97] Examples of this are not hard to find: during a memory slip in a performance, do you really think that it is because you could not play the passage properly if you were given the chance to use the score the second time? Or, if you experience a stage-fright "blank mind" scenario, is it really proof that you have no procedural memory of the piece at all? No. And no.
→ Once our "muscle memory" (procedural memory) is well established for a given piece, repeatedly repeating it more, with the hope that *more* procedural memory will translate into *more* recall of it during performance, is mistaken.
→ Given that motor memories are easier to make than to un-make, careful attention should be given to learning each movement with correct biomechanics and correct sounds from the outset of learning each movement.

> → Given that well-established muscle memory is procedurally reliable—I've not forgotten how to ride a bike yet—our role as a pianist, when performing, from a motor-system point of view, is to facilitate the sequencing of chunks of information. This is done by *listening for the musical-emotional sound images* that we have already trained our movements to attached themselves to, and/or by *following the cognitive sequences* of the declarative details that we have taught our minds, so that they will trigger the upcoming motor actions.
> 5. *Reconsolidation*—when old memories are recalled, they are simultaneously altered by the new information applied to them.
> → This is why we tend to feel different about a piece that we have not played for a long period of time.

- *In general, practicing more and practicing regularly helps.*

"The strongest neural structural effects are driven by "paced learning"— that is, learning that is "progressive and repetitive."[98] Broadly, this is what most pianists do (or know they should do): to practice regularly and improve upon what they have learned in the previous session. Learning that is spaced out in time ("spaced learning") and varied in content ("interleaved learning") also tends to be more effective than learning that has no variety or occurs all in one go.[99] It is what our understanding of neuroplasticity (and metaplasticity) would have us expect:

> **that gradually and regularly adding new nerve connections onto previous connections, using a variety of cognitive domains, while maintaining interest in what we are learning, works.**[100]

Generally, practicing *every day* is likely to be more beneficial than practicing *every other day*, given that most motor skills decay in a time-dependent fashion[101] and that "as the time interval between practice sessions is extended, it prevents the new internal model from being activated."[102]

But to practice *very many times per day* may cause its own problems too, should the phenomenon of *interference* take effect—where the learning of new information interferes with the recall of information that has just recently been learned. Busy musicians may experience this phenomenon when trying to learn too much music in too short a time-frame and become frustrated that neither the new material is sinking in nor the previously learned material is being remembered. Paradoxically, interference is made worse when the material being learned is highly *similar* to the material that has just been learned (compared to *interleaved learning*, where the type of material being learned is varied).

The problem of interference can easily be demonstrated in beginner pianists by asking them, for example, to learn too many new major and minor scales in one session—where the similarity of all the scale patterns overwhelms the brain's ability to differentiate them and store them separately. In professionals, the equivalent might occur when trying to learn an entire Bach *Contrapunctus* in one sitting, or too many pages of a Boulez Sonata, where too much "similar" material makes the new memories overlap and become jumbled.

Physiologically, with interference, there has not been enough time for each dose of information to be consolidated into the neuronal web before the next dose of information has arrived. In such situations, as a (possible) suggestion, some hours of rest time may be needed for the brain to absorb the new material[103] before adding further material to it. Or, alternatively, practicing using different modalities may help to avoid the interference in the first place. In principle, when it comes to consolidating new memories, introducing regular periods of rest is likely to enhance learning outcomes compared to no or little rest—so long as the brain has enough material upon which to digest during those periods of rest.

The other way to help consolidation is to *vary* the way in which the material is learned. There are no limits to how many ways this can be done, and a skilled learner will have many personal favorites which work well for them. As the pianist Yonty Solomon encouraged, "find multiple solutions [to your piano playing problems], not just one."[104]

Furthermore, bringing variety to your practice "not only strengthens the very specific task at hand but has been shown to positively boost other, related skills"—this is called *generalizability*.[105] A willingness to experiment with a variety of solutions rather than pursuing just one would appear to have a solid evidence base.

Based on all the above principles, examples of bad practice might include:

- cramming the learning of *too much new material* into *too few days*;
- repeating too much *of the same thing* during any single practice session;
- not bringing enough *variety* into your practice sessions (different pieces, different speeds, different dynamics, different rhythms, different characterisations, different instruments, different sounds, different feelings, different sitting positions, different audiences etc.);

- *failing to follow up* one practice session with another practice session later in the day or the next day;
- *failing to revise* the material that was learned during the previous session before adding new material to it.

- *Bursts of practice that last only a few minutes can be of value, but what is learned is less likely to be remembered.*

Permanent changes in the structure of the brain (plasticity) can occur following very short periods of practice. This has been shown for single doses of learning that last only a few minutes[106] and also following short episodes of practice of twenty-minute durations.[107] The early stage joining (and signaling) of nerves to each other is called *synaptic consolidation* and it "is accomplished within the first minutes to hours after learning."[108]

As useful as a very small dose of practice might seem, however, when we learn something new, our recall of it will be fragile compared to if a larger dose of practice had been taken—"extensive practice is necessary for the consolidation of a new internal model."[109] Too small a dose of learning seems to reduce the chances of it being recalled long-term,[110] which is hardly surprising but does serve to confirm that "enough" of a dose of practice needs to occur for a new internal model to become established and remember-able for the next occasion it is revisited.

> *"The efficiency and size of synapses may be modified in a time window of seconds to minutes, while the growth of new synapses and dendrites may require hours to days. An increase in gray matter density, [...] needs at least several weeks. White matter density also increases as a consequence of musical training."*[111]

- *Resting helps learning.*

As important as it is to practice enough during any single session, much of the learning of our motor skills continues to occur *in between* practice sessions—i.e., during periods of rest. This is because even though our mind takes a break, the nerves continue working, making their connections:

> *"Motor skill learning depends on de novo synthesis of proteins in the motor cortex after training"*[112] *and taking regular breaks is "critical for dynamic motor memory stabilization."*[113]

In fact, the motor-skills learning done by the brain during breaks is just as useful as the learning done during physical practice—"learning improves often as much and sometimes more during rest (memory consolidation and/or insight generation processes) than during a practice session itself."[114] Resting gives our brain the time it needs to consolidate what it has just learnt and to avoid the information jumble that it might otherwise get itself into. To "only bite off what you can chew" remains wise advice.

Furthermore, resting allows the brain to enter *daydreaming mode*. This is its most habitual mode and is "where connections occur and creativity happens."[115] The regular daily walks that Beethoven, Tchaikovsky, Mahler, Satie and Britten took, amongst others, might be considered deliberate attempts to allow for this creative daydreaming mode to be exercised. Pianists, as interpreters, a sure to benefit from this creative mode of the mind too.

The ultimate rest, sleep, should also be considered as an important factor in the acquisition of motor skills. During sleep, synaptic pruning occurs, where weaker synapses are left to wither away, and the more present short-term memories are repeated and consolidated into longer-term memories.[116] Somewhat fantastically, sleep *improves* motor skills too[117]—to the extent that, according to one study, "a night of sleep results in a 20% increase in motor speed without loss of accuracy."[118] The importance of the rest phase in learning has been recognized by experienced pianists:

- "I don't really get the results of what I practice today, the next day, or the next day, but probably from one to two weeks later."—Jorge Bolet[119]
- "The pieces I forget first [are those] when I don't allow things to sink in."—Misha Dichter[120]
- "Learn a piece as best you can up to a certain point, and then drop it [...] in that period of having been dropped, it will have matured."—Leon Fleisher[121]

- *Learn properly or do not learn at all.*

Learning bad motor habits is highly counterproductive and should be avoided at all times. It costs us (theoretically) at least two units of practice time for the price of one: firstly, time is spent learning the skill badly; and secondly, the re-learning of the skill properly will be more time consuming than if it had been learned properly the first time (because of it having to compete with the previously learned neuro-motor pathways. The formidable effort required to re-learn entrenched, unwanted pianistic movements, especially those that have been emotionalized, is well recognized by performers and scientists:

> *"The [biological] cost of unlearning may be much higher than learning"*[122] because *"the unlearning of bad habits is just the spawning of a new, competing memory, not erasure of the existing memory"*[123] and *"once a slow motor*

memory has been established, large performance errors [i.e., learning to play it in different ways] may not be able to change it."[124]

The discipline of elite sportspeople to redress motor errors immediately upon their recognition ought to inspire us to do the same. Famed golfer, Tiger Woods knew the drill. At his peak, his coach remarked: "He makes mistakes, but then you watch him go about his business and he doesn't make that mistake twice."[125] Interestingly, practicing with a degree of discipline not only prevents bad motor habits from being learned but improves the success of the learning itself, where "movement corrections driven by a failure to successfully achieve movement goals underpin motor memories."[126] To strive, err, and correct, appears to be a time-proven recipe for effective learning.

- *Focus your attention, don't dilute it.*

Finally, despite the sense of needing to attend to a multitude of tasks during any practice session, at any single moment, our minds can *focus on only one thing at a time*. Whether it be learning notes, improving biomechanics, experimenting with phrasing or any other musical concept, we should engage with it, and with it alone. It is neurophysiologically impossible to divide our attention between two tasks simultaneously, and we should ignore the temptation to try. The neuroscientist Ramachandran states clearly: "Even though you've got one hundred billion nerve cells, you can't have two overlapping patterns [...] there is a bottleneck of attention. You can only allocate your attentional resources to one thing at a time."[127]

Although we can shift our attention rapidly between two points of interest (giving us the impression that we are focusing on two things at once), this only divides our attention between them and dilutes the learning that could have otherwise occurred if we had remained intently focused on each task individually. During teaching sessions, this rule is frequently breached by teachers who (unwittingly) might demand of a student to improve two aspects of their playing simultaneously during a single repetition of a passage—e.g., like experimenting with *rubato* while trying to optimize thumb movements. It doesn't work. Neither aspect gets learned properly and the quality of our learning is made worse. We can alternate between two points of attention, but not superimpose them.

> When practicing, our "attention baton" needs to be passed from one specific pianistic problem to the next. The mind cannot superimpose two points of attention. Focusing on one problem at a time is the only way to get to the bottom of each of our pianistic problems.

PROCESS OPTIMIZATION

"We are what we repeatedly do. Excellence, then, is not an act but a habit"[128]—Aristotle

Next, we look at the *process* of practicing and how it can be improved to optimize pianism. Process optimization is big business in most areas of human professional endeavor where consistent, high-quantity and high-quality outputs are required of the activity (e.g., sports, science, medicine, business, finance, industry, marketing, etc.)

The topic is generally neglected in piano pedagogy, where advice on *how to play like an expert* is readily available but advice on *how to increase the chances of how to play like an expert* is scarce. The difference between the two, however, in terms of outcomes, may be considerable. This is why: anybody can offer advice about how to get from learning point A to learning point B with respect to any aspect of pianism, but knowing how to get from A to B *the quickest, the easiest* and *the safest*, is a very different type of advice. It is the advice that we want, because if we can get to B quickly, we can then advance to C, and then to D, and so on, quickly, though the endless chain of skill acquisition that we, eventually, call *expertise*.

Admittedly, playing the piano is not a skills acquisition race, but *if* we are aiming for the letter Z with our pianism (virtuosic pianism) and *if* our career goals depend on it, to accumulate pianistic skills quickly and reliably over shorter periods of time may be the deciding factor in whether we can learn to play difficult pieces *at all*, with *artistic depth*, at *short notice* or *without injury*. These are necessary requirements of being a professional pianist.

The idea of process optimization may rub some pianists the wrong way, with its (objective) percepts of logic, maths and reasoning conflicting with the (subjective) artistic percepts of creativity, freedom and emotions. But, as Part I explained, our negatively charged emotional responses to percept-reality-mismatched information do not always work in our favor.

It is hypocritical too to deny the importance of an objective approach to optimizing pianism given that the daily lives of pianists are constantly and consistently being assessed using *objective* criteria in lessons, exams, master classes and competitions: e.g., mechanical elements ("his fingers were too-curled"); mental elements ("she lost points because of her memory slips"); and musical elements ("his playing didn't have any rhythmic energy")—the very objective problems that an optimized process of practicing is addressing.

To a career-driven pianist, increasing the chances of improving *needs* to matter. Practice time is always limited and high-quality outcomes are always expected. The use of time *is* important. Time *must* be spent on tasks that provide us with gains and limit our losses, and to repeat such tasks with (appropriate) frequency.

Leverage and Compensation Errors

Objectively, our pianism can be thought of as a system of interconnecting parts. Our ideas go into it, and via its internal workings, something involving movement and sound comes out of it. If it is done well, music may result. This concept is described by the 3Ms of Pianism (see chapter 5) where our central beliefs about pianism will feed into its realities: its Mechanical, Mental and Musical outputs.

For any system to work, *each part* must work, and *each connection* between each part must work. If there is a weak part, the overall performance of the system will suffer—like having a flat tyre on a car. If there is a weak connection, the overall performance of the system will also suffer—like not knowing how to change gears.

In piano playing, the parts of our system that matter are our 3Ms—our Musical ideas, our Mechanical ability to produce them, and our Mental capacity to coordinate them. Note how "playing Bartok etudes" is *not* part of the system. "Winning a competition" is *not* a part. Nor is "studying with someone famous." Though engaging in such activities might help us, none of them *necessarily* improve our Ms, which, when all is said and done, is all that matters, pianistically speaking.

Assessing your pianism using the 3M triangle is a quick and easy way to find out which parts of your system are not working well. Errors must be sought and corrected, because despite the strengths in your pianism, any weaknesses may negatively affect the overall performance. And this negative impact may be fourfold:

#1—If a specific aspect doesn't work, that aspect of your playing will be weak.
#2—If a specific aspect doesn't work, other aspects of your playing that depend on it may not work either.
#3—If a specific aspect doesn't work, other parts of your system may be burdened by having to take on an extra role.
#4—If a specific aspect doesn't work, the burden taken on by other parts of your system may not be well suited to taking on that role and may suffer.

The theory may sound complicated, but the reality isn't. Imagine the following example:

- Primary Error = 5th finger touch angle is poor (Mechanical problem)

    #1 → momentum transfer into the key is less. (Mechanical error)
    #2 → volume of 5th finger is too soft. (Musical compromise)
    #3 → the small muscles of the 5th finger have to work harder to create more momentum for the keystroke. (Mechanical compensation)
    #4 → the small joints of the 5th finger and the small muscles controlling them become injured from having the burden of too much work. (further Mechanical compromise)

In this example, the pianist gets four problems for the price of one. It is an example of *negative leverage*. In piano playing we want to *benefit* from leverage—where extra output (pianism) is gained for no added effort (practice)—not suffer from it. Negative leverage acts like a disease. It significantly burdens the overall performance of our pianism for having only one small thing wrong with it.

Consider the following list of primary errors and the secondary compensation errors that could result from them:

- Poor keystroke coordination . . .

    → tight wrist, increased height of finger lift, over-practice to make up for it, limited technical possibilities, avoidance of certain repertoire.

- Poor key control when playing softly . . .

    → overuse of the *una corda* pedal to ensure reliability of soft volumes.

- Poor articulation and key control . . .

    → overuse of the sustain pedal to cover it up, avoidance of certain repertoire.

- Poor understanding of inertia and movement arcs . . .

    → overuse of arm muscles, tightness, less key control, inappropriate slower speeds.

- Insecurity with memory . . .

    → over-repeatedly practicing the same passage to try to "secure" it to memory.

- Poor anticipatory planning…

    → slower speeds, less accuracy, less sound control, poorer memory.

    Consider how much negative leverage exists in your pianism and how many of your pianistic issues would disappear if you could diagnose and treat the primary error.

Fix Your Weaknesses—Leverage Your Practice in Your Favor

By addressing your Beliefs, your 3 Ms and your Process, you should very quickly be able to come up with two lists of "things to improve"—things you *need* to improve and things you *want* to improve. Your daily practice needs to address these lists. It is where the easy rewards are made in improving your pianism.

In addition to your own lists, you should think to add some of the following tasks to it too:

- *Beliefs*: believing that you can be amazing; letting go of any previous beliefs that prevent you from being able to be amazing; adopting new beliefs that allow you to improve the realities of your 3 Ms.
- *Music*: being creative and original; being inspired with purpose; exploiting any single element of the music to see what its maximal musical effect could be; exploiting elements of the music which you tend to neglect.
- *Mental*: concentrating intensely on the sounds you want to make and the sounds you actually make; mentally rehearsing your ideal music; mentally rehearsing your ideal movements.
- *Mechanics*: eliminating inefficiencies in your postures, finger-hand positions and movements; avoiding any extreme joint positions; avoiding the repetition of physical movements until you have a musical purpose for them.
- *Process*: having a practice strategy that improves strengths and weaknesses; scheduling and distributing your practice time better to maximize productivity; immediately correcting the primary source of errors.

Incremental Gains and Compound Interest

Another principle that underlies system performance improvement, is to appreciate that large improvements do not need to arise from singular, large gains, but can (and probably should) arise from higher frequency, smaller gains across the many subcomponents of the system. Professional sportspeople are experts at exploiting this principle in their daily practice: "those little small steps and those little small things can add up to massive things"[129] (Michael Phelps, Olympic swimming champion); "focus on progression," "compound the improvements," and improvement of performance by "the aggregation of marginal gains"[130] (Sir Dave Brailsford, coach of the uber-successful British Cycling team between 2003–14); "I'm not out there sweating for three hours every day just to find out what it feels like to sweat"[131] (Michael Jordan, legendary basketball player).

The strategy of improving skills *frequently* and *step-by-step* works because of the physiological reasons that underlie it: each increment of improvement is biologically achievable (because the brain already has a neural scaffolding upon which to add the new information) and, secondly, because of the regularity of the improvements, each improvement is more likely to not be forgotten. Mathematically, small, frequent gains result in exponentially large gains over time. (For example, improving something 1 percent daily, each day, for 365 days leads to a 3778 percent improvement. Doing the opposite, leads to a 97.5 percent loss.)

Although such percentages are mathematical (and won't translate into physiological gains in the same way), it does shows us that small, regular improvements can result in significant performance gains relatively quickly. Obviously, compounding gains—not losses—is the biological goal of our practice. Interestingly, the principle of eliminating the compounding of losses (errors) is at the forefront of other disciplines too, for example, in medicine, it is *primum non nocere*—"first, do no harm" (from the Hippocratic Oath); in finance, "first, don't lose [money]"[132] (Warren Buffett); and, amusingly, in architecture, "You can use an eraser on the drafting table or a sledgehammer on the construction site."[133] (attr. Frank Lloyd Wright). Small errors become big errors very quickly when they are repeated frequently.

Strategically, because of the enormous effect that it has on pianistic outcomes, the process of practicing ought to be seen as a tool in its own right to help improve performance. Michael Phelps focused his training sessions around "what I needed to do" and improve the "small little things [that made it work]."[134] We could follow his lead. Phelps created his own daily "to do" lists. He exploited the mathematical principles of compound interest and leverage by putting his efforts into improving what he most needed to improve. He was as engaged with *improving the process* of improvement just as he was with improving the "3 Ms" of his swimming. He was constantly improving the average of his previous learnings.[135]

The "small little things" that make your pianism work will be found in your 3 Ms. If your fingers don't move properly (Mechanics), they don't know where they should be moving (Mental skills), or don't produce anything interesting when they move (Music), there are a lot of "small little things" to put onto your to-do list.

Reward-to-Risk Ratios

Shifting the balance of our efforts toward actions that are *more useful* ("reward") rather than *less useful* ("risk") is another way of thinking about process optimization. In mathematical terms, this could be called improving the *reward-to-risk ratio* of our actions. Logically, to improve our practice, we should be looking to improve the ratios of all our actions. However, because we are not trained to think in terms of reward and risk, it is highly unlikely that we, or our teachers, are ever fully aware of the reward-to-risk ratios of the actions that we participate in. Risks tend to be hidden from our thinking (recall Part I).

As a way of understanding the reward-to-risk ratios of our actions, it can be useful to separate rewards and risks into individual categories. Doing this can help to expose the quality, or lack thereof, of the decisions that we make. Table 7.2 shows how this could be done.

Analyzing our actions this way will not necessarily tell us definitely whether the reward-to-risk ratio of that action is in our favor, but it will give us a better understanding of whether an action is worth repeating, how it could be improved, and what its outcomes might be if repeated many times. This, over the long term will count for a lot.

Table 7.1. Rewards and Risks of Your Pianistic Decisions

REWARD:	RISK:
Improved Pianism	Time spent
Improved Musical outcome	Effort exerted
Improved Mechanical outcome	Muscle fatigue
Improved Mental outcome	Injury risk, pain, or injury
Pleasure and Enjoyment	Psychological fatigue and stress
Endorsement (career, recognition, awards, etc.)	Money spent (on teachers, courses, institutions, doctors, etc.)

Table 7.2. Discovering the Reward-to-Risk Ratio of Pianistic Actions

Action: *Regularly practicing eight hours per day*	
Possible Rewards:	• Pianism improves more than if only practicing four hours. • Reach short-term and long-term pianistic goals earlier. • Learn more repertoire. • Eight hours of practicing enjoyment per day instead of just four.
Possible Risks:	• Regularly practicing eight hours per day is a lot—is it all translating itself into pianistic gains? Could the same outcomes be achieved with less practice? • Eight hours per day of physical practice is likely to push muscles, ligaments and joints beyond their physiological adaptable limits, thus making injury risk very high. • Mental fatigue, motivation problems and burnout are likely. • Eight hours of piano practice means eight hours of *not* doing something else—something that might be equally beneficial (or enjoyable) to your career or life in general.
Reflection and Summary:	• Probably, eight hours of physical practice is unnecessary and unhelpful. • Probably, devoting some time to mental practice could help. • Probably, the pain in your wrist may ease if you reduce the hours of physical work. • Probably, your learning speed (and recall) would improve if you divided the eight hours into different activities, shorter in duration, though more frequent. • Probably, if you practiced less hours, you could sustain motivation and attention better over the long term.
Conclusion:	• The reward-to-risk ratio of this action could probably be easily improved by applying some science: by inserting more rest periods, more mental practice and by maintaining better concentration during the periods of physical practice.

Do You Gamble with Your Pianism?

Consider the following thought experiment. You are asked to reflect on your productivity. Mathematically, productivity is the result of increasing the frequency and amount of *what you want to occur* (gain, reward) while minimizing the frequency and amount of *what you don't want to occur* (loss, risk).

> *What does pianistic productivity look like for you? What do you want your pianism to produce? What don't you want it to produce?*

Although, as pianists, we may not consider ourselves as gamblers, we are still subjected to the same rules as gamblers. For example, if you choose to practice Hanon exercises for 15 minutes a day, you have "bought" the idea that *that* 15 minutes spent will offer a better reward:risk profile than spending it on something else. But is it? What do you know about its rewards and what do you know about its risks? Are the odds in your favor? If "15 minutes per day of Hanon" were a pianistic trade, would you want to bet on it repeatedly?

What if you had practiced 15 minutes of a Bach Prelude instead? Would that be a better reward:risk transaction relative to what you are wanting to produce? Or, what if you divided the 15 minutes into 5 minutes of Bach, 5 minutes of Chopin, and 5 minutes of Liszt? Or 5 minutes of Bartok, 5 minutes of Ligeti, and 5 minutes of Stockhausen? Or 5 minutes of singing, 5 minutes of improvisation, and 5 minutes of feeling joyful while playing? And why 15 minutes? Why not 10 minutes, or 20, or some other quantity? Have you tested any of them?

To the point: why have you invested in the activity *at all*? What was it that you hoped to achieve with the 15 minutes of Hanon? Could you have made a better pianistic trade for the same cost of that 15 minutes of time—like targeting some of the tasks on your "3M to-do" list?

We trade "pianistic ideas" (using our time, effort and money) in the hope that they will go up in value (better pianism, enjoyment, career success) but with the risk that they may fall in value (worse pianism, injury and unhappiness).

Consider the reward-to-risk ratios *for you*, with *your goals*, and *your level of pianism* of the following actions:

- practicing lots of scales and exercises?
- paying lots of money to learn from a famous teacher?
- having a clear musical image in your head of each phrase of the piece before you play it?
- spending half your practice time on mental practice?
- entering a competition?
- buying an expensive piano?
- learning how to improvise?
- insisting on perfect touch mechanics in difficult passages?
- playing with a slouched posture?

- performing Scriabin's Etude in 9ths?
- using meditation, self-hypnosis and visualization techniques to mentalize ideal performance scenarios?
- understanding how singers vary airspeed when singing?
- warming up before a performance?
- reducing your amount of daily practice?
- sharing a drink with the festival's artistic director?
- playing through pain?
- wearing red socks in your Carnegie Hall concert?
- reading this book?

NOTES

1. Ericsson, Anders. *Peak: Secrets from the New Science of Expertise*. Boston: Houghton Mifflin Harcourt, 2016.

2. Altenmüller, Eckart, Jürg Kesselring, and Mario Wiesendanger. *Music, Motor Control and the Brain*. Oxford: Oxford University Press, 2006, 41.

3. Gould, Glenn. 2012. *The Glenn Gould Collection: Johannes Brahms Ballades, Rhapsodies & Intermezzi*. CD booklet. Sony Music Entertainment Classical.

4. Simonsmeier, B. A., et al (2021). Keller, P.E. (2012). Zatorre, R., Chen, J., & Penhune, V. (2007). Also, *The Mindful Musician* by Cornett (2019) contains useful, practical information about the topic for musicians.

5. Anecdotally, too, it would seem he was correct – his performing repertoire was enormous. See: Gieseking, Walter, and Karl Leimer. *Piano Technique*. 1932. Reprint, New York: Dover Publications, 1972.

6. Altenmüller, Eckart, Jürg Kesselring, and Mario Wiesendanger. *Music, Motor Control and the Brain*. Oxford: Oxford University Press, 2006, 173–88.

7. Altenmüller, Eckart, Jürg Kesselring, and Mario Wiesendanger. *Music, Motor Control and the Brain*. Oxford: Oxford University Press, 2006, 176.

8. Altenmüller, Eckart, Jürg Kesselring, and Mario Wiesendanger. *Music, Motor Control and the Brain*. Oxford: Oxford University Press, 2006, 39.

9. Stachó, László. "Mental Virtuosity: A New Theory of Performers' Attentional Processes and Strategies." *Musicae Scientiae* 22, no. 4 (November 13, 2018): 539–57. doi:https://doi.org/10.1177/1029864918798415.

10. Stephan, Marianne A, Carlotta Lega, and Virginia B Penhune. "Auditory Prediction Cues Motor Preparation in the Absence of Movements." *NeuroImage* 174 (July 1, 2018): 288–96. doi:https://doi.org/10.1016/j.neuroimage.2018.03.044.

11. Gieseking, Walter, and Karl Leimer. *Piano Technique*. 1932. Reprint, New York: Dover Publications, 1972.

12. Chaffin, Roger, Gabriela Imreh, and Mary E Crawford. *Practicing Perfection*. Mahwah, NJ: Lawrence Erlbaum, 2002, 611.

13. Ranganathan, Vinoth K., Vlodek Siemionow, Jing Z. Liu, Vinod Sahgal, and Guang H. Yue. "From Mental Power to Muscle Power—Gaining Strength by Using the Mind." *Neuropsychologia* 42, no. 7 (2004): 944–56. doi:https://doi.org/10.1016/j.neuropsychologia.2003.11.018;

Rieger, Martina, Shaun G. Boe, Tony, Victoria, and Stephan F. Dahm. "A Theoretical Perspective on Action Consequences in Action Imagery: Internal Prediction as an Essential Mechanism to Detect Errors." *Psychological Research* 88 (March 24, 2023). doi:https://doi.org/10.1007/s00426-023-01812-0.

14. Gallo, Carmine. "3 Daily Habits of Peak Performers, according to Michael Phelps' Coach." *Forbes*, August 8, 2016. http://www.forbes.com/sites/carminegallo/2016/05/24/3-daily-habits-of-peak-performers-according-to-michael-phelps-coach/.

15. Williamon, Aaron. *Musical Excellence: Strategies and Techniques to Enhance Performance*. Oxford: Oxford University Press, 2004, 227. A guide to some evidence-based strategies for mental rehearsal can be found in the same book, pp. 221–45.

16. See chapter 4 on Learned Movement in: Helding, Lynn. *The Musician's Mind: Teaching, Learning, and Performance in the Age of Brain Science*. Lanham, MD: Rowman & Littlefield, 2020.

17. Lipatti, Dinu. "Letter from Dinu Lipatti to a Student." *Musicandhealth.co.uk*, 2024. https://www.musicandhealth.co.uk/articles/Lipatti.html.

18. Stachó, László. "Mental Virtuosity: A New Theory of Performers' Attentional Processes and Strategies." *Musicae Scientiae* 22, no. 4 (November 13, 2018): 539–57. doi:https://doi.org/10.1177/1029864918798415, 552.

19. "the very existence of anticipatory imagery suggests that retrieving stored sequences of any kind involves predictive readout of upcoming information before the actual sensorimotor event." Leaver, A. M., J. Van Lare, B. Zielinski, A. R. Halpern, and J. P. Rauschecker. "Brain Activation during Anticipation of Sound Sequences." *Journal of Neuroscience* 29, no. 8 (February 25, 2009): 2477–85. doi:https://doi.org/10.1523/jneurosci.4921-08.2009.

20. For exceptional speeds of virtuosity to occur, exceptional speeds of memory retrieval are required. See: Stachó, László. "Mental Virtuosity: A New Theory of Performers' Attentional Processes and Strategies." *Musicae Scientiae* 22, no. 4 (November 13, 2018): 539–57. doi:https://doi.org/10.1177/1029864918798415.

21. Keller, Peter E. "Mental Imagery in Music Performance: Underlying Mechanisms and Potential Benefits." *Annals of the New York Academy of Sciences* 1252, no. 1 (April 2012): 206–13. doi:https://doi.org/10.1111/j.1749-6632.2011.06439.x.

22. Rosenbaum, David A. *Human Motor Control*. Academic Press, 2016.

23. Bernardi, Nicolò F., Matteo De Buglio, Pietro D. Trimarchi, Alfonso Chielli, and Emanuela Bricolo. "Mental Practice Promotes Motor Anticipation: Evidence from Skilled Music Performance." *Frontiers in Human Neuroscience* 7 (2013). doi:https://doi.org/10.3389/fnhum.2013.00451.

24. Leaver, A. M., J. Van Lare, B. Zielinski, A. R. Halpern, and J. P. Rauschecker. "Brain Activation during Anticipation of Sound Sequences." *Journal of*

Neuroscience 29, no. 8 (February 25, 2009): 2477–85. doi:https://doi.org/10.1523/jneurosci.4921-08.2009.

25. Frank, Cornelia, William M. Land, Carmen Popp, and Thomas Schack. "Mental Representation and Mental Practice: Experimental Investigation on the Functional Links between Motor Memory and Motor Imagery." Edited by Cosimo Urgesi. *PLoS ONE* 9, no. 4 (April 17, 2014): e95175. doi:https://doi.org/10.1371/journal.pone.0095175.

26. "mental practice promotes the cognitive adaptation process during motor learning." See: Frank, Cornelia, William M. Land, Carmen Popp, and Thomas Schack. "Mental Representation and Mental Practice: Experimental Investigation on the Functional Links between Motor Memory and Motor Imagery." Edited by Cosimo Urgesi. *PLoS ONE* 9, no. 4 (April 17, 2014): e95175. doi:https://doi.org/10.1371/journal.pone.0095175.

27. "In his own words: his secrets"—quoted in *Golf Digest*, 1972. Taken from: https://www.golfdigest.com/story/jack-nicklaus-secrets,

28. Simonsmeier, Bianca A., Cornelia Frank, Hanspeter Gubelmann, and Michael Schneider. "The Effects of Motor Imagery Training on Performance and Mental Representation of 7- to 15-Year-Old Gymnasts of Different Levels of Expertise." *Sport, Exercise, and Performance Psychology* 7, no. 2 (May 2018): 155–68. doi:https://doi.org/10.1037/spy0000117.

29. Lappi, Otto. "The Racer's Mind—How Core Perceptual-Cognitive Expertise Is Reflected in Deliberate Practice Procedures in Professional Motorsport." *Frontiers in Psychology* 9 (August 13, 2018). doi:https://doi.org/10.3389/fpsyg.2018.01294.

30. Morris, Tony, Michael Spittle, and Anthony P. Watt. *Imagery in Sport*. Champaign, Ill.: Human Kinetics, 2005.

31. Lappi, Otto. "The Racer's Mind—How Core Perceptual-Cognitive Expertise Is Reflected in Deliberate Practice Procedures in Professional Motorsport." *Frontiers in Psychology* 9 (August 13, 2018). doi:https://doi.org/10.3389/fpsyg.2018.01294. Interestingly, he points out that accidents in racing tend to occur when multi-sensory cues that the driver normally expect to have during a race are different or absent – like driving in unusual weather conditions, or when driving a car with a slightly different set up. Respectively, pianists are no different.

32. As the musicologist Gary McPherson has shown, one of the main factors that separates the skill development of students is their ability to recognize mistakes. This correlates directly to how well defined their mental representations were of the pieces in the first place. As inexperienced pianists have poorly formed mental images of what they are aiming for, their practice tends to be more aim-less and, therefore, less productive. See Ericsson, Anders. *Peak: Secrets from the New Science of Expertise*. Boston: Houghton Mifflin Harcourt, 2016, 83.

33. Zull, James E. "Key Aspects of How the Brain Learns." *New Directions for Adult and Continuing Education* 2006, no. 110 (2006): 3–9. doi:https://doi.org/10.1002/ace.213, 4.

34. Ericsson, Anders. *Peak: Secrets from the New Science of Expertise*. Boston: Houghton Mifflin Harcourt, 2016.

35. Altenmüller, Eckart, and Shinichi Furuya. "Brain Plasticity and the Concept of Metaplasticity in Skilled Musicians." *Advances in Experimental Medicine and Biology*, 2016, 197–208. doi:https://doi.org/10.1007/978-3-319-47313-0_11.

36. Zull, James E. "Key Aspects of How the Brain Learns." *New Directions for Adult and Continuing Education* 2006, no. 110 (2006): 3–9. doi:https://doi.org/10.1002/ace.213, 4.

37. Yin, Henry H., Shweta Prasad Mulcare, Monica R. F. Hilário, Emily Clouse, Terrell Holloway, Margaret I. Davis, Anita C. Hansson, David M. Lovinger, and Rui M. Costa. "Dynamic Reorganization of Striatal Circuits during the Acquisition and Consolidation of a Skill." *Nature Neuroscience* 12, no. 3 (February 8, 2009): 333–41. doi:https://doi.org/10.1038/nn.2261.

38. Altenmüller, Eckart, Jürg Kesselring, and Mario Wiesendanger. *Music, Motor Control and the Brain*. Oxford: Oxford University Press, 2006, 297.

39. "safeguards must therefore be in place to prevent the saturation of LTP or LTD, which could ultimately compromise the ability of networks to discriminate events and store information." In: Abraham, Wickliffe C. "Metaplasticity: Tuning Synapses and Networks for Plasticity." *Nature Reviews Neuroscience* 9, no. 5 (May 2008): 387–87. doi:https://doi.org/10.1038/nrn2356.

40. Owens, Melinda T., and Kimberly D. Tanner. "Teaching as Brain Changing: Exploring Connections between Neuroscience and Innovative Teaching." *CBE—Life Sciences Education* 16, no. 2 (June 2017): fe2. doi:https://doi.org/10.1187/cbe.17-01-0005.

41. Williamon and Egner identify this feature in their Skilled Memory Theory – that while existing knowledge structures are used to store new information, the ability to encode new information and retrieve old information from these structures improves with practice. See: Altenmüller, Eckart, Jürg Kesselring, and Mario Wiesendanger. *Music, Motor Control and the Brain*. Oxford: Oxford University Press, 2006, 32–33.

42. "early learning experiences in skill acquisition will raise scaffolding for later expertise in this very skill." From: Altenmüller, Eckart, and Shinichi Furuya. "Brain Plasticity and the Concept of Metaplasticity in Skilled Musicians." *Advances in Experimental Medicine and Biology*, 2016, 197–208. doi:https://doi.org/10.1007/978-3-319-47313-0_11.

43. "Emotion is the foundation of learning. The chemicals of emotion act by modifying the strength and contribution of each part of the learning cycle." Zull, James E. "Key Aspects of How the Brain Learns." *New Directions for Adult and Continuing Education* 2006, no. 110 (2006): 3–9. doi:https://doi.org/10.1002/ace.213.

44. "the fixation of incorrect motor programs happens especially intensely under the influence of anxiety and stress hormones." Altenmüller, Eckart, Jürg Kesselring, and Mario Wiesendanger. *Music, Motor Control and the Brain*. Oxford: Oxford University Press, 2006, 262.

45. Altenmüller, Eckart, and Shinichi Furuya. "Brain Plasticity and the Concept of Metaplasticity in Skilled Musicians." *Advances in Experimental Medicine and Biology*, 2016, 197–208. doi:https://doi.org/10.1007/978-3-319-47313-0_11.

46. The scaffolding concept helps to explain other concepts like *associative learning* and *associative memory*. See: Altenmüller, Eckart, Jürg Kesselring, and Mario Wiesendanger. *Music, Motor Control and the Brain*. Oxford: Oxford University Press, 2006.

47. This large cross-networking of nerves probably explains the bigger than usual *corpus callosum* in musicians—a central nerve highway of the brain that connects millions of nerves track between the lobes and hemispheres. See: Schlaug, G. "Increased Corpus Callosum Size in Musicians." *Neuropsychologia* 33, no. 8 (August 1995): 1047–55. doi:https://doi.org/10.1016/0028-3932(95)00045-5; Hyde, K. L., J. Lerch, A. Norton, M. Forgeard, E. Winner, A. C. Evans, and G. Schlaug. "Musical Training Shapes Structural Brain Development." *Journal of Neuroscience* 29, no. 10 (March 11, 2009): 3019–25. doi:https://doi.org/10.1523/jneurosci.5118-08.2009.

48. Altenmüller, Eckart, and Shinichi Furuya. "Brain Plasticity and the Concept of Metaplasticity in Skilled Musicians." *Advances in Experimental Medicine and Biology*, 2016, 197–208. doi:https://doi.org/10.1007/978-3-319-47313-0_11.

49. Chaffin, Roger, Gabriela Imreh, and Mary E Crawford. *Practicing Perfection*. Mahwah, NJ: Lawrence Erlbaum, 2002, 52.

50. Chaffin, Roger, Gabriela Imreh, and Mary E Crawford. *Practicing Perfection*. Mahwah, NJ: Lawrence Erlbaum, 2002, 38.

51. Chaffin, Roger, Gabriela Imreh, and Mary E Crawford. *Practicing Perfection*. Mahwah, NJ: Lawrence Erlbaum, 2002, 39 & 46.

52. Chaffin, Roger, Gabriela Imreh, and Mary E Crawford. *Practicing Perfection*. Mahwah, NJ: Lawrence Erlbaum, 2002, 55.

53. Chaffin, Roger, Gabriela Imreh, and Mary E Crawford. *Practicing Perfection*. Mahwah, NJ: Lawrence Erlbaum, 2002, 40.

54. Chaffin, Roger, Gabriela Imreh, and Mary E Crawford. *Practicing Perfection*. Mahwah, NJ: Lawrence Erlbaum, 2002, 45.

55. Chaffin, Roger, Gabriela Imreh, and Mary E Crawford. *Practicing Perfection*. Mahwah, NJ: Lawrence Erlbaum, 2002, 45.

56. Chaffin, Roger, Gabriela Imreh, and Mary E Crawford. *Practicing Perfection*. Mahwah, NJ: Lawrence Erlbaum, 2002, 46.

57. Chaffin, Roger, Gabriela Imreh, and Mary E Crawford. *Practicing Perfection*. Mahwah, NJ: Lawrence Erlbaum, 2002, 47.

58. Lister-Sink, Barbara. "Freeing the Caged Bird." DVD. *Wingbound International and Lister-Sink Institute & Foundation*, 2017. https://www.lister-sink.org/freeing-the-caged-bird/.

59. Even the word *emotion* suggests the link between expression and motion: from the Latin term *emovere*, meaning "to move out."

60. Pease, Allan, and Barbara Pease. *The Definitive Book of Body Language: How to Read Others' Attitudes by Their Gestures*. London: Orion, 2017.

61. Cooke, James Francis. *Great Pianists on Piano Playing: Godowsky, Hofmann, Lhévinne, Paderewski, and 24 Other Legendary Performers*. Mineola, NY: Dover Publications, 1999, 77.

62. Because the index finger is the finger that is most strongly linked to emotions, gesture and communication, it is often the finger that demonstrates the most

emotionalization. Strange, awkward and bizarre pianistic movements are commonly seen with this finger.

63. One not-to-be-named teacher (from a famous London institution) once admitted that he had stopped bothering trying to eliminate strongly emotionalized movements and gestures in his students. He conceded that getting students to calm down their bodies and control their unwanted movements in the practice room was rarely successful because the unwanted movements would invariably return when the emotional triggers returned during performances. The teacher failed to recognize that the solution was not to dampen their emotions in the practice room, but to re-wire them to maintain the same emotional intensity in the sound but not in the muscles.

64. The association between mental state and posture/movement style is well known to psychiatrists. It is assessed in the standard psychiatric Mental State Examination (MSE).

65. In chronic pain, the nerves, their receptors, the amount and types of neurotransmitters used, and the strengths of the different types of nerve connections that are made, undergo permanent adaptive changes. "Once in the CNS [Central Nervous System], transformation [of the nerve signal] is the process of biological modulation of the signal. Finally, perception is the interpretation of the signal by cognitive and emotional responses in the brain, which considers context, past experiences, and expectations." From: Christiansen, S, and S Cohen. "Chronic Pain: Pathophysiology and Mechanisms." In *Essentials of Interventional Techniques in Managing Chronic Pain*, 15–25. New York: Springer International Publishing, 2018.

66. Here, somatic education techniques like Feldenkrais method and Alexander technique may be useful to the extent that they encourage physiologically comfortable playing while promoting an awareness and correction of extraneous movements. Like eating vegetables, however, they won't turn you into a virtuoso – though they might help prevent you from *not* being able to become one. See: Jain, Sanjiv, Kristy Janssen, and Sharon DeCelle. "Alexander Technique and Feldenkrais Method: A Critical Overview." *Physical Medicine and Rehabilitation Clinics of North America* 15, no. 4 (November 2004): 811–25. doi:https://doi.org/10.1016/j.pmr.2004.04.005.

67. Brutus Alwaysmind. "Schiff on Bach." *YouTube*, April 10, 2021. https://www.youtube.com/watch?v=RxK1hY6vHNk.

68. Hambrick, David Z., Brooke N. Macnamara, Guillermo Campitelli, Fredrik Ullén, and Miriam A. Mosing. "Beyond born versus made: A new look at expertise." In *Psychology of Learning and Motivation*, vol. 64, pp. 1–55. San Diego, CA: Academic Press, 2016.

69. Ericsson, K Anders, ed. *The Road to Excellence: The Acquisition of Expert Performance in the Arts and Sciences, Sports, and Games*. New York: Psychology Press, 2013.

70. Quote from his student Kirnberger and the biographer Forkel. See: Forkel, Johann Nikolaus, and Charles Sanford Terry. *Johann Sebastian Bach, His Life; Art, and Work*. London: Constable, 1970.

71. Ericsson, Anders. *Peak: Secrets from the New Science of Expertise*. Boston: Houghton Mifflin Harcourt, 2016.

72. Ericsson, K. Anders. "Deliberate Practice and Acquisition of Expert Performance: A General Overview." *Academic Emergency Medicine* 15, no. 11 (November 2008): 988–94, 992.

73. Bjork, Robert A. *Metacognition*. Edited by Janet Metcalfe and Arthur P. Shimamura. Cambridge: The MIT Press, 1994. doi:https://doi.org/10.7551/mitpress/4561.001.0001.

74. Williamon, Aaron. *Musical Excellence: Strategies and Techniques to Enhance Performance*. Oxford: Oxford University Press, 2004, 31.

75. Altenmüller, Eckart, Jürg Kesselring, and Mario Wiesendanger. *Music, Motor Control and the Brain*. Oxford: Oxford University Press, 2006, 296.

76. As a bonus too, when learning tasks that are interesting and challenging, it "enhances long-term retention of motor skills." Kantak, Shailesh S., and Carolee J. Winstein. "Learning–Performance Distinction and Memory Processes for Motor Skills: A Focused Review and Perspective." *Behavioural Brain Research* 228, no. 1 (March 2012): 219–31. doi:https://doi.org/10.1016/j.bbr.2011.11.028.

77. Liszt, Franz. *The Collected Writings of Franz Liszt. Volume 2, Essays and Letters of a Travelling Batchelor of Music*. Edited and translated by Janita R. Hall-Swadley. Lanham, MD: Scarecrow Press, 2012, 22.

78. Williamon, Aaron. *Musical Excellence: Strategies and Techniques to Enhance Performance*. Oxford: Oxford University Press, 2004, 26.

79. Attributed to Henry Ford. See: Quoteinvestigator.com. "Whether You Believe You Can Do a Thing or Not, You Are Right – Quote Investigator," February 4, 2015. https://quoteinvestigator.com/2015/02/03/you-can/.

80. Schwartz, David J. *The Magic of Thinking Big*. 1959. Reprint, New York: Penguin, 2014.

81. Ng, Betsy. "The Neuroscience of Growth Mindset and Intrinsic Motivation." *Brain Sciences* 8, no. 2 (January 26, 2018): 20. doi:https://doi.org/10.3390/brainsci8020020.

82. Hambrick, David Z., Brooke N. Macnamara, Guillermo Campitelli, Fredrik Ullén, and Miriam A. Mosing. "Beyond born versus made: A new look at expertise." In *Psychology of Learning and Motivation*, vol. 64, pp. 1–55. San Diego, CA: Academic Press, 2016.

83. Dweck, Carol S., and Ellen L. Leggett. "A Social-Cognitive Approach to Motivation and Personality." *Psychological Review* 95, no. 2 (1988): 256–73. doi:https://doi.org/10.1037//0033-295x.95.2.256.

84. Wulf, Gabriele, and Rebecca Lewthwaite. "Optimizing Performance through Intrinsic Motivation and Attention for Learning: The OPTIMAL Theory of Motor Learning." *Psychonomic Bulletin & Review* 23, no. 5 (January 29, 2016): 1382–1414, 1384.

85. Hambrick, David Z., Brooke N. Macnamara, Guillermo Campitelli, Fredrik Ullén, and Miriam A. Mosing. "Beyond born versus made: A new look at expertise." In *Psychology of Learning and Motivation*, vol. 64, pp. 1–55. San Diego, CA: Academic Press, 2016.

86. Klavierplus. "Stephen Hough on Practice of Practising." *YouTube*, January 12, 2014. https://www.youtube.com/watch?v=VGBIgsoM4ng.

87. Ericsson, Anders. *Peak: Secrets from the New Science of Expertise*. Boston: Houghton Mifflin Harcourt, 2016.

88. "advanced performers should be presented with cases just above their current level of ability" – Ericsson, K. Anders. "Deliberate Practice and Acquisition of Expert Performance: A General Overview." *Academic Emergency Medicine* 15, no. 11 (November 2008): 988–94, 992.

89. Williamon, Aaron. *Musical Excellence: Strategies and Techniques to Enhance Performance*. Oxford: Oxford University Press, 2004, 26–29.

90. Jensen, Anthony K. "Goethe, Johann Wolfgang von | Internet Encyclopedia of Philosophy." *Internet Encyclopaedia of Philosophy*. Accessed September 29, 2024. https://iep.utm.edu/goethe/.

91. Ericsson, K. Anders, Ralf T. Krampe, and Clemens Tesch-Römer. "The Role of Deliberate Practice in the Acquisition of Expert Performance." *Psychological Review* 100, no. 3 (1993): 363–406. doi:https://doi.org/10.1037/0033-295X.100.3.363, 393–94.

92. Hambrick, David Z., Brooke N. Macnamara, Guillermo Campitelli, Fredrik Ullén, and Miriam A. Mosing. "Beyond born versus made: A new look at expertise." In *Psychology of learning and motivation*, vol. 64, pp. 1–55. San Diego, CA: Academic Press, 2016.

93. Newell, Karl M., Gottfried Mayer-Kress, S. Lee Hong, and Yeou-Teh Liu. "Adaptation and Learning: Characteristic Time Scales of Performance Dynamics." *Human Movement Science* 28, no. 6 (December 2009): 655–87. doi:https://doi.org/10.1016/j.humov.2009.07.001; Smith, Maurice, Ali Ghazizadeh, and Reza Shadmehr. "Interacting Adaptive Processes with Different Timescales Underlie Short-Term Motor Learning." Edited by James Ashe. *PLoS Biology* 4, no. 6 (May 23, 2006): e179. doi:https://doi.org/10.1371/journal.pbio.0040179.

94. Helding, Lynn. *The Musician's Mind: Teaching, Learning, and Performance in the Age of Brain Science*. Lanham, MD: Rowman & Littlefield, 2020.

95. "Chunking" is a skill that can be developed in its own right. It is easy to learn, and it helps music to be played (recalled) at very fast speeds. Practical tips can be found in: Iott, Sheryl. *Thinking and Playing Music: Intentional Strategies for Optimal Practice and Performance*. Lanham, MD: Rowman & Littlefield Publishers, 2021.

96. Helding, Lynn. *The Musician's Mind: Teaching, Learning, and Performance in the Age of Brain Science*. Lanham, MD: Rowman & Littlefield, 2020.

97. Svard, Lois. *The Musical Brain*. Oxford: Oxford University Press, 2023, 94.

98. Altenmüller, Eckart, Jürg Kesselring, and Mario Wiesendanger. *Music, Motor Control and the Brain*. Oxford: Oxford University Press, 2006, 296.

99. Svard, Lois. *The Musical Brain*. Oxford: Oxford University Press, 2023, 104; Lin, Chien-Ho Janice, Ming-Chang Chiang, Barbara J. Knowlton, Marco Iacoboni, Parima Udompholkul, and Allan D. Wu. "Interleaved Practice Enhances Skill Learning and the Functional Connectivity of Fronto-Parietal Networks." *Human Brain Mapping* 34, no. 7 (February 22, 2012): 1542–58. doi:https://doi.org/10.1002/hbm.22009.

100. Pascual-Leone, Alvaro. "The brain that plays music and is changed by it." *Annals of the New York Academy of Sciences* 930, no. 1 (2001): 315–329.

101. Krakauer, John W., Claude Ghez, and M. Felice Ghilardi. "Adaptation to visuomotor transformations: Consolidation, interference, and forgetting." *Journal of Neuroscience* 25, no. 2 (2005): 473–78; Yamada, Chiharu, Yoshihiro Itaguchi, and Kazuyoshi Fukuzawa. "Effects of the Amount of Practice and Time Interval between Practice Sessions on the Retention of Internal Models." Edited by Karsten Witt. *PLOS ONE* 14, no. 4 (April 16, 2019): e0215331. doi:https://doi.org/10.1371/journal.pone.0215331.

102. Yamada, Chiharu, Yoshihiro Itaguchi, and Kazuyoshi Fukuzawa. "Effects of the Amount of Practice and Time Interval between Practice Sessions on the Retention of Internal Models." Edited by Karsten Witt. *PLOS ONE* 14, no. 4 (April 16, 2019): e0215331. doi:https://doi.org/10.1371/journal.pone.0215331.

103. If the second task intrudes within the first few hours of having learned the first task, interference tends to be strong and the first task is less well remembered. See: Shadmehr, Reza, and Thomas Brashers-Krug. "Functional Stages in the Formation of Human Long-Term Motor Memory." *The Journal of Neuroscience* 17, no. 1 (January 1, 1997): 409–19. doi:https://doi.org/10.1523/jneurosci.17-01-00409.1997.

104. Self-reported, from lessons at the Australian National Academy of Music in 1999.

105. Helding, Lynn. *The Musician's Mind: Teaching, Learning, and Performance in the Age of Brain Science*. Lanham, MD: Rowman & Littlefield, 2020.

106. Kelley, Paul, and Terry Whatson. "Making Long-Term Memories in Minutes: A Spaced Learning Pattern from Memory Research in Education." *Frontiers in Human Neuroscience* 7 (2013). doi:https://doi.org/10.3389/fnhum.2013.00589.

107. Bangert, Marc, and Eckart Altenmüller. "Mapping Perception to Action in Piano Practice: A Longitudinal DC-EEG Study." *BMC Neuroscience* 4, no. 1 (2003): 26. doi:https://doi.org/10.1186/1471-2202-4-26, 148.

108. Dudai, Yadin. "The Neurobiology of Consolidations, Or, How Stable Is the Engram?" *Annual Review of Psychology* 55, no. 1 (February 2004): 51–86. doi:https://doi.org/10.1146/annurev.psych.55.090902.142050.

109. Yamada, Chiharu, Yoshihiro Itaguchi, and Kazuyoshi Fukuzawa. "Effects of the Amount of Practice and Time Interval between Practice Sessions on the Retention of Internal Models." Edited by Karsten Witt. *PLOS ONE* 14, no. 4 (April 16, 2019): e0215331. doi:https://doi.org/10.1371/journal.pone.0215331.

110. Ghanamah, Rafat, Hazar Eghbaria-Ghanamah, Avi Karni, and Esther Adi-Japha. "Too Little, Too Much: A Limited Range of Practice 'Doses' Is Best for Retaining Grapho-Motor Skill in Children." *Learning and Instruction* 69 (October 1, 2020): 101351. doi:https://doi.org/10.1016/j.learninstruc.2020.101351.

111. Altenmüller, Eckart, and Shinichi Furuya. "Apollos Gift and Curse: Making Music as a Model for Adaptive and Maladaptive Plasticity." *E-Neuroforum* 23, no. 2 (January 24, 2017). doi:https://doi.org/10.1515/nf-2016-a054.

112. Luft, A. R., M. Buitrago, T. Ringer, J. Dichgans, and J. Schulz. "Motor Skill Learning Depends on Protein Synthesis in Motor Cortex after Training." *Journal of Neuroscience* 24, no. 29 (July 21, 2004): 6515–20. doi:https://doi.org/10.1523/jneurosci.1034-04.2004.

113. Overduin, Simon A, Andrew G Richardson, Courtney E Lane, Emilio Bizzi, and Daniel Z Press. "Intermittent Practice Facilitates Stable Motor Memories." *The*

Journal of Neuroscience 26, no. 46 (November 15, 2006): 11888–92. doi:https://doi.org/10.1523/jneurosci.1320-06.2006.

114. Newell, Karl M., Gottfried Mayer-Kress, S. Lee Hong, and Yeou-Teh Liu. "Adaptation and Learning: Characteristic Time Scales of Performance Dynamics." *Human Movement Science* 28, no. 6 (December 2009): 655–87. doi:https://doi.org/10.1016/j.humov.2009.07.001.

115. See chapter, "How learning works" in: Helding, Lynn. *The Musician's Mind: Teaching, Learning, and Performance in the Age of Brain Science.* Lanham, MD: Rowman & Littlefield, 2020.

116. Walker, Matthew P., and Robert Stickgold. "Sleep-Dependent Learning and Memory Consolidation." *Neuron* 44, no. 1 (September 2004): 121–33. doi:https://doi.org/10.1016/j.neuron.2004.08.031.

117. Krakauer, John W., Claude Ghez, and M. Felice Ghilardi. "Adaptation to visuomotor transformations: consolidation, interference, and forgetting." *Journal of Neuroscience* 25, no. 2 (2005): 473-478.

118. Walker, Matthew P., and Robert Stickgold. "Sleep-Dependent Learning and Memory Consolidation." *Neuron* 44, no. 1 (September 2004): 121–33. doi:https://doi.org/10.1016/j.neuron.2004.08.031.

119. Chaffin, Roger, Gabriela Imreh, and Mary E Crawford. *Practicing Perfection.* Mahwah, NJ: Lawrence Erlbaum, 2002, 44.

120. Chaffin, Roger, Gabriela Imreh, and Mary E Crawford. *Practicing Perfection.* Mahwah, NJ: Lawrence Erlbaum, 2002, 53.

121. Chaffin, Roger, Gabriela Imreh, and Mary E Crawford. *Practicing Perfection.* Mahwah, NJ: Lawrence Erlbaum, 2002, 47.

122. Criscimagna-Hemminger, S. E., and R. Shadmehr. "Consolidation Patterns of Human Motor Memory." *Journal of Neuroscience* 28, no. 39 (September 24, 2008): 9610–18. doi:https://doi.org/10.1523/jneurosci.3071-08.2008.

123. Criscimagna-Hemminger, S. E., and R. Shadmehr. "Consolidation Patterns of Human Motor Memory." *Journal of Neuroscience* 28, no. 39 (September 24, 2008): 9610–18. doi:https://doi.org/10.1523/jneurosci.3071-08.2008.

124. Criscimagna-Hemminger, S. E., and R. Shadmehr. "Consolidation Patterns of Human Motor Memory." *Journal of Neuroscience* 28, no. 39 (September 24, 2008): 9610–18. doi:https://doi.org/10.1523/jneurosci.3071-08.2008.

125. Gregory, Sean. "Tiger at the Masters: An Ultimate Test of Toughness." *TIME.* nextgen, April 5, 2010. https://time.com/archive/6907036/tiger-at-the-masters-an-ultimate-test-of-toughness/.

126. Leow, Li-Ann, Welber Marinovic, Aymar de Rugy, and Timothy J Carroll. "Task Errors Drive Memories That Improve Sensorimotor Adaptation." *The Journal of Neuroscience* 40, no. 15 (February 6, 2020): 3075–88. doi:https://doi.org/10.1523/jneurosci.1506-19.2020.

127. Ramachandran in The Reith Lectures. See: BBC. "BBC Sounds – the Reith Lectures – Available Episodes," 2003. https://www.bbc.co.uk/sounds/series/p00ghvck.

128. Paraphrased by Will Durant. Cited in Soschner, Chris. "Aristotle Never Said, 'We Are What We Repeatedly Do. Excellence, Then, Is Not an Act, but a

Habit.'" *Illumination*, March 16, 2022. https://medium.com/illumination/aristotle-never-said-we-are-what-we-repeatedly-do-excellence-then-is-not-an-act-but-a-habit-215451129bed#:~:text=After%20quoting%20a%20phrase%20from.

129. Martin, Emmie. "23-Time Gold Medalist Michael Phelps Uses a Simple Trick to Stay Focused on His Goals." *CNBC*, January 1, 2019. https://www.cnbc.com/2018/12/20/michael-phelps-strategy-for-reaching-his-goals.html.

130. Harrell, Eben. "How 1% Performance Improvements Led to Olympic Gold." *Harvard Business Review*, October 30, 2015. https://hbr.org/2015/10/how-1-performance-improvements-led-to-olympic-gold.

131. Levin, Marissa. "The 1 Thing You Need for Success, according to Michael Jordan and Tony Robbins." *Inc.com*. Inc., July 24, 2017. https://www.inc.com/marissa-levin/tony-robbins-and-michael-jordan-attribute-their-su.html#:~:text=He%20ruminates%20on%20his%20own.

132. www.youtube.com. "Warren Buffett: 'Rule #1: Never Lose Money. Rule #2: Never Forget Rule #1.'" Grahamvalue, 2018. https://www.youtube.com/watch?v=vCpT-UmVf3g.

133. Quoteinvestigator.com. "The Architect's Most Effective Tools Are the Eraser in the Drafting Room and the Wrecking Bar on the Job – Quote Investigator," January 31, 2016. https://quoteinvestigator.com/2016/01/30/eraser/.

134. Martin, Emmie. "23-Time Gold Medalist Michael Phelps Uses a Simple Trick to Stay Focused on His Goals." *CNBC*, January 1, 2019. https://www.cnbc.com/2018/12/20/michael-phelps-strategy-for-reaching-his-goals.html

135. Mattar, Andrew, Mohammad Darainy, and David J Ostry. "Motor Learning and Its Sensory Effects: Time Course of Perceptual Change and Its Presence with Gradual Introduction of Load." *Journal of Neurophysiology* 109, no. 3 (February 1, 2013): 782–91. doi:https://doi.org/10.1152/jn.00734.2011.

Chapter 8

Musical Skills

"Imagination creates reality."[1]—Wagner

Regarding the Musical aspects of our playing, our beliefs about pianism should be encouraged to be as free and creative as possible. Unlike the Mechanical and Mental aspects of pianism, where the proper application of facts will help us to thrive, there is everything to gain and nothing to lose by dreaming of the impossible and believing in artistic outcomes that have not yet been imagined. This is what the science would say.

ARTISTIC VISION—MIND OVER MATTER

We practice to realize our artistic ideas. Whether our practice is dominated by mechanical or mental work, the reach of our artistic ideas sets the maximum possible endpoint for our pianism. Were mechanical excellence or mental skills our endpoints, then playing the piano would be classified as a sport or a memory competition—but it is not, unless we are in a cheap and dirty piano competition.

But we are not here for such competitions. We are here to express. And to share. And it is in the wordless abstractions of our minds that we feel our ideas and push them into reality through our touch. Realizing ideas are our goals—not mastering our double trills—and although such goals may seem ephemeral, they are what will shape our pianism long term, as our entire motor-sensory cognitive system *learns to try and realize them.*

It is only fitting, therefore, that we extend our creative abilities as much as possible to come up with new ideas, new feelings and new relationships between the elements available to us. This requires freeing ourselves from any restrictive doctrines that might be holding us back. We can learn from others how to do this, as the inspired Australian painter Di Bresciani describes how she feels her way toward the impossible with her brush until it becomes reality:

"How to discover a dancing blue, a shimmering? The pleasure of the paint on the surface begins to 'speak,' enticing the brush and the mind to follow—creating, evolving, emerging, what seems to be inevitable and yet impossible—the sky is dancing."[2]

We may learn from great pianists too, some of whom are well known to us:

- *"Follow freely the ideal you've set for yourself."*[3]—Frédéric Chopin
- *"[I want to] throw a lance as far as possible into the boundless realm of the future."*[4]—Franz Liszt
- *"When you play, never mind who listens to you."*[5]—Robert Schumann
- *"Es muss alles möglich zu machen sein"* [it must be possible].[6]—J. S. Bach
- *"Do you think I care for your lousy fiddle when the spirit is upon me?"*[7]—L. van Beethoven
- *"I want to risk, to dare. I want to be surprised by what comes out. I want to enjoy it more than the audience"*[8]—Artur Rubinstein
- *"In the realm of music, there are no limitations or boundaries. It is a world of infinite possibilities."*[9]—Anton Rubinstein
- *"I take terrible risks [...] I am never afraid to dare."*[10]—Vladimir Horowitz

Ambitious creative thinking drove the motor-skills development of Franz Liszt. His attitude to pianism is worth examining in detail. Consistently, throughout his life he chose to push the boundaries of his own musical thinking *and then* find ways of how to present them through the piano. Though, in his youth, he practiced much—"provided I don't go mad [from practicing], you will find in me an artist!"[11]—we repeatedly notice the tremendous artistic drive behind his work ethic. We ought to view his impressive technique *as a consequence* of his impressive thinking.

His masterclasses, given to some of the best young pianists of the day, never addressed mechanical issues, except in the most general sense, and his imploring of his students *to realize metaphors through sound* was as fervent as it was unrelenting.[12] Consistent with this approach to nurturing imagination, was his insistence that all pianists study composition too.[13]

The determined pursuit of musical ideas is a powerful driving force for our motor system to learn its skills. And, as the scientists (no less!) tell us, they are even more powerful than focusing on the motor system itself: "Instructions or feedback that promote an external focus of attention by directing concentration to a relevant and appropriate external goal [e.g., a musical idea] are reliably more helpful than internal attention focused on body parts or movement coordination."[14]

"Going for the music" rather than "going for the notes" should, therefore, be at the forefront of our thinking. Time spent improving the mechanical aspects of our techniques should never distract us from this primary goal.[15] Even Horowitz, the technical wizard that he was, pointed out the mistake of aiming for technical perfection rather than musical perfection—"perfection itself is imperfection." Pianists, teachers and musical educational systems might benefit from embracing similar attitudes, where the pursuit of interesting and meaningful musical outcomes is rewarded, and where "note perfection," whether present or not, is regarded as a by-product of the endeavor.

> *Do you think Horowitz's ability to shape melody, balance textures and capture your interest happened by accident? Do you think it was by chance that Michelangeli achieved such unreal levels of live-performance accuracy,[16] that Artur Rubinstein's playing was so personally warm and charming[17] or that Gould's interpretations were so stylistically subversive?[18] The pianism of these pianists was a by-product of them striving to achieve such individual musical goals.*

Listening—the Most Important Skill of All?

If realizing our musical ideas is our goal, then the importance of the skill of listening becomes glaringly obvious. Listening is more than just hearing. Listening seeks to understand as it evaluates whether sounds contain or don't contain certain information. Listening is the tool that marries your technique to your musical vision. As a musician, it is one of our greatest weapons. Artists in other domains also have their listening equivalents. As a chef, the equivalent is *taste*—the ability to discern through taste—as the great *sushi* chef Jiro Ono described:

> *"You need to develop a palate capable of discerning good and bad. Without good taste, you can't make good food. If your sense of taste is lower than that of the customers, how will you impress them? [...] If I had his [Joël Robuchon's] tongue and nose, I could probably make even better food."*[19]

Listening is a skill that one can never have too much of, for the better that we can detect the differences in sound (and meaning) between what we *want* to hear (the ideal) and what we *actually* hear (the reality), the better are our chances of realising them. Though such advice is not new in pedagogy, we cannot ignore its central importance in developing motor skills in musicians:

- *"Only trained ears are capable of noticing the fine inexactitudes and unevennesses, the eliminating of which, is necessary to a perfect technique."*[20] —Walter Gieseking
- *"Practice it at night in the dark] only then does the hearing function with all its sensitivity [...] you can really hear yourself, noticing every fault."*[21] —Frédéric Chopin
- *"think music, and nothing but music, all the time, down to the smallest detail even in technic"*[22] —Harold Bauer
- *"He is simply hearing every tone, knowing exactly what effect he wishes to produce and how to do it. In fact, he was practically two persons in one—the listener and the performer."*[23] —Amy Fay's observation of Franz Liszt.

Listening Boosts Your Learning Efficiency

Any pianist who "thinks big" (musically) *and* who "listens big" (for the music) is far more likely to achieve excellence than one who doesn't. This is not just pedagogical propaganda; it is science calling out to us. By making musical goals as ambitious as possible, our brain, our muscles, and all the different cells involved in the coordination of our movements will be required to adapt *more* to reach them. And secondly, by listening attentively, the best feedback will be given to our motor system to help it adjust to those musical goals.

Mathematically, by listening for an ideal and making the best mechanical adjustments each time to achieve it, it equates to having *more chance* of *more gain* per action. From a pedagogical perspective, pressing the repeat button on this strategy can hardly be surpassed, because over time, as we continue to improve each component of this play-listen loop (see figure 8.1.),

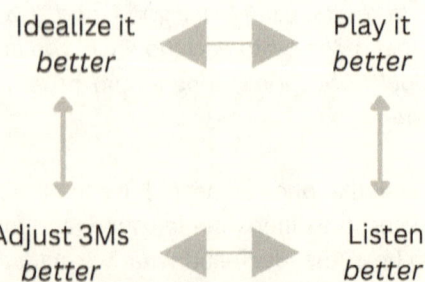

Figure 8.1. Idealize, Play, Listen, Adjust. Repeat. Author created

the reward:risk ratio of our learning becomes increasingly favorable, and our pianism cannot do anything else but continue to improve in the areas of piano playing that matter most—the 3 Ms.

With near certainty, every expert player will be using this loop. It is unavoidable. If we look closely, we can see that Chopin used it to teach his students too: to pursue ideal (internal) musical images using proper mechanics while intensely listening to/for them:

1. *Idealize It*
   - Chopin: "Imagine [...] listening to the most beautiful performance in the world."[24]
     → the ambitious musical conception means that the maximum possible outcome is very high.
2. *Play It*
   - Chopin: "Make yourself want to hear it,"[25] and "Hear [visualize] yourself playing it."[26]
     → the strong intention to release the musical conception increases the chances that your ideal (rather than something else) will be realized.
3. & 4. *Listen and Adjust*
   - Chopin: "Always listen to yourself."
     → the higher the quality of the listening, the higher the chance that you will be able to adapt your body to achieve what you are aiming for.

BE A "SOUND CHEF"—MIX-ING AND MAX-ING THE ELEMENTS

As musicians, we should demand of ourselves that we are experts at communicating through the medium of *sound*. Sound is our business. We are not painters, dancers or film directors. We are *sound* artists: we *make* sounds and we *present* sounds, mixing them and emphasizing certain aspects of them to produce its effects. As Anton Rubinstein stated, "a musician's duty is to communicate with the audience through the medium of music."[27]

All of the elements of music are available to *any* pianist and, like a chef, we are free to choose to make any dish of music and present it in any way that we want. The textbox on the next page shows us what these options are. There are no barriers preventing us from accessing the whole universe of musical possibilities except for our own self-imposed beliefs and our audience's willingness to participate in them. As a musician, excuses for not trying to be maximally musically creative are indefensible. It limits musical outcomes. It limits pianistic outcomes. And it limits the existential joy of being a free artist.

"To play a wrong note is insignificant; to play without passion is inexcusable";
"Music is a higher revelation than all wisdom and philosophy."—Beethoven[28]

Elements That Can Be Manipulated

Before presuming that we are actually extracting all the possibilities of expression from the musical elements at our disposal, it is worth remembering what those elements are.

Sound & Music elements:
- Tempo
- Phrasing and form
- Rhythm and accent
- Dynamics (and silence)
- Harmony
- Melody
- Register
- Texture and Instrumentation
- Characterization
- Rubato and rhetoric
- Style and Emotion
- Etc.

Non-Sound & Non-Music elements:
- Gestures
- Visual appearance
- Staging and acoustics
- Lighting
- Venue and location
- Instrument type, quality and voicing
- Audience selection
- Programming
- Marketing story
- Time and day of concert
- Etc.

As pianists, the interpretation of the elements of the first group, *Sound & Music*, occupy most of our time—and rightly so: they define us as musicians, and they are the features that a serious listener might identify us by if using *only* the sense of hearing. Some pianists are often immediately recognisable in this regard (e.g., Rachmaninoff's stretched rubatos and rhythmic verve; Gould's unusual characterisations; Horowitz's extreme sound contrasts; Schiff's fluid lyricism and improvised ornamentation, etc.).

> *As painters of sound, we cannot just join the composer's dots on the page with straight lines and expect artistic miracles to occur. We must use the dots, mix them and manipulate them to create the musical pictures that we want our audiences to experience. There are an unlimited number of ways to do this.*

As performers, however, sound is not the only factor involved in the transmission of expression. Unless we are studio-only recording pianists, we cannot ignore the potential of the *Non-Sound* and *Non-Music* elements to improve (or ruin) the experience for our listeners—irrespective of the quality of the music being offered. It is not difficult to find examples of pianists who exploit such elements, be it Richter's single-lamp lighting experience, Lang Lang's charismatic gestures, Michelangeli's off-stage mystique, or those with captivating dress styles and appearances—all factors that have nothing to do with sound but nevertheless alter the audience's experience of it. The emphasis that pop musicians give to non-sound and non-music elements can be recognized here, as they exploit such elements to alter the experience of their music for their listeners.

The exploration of *all* the elements, and the choosing of which ones to exaggerate and which ones to minimise, when, and by how much, is the essence of what interpretation is all about. As the neuroscientist V. S. Ramachandran remarked: "[artists seek] to not only capture the essence of something but also to amplify it in order to more powerfully activate the same neural mechanisms that would be activated by the original object."[29]

And depending on the degree of amplification, and the observer who judges it, the affect of that amplification will be considered to be artistically *agreeable* or *disagreeable*—or, in Ramachandran's words, to be "lawful or "unlawful."[30] As musicians, whether as composers or performers, we are constantly making decisions about which elements of the music are to be exaggerated more or less, and depending on what we choose, our listeners will be pleased or dis-pleased by our attempts. The textbox on the following page offers practical suggestions about how we can widen the scope of our interpretative skills—and alter the impact of our performances— by experimenting with the elements available to us.

Experimenting with the Elements

Consider the amplifications, distortions, and lawfulness (or not) of the interpretations of the great pianists. How do they manipulate the elements to produce their effect on you? How do *you* manipulate the elements to produce your effect on others? Do you take full advantage of the expressive potential of the *Sound & Music* and *Non-Sound & Non-Music* elements available to you?

- In the piece that you are playing, what elements do you enhance or diminish (or ignore) to alter the sensory or emotional experience of your listeners?
- What elements of the music do you think the composer wishes to have exploited?
- What elements of the music do you habitually emphasize more than others? Why?
- Do you have a tendency to neglect certain elements? Why?
- What do your interpretative choices tell you about your pianistic beliefs
- What would happen to your pianism if you invested more time in exploiting the areas that you habitually neglected?
- How could the non-music elements of your performance be altered to achieve the sound experience that you seek? For example, does the venue in which you perform (e.g., its size, acoustics, instrument, etc.) allow you to fulfill your musical goals? Could the stage lighting enhance the experience? Could programme notes or marketing strategies help to prime the audience's attention toward specific aspects of the music—the same aspects that you are trying to exploit through your playing? Is the standard piano recital format even the right pathway for you?

Push the boundaries of what you think is possible with each of the elements. Get out of your comfort zone. Try the opposite of what you would normally do. Experiment with extremes of expression. Break out of your self-confirmation biases. Increase the range of your aesthetic options and recognize how much more interesting your piano playing could be.

MAKE FRIENDS WITH YOUR MEDIUM—WORK WITH REALITY

As just discussed, playing the piano involves manipulating musical and non-musical elements in order to realize artistic ideas. These manipulations occur, chiefly, in three physical locations (see Figure 8.2):

1. The composer (the provider of the sound ideas)
2. The instrument-performer (the producer and manipulator of sound)
3. The listener in an acoustic space (who experiences the sound)

When any of these three factors are altered, so too is the experience of the participants of the performance. Our job, as performers, is to make manipulations within this performance space to shift the experience of its participants *in the direction that we want.* The textbox below shows examples of how these manipulations can work for us or against us.

> **Same Pianism, Different Experience.**
>
> Compare, for example, the experience of listening to a performance of three late Beethoven sonatas in two different scenarios:
>
> - Scenario A: played on a digital piano in a classroom full of noisy kids.
> - Scenario B: played on a high-quality grand-piano in a quiet hall with good acoustics to an audience of attentive listeners.

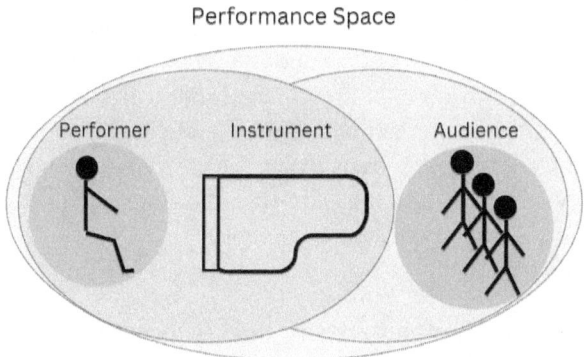

Figure 8.2. Manipulating the Medium. Altering the Experience. Author created

Supposing that the pianist's performance of the sonatas is the same (pianistically speaking), the outcome of the musical experience in these different scenarios, for both the performer and the listeners, is likely to be very different. The composer's music hasn't changed, nor has the pianist's performance of it, but the non-musical elements within the medium in which the music has been shared has been altered, and with it, so has each participant's experience of it.

Irrespective of the quality of the pianist's pianism in scenario A, the piano, the acoustic and the listeners were not conducive to the pianist being able to realize their intended musical goal (which *was*, however, possible in scenario B). The experience may still have been meaningful, of course, but not in the way that was intended.

Different Pianism, Same Experience.

On other occasions, for the same reasons, though in reverse, the musical experience for the pianist and the audience is often meaningful and pleasurable *irrespective* of the quality of the pianism that is being offered. There are many instances where this occurs, like when listeners are "in love" with the performer (e.g., a friend, a living legend of the piano world, a likable personality), "in love" with the piece (e.g., it's your favorite), "in love" with the occasion (e.g., a wedding, an encore, sharing the experience with a beloved) or "in love" with the larger aesthetic goals that the pianist is offering (e.g., conformist interpretations, subversive interpretations, a contribution to a social cause). In such situations, it can be largely irrelevant whether the pianism is of high or low quality—the shared meaning of the intended experience may still be the same.

Professional pianists are constantly dealing with the above two scenarios in real life: most commonly, when great effort has been spent preparing for a recital only to find that it has to be performed on a poor-quality instrument with a poor acoustic; or, on the flip-side, when audiences react enthusiastically to a performance while remaining oblivious to how bad the pianism was. Both circumstances can challenge our sense of purpose as a pianist.

Appropriately, much of our practice time is spent on learning and interpreting notes, but as this book suggests, the performance of those notes (as music) may not always translate into the experience that we presume will occur if we fail to take into account *all* the factors that exist within our musical medium—of which *the audience* is one.

> *If we only consider ourselves in the equation of the experience, we must also learn to accept the disappointments that accompany our failing to appreciate the full reality of the situation—that our great playing may fall on deaf ears, deaf pianos, deaf acoustics, deaf judges and deaf critics.*

The smallest of alterations made to our medium can have the biggest of impacts on the experience that our pianism provides. These may include: mechanical choices about what type of keystroke to use (affecting momentum and playability), interpretative choices about what elements of the music to amplify (affecting stylistic lawfulness), the choice of repertoire (is it well-known or new music), our appearance (does it enhance or distract), our gestures (what meaning to they add), the choice of piano and venue (will it facilitate your goals), the tone of your marketing (what does it anticipate), the comfort of the seating (will it annoy), how much wine the audience has drunk (more manipulatable) or, simply, how we greet the audience when we walk out on stage (empathy to sharing ideas).

Different changes will cause different effects on different people and there is no suggestion here that one can (or should) try to please everyone, but to be naive to the existence of the factors that contribute to the performance experience is to welcome the frustrations that come with them: like the pain of becoming injured (your body is part of the medium), the frustration that the instrument doesn't work well (the piano is part of the medium) or the despair that your audience doesn't recognize your genius (the audience is part of the medium). I will always thank the kind lady who told me after a concert that she could not enjoy my playing because my shoes were dirty (I had to navigate puddles of water outside the concert hall as I arrived late during a thunderstorm).

To be in tune with all the elements that exist within our musical medium, and to be able to adapt to them, we, as pianists, need to make friends with them. We need to make friends with ourselves, our instrument, and the space in which we perform. If not, we deny ourselves opportunities: we deny ourselves full access to the reality of the performance interaction. Herrigel's archer knew what to do:

> *"enter into friendly relations with whatever appears on the scene"*—
> *"[performance is] a contest of the archer with himself"*[31]

As discussed, when we play a note, we receive sensory feedback from the key, kinaesthetic feedback from our movements, as well as auditory and emotional feedback. These haptic processes,[32] along with all our other sensory inputs, alter us physiologically, which, in turn, affect how we judge the notes played and how we plan for the notes that lie ahead. The situation is dynamic as we simultaneously give to and respond to the medium in which we operate.

> *Simultaneously, pianists are three entities in one: an element within the medium, an element that manipulates it, and an element that is manipulated by it. The state of our mind and body alters how we play. Different pianos alter how we play. Different audiences and acoustic spaces alter how we play. There is a constant exchange of information between ourselves and the environment and a constant exchange of information between ideas and reality.*

Being open to the feedback of our musical medium, and adapting to it, is vitally important. To deny it, is to deny that there is a connection between what we are doing and what is happening around us. This rarely ends well. Ignoring the feedback from our medium risks any of the following from occurring:

- being unable to control the key,
- being unable to control the sound,
- being unable to adapt to different acoustics,
- being unable to recognize inefficiencies in your movements,
- being unable to recognize errors in your sounds,
- being unable to recognize that you are causing yourself injury, and
- being unable to recognize that your audience is bored.

Teaching ourselves to be open to the feedback of our medium is the optimal pathway to proceed. It allows our beliefs to integrate better with the reality in which they exist. (Recall figure 1.3 in chapter 1.) It allows us to make adaptations to improve our situation. Making friends with our medium, and everything in it, provides us with the pre-conditions for becoming at one with our pianism, physically and emotionally. It creates the conditions for absolute key control, sensory and emotional unity with sound, the inner flow of the music, a love of the presence of the audience and a respect for the health of our body.

Liszt professed that "the piano is me" and it makes us wonder to what degree of "one-ness" he had with his instrument, music, and the non-music elements of his medium. Whether "one-ness" is physical or metaphorical, the distinction becomes irrelevant when performing because this is how we *experience* music, as a player and as an observer, as Schumann observed of Liszt:

"He [Liszt] first played with the public as if to try it, then gave it something more profound, until every single member was enveloped in his art; and then the whole mass began to rise and fall precisely as he willed it."[33] *"[Liszt had] in so high a degree [...] the power of subjugating, elevating and leading the public."*[34]

Thinking of ourselves as "experience creators" who *use* all that is available to us, rather than "note creators" who *hope* that experience will occur, is one way of shifting the focus of our practice to include musical-experiential outcomes, not just pianistic outcomes. Could our outcomes be different if we treated the piano as a "metaphor maker" or a "magic machine" rather than a stiff piece of wood and metal with parochial rules attached to it?

Consider the importance of the following interactions (that all occur within the musical medium) that can affect the musical experience.

Pianist-Piano Interactions

When we play the piano, we touch the keys with the intention of making music through sound. At the same time, the mechanical action of the key and the sound of the instrument provide us with sensory and acoustic feedback. Responding to this feedback allows us to immediately make adjustments to our touch and sound. Conversely, not responding to the feedback leads to pianistic nonsense, of pressing down keys without regard for the mechanical idiosyncracies or the sounds they produce. Such are the outcomes cultivated by pianists who engage in the repetition of mindless, motor exercises that strive to dominate the instrument rather than work with it. Problems associated with ignoring the feedback from the instrument may include the following:

- Getting frustrated with your instrument because of the feel of its action, its sound quality, its dynamic range, its pedals, its tuning, its seat height, etc.
- Failing to exploit the best range of volumes and sound qualities for the instrument that you are playing.
- Poor key control and dynamic inconsistencies.
- An unrealistic expectation that you will be able to replicate the same level of technical precision and control when playing on an instrument that is unfamiliar to you.
- Over-playing (i.e., trying to get more volume out of an instrument than is possible), leading to excessive thump (percussive) sounds.
- Injury because of failing to recognize the limits of the piano (and your body).

Pianist-Audience Interactions

When we perform, we share music with our audience and (presumably) try to influence them with it. At the same time, our audience exerts an influence over us. This influence can have a major effect on our pianism: affecting our mental performance (concentration, memory), influencing our musical choices (by making changes to style and emotional ranges) and altering our mechanical performance (emotional responses affect muscle control). Depending on how we manage "the presence of an audience," the effect on our pianism may be positive or negative. Certainly, if the audience wasn't there, our pianism would be very different.[35] Given this interaction, some questions can be asked:

- What would happen to your stress levels on stage (and off stage) if you knew that the audience was also your friend and supportive of your pianism (and your mistakes) rather than being an unknown, scary, judging machine? Could you re-frame the pianist-audience relationship into a "you and them" experience, or better, "you are them," rather than a "you versus them" contest?
- How do you respond to the unwanted noises that come from the audience (e.g., inappropriate coughing, ringing phones, air-conditioner humming, poorly timed clapping, etc.)? Do you incorporate them into your medium or do you expect them to never occur?[36]
- How might your audiences respond if you embraced their attitudes and satisfied their needs? Could you reduce your level of frustration at them for failing to understand your interpretations, or could you reduce their level of frustration at you for failing to understand their expectations regarding interpretative extremes, gestures, choice of repertoire or style of presentation etc.

Pianist-Music Interactions

When we perform, we influence how it sounds by the interpretive choices that we make. Yet although we might presume the role of creator when we perform, we are often unaware that, simultaneously, the composers are making puppets out of us *as their music plays us*, affecting our emotions, our thinking and highjacking our body movements.[37] As musicians, a willingness to allow music to "flow through us" would be much more in keeping with the truth that our role as a performer is as much a *facilitator* and *participant* of the musical experience as it is a creator of it. The distinction is subtle, yet valuable, as it prevents us from subjugating elements of the music that could otherwise be used to help us realize the full potential of the musical experience. Here, some more questions can be asked:

- How willing are you to allow the music to speak through you versus you imposing your will upon it?
- Do you impose your own personal emotional stamp upon the music before you have understood all its elements or listened to what it is trying to say?
- Do you fail to enjoy the music of certain composers because you have emotionally blocked it out before you have emotionally allowed it in?
- Does your psychological approach to piano playing (and the beliefs it contains) prevent you from engaging in certain musical styles, i.e., does your insistence in using certain keystrokes, accents, articulations, dynamics, tempos, rubatos, or pedaling cause all your interpretations to sound the same, regardless of the composer you are playing?

Pianist-Pianist Interactions

Finally, it must be remembered that our mind is in constant exchange with our physical body, and as much as we may wish to impose our will upon our body, our body is constantly giving us feedback as to the suitability and sustainability of the orders it receives. Some examples that demonstrate this two-way exchange include the following:

- Do you get frustrated with yourself because you make mistakes or do you accept mistakes as feedback that something within your pianism needs improving?
- Are you patient with yourself, your level of skill, and your progress?
- Do you ignore the warning signs of pain in your body (physical feedback) and hope that they will just go away?

All of the above-listed problems result from not having learned the skill of making friends with your medium. They are self-inflicted problems. They have nothing to do with how talented you are, how good your technique is or how much you practice. To a large extent, they are extensions of our self-confirmation biases—where, having already convinced ourselves of the superiority of our own assumptions, we subjugate reality and ignore its feedback.

The open mindsets of the following pianists and teachers demonstrate their awareness of the need to embrace the realities of their pianism, to make friends with their instrument, the music, the audience and, indeed, themselves:

- "The piano should become something loving to you."[38]—Dorothy Taubman
- "He [the pianist] should not have to struggle with the instrument, or impose his will tyrannically upon it [...] On the contrary, the player should make friends with the piano and assure himself of its services [...] He should give the instrument its due by showing how capable it is of transforming itself."[39]—Alfred Brendel
- "There are no bad pianos, only bad pianists."[40]—Ferruccio Busoni
- "When I walk out and see the friendly grin of those eighty-eight keys reassuring me, inviting me, I love them, and then everything falls into place."[41]– Lili Kraus
- "When I make music, I am in love with music. Actually, when I play, I make love."[42] "My audience, for me, is something that I love . . . I come before them as a loved one . . . and I play with all my heart."[43]—Artur Rubinstein
- "I let go completely and feel myself as being part of the universe [...] I just sat there and listened to myself."[44]—Peter Feuchtwanger

AESTHETICS AND YOUR PIANISM—SHARING EXPECTATIONS

Lastly, in our eternal pursuit of trying to share artistic ideas with our audiences, we must reflect upon the aesthetic criteria that we, and our audiences, operate under. As with any artistic creations, irrespective of our perception of the quality of our own artistic performances, if the aesthetic criteria that we use is not shared by our audience, both we and our audience may end up being disappointed by the interaction, where our feelings of meaning and pleasure may be *mismatched* with those of our audience.[45] It happens because "aesthetic value does not rest on the micro or macro features of a piece, per se, but on how one responds to those features."[46]

Somewhat deceptively, when we perform within a typical classical-music recital-hall venue, the aesthetic rules and expectations of the performer and the audience are usually similar enough that we do not notice their existence, less so any differences between them. For example: if a professional pianist presents a recital of Schubert Sonatas in a "standard" interpretative way to an audience that is trained to listen to them using the same "standard" aesthetic criteria, then it is more likely that the audience will have no trouble in understanding the meaning of the pianist's manipulations and be able to respond to them.

Large differences in the aesthetic criteria used by the pianist and the audience, however, risk violating the unwritten aesthetic contract that supposedly exists between the two participants. Predictably, the mismatch in the criteria may cause boredom (lack of interest), disgust (lack of pleasure) or bemusement (uncertainty of meaning) in the listener. New music and new musical styles are constantly at risk of evoking such negative responses. Unfairly, they are the negative responses that our now-celebrated composers (and most innovative pianists too) had to endure during their lifetimes. Just ask Beethoven, or Mahler, or Stravinksy.[47]

Within a modern context, common examples of aesthetic clashes ("disagreements of interpretation") between pianists and audiences might include:

- playing with unusual rubatos, tempi, or agogics;
- using the score when performing a standard repertoire concerto;
- not delivering a note-perfect performance, especially on a recording;
- using a period instrument instead of a modern instrument;
- presenting music with electronics in a classical music venue;
- adding extra notes to the score;
- playing (or not playing) all the repeats in baroque or classical works;
- using too large (or too small) visible gestures.

The clashes are a result of the mismatch in the expectations between the performer and its audience members—not about who is right or wrong. Here are some more specific examples of what can happen when your aesthetic expectations as an artist are poorly aligned to those of the audience:

- your fine performance of the music of Gibbens and Boulez failed to receive much applause.
  - → i.e., the audience didn't know how to appreciate those musical aesthetics.
- you were disappointed with your technically poor performance but the audience loved your showmanship.
  - → i.e., the audience valued something different to technical perfection.
- you did not win the competition even though you were the best pianist.
  - → i.e., your style of playing didn't resonate with the criteria of the jury.
- the paucity of your gestures bored the uninformed audience.
  - → i.e., the audience needed different visual clues to appreciate the music.
- your use of *rubato* in Mozart lead to a 1-star review in one country and a 5-star review in another.
  - → i.e., aesthetic tastes differ between different groups of people.
- some teachers recommend Hanon while other teachers don't.
  - → i.e., some teachers are mechanically focused, while others are musically focused.
- your teacher criticized your *cantabile* because of your curved-fingered touch.
  - → i.e., their aesthetic belief system associates curved fingers with tense muscles, and tense muscles with a tense sound, hence their value judgment of "bad" *cantabile*.

- you feel nervous performing in a masterclass, or in front of a (new) audience.
    → i.e., you are scared because you do not (yet) know the aesthetic criteria of the audience (and are yet to win them over with yours).

It is neither right nor wrong that there is a mismatch of aesthetic expectations between the artist and the audience. The point is, that it should be expected and anticipated. The levels of pleasure and meaning that each participant derives from any performance will be affected by the aesthetic assumptions that each participant brings to the occasion—aesthetic assumptions that may not even be consciously known.

To avoid the resentment that you feel when audiences fail to acknowledge the aesthetic virtues of your performances, it is worth thinking about what your and your audience's aesthetic expectations actually are (or could be) and to figure out a way to make them find common ground. The textbox below explains the dilemma.

To Whom Does One Play?

On a neurocognitive level, for meaning and pleasure to be derived from your performance, your listeners' mental blueprint of "what needs to happen, aesthetically," will need to overlap with yours. Irrespective of how much you excite your own blueprint, if you do not provide enough stimulus to excite theirs, boredom, bemusement or disgust are likely to result.

Imagine playing a Bach keyboard *Partita* to the following listeners:

- The jury of an international piano competition
- A mixed group of "non-musical" friends and acquaintances in a private setting
- A "cultured" audience at Wigmore Hall
- An indigenous tribe of people from the Amazon rainforest
- J. S. Bach

Each of the above listeners will have a different mental blueprint of what to expect from the listening experience. This will, in turn, affect their aesthetic response to it. For example, the jury of the international competition are likely to expect note perfection, well-presented musical lines and sound organization, a coherent presentation of form and character and some sort of "acceptably original yet still conforming" style. The group of non-musical friends, however, who are likely to be less knowledgable (and less concerned) with such criteria, may be satisfied enough that the music of Bach wafts over them, giving them some pleasant occasion to reflect upon life while providing them with a feeling of being cultured for having listened to a performance of classical music at all. The audience members at Wigmore Hall may be more diverse, but being a self-selected group of people for having chosen to attend a piano recital with Bach in it, they probably already have personal opinions about how Bach "should" sound, how Bach on a piano "should" sound, and even how the specifics of the Partita movements "should" sound. They might be wrong on all accounts (from your point of view) but as they are your audience, their views cannot be dismissed. Performing to an indigenous group of Amazoneans who have never heard Western Classical music before, less a Bach Partita, are likely to respond differently again. I resist predicting their response, but they will, nevertheless, like everybody else, map your performance of the Bach Partita against their expectations of what music is for, what a performer is supposed to do, and possibly, what such a musical event is supposed to achieve. Performing to Bach himself is anyone's guess.

Evidently, *our* experience of the performance will be shaped by the values that we have learned to assign to the various components that make up the performance experience. Quite possibly, our performance of the Bach Partita could meet all our criteria of musical and technical excellence but still be met with a tepid mix of emotional responses from the many different audience participants.

What we choose to do about the discrepancy in individuals' aesthetic responses to our playing raises important questions. Should we try to *please* the audience, *ignore* the audience, *teach* the audience, *challenge* the audience, *lead* the audience or *engage* with them in some other kind of way? Principally: *For whom do we play, and for what purpose?*

The question is innocuous, but its consequences are very real. Our answer reveals to us our beliefs about what it means to be a pianist and what it means to be an audience, and this will influence the type of pianist that we choose to become: affecting how we prepare music, where we invest our time, what elements we choose to perfect, and how we will perform music. It also informs us about whether what we are striving for is actually going to be appreciated by the audiences that we (think) we are going to play to.

To avoid pianistic, emotional, professional and health disasters later, it seems reasonable to ask now: what is the goal of your thousands of hours of practice? And why do you believe in that goal?

Ultimately, the aesthetic criteria that we value in our pianism is our choice. And although many teachers and institutions of western-art music direct us toward well-worn scripts of what the aesthetic criteria should be, we need not be servants to them. Irrespective of how much anybody knows about the aesthetic predilections of any given composer—do we really know how Chopin would have played on a modern Steinway?—as performers, we will still have to solve the problem of how to convince contemporary audiences of the meaning of those aesthetics.[48]

The solution to how to convince audiences comes back to the choices that we make about the degrees of distortion of the musical and non-musical elements available to us—of stimulating our audience's brains with sensory material that mixes *what is expected* with *what is unexpected*, of *conforming too much* or *not conforming enough* to audiences' expectations, and of constructing interpretations that balance what is *lawful* with what is *unlawful*.

How cleverly we manipulate our musical medium is what will determine the artistic success of our pianism, not whether we practice Hanon, use arm-weight or channel energy through our bodies. As an example of a pianist-composer who had to deal with the challenges of finding this balance, Beethoven's compositions (and original performances) immediately come to mind, where he worked within traditional structures ("expected" harmonies, styles, forms, agogics, etc.) but only to establish a reference point upon which to break free from their rules (with "unexpected" harmonies, styles, forms, agogics etc.). But any composer (or interpreter) seeking to be both original *and* understood has to deal with the same dilemma: where to be too original risks being misunderstood, and not original enough, risks being boring.

When playing for an exam, an international competition, a Carnegie Hall recital, a recording, a private post-dinner soirée, a fundraising benefit concert, a concert for kids, or simply playing for yourself, the aesthetic criteria of each group of listeners will be different. This must be kept in mind. Playing a recital of highly refined Couperin, a Stockhausen Klavierstück and some late Beethoven Bagatelles to a troop of monkeys may provide them with the same dose of aesthetic profundity as playing them Twinkle Star or Chopsticks if they can't relate to the aesthetic criteria that you have chosen.

Ultimately, as pianists, we need to take ownership of the challenges of finding convincing ways to share our aesthetic interests (and those of our composers) with those of a diverse range of listeners. It is a difficult task and represents one of the highest skills that a performer can master: to create a shared aesthetic experience that is both pleasurable and meaningful and to do so without the listener having the faintest idea of how it was done.

> *"... for them to think they have dreamed, for an instant, of an imaginary country, nowhere to be found because imaginary."*[49]—Claude Debussy

NOTES

1. Goodreads.com. "A Quote by Richard Wagner," 2024. https://www.goodreads.com/quotes/1056017-imagination-creates-reality.

2. Bresciani, Di. *Di Bresciani: A New Look at Australian Light*. Berkeley, CA: Hardie Grant Books, 2022, 222.

3. Eigeldinger, Jean-Jacques. *Chopin: Pianist and Teacher as Seen by His Pupils*. Cambridge, Cambridgeshire; New York: Cambridge University Press, 1986, 12.

4. Walker, Alan. *Franz Liszt / Vol. 3, the Final Years, 1861–1886*. Ithaca, NY: Cornell University Press, 1997, 455.

5. Schumann, Robert. *Advice to Young Musicians*. Translated by H Pierson. New York: J. Schuberth & Co, 1860, 10.

6. Quote from his student Kirnberger and the biographer Forkel. See: Forkel, Johann Nikolaus, and Charles Sanford Terry. *Johann Sebastian Bach, His Life; Art, and Work*. London: Constable, 1970.

7. Goodreads.com. "A Quote by Ludwig van Beethoven," 2024. https://www.goodreads.com/quotes/4103660-to-play-a-wrong-note-is-insignificant-to-play-without#:~:text=Quote%20by%20Ludwig%20van%20Beethoven.

8. La Musica. "Artur Rubinstein," January 29, 2016. https://lamusica808.wordpress.com/2016/01/29/artur-rubinstein/.

9. Bookey.app. "30 Best Anton Rubinstein Quotes with Image | Bookey," 2023. https://www.bookey.app/quote-author/anton-rubinstein.

10. Greenberg, Robert. "Music History Monday: The Beloved Son Returns – Robert Greenberg – Medium." *Medium*, April 20, 2020. https://medium.com/@rgreenbergmusic/music-history-monday-the-beloved-son-returns-b671f28ec1b7.

11. Liszt, Franz. *The Collected Writings of Franz Liszt. Volume 2, Essays and Letters of a Travelling Batchelor of Music*. Edited and translated by Janita R. Hall-Swadley. Lanham, MD: Scarecrow Press, 2012, 22.

12. "Picture the image [...] and the body will find its own way." See: Walker, Alan. *Franz Liszt / Vol. 3, the Final Years, 1861–1886*. Ithaca, NY: Cornell University Press, 1997, 232.

13. A rule that he enforced, while president of the Royal Academy in Budapest.

14. Wulf, Gabriele, and Rebecca Lewthwaite. "Optimizing Performance through Intrinsic Motivation and Attention for Learning: The OPTIMAL Theory of Motor Learning." *Psychonomic Bulletin & Review* 23, no. 5 (January 29, 2016): 1382–1414, 1404.

15. Note, improvised music also fits into this framework. Though its notes may not be predefined, its goals very much are (e.g., how the elements of the music are

going to be explored, what the parameters of the improvisation will be, and what sort of stylistic outcomes are sought).

16. Australian pianist Stephen McIntyre, during a period of study with Michelangeli, recalls the obsessive focus that Michelangeli gave to optimizing finger and hand movements (developing his own code of symbols which he wrote onto his scores) to ensure their perfection.

17. Recall how Rubinstein always used to choose somebody in the crowd to play to, to help him personalize the expression of his performances.

18. In many of his interviews, Gould describes his deliberate attempts to be nonconformist. For example, watch his discussion of how he chose to interpret Mozart's K.331 piano sonata. See: www.youtube.com. "I Asked 6 Pianists What They Think of Glenn Gould (Ft. Ax, Fleisher, Bernstein, et Al)." tonebase Piano, August 9, 2022. https://www.youtube.com/watch?v=dgUnUd9oBSc.

19. Gelb, David. *Jiro Dreams of Sushi*. Magnolia Pictures, 2001.

20. Gieseking, Walter, and Karl Leimer. *Piano Technique*. 1932. Reprint, New York: Dover Publications, 1972, 9.

21. Eigeldinger, Jean-Jacques. *Chopin: Pianist and Teacher as Seen by His Pupils*. Cambridge, Cambridgeshire; New York: Cambridge University Press, 1986, 28.

22. Cooke, James Francis. *Great Pianists on Piano Playing: Godowsky, Hofmann, Lhévinne, Paderewski, and 24 Other Legendary Performers*. Mineola, NY: Dover Publications, 1999, 77.

23. Brent-Smith, A. "A Study of Franz Liszt." *The Musical Times* 70, no. 1035 (May 1, 1929): 401–3. doi:https://doi.org/10.2307/915233.

24. Eigeldinger, Jean-Jacques. *Chopin: Pianist and Teacher as Seen by His Pupils*. Cambridge, Cambridgeshire; New York: Cambridge University Press, 1986, 12.

25. Eigeldinger, Jean-Jacques. *Chopin: Pianist and Teacher as Seen by His Pupils*. Cambridge, Cambridgeshire; New York: Cambridge University Press, 1986, 12.

26. Eigeldinger, Jean-Jacques. *Chopin: Pianist and Teacher as Seen by His Pupils*. Cambridge, Cambridgeshire; New York: Cambridge University Press, 1986, 12.

27. Bookey.app. "30 Best Anton Rubinstein Quotes with Image | Bookey," 2023. https://www.bookey.app/quote-author/anton-rubinstein.

28. Goodreads.com. "Ludwig van Beethoven Quotes (Author of Beethoven's Letters)," 2019. https://www.goodreads.com/author/quotes/40589.Ludwig_van_Beethoven.

29. Ramachandran, Vilayanur S, and William Hirstein. "The Science of Art: A Neurological Theory of Aesthetic Experience." *Journal of Consciousness Studies* 6 (June 1, 1999): 15–41.

30. BBC. "BBC Sounds – the Reith Lectures – Available Episodes," 2003. https://www.bbc.co.uk/sounds/series/p00ghvck.

31. Herrigel, Eugen. *Zen in the Art of Archery: With an Introduction by D.T. Suzuki*. Translated by R.F.C. Hull. 1953. Reprint, New York: Vintage Books, 1971.

32. Papetti, Stefano, and Charalampos Saitis, eds. *Musical Haptics*. Cham, Switzerland: Springer International Publishing, 2018.

33. Davies, James Q. *Romantic Anatomies of Performance*. Berkeley: University of California Press, 2014.

34. Ginsborg, Jane. "'The Brilliance of Perfection' or 'Pointless Finish'? What Virtuosity Means to Musicians." *Musicae Scientiae* 22, no. 4 (November 13, 2018): 454–73. doi:https://doi.org/10.1177/1029864918776351.

35. A comprehensive account of the problems (and solutions) that occur because of the presence of an audience can be found in: Nagel, Julie Jaffee. *Managing Stage Fright: A Guide for Musicians and Music Teachers*. Oxford: Oxford University Press, 2017.

36. "'making friends' with the distraction" and finding "creative solutions in order to address these disruptions" are accepted strategies. See, respectively: Williamon, Aaron. *Musical Excellence: Strategies and Techniques to Enhance Performance*. Oxford: Oxford University Press, 2004, 237; Toner, John, and Aidan Moran. "Enhancing Performance Proficiency at the Expert Level: Considering the Role of 'Somaesthetic Awareness.'" *Psychology of Sport and Exercise* 16 (January 2015): 110–17. doi:https://doi.org/10.1016/j.psychsport.2014.07.006. Other useful mindset solutions are given in: Cornett, Vanessa. *The Mindful Musician*. Oxford: Oxford University Press, 2019.

37. That there are so many self-proclaimed experts of the great piano works of the great composers – because of the argument that they "feel the music deeper than everybody else" or "have a special understanding" with the composer – is more of a tribute to these composers' skill in manipulating us than us having any special ability to interpret their music. We *feel* like we can interpret it better because they have already made us feel like we understand it, though without us realizing.

38. Santiago, Kathy. "Point of Sound." *Pointofsound.com*, 2024. http://www.pointofsound.com/taubintro.html.

39. Brendel, Alfred. *Musical Thoughts & Afterthoughts*. Robson Books Limited, 1976, 129.

40. Rosen, Charles. *Piano Notes: The World of the Pianist*. New York: Free Press, 2002, 86.

41. Chaffin, Roger, Gabriela Imreh, and Mary E Crawford. *Practicing Perfection*. Mahwah, NJ: Lawrence Erlbaum, 2002, 62.

42. PianoLegendaryVideos. "Arthur Rubinstein: The Music Hero (Mini Documentary)." *YouTube*, July 15, 2019. https://www.youtube.com/watch?v=3H7nzTLVksU.

43. *Translated from German: "Mein Publikum für mich ist etwas was ich liebe... Ich komme zum Publikum wie einer Geliebten... Ich spiele mit meinem ganzen Herz."* The Piano Experience. "Arthur Rubinstein Explains Why He Will Never Perform in Germany Again (1965)." *YouTube*, May 14, 2021. https://www.youtube.com/watch?v=Lewd24QPeNs.

44. Blido, Stefan. "Texts." *Peter-Feuchtwanger.de*, 2024. http://www.peter-feuchtwanger.de/english-version/texts/.

45. To simplify the discussion of aesthetics, "meaning" and "pleasure" will be used as the terms to qualify the value of aesthetic interactions. See: Chatterjee, Anjan. *The Aesthetic Brain: How We Evolved to Desire Beauty and Enjoy Art*. New York: Oxford University Press, 2015.

46. Friedmann, Jonathan L. *Musical Aesthetics: An Introduction to Concepts, Theories, and Functions*. Newcastle-upon-Tyne: Cambridge Scholars Publishing, 2018, Preface, viii.

47. About the premiere of his *The Rite of Spring*, Stravinsky said about the audience that "[they] came for *Scheherazade* or *Cleopatra*, and they saw *Le Sacre du Printemps*. They were very shocked. They were very naïve and stupid people." Jones, Josh. "Igor Stravinsky Remembers the 'Riotous' Premiere of His Rite of Spring in 1913: 'They Were Very Shocked. They Were Naive and Stupid People.'" *Open Culture*, 2018. https://www.openculture.com/2018/04/igor-stravinsky-remembers-the-riotous-premiere-of-his-rite-of-spring.html.

48. Deciding whether or not to follow the metronome markings of composers is always a good example of this, where to follow them correctly may risk annoying members of your audience who are already accustomed to a speed that they know.

49. Dayan, Peter. "On Nature, Music, and Meaning in Debussy's Writing." *19th-Century Music* 28, no. 3 (2005): 214–29. doi:https://doi.org/10.1525/ncm.2005.28.3.214, 218.

Movement Optimization Exercises

The following exercises teach the core movements of piano playing. All other movements are adaptations or derivatives of them. Like learning how to swing a golf club or a tennis racquet, they should only take a few weeks or months to learn but will take years to fine tune over the years of playing challenging repertoire. The square brackets "[ ]" indicate the scientific reason why the task is important, the reasons for which can be found in the chapters of the book. Multiple videos explaining these movements can also be found via links at www.cameronroberts.com.au.

THE "TRIPLE-STROKE"—"FALL, PLAY & ROLL"

Part 1 (one note):

FALL with the hand:

- Assume and maintain a natural hand position at all times (natural arches, natural curves etc.) [this optimizes strength of muscle contractions and minimizes fatigue].
- Let your hand (or hand and forearm together) bounce lightly in and out of the keys [these masses correlate best with ideal m-v combinations] as though it moved like a marionette puppet [learn to independently observe your movements without always being psychologically attached to them. This helps to minimize emotionalization of movements], being lifted up out of the keys by imaginary strings [helps the preparatory backswing movement] and being allowed to fall back down into them without needing to try [they learn to use gravity], without ever feeling stuck or restricted to being

in any position at any time [muscles learn to feel that they can move to any location at any time without undue tension].
- If anything, imagine that the keys were not even there, learning to enjoy the movement and the sound that it makes [remove the psychological tension associated with obsessing over mechanics or the accuracy of the movement].

PLAY with the finger:

- Choose a finger to land on (e.g., the thumb). Choose a scale to play (e.g., C major or D flat major). Play the scale using only the thumb (1 octave), and *as the hand falls into the key*, play the thumb *downward* into the key (not across it). [This coordination of the finger and hand summates the masses of your keystroke during the window of opportunity]. A drop into the key from a few centimeters above it is enough [piano playing rarely requires more than this].

ROLL with the forearm:

- As the finger plays with the hand into the key, add some forearm rotation to the keystroke too.
- The roll of the forearm should coincide exactly with the keystroke [to add to the momentum of the keystroke during the window of opportunity]. A forearm roll of 1–2 centimeters is enough [piano playing rarely requires more than this].

*This is the "triple-stroke": coordinating the movements of the finger, the hand and the forearm to play into the key during the window of opportunity.

Further training steps:

- Instead of a scale, play the notes of an arpeggio using just the thumb (e.g., over 2–3 octaves).
- Then, instead of an arpeggio, play notes at intervals of an octave (over 3–4 octaves).
- Then, learn to play notes at *any interval across the keyboard*, bouncing freely and easily onto any note (like a pogo stick). [Learn the momentum benefits of circular movements, not zig-zag movements, and learn *not* to stop the fall of your hand into the key even if notes are at wide intervals from each other, an essential skill needed in fast, leaping passagework]

*The *same sense of physical and mental ease* should be felt whether you are playing notes that are next to each other or are multiple octaves apart. [Learn to enjoy leaps, not panic about them]

- After some weeks of training your muscles, gradually speed up your bounces, or try to play some simple pieces using only your thumbs (e.g., the Preludes in C major and C# major of Bach's Well-Tempered Klavier are good challenges).
- Learn to do all of the above for each of the five fingers. [so that there are no mechanical problems with any of your fingers, which will help to prevent compensation errors]

Part 2 (two notes):

Now, learn to play two notes in succession:

- As with the first note played, the second note played also uses the "Fall, Play and Roll" triple-stroke.
- The 2nd finger should learn to play *during the same bounce of the hand into the key.*
- Any two notes can be chosen for the exercise, but let us continue in logical order, using the 1st and 2nd fingers.
- Here, learn to make the 1st finger the "go-to" note, receiving the emphasis and most of the momentum of the hand-drop into the keys. The 2nd finger should be played lighter and without emphasis.

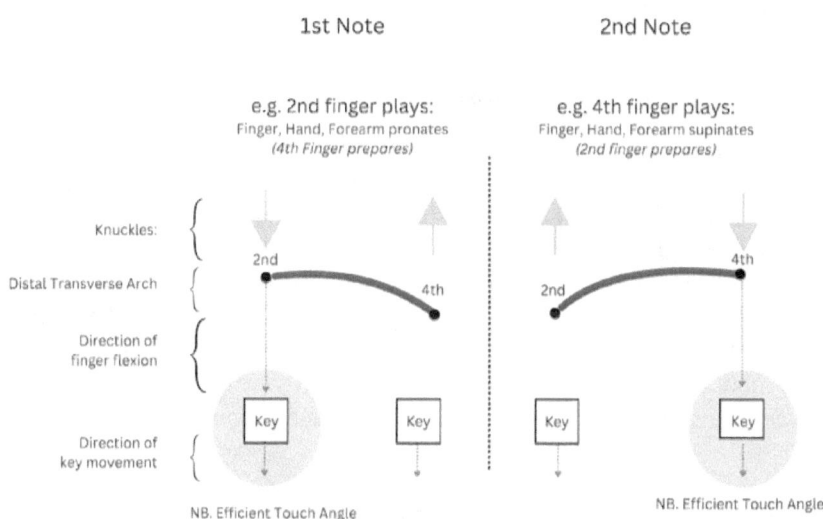

Figure 8.3. The "Triple-Stroke" (When Playing Two Consecutive Notes). Author created

- Importantly, the forearm must learn to supinate during the backswing of the thumb, pronate when playing it (which assists with the backswing preparation of the 2nd finger), then supinate again when the 2nd finger plays into the key.

Further training steps:

- Instead of using the notes of a scale, play the two-note sequence using the notes of an arpeggio as the "go-to" notes. Then, use octave notes as the "go-to" notes.
- Once the movements are learned (regardless of the interval of the leap), they should be played gradually quicker and with some intentional musical shape.

*Again, the *same sense of physical and mental ease* should be felt whether you are playing notes that are next to each other or are multiple octaves apart.

Parts 3 to 5 (three to five notes):

Now, learn to play three to five notes in succession using the same advice as in Part 2. Ensure comfort, natural arches and proper mechanical action of all fingers at all times. With more fingers being played, it is common that some fingers will start to misbehave and adopt inefficient mechanical keystrokes. Do not allow it. Slow down and return to Parts 1 and 2 if necessary. Do not cut corners in learning these steps.

Part 6 (change the "go-to" note):

Repeat steps 2 to 5 but now make the 2nd note of the note sequence the "go-to" note, which is to say, the 2nd finger will receive the emphasis and most of the momentum of the hand when it falls onto the keyboard.

Then, repeat for the 3rd, 4th, and 5th fingers, teaching them also how to be the "go-to" notes. [Piano playing requires learning how to fall onto groups of notes *and* learning how to emphasize the right ones within that group, whether they appear at the beginning of the note sequence or elsewhere throughout it. Learning how to do this within one hand drop makes the finger movements and the gesture unified in concept and action.]

Part 7 (change the direction of the sequence):

Repeat all the previous steps but now use a descending note sequence (rather than ascending). I.e., start with the 5th finger alone, then proceed to a 5-4 sequence, then 5-4-3 etc. Note how the 5th finger will need pronation in its backswing and supination in its downswing—the opposite to the thumb.

Part 8 (other applications: different sequences, different directions):

Instead of playing groups of notes that have only adjacent notes (as above), play groups of notes that have different intervals within them, e.g., triads, dominant 7ths, or other chords that span less than an octave. Later, play groups of notes where the group itself spans across more than an octave, like those in Chopin Op.10, No.1. Also, choose groups of notes that involve different note sequences and different note emphases, e.g., instead of playing a finger sequence 1-2-3-4, play 2-1-3-4 or 3-1-2-4, etc. (underlined number indicates the "go-to" note). Musical examples that already require such variations of emphasis include:

- Bach: Prelude (From WTK Bk.1 in D minor). Bar 1. R.H.: 4-2-1 / 4-2-1 etc.
- Beethoven: Sonata Op. 27, No. 2, 3rd movement. Bar 1. R.H.: 1-2-4-5 / 1-2-3-5 / 1-2-4-5 / 1-2-4-5 etc.
- Chopin: *Étude* Op. 10, no. 4. Bar 5. L.H.: 3-2 / 4-3-2-1 / 4-3-2-1 / 4-3-2-1/ 4-3 etc.

Comments and Tips:

- Note that as the coordination of your keystroke improves, the amount of physical movement required to play the notes (backswing and downswing) reduces. This is efficiency. It means that your triple-strokes and your preparatory movements between them are coordinated and that you have minimized physical effort. Finger lifts, hand lifts and forearm rotations that go beyond a few centimeters above the key surface are rarely, if ever, required in piano playing for mechanical purposes.
- Note that as the speed of your passagework increases, *the limiting factor for being able to play faster will not be your mechanics* but your mental agility—the speed at which your mind can "see," "hear," and "plan" ahead for the next group of notes about to be played. Reminding yourself of this should prevent you from wasting time "strengthen your fingers" or doing meaningless repetitions of the same passage when it is neither your mechanics nor your muscles that are slowing you down.
- The intended outcome of these exercises is to learn how to play any sequence of notes on the piano with correct biomechanics *and* quick mental preparation. The skill, once acquired, should be applied to musical examples, as the emotions of playing will likely interfere with your now

perfect biomechanics, and you will have to learn how to accommodate both needs at the same time.

Ultimately, it should make no difference to you whether the groups of notes that you play on the keyboard are adjacent to each other or spread far apart across the keyboard—the mechanics of playing the piano are always the same, and they are not difficult to learn. Once learned, the limiting factor in your playing will be mental (speed of recall) or musical (are you interesting?)

THE BUTTERFLY EXERCISE

This exercise encourages you to become comfortable with forearm rotation in both directions (pronation and supination), and to learn how to coordinate it with your finger-strokes.

Step 1:

Place both hands on the keyboard using the comfortable notes: E, F#, G#, A#, C. ("Chopin position")

Step 2:

Gently hold down the thumb notes of both the R.H. and L.H (the L.H. thumb will be on middle *C*., the R.H. thumb will be on the *E* a third above it). During the exercise, the thumbs will serve as mechanical pivot points for the forearm rotation.

Step 3:

Begin by playing using the 5th finger. Prepare the 5th finger keystroke with a small backstroke of the finger. For the purposes of this exercise, exaggerate the pronation rotation of the forearm during the backswing of the finger-stroke so that the backs of each hand move toward each other (like the wings of a butterfly). This may cause the elbows to stick slightly outwards from the body. Don't worry; the point of the exercise is to become accustomed to pronating the forearm *more than it usually does* during the backswing of the 5th finger so that more supination is available to be used during the downstroke of the finger into the key [to add to the momentum of the keystroke without requiring the small muscles of the 5th finger to exert extra effort].

Step 4:

When the finger plays into the key, it should coincide with the fall of the hand and the rotation of the forearm into the key (again, the triple-stroke).

Step 4:

The same movement should then be learned for the 4th, 3rd, and 2nd fingers.

Step 5:

Repeat the same steps as above, but instead of using thumbs as the pivot points, use the 5th fingers. This time, exaggerate the (supination) rotation of the forearm during the backswing so that the palms of each hand face each other. Then allow the forearm to pronate when the finger plays its downstroke. Learn to coordinate the keystrokes of the thumb, and then the 2nd, 3rd, and 4th fingers.

Comments and Tips:

- When rotating your forearms, you may benefit by imagining that your hand rolls upon a soft ball which sits beneath the palm of your hand (keeping the natural arches of your hand) and that your fingers reach "over" this ball before playing down into the key.
- Once a slow keystroke is learned, learn to develop a faster keystroke, then, ultimately, a fast keystroke (that moves rapidly in and out of the key, *staccatissimo*, like a snake bite). Such fast strokes will require quick finger speeds, quick forearm rotations, and generally smaller movements (to reduce inertia).
- This quick keystroke (and preparation) is what is used in fast trills, tremolos, Alberti basses, or works requiring very fast rotation movements, like Chopin's *Étude* Op. 25, No. 11, or Stravinsky's Etude Op. 7, No. 4.

WHAT LEAP? JUST PLAY!

This exercise teaches you to coordinate your finger-stroke with forearm rotation over any interval of the keyboard.

Step 1:

- Choose any pair of fingers for this exercise (e.g., start with fingers 1 and 5).

Step 2:

- Choose any note to start on, then play each finger alternately such that the interval between them gradually increases from a semitone up to 2 to 3 octaves apart and then decreases the interval until the two fingers are back to where they started (a semitone apart). [This encourages the arc (circular) motion between notes, and helps to promote the idea that whether successive notes are adjacent or far apart, the mechanical approach to playing them is the same—"don't leap, just play"].

Comments and Tips:

- Play each note using a perfectly executed triple-stroke (like in Step 1 above) *regardless of whether the notes are at intervals close together or far apart.*
- The hand should remain in a state of comfort at all times with natural arches maintained and fingers *not* stretched out. Overcome the urge to stretch out your fingers when the interval between each note becomes larger. [Avoiding stretching avoids muscle fatigue].
- Train your hand to feel free to move anywhere across the keyboard, moving in an arc-like trajectory between one note and the next, and never feeling "stuck" in any single keyboard location. Liszt's *La Campanella* and the L.H in Brahms's 1st Piano Concerto, 3rd Movement, 2nd subject are good musical examples of needing to use this movement [and prove the importance of looking at the to-be-leaped-to note before leaping].

CHOPIN'S TRIPLE-STROKE AND SIDEWAYS GLIDE

Although all piano playing uses the above skills, the most obvious examples of *needing* to use them are found in Chopin's *Études*. In fact, apart from their musical value, it would seem that many of these etudes were written with the specifically purpose to teach these core biomechanical movements: *to teach us how* to play difficult piano passages, not just daring us to see if we can survive them. Examples, from his Op. 10, are given below. It is especially interesting to observe how, when Chopin asks for the hand to move from one group of notes to another, even though the thumb may be the first finger of that hand group to fall into the key, it is usually *not* the thumb that will receive the emphasis of that group. The "go-to" note is usually a different finger of that group.

- Op.10, no.1
  bar 1: hand falls onto the finger group 1-2-4-<u>5</u> (R.H.) with fingers 1-2-4 acting as passing notes to the 5th finger, the go-to note.
- Op.10, no.4
  bar 1: hand falls onto the finger group 1-2-<u>3</u>-4 (R.H.) with the 3rd finger the go-to note.

bar 2: hand falls onto the finger group 1-2-1-4 (R.H.), (or 1-2-1-5) but 1st finger marks the bottom of the fall and is, hence, the go-to note.

bar 5: hand falls onto the finger group 4-3-2-1 (L.H.) with the 2nd finger the go-to note.

bar 6: hand falls onto the finger group 3-2-3-1 (L.H.) with the 3rd finger the go-to note.

bar 7: hand falls onto the finger group 5-2-1-3 (L.H.) with the 5th finger the go-to note.

- Op.10, no.8

  bar 1: hand falls on the finger group 4-3-2-1 (R.H.) with the 4th finger the go-to note.

  bar 2: hand falls on the finger group 1-2-3-4 (R.H.) with the 2nd finger the go-to note

  bar 3: hand falls on the finger group 4-3-2-1 (R.H.) with the 2nd finger the go-to note.

  bar 4: hand falls on the finger group 1-2-3-4 (R.H.) with the 4th finger the go-to note.

- Op.10, no.10

  Almost every phrase has a different placement of R.H. accents indicating where the emphasis of the triple-stroke should be placed.

- Op.10, no.11

  Every broken chord is essentially a group for 3 or 4 notes with the top note the go-to note and the notes preceding it acting as appoggiaturas (effectively, very similar to Op.10, No.1)

- Op.10, no.12

  bars 1–2, L.H. falls on the finger group (2 or 1)-1-2-4-3 with the 2nd finger the go-to note.

  bars 29–32, L.H. falls on the finger group 5-4-2-1 with the 2nd finger the go-to note.

What is also unique about Chopin's etudes, is that if the biomechanics of one's movements are not optimized, it becomes very difficult to play them *at all*—in short bursts, perhaps, or with early onset fatigue, perhaps, but in any sustainable fashion, unlikely. The perfect timing and amount of the finger-stroke *with* the right amount of hand drop *with* the right amount of forearm rotation are prerequisites for success, not options. Too much hand and forearm movement will lead to too slow, heavy and loud playing; and too much finger movement, especially played at loud volumes in stretched positions, will fatigue the muscles too quickly.

Chopin seems to demand that we get this biomechanical balance exactly correct right from the start, as the opening etude Op. 10, No. 1, demands of us, with its long uninterrupted sequence of notes played at velocity *and* at wide intervals. Because of this novel combination, a smooth, sideways gliding movement of the forearm *must* also accompany the hand as it moves up and down the keyboard so that the hand can *maintain its natural shape, its natural arches* and *minimize the stretching*. This is the challenge of the etude: that a constant string of wide intervals must be learned to be played at speed *as though they were small intervals*.

To assist us in how to play it, Chopin provides us with two secret clues (as he does in much of his piano writing). The first, is his use of the ">" symbol, which he uses to indicate the go-to note of each hand drop. For example, in the opening of Op. 10, No. 1, the R.H. notes are grouped in fours, using fingers 1-2-4-5. Obviously, the hand begins its drop into the keys with the thumb, but as the ">" is marked on the 5th finger, this is the go-to note (not the thumb) and should mark the *bottom* of the hand drop. The other notes are passing notes that lead to the 5th finger.

At the same time, given that there is very little time between playing the 1st finger and the 5th finger, the hand and the forearm must learn *to move quickly, laterally*, otherwise the 5th finger will be played in an extended, stretched out position—the opposite of what we want—and a cause of the muscle fatigue that this piece will otherwise generate. Additionally, given that there is little time between playing the 5th finger and the 1st finger (of the next group of notes), when the 5th finger plays its note, the 1st finger must *already* have prepared its backswing. (Mastery of the three biomechanical exercises, previously mentioned, should make this movement feel easy.) If the 1st finger is not well-prepared before it plays, your hand will be required to shift as a unit abruptly laterally to make up for the lost time. This will add volatility to your movement and musical accents and bumps which interfere with the *legato* effect that Chopin requests.

Thus, we recognize that continuity of hand motion becomes an essential feature of this etude, as it is in many others. Such advice is no secret (Mikuli, Chopin's student, commented on it[1]) but the mechanical and physiological rationale behind it, just given, perhaps is.

> **Objectively, pianism works better when a** *comfortable hand posture (i.e., neutral joint positions)* **moves** *flowingly*—**compared to an** *uncomfortable hand posture (i.e., outstretched hands and fingers)* **that moves** *abruptly*. **Evidently, virtuosic piano playing and physiologically healthy playing are not just** *hopefully* **compatible but** *necessarily* **compatible.**

That the maintenance of a comfortable hand position is essential to the pianistic success of this etude (and many others), tells us that we must let go of some of the pedantic misadventures that often accompany the teaching of it: like the idea of needing to maintain finger legato, of needing to endure extreme stretches, of needing to pass the thumb under the hand, or of learning to train all notes to be equal through a diverse range of exercises. Such teachings are impediments to the biomechanical and physiological optimization of the piece.

Instead, our goals with this piece, and any other, ought to be to use comfortable, coordinated, smooth and flowing movements, and to fuse such movements with musical gestures and sound. This type of fusion is the type of *legato* that Chopin is asking for—a haptic one, a kinaesthetic one, a musical one and a metaphorical one—him knowing full well the absurdity of trying to maintain finger legato durings such fleet-footed passagework.[2]

OPTIMIZING PIANISM—A WORKING CHECKLIST

Mechanical

- When you play, are you at ease mentally and physically with yourself, your instrument and the environment?
- Do you maintain comfortable hand positions, neutral joint ranges and good arches as much as possible?
- Have you optimized the mechanics of the notes being played?
- Have you optimized the mechanics of your movements between the notes, i.e., that get you from one note to the next (including leaps)?
- Are you coordinating the right amount of finger, hand and forearm movement for each musical passage that you play?
- Could a little hand drop or a little forearm rotation spare your fingers (and the muscles that move them) from needing to work so hard?
- Could your movements relate to musical gestures more naturally?
- Are any of your movements jerky, stressed, unnecessary, distracting, extreme in their positions, or overly emotionalized?

Mental

- When practicing, do you have an artistic vision for the piece and a clear mental image of the music (with its ideal sounds and movements) before you play them?
- When playing, do you check that your internal image of the music (and its ideal sounds and movements) is being realized?
- If your internal image is not being realized, do you immediately make corrections to ensure that it is?

- Do you challenge yourself using a variety of motor-sensory modalities to consolidate learning and memorizing?
- Are you exploiting the benefits of mental practice and visualization techniques?
- Do you engage in tasks that occupy your interest and are emotionally rewarding?
- Do you take regular breaks, including getting lots of sleep?

Music

- Is your artistic vision of the music original, inspired or in some way, extraordinary?
- Is the expressive purpose of each note, phrase and piece clear to you?
- Have you experimented with all the elements of the music to explore their "lawful" and "unlawful" limits and extract maximum expression?
- Objectively, should the notes that you are playing be played louder/softer, longer/shorter or earlier/later?
- Do you capture the sensory and emotional attention of your listeners at all times?
- Have you thought about what will provide pleasure or meaning to your listeners?

Process

- Do you maintain a positive mindset and an expectation of future success?
- Do you have a clear "to do" list to prioritize your learning tasks?
- Have you thought about the risks of what you are doing?
- Are you addressing the limiting factors in your playing (Beliefs, Mechanics, Mental, Musical, or Process)?
- Do you ensure that each learning step adds comfortably to what was previously learnt?
- Do you divide your weekly time appropriately to provide a balance between depth of learning and frequency of learning?
- Is your practice session today going to bring you closer to becoming extraordinary or are you just pushing notes and passing time?

NOTES

1. Read Mikuli's introductory notes in: Chopin, Frédéric. *Etudes*. Edited by Carl Mikuli. New York: G. Schirmer, Inc., 1943.

2. The performances of Op. 10, No.1 by Garrick Ohlsson, Valentina Lisitsa and Rubinstein are, from a biomechanical point of view, exemplary. Their videos are worth studying in slow motion, as are those of Sokolov (Op. 25, No. 12), Horowitz (Op. 10, No. 8) and Richter (Op. 10, No. 4).

Appendix A—Case Study 1
Playing mf *with Different Touch Masses*

Momentum = 1, Touch mass = 2 kg
Using:

m_{touch} = 2 kg
v_{touch} = 0.5 m/s
m_{key} = 0.1 kg

we obtain:

$$\begin{aligned} p_{in} &= m_{touch} \cdot v_{touch} \\ &= 2 \cdot 0.5 \\ &= 1 \end{aligned}$$

Upon impact, the key will accelerate (because it receives a force from the pianist), and it will continue to accelerate until the force is stopped. At the moment of hammer escapement, in order to produce a *mf* volume, v_{hammer} will need to be traveling at around 2.5 m/s, which means that v_{key} will need to be traveling at around 0.5 m/s (applying a leverage of 5:1) at the moment of escapement. Thus,

$$\begin{aligned} p_{out} &= p_{touch} + p_{key} \\ &= (m_{touch} \cdot v_{touch}) + (m_{key} \cdot v_{key}) \\ \Rightarrow 1 &= (2 \cdot v_{touch}) + (0.1 \cdot 0.5) \\ \Rightarrow v_{touch} &= 0.475 \end{aligned}$$

Presuming that m_{touch} remains unchanged during the window of opportunity, note how v_{touch} has dropped only minimally from 0.5 m/s to 0.475 m/s during this time.

Momentum = 1. Touch mass = 0.1 kg
Using:

m_{touch} = 0.1 kg
m_{key} = 0.1 kg
p_{in} = 1

we obtain:

$p_{in} = m_{touch} \cdot v_{touch}$
$\Rightarrow 1 = 0.1 \cdot v_{touch}$
$\Rightarrow v_{touch} = 10$

Thus, using a small touch mass of 0.1 kg, to produce the same *mf* volume, the pianist's finger will need to be traveling at 10 m/s, and at the moment of escapement, v_{key} will need to be the same as before (0.5 m/s). Hence:

$p_{out} = (m_{touch} \cdot v_{touch}) + (m_{key} \cdot v_{key})$
$\Rightarrow 1 = (0.1 \cdot v_{touch}) + (0.1 \cdot 0.5)$
$\Rightarrow v_{touch} = 9.5$

Note that on this occasion, v_{touch} has changed more, by 0.5 m/s (compared to 0.025 m/s). In practice, although the reduction in speed is proportionally the same in both touches, (a reduction of 5 percent) the lighter touch might be felt by pianists to cause more difficulty in controlling the speed of the key's descent. This is because any *slight* change in m_{touch}—say, increasing it by 100 g (e.g., from 0.1 kg to 0.2 kg)—will cause a relatively *large* decrease in v_{touch} (by a factor of 2) to produce the same momentum. By comparison, if the larger m_{touch} (2 kg) were chosen, the same *slight* increase in m_{touch} by 100 g (e.g., from 2.0 kg to 2.1 kg) would cause a relatively *insignificant* change in v_{touch} (by a factor of approximately 1.05) to produce the same momentum.

Appendix B—Case Study 2
Comparing Momentum Transfers for Elastic and Inelastic Collisions

Momentum = 1, Touch mass = 2 kg (Elastic Collision)
Using:

p_{in} = 1 kg.m/s
m_{touch} = 2 kg
v_{touch} = 0.5 m/s
m_{key} = 0.1 kg

$$\begin{aligned} p_{in} &= p_{out} \\ \Rightarrow m_{touch} \cdot v_{touch} &= m_{key} \cdot v_{key} \\ \Rightarrow 2 \cdot 0.5 &= 0.1 \cdot v_{key} \\ \Rightarrow v_{key} &= 10 \end{aligned}$$

Momentum = 1, Touch mass = 0.1 kg (Elastic Collision)

p_{in} = 1 kg.m/s
m_{touch} = 0.1 kg
v_{touch} = 10 m/s
m_{key} = 0.1 kg

$$\begin{aligned} p_{in} &= p_{out} \\ \Rightarrow m_{touch} \cdot v_{touch} &= m_{key} \cdot v_{key} \\ \Rightarrow 0.1 \cdot 10 &= 0.1 \cdot v_{key} \\ \Rightarrow v_{key} &= 10 \end{aligned}$$

Momentum = 1, Touch mass = 2 kg (Inelastic Collision)
Using:

p_{in} = 1 kg.m/s
m_{touch} = 2 kg
v_{touch} = 0.5 m/s
m_{key} = 0.1 kg

$$
\begin{aligned}
p_{in} &= p_{out} \\
\Rightarrow m_{touch} \cdot v_{touch} &= (m_{touch} + m_{key}) \times v_{touch+key} \\
\Rightarrow 2 \cdot 0.5 &= (2 + 0.1) \times v_{touch+key} \\
\Rightarrow v_{touch+key} &= \mathbf{0.476}
\end{aligned}
$$

Momentum = 1, Touch mass = 0.1 kg (Inelastic Collision)
Using:

p_{in} = 1 kg.m/s
m_{touch} = 0.1 kg
v_{touch} = 10 m/s
m_{key} = 0.1 kg

$$
\begin{aligned}
p_{in} &= p_{out} \\
\Rightarrow m_{touch} \cdot v_{touch} &= (m_{touch} + m_{key}) \cdot v_{touch+key} \\
\Rightarrow 0.1 \cdot 10 &= (0.1 + 0.1) \cdot v_{touch+key} \\
\Rightarrow v_{touch+key} &= \mathbf{5}
\end{aligned}
$$

Appendix C—Ideal Touch Masses (and $m\text{-}v$ Zones) for Different Dynamics

To achieve a *ff* tone ($v_{touch+key}$ = 2.5 m/s):
Using:

$$m_{touch} \cdot v_{touch} = (m_{touch} + m_{key}) \cdot v_{touch+key}$$

if m_{touch} = 2.0 => v_{touch} = 1.58 (p_{in} = 3.16)
if m_{touch} = 1.5 => v_{touch} = 1.60 (p_{in} = 2.41)
if m_{touch} = 1.0 => v_{touch} = 1.65 (p_{in} = 1.65)
if m_{touch} = 0.5 => **v_{touch} = 1.80** (**p_{in} = 0.90**)
if m_{touch} = 0.25 => v_{touch} = 2.10 (p_{in} = 0.53)
if m_{touch} = 0.1 => v_{touch} = 3.00 (p_{in} = 0.30)
if m_{touch} = 0.05 => v_{touch} = 7.50 (p_{in} = 0.38)

To achieve a *pp* tone ($v_{touch+key}$ = 0.1 m/s):
Using:

$$m_{touch} \cdot v_{touch} = (m_{touch} + m_{key}) \cdot v_{touch+key}$$

if m_{touch} = 2.0 => v_{touch} = 0.105 (p_{in} = 0.21)
if m_{touch} = 1.5 => v_{touch} = 0.107 (p_{in} = 0.16)
if m_{touch} = 1.0 => v_{touch} = 0.11 (p_{in} = 0.11)
if m_{touch} = 0.5 => v_{touch} = 0.12 (p_{in} = 0.06)
if m_{touch} = 0.25 => v_{touch} = 0.14 (p_{in} = 0.04)
if m_{touch} = 0.1 => **v_{touch} = 0.20** (**p_{in} = 0.02**)
if m_{touch} = 0.05 => v_{touch} = 0.30 (p_{in} = 0.015)

Appendix C—Ideal Trends Masses (and Forces) for Different Dynamics

Bibliography

VIDEOS

Brutus Alwaysmind. "Schiff on Bach." *YouTube*, April 10, 2021. https://www.youtube.com/watch?v=RxK1hY6vHNk.

Erick Martinez. "Glenn Gould Scriabin Op. 57 Recording Session the Paths of Music." *YouTube*, November 7, 2017. https://www.youtube.com/watch?v=fMuZUC18gDs.

Klavierplus. "Stephen Hough on Practice of Practising." *YouTube*, January 12, 2014. https://www.youtube.com/watch?v=VGBIgsoM4ng.

Lister-Sink, Barbara. "Freeing the Caged Bird." DVD. *Wingbound International and Lister-Sink Institute & Foundation*, 2017. https://www.lister-sink.org/freeing-the-caged-bird/.

Music Academy of the West. "Leon Fleisher Solo Piano Masterclass July 13, 2015." *YouTube*, July 29, 2015. https://www.youtube.com/watch?v=EGRnYBxx2Y8.

PianoLegendaryVideos. "Arthur Rubinstein: The Music Hero (Mini Documentary)." *YouTube*, July 15, 2019. https://www.youtube.com/watch?v=3H7nzTLVksU.

pianopera. "Basic Principles in Piano Playing as Taught by Josef & Rosina Lhévinne, Explained by John Browning." *Www.youtube.com*, August 23, 2017. https://www.youtube.com/watch?v=Eru9FDvUfz4.

The Piano Experience. "Arthur Rubinstein Explains Why He Will Never Perform in Germany Again (1965)." *YouTube*, May 14, 2021. https://www.youtube.com/watch?v=Lewd24QPeNs.

thepolonaise. "Vladimir Horowitz - Variation on a Theme of Bizet's - Carmen." *YouTube*, November 29, 2006. https://www.youtube.com/watch?v=WV_Nh884PKg.

tonebase Piano. "Ten Piano Technique Tips from Garrick Ohlsson." *YouTube*, August 12, 2024. https://www.youtube.com/watch?v=FWGZUHJQMrc.

www.youtube.com. "I Asked 6 Pianists What They Think of Glenn Gould (Ft. Ax, Fleisher, Bernstein, et Al)." tonebase Piano, August 9, 2022. https://www.youtube.com/watch?v=dgUnUd9oBSc.

www.youtube.com. "Warren Buffett: 'Rule #1: Never Lose Money. Rule #2: Never Forget Rule #1.'" Grahamvalue, 2018. https://www.youtube.com/watch?v=vCpT-UmVf3g.

WEB PAGES

BBC. "BBC Sounds – the Reith Lectures – Available Episodes," 2003. https://www.bbc.co.uk/sounds/series/p00ghvck.

BIO10NUMB3R5. "Reaction Times to Sound, Light and Touch – Human Homo Sapiens – BNID 110800," 2012. https://bionumbers.hms.harvard.edu/bionumber.aspx?s=n&v=4&id=110800.

Bookey.app. "30 Best Anton Rubinstein Quotes with Image | Bookey," 2023. https://www.bookey.app/quote-author/anton-rubinstein.

Bruceduffie.com. "Piano Technician Franz Mohr," 1992. http://www.bruceduffie.com/mohr.html.

darrylspiano. "Sonata Deformed: An Injured Musician's Chronicle Pt.1." *Darryl's Piano*, March 5, 2018. https://darrylspiano.com/2018/03/04/sonata-deformed-an-injured-musicians-chronicle-pt-1/.

Gallo, Carmine. "3 Daily Habits of Peak Performers, according to Michael Phelps' Coach." *Forbes*, August 8, 2016. http://www.forbes.com/sites/carminegallo/2016/05/24/3-daily-habits-of-peak-performers-according-to-michael-phelps-coach/.

Goodreads.com. "A Quote by Ludwig van Beethoven," 2024. https://www.goodreads.com/quotes/4103660-to-play-a-wrong-note-is-insignificant-to-play-without#:~:text=Quote%20by%20Ludwig%20van%20Beethoven.

Goodreads.com. "Ludwig van Beethoven Quotes (Author of Beethoven's Letters)," 2019. https://www.goodreads.com/author/quotes/40589.Ludwig_van_Beethoven.

Goodreads.com. "A Quote by Richard Wagner," 2024. https://www.goodreads.com/quotes/1056017-imagination-creates-reality.

Jensen, Anthony K. "Goethe, Johann Wolfgang von | Internet Encyclopedia of Philosophy." *Internet Encyclopaedia of Philosophy*. Accessed September 29, 2024. https://iep.utm.edu/goethe/.

Jones, Josh. "Igor Stravinsky Remembers the 'Riotous' Premiere of His Rite of Spring in 1913: 'They Were Very Shocked. They Were Naive and Stupid People.'" *Open Culture*, 2018. https://www.openculture.com/2018/04/igor-stravinsky-remembers-the-riotous-premiere-of-his-rite-of-spring.html.

Harrell, Eben. "How 1% Performance Improvements Led to Olympic Gold." *Harvard Business Review*, October 30, 2015. https://hbr.org/2015/10/how-1-performance-improvements-led-to-olympic-gold.

La Musica. "Artur Rubinstein," January 29, 2016. https://lamusica808.wordpress.com/2016/01/29/artur-rubinstein/.

Levin, Marissa. "The 1 Thing You Need for Success, according to Michael Jordan and Tony Robbins." *Inc.com*. Inc., July 24, 2017. https://www.inc.com/marissa-levin

tony-robbins-and-michael-jordan-attribute-their-su.html#:~:text=He%20ruminates%20on%20his%20own.

Lipatti, Dinu. "Letter from Dinu Lipatti to a Student." *Musicandhealth.co.uk*, 2024. https://www.musicandhealth.co.uk/articles/Lipatti.html.

Martin, Emmie. "23-Time Gold Medalist Michael Phelps Uses a Simple Trick to Stay Focused on His Goals." *CNBC*, January 1, 2019. https://www.cnbc.com/2018/12/20/michael-phelps-strategy-for-reaching-his-goals.html

Milanovic, Therese. "The Taubman Approach to Piano Technique." *The Piano Teacher*, May 6, 2014. http://thepianoteacher.com.au/articles/the-taubman-approach-to-piano-technique/.

National Institute of Neurological Disorders and Stroke. "Repetitive Motion Disorders Information Page | National Institute of Neurological Disorders and Stroke." *Nih.gov*, July 19, 2024. https://www.ninds.nih.gov/Disorders/All-Disorders/Repetitive-Motion-Disorders-Information-Page.

Oxford Centre for Evidence-Based Medicine. "Oxford Centre for Evidence-Based Medicine: Levels of Evidence (March 2009)—Centre for Evidence-Based Medicine, University of Oxford." *Www.cebm.ox.ac.uk*, 2009. https://www.cebm.ox.ac.uk/resources/levels-of-evidence/oxford-centre-for-evidence-based-medicine-levels-of-evidence-march-2009.

Quoteinvestigator.com. "It Ain't What You Don't Know That Gets You into Trouble. It's What You Know for Sure That Just Ain't So." Accessed September 20, 2024. https://quoteinvestigator.com/2018/11/18/know-trouble/#note-20795-2.

Quoteinvestigator.com. "The Architect's Most Effective Tools Are the Eraser in the Drafting Room and the Wrecking Bar on the Job – Quote Investigator," January 31, 2016. https://quoteinvestigator.com/2016/01/30/eraser/.

Quoteinvestigator.com. "Whether You Believe You Can Do a Thing or Not, You Are Right – Quote Investigator," February 4, 2015. https://quoteinvestigator.com/2015/02/03/you-can/.

Santiago, Kathy. "Point of Sound." *Pointofsound.com*, 2024. http://www.pointofsound.com/taubintro.html.

Soschner, Chris. "Aristotle Never Said, 'We Are What We Repeatedly Do. Excellence, Then, Is Not an Act, but a Habit.'" *Illumination*, March 16, 2022. https://medium.com/illumination/aristotle-never-said-we-are-what-we-repeatedly-do-excellence-then-is-not-an-act-but-a-habit-215451129bed#:~:text=After%20quoting%20a%20phrase%20from.

NEWS/MAGAZINE

Avery, Brett. "In His Own Words: Jack Nicklaus on 'His Secrets' – Golf Digest." *Golf Digest*, June 3, 2010. https://www.golfdigest.com/story/jack-nicklaus-secrets.

Del Pico-Taylor, Maria, and S. Tammam. "The Wisdom of Dorothy Taubman." *Clavier*, 2005.

Greenberg, Robert. "Music History Monday: The Beloved Son Returns – Robert Greenberg – Medium." *Medium*, April 20, 2020. https://medium.com/@rgreenbergmusic/music-history-monday-the-beloved-son-returns-b671f28ec1b7.

Gregory, Sean. "Tiger at the Masters: An Ultimate Test of Toughness." *TIME*. nextgen, April 5, 2010. https://time.com/archive/6907036/tiger-at-the-masters-an-ultimate-test-of-toughness/.

Holland, Bernard. "Vladimir Horowitz, Titan of the Piano, Dies." *Nytimes.com. The New York Times*, November 6, 1989. https://www.nytimes.com/1989/11/06/obituaries/vladimir-horowitz-titan-of-the-piano-dies.html.

Kohn, David. "What Athletes See." *The Atlantic*. The Atlantic, November 18, 2015. https://www.theatlantic.com/health/archive/2015/11/what-athletes-see/416388/#.

Liszt, Franz. *La Gazette musicale*. February 11, 1838.

McElvery, Raleigh. "How the Brain Links Gestures, Perception and Meaning." *Quanta Magazine*, March 25, 2019. https://www.quantamagazine.org/how-the-brain-links-gestures-perception-and-meaning-20190325/.

Picasso, Pablo. "Picasso Speaks: A Statement by the Artist." *The Arts: An Illustrated Monthly Magazine Covering All Phases of Ancient and Modern Art*, vol. 3, no. 5, January–June 1923, p. 315.

MUSICAL SCORES

Chopin, Frédéric. *Etudes*. Edited by Carl Mikuli. New York: G. Schirmer, Inc., 1943.

Grainger, Percy. *The Man I Love. In a transcription for the piano by the composer* (orig. George Gershwin). New York: Harms. 1944.

London College of Music. *Piano: Grade 3. Piano 2018–2020*. University of West London, LCM publications. (2017): 1–44.

FILMS

Gelb, David. *Jiro Dreams of Sushi*. Magnolia Pictures, 2001.

THESIS/DISSERTATION

Barris, Coralie Sian. "An examination of learning design in elite springboard diving." PhD diss., Queensland University of Technology, 2013.

Milanovic, Therese. "Learning and Teaching Healthy Piano Technique: Training as an Instructor in the Taubman Approach," 2011.

OTHER

Bookspan, M. 1987. *Claudio Arrau – The 80th Birthday Recital.* Liner notes. West Long Beach, NJ: Kultur.

Gould, Glenn. 2012. *The Glenn Gould Collection: Johannes Brahms Ballades, Rhapsodies & Intermezzi.* CD booklet. Sony Music Entertainment Classical.

BOOKS/ARTICLES

Abolins, Valters, Alex Stremoukhov, Caroline Walter, and Mark L. Latash. "On the Origin of Finger Enslaving: Control with Referent Coordinates and Effects of Visual Feedback." *Journal of Neurophysiology* 124, no. 6 (December 1, 2020): 1625–36. doi:https://doi.org/10.1152/jn.00322.2020.

Abraham, Wickliffe C. "Metaplasticity: Tuning Synapses and Networks for Plasticity." *Nature Reviews Neuroscience* 9, no. 5 (May 2008): 387–87. doi:https://doi.org/10.1038/nrn2356.

Ackermann, Bronwen J. "How Much Training Is Too Much?" *Medical Problems of Performing Artists* 32, no. 1 (March 1, 2017): 61–62. doi:https://doi.org/10.21091/mppa.2017.1011.

Adams, Andrew, and Bradley Martin. "The Man behind the Virtuoso Pianist: Charles-Louis Hanon's Life and Works." *Hanon-Online*, 2014. https://www.hanon-online.com/the-man-behind-the-virtuoso-pianist-charles-louis-hanon-s-life-and-works-p1/.

Adams, Debi. "An Introduction to the Alexander Technique for Pianists and Their Teachers." *Debi Adams, Alexander Technique.* Debi Adams, Alexander Technique, July 10, 2012. https://debiadamsat.com/about/an-introduction-to-the-alexander-technique-for-pianists-and-their-teachers/.

Alford, Robert R., and Andras Szanto. "Orpheus Wounded: The Experience of Pain in the Professional Worlds of the Piano." *Theory and Society* 25, no. 1 (February 1996): 1–44. doi:https://doi.org/10.1007/bf00140757.

Altenmüller, Eckart. "Focal Dystonia: Advances in Brain Imaging and Understanding of Fine Motor Control in Musicians." *Hand Clinics* 19, no. 3 (August 2003): 523–38. doi:https://doi.org/10.1016/s0749-0712(03)00043-x.

Altenmüller, Eckart, and Shinichi Furuya. "Apollos Gift and Curse: Making Music as a Model for Adaptive and Maladaptive Plasticity." *E-Neuroforum* 23, no. 2 (January 24, 2017). doi:https://doi.org/10.1515/nf-2016-a054.

Altenmüller, Eckart, and Shinichi Furuya. "Brain Plasticity and the Concept of Metaplasticity in Skilled Musicians." *Advances in Experimental Medicine and Biology*, 2016, 197–208. doi:https://doi.org/10.1007/978-3-319-47313-0_11.

Altenmüller, Eckart, Jürg Kesselring, and Mario Wiesendanger. *Music, Motor Control and the Brain.* Oxford: Oxford University Press, 2006.

Askenfelt, Anders. "Measuring the motion of the piano hammer during string contact." *Department for Speech, Music and Hearing KTH Sweden: Quarterly Progress and Status Report* (1991).

Askenfelt, Anders. "Observations on the transient components of the piano tone." *Speech Transmission Laboratory – Quarterly Progress and Status Report* 90, no. 4 (July 28, 1993): 15–22.

Askenfelt, Anders, ed. *Five Lectures on the Acoustics of the Piano*. Stockholm: Royal Swedish Academy of Music, 1990.

Askenfelt, Anders, and Erik V Jansson. "From Touch to String Vibrations. II: The Motion of the Key and Hammer." *Journal of the Acoustical Society of America* 90, no. 5 (November 1, 1991): 2383–93. doi:https://doi.org/10.1121/1.402043.

Askenfelt, Anders, Alexander Galembo, and Lola L. Cuddy. "On the Acoustics and Psychology of Piano Touch and Tone." *Journal of the Acoustical Society of America* 103, no. 5 Supplement (May 1, 1998): 2873–73. doi:https://doi.org/10.1121/1.421527.

Bangert, Marc, and Eckart Altenmüller. "Mapping Perception to Action in Piano Practice: A Longitudinal DC-EEG Study." *BMC Neuroscience* 4, no. 1 (2003): 26. doi:https://doi.org/10.1186/1471-2202-4-26.

Bangert, Marc, Thomas Peschel, Gottfried Schlaug, Michael Rotte, Dieter Drescher, Hermann Hinrichs, Hans-Jochen Heinze, and Eckart Altenmüller. "Shared Networks for Auditory and Motor Processing in Professional Pianists: Evidence from FMRI Conjunction." *NeuroImage* 30, no. 3 (April 2006): 917–26. doi:https://doi.org/10.1016/j.neuroimage.2005.10.044.

Barnes, Christopher. *The Russian Piano School*. London: Kahn and Averill, 2008.

Behne, Klaus-Ernst, and Clemens Wöllner. "Seeing or Hearing the Pianists? A Synopsis of an Early Audiovisual Perception Experiment and a Replication." *Musicae Scientiae* 15, no. 3 (August 15, 2011): 324–42. doi:https://doi.org/10.1177/1029864911410955.

Berman, Boris. *Notes from the Pianist's Bench*. New Haven, CT: Yale University Press, 2000.

Bernardi, Nicolò F., Matteo De Buglio, Pietro D. Trimarchi, Alfonso Chielli, and Emanuela Bricolo. "Mental Practice Promotes Motor Anticipation: Evidence from Skilled Music Performance." *Frontiers in Human Neuroscience* 7 (2013). doi:https://doi.org/10.3389/fnhum.2013.00451.

Bernstein, Nikolai. *Coordinate and Regulation of Movements*. Oxford: Pergamon Press, 1967.

Bjork, Robert A. *Metacognition*. Edited by Janet Metcalfe and Arthur P. Shimamura. The MIT Press, 1994. doi:https://doi.org/10.7551/mitpress/4561.001.0001.

Blido, Stefan. "Stefan Blido: Zen in the Art of Playing the Piano." *Peter-Feuchtwanger.de*. Accessed September 27, 2024. http://www.peter-feuchtwanger.de/english-version/texts/stefan-blido-zen-in-the-art-of-playing-the-piano/index.html.

Blido, Stefan. "Texts." *Peter-Feuchtwanger.de*, 2024. http://www.peter-feuchtwanger.de/english-version/texts/.

Boutillon, Xavier. "Model for Piano Hammers: Experimental Determination and Digital Simulation." *Journal of the Acoustical Society of America* 83, no. 2 (February 1, 1988): 746–54. doi:https://doi.org/10.1121/1.396117.

Bowen, Catherine. *Free Artist*. New York: Random House, 1939.

Bragge, Peter, Andrea Bialocerkowski, and Joan McMeeken. "A Systematic Review of Prevalence and Risk Factors Associated with Playing-Related Musculoskeletal Disorders in Pianists." *Occupational Medicine* 56, no. 1 (November 7, 2005): 28–38. doi:https://doi.org/10.1093/occmed/kqi177.

Brée, Malwine, Arthur Elson, and Seymour Bernstein. *The Leschetizky Method: A Guide to Fine and Correct Piano Playing.* Mineola, NY: Dover, 1997.

Breithaupt, Rudolf Maria. *Natural Piano-Technic. Vol. II. School of Weight-Touch . . . Preliminary to Intermediate Grade ... Translation by John Bernhoff.* Translated by John Bernhoff. Leipzig: C. F. Kahnt Nachfolger., 1909.

Brendel, Alfred. *Musical Thoughts & Afterthoughts.* Robson Books Limited, 1976.

Brent-Smith, A. "A Study of Franz Liszt." *The Musical Times* 70, no. 1035 (May 1, 1929): 401–3. doi:https://doi.org/10.2307/915233.

Bresciani, Di. *Di Bresciani: A New Look at Australian Light.* Berkeley, CA: Hardie Grant Books, 2022.

Bresciani, Jean-Pierre, Marc O. Ernst, Knut Drewing, Guillaume Bouyer, Vincent Maury, and Abderrahmane Kheddar. "Feeling What You Hear: Auditory Signals Can Modulate Tactile Tap Perception." *Experimental Brain Research* 162, no. 2 (December 10, 2004): 172–80. doi:https://doi.org/10.1007/s00221-004-2128-2.

Broughton, Mary C., and Catherine J. Stevens. "Analyzing Expressive Qualities in Movement and Stillness: Effort-Shape Analyses of Solo Marimbists' Bodily Expression." *Music Perception: An Interdisciplinary Journal* 29, no. 4 (April 1, 2012): 339–57. doi:https://doi.org/10.1525/mp.2012.29.4.339.

Bruser, Madeline. *The Art of Practicing.* New York: Crown, 2013.

Busby, Jim. *Grand Piano Regulation.* Piano Technician Tutorials. Apple Books, 2016. https://books.apple.com/us/book/grand-piano-regulation/id1135106813.

Cairns, Simeon P. "Lactic Acid and Exercise Performance." *Sports Medicine* 36, no. 4 (2006): 279–91. doi:https://doi.org/10.2165/00007256-200636040-00001.

Carr, Elizabeth. *Shura Cherkassky.* Lanham, MD: Scarecrow Press, 2006.

Chaffin, Roger, Gabriela Imreh, and Mary E. Crawford. *Practicing Perfection.* Mahwah, NJ: Lawrence Erlbaum, 2002.

Chatterjee, Anjan. *The Aesthetic Brain: How We Evolved to Desire Beauty and Enjoy Art.* New York: Oxford University Press, 2015.

Christiansen, S., and S. Cohen. "Chronic Pain: Pathophysiology and Mechanisms." In *Essentials of Interventional Techniques in Managing Chronic Pain*, 15–25. New York: Springer International Publishing, 2018.

Cole, Jonathan, and Barbara Montero. "Affective Proprioception." *Janus Head* 9, no. 2 (2007): 299–317. doi:https://doi.org/10.5840/jh2006922.

Colosio, Marco, Anna Shestakova, Vadim V. Nikulin, Evgeny Blagovechtchenski, and Vasily Klucharev. "Neural Mechanisms of Cognitive Dissonance (Revised): An EEG Study." *The Journal of Neuroscience* 37, no. 20 (April 24, 2017): 5074–83. doi:https://doi.org/10.1523/jneurosci.3209-16.2017.

Conklin, Harold A. "Design and Tone in the Mechanoacoustic Piano. Part I. Piano Hammers and Tonal Effects." *Journal of the Acoustical Society of America* 99, no. 6 (June 1, 1996): 3286–96. doi:https://doi.org/10.1121/1.414947.

Connors, Michael H., and Peter W. Halligan. "A Cognitive Account of Belief: A Tentative Road Map." *Frontiers in Psychology* 5 (February 13, 2015). doi:https://doi.org/10.3389/fpsyg.2014.01588.

Cook, Nicholas. "Beyond the Notes." *Nature* 453, no. 7199 (June 2008): 1186–87. doi:https://doi.org/10.1038/4531186a.

Cooke, James Francis. *Great Pianists on Piano Playing: Godowsky, Hofmann, Lhévinne, Paderewski, and 24 Other Legendary Performers*. Mineola, NY: Dover Publications, 1999.

Cornett, Vanessa. *The Mindful Musician*. Oxford: Oxford University Press, 2019.

Criscimagna-Hemminger, S. E., and R. Shadmehr. "Consolidation Patterns of Human Motor Memory." *Journal of Neuroscience* 28, no. 39 (September 24, 2008): 9610–18. doi:https://doi.org/10.1523/jneurosci.3071-08.2008.

Cruder, Cinzia, Marco Barbero, Pelagia Koufaki, Emiliano Soldini, and Nigel Gleeson. "Prevalence and Associated Factors of Playing-Related Musculoskeletal Disorders among Music Students in Europe. Baseline Findings from the Risk of Music Students (RISMUS) Longitudinal Multicentre Study." Edited by Feng Pan. *PLOS ONE* 15, no. 12 (December 9, 2020): e0242660. doi:https://doi.org/10.1371/journal.pone.0242660.

Culver, Charles A. *Musical Acoustics*. Philadelphia: Blakiston Company, 1947.

D'Ausilio, Alessandro. "Mirror-like Mechanisms and Music." *The Scientific World JOURNAL* 9, no. 9 (2009): 1415–22. doi:https://doi.org/10.1100/tsw.2009.160.

Davidson, Jane W. "Bodily Movement and Facial Actions in Expressive Musical Performance by Solo and Duo Instrumentalists: Two Distinctive Case Studies." *Psychology of Music* 40, no. 5 (August 20, 2012): 595–633. doi:https://doi.org/10.1177/0305735612449896.

Davidson, Jane W. "Visual Perception of Performance Manner in the Movements of Solo Musicians." *Psychology of Music* 21, no. 2 (April 1993): 103–13. doi:https://doi.org/10.1177/030573569302100201.

Davies, James Q. *Romantic Anatomies of Performance*. Berkeley: University of California Press, 2014.

Dayan, Peter. "On Nature, Music, and Meaning in Debussy's Writing." *19th-Century Music* 28, no. 3 (2005): 214–29. doi:https://doi.org/10.1525/ncm.2005.28.3.214.

Dobelli, Rolf. *The Art of Thinking Clearly*. London: Sceptre, 2014.

Donovan, Sandy. *Hypatia: Mathematician, Inventor, and Philosopher*. Minneapolis, MN: Compass Point Books, 2008.

Dossey, Larry. "Compasses, Craziness, and the Thieves of Reason: How Thinking Goes Wrong." *EXPLORE* 12, no. 5 (September 2016): 295–301. doi:https://doi.org/10.1016/j.explore.2016.06.007.

Dounskaia, Natalia. "Control of Human Limb Movements: The Leading Joint Hypothesis and Its Practical Applications." *Exercise and Sport Sciences Reviews* 38, no. 4 (October 2010): 201–8. doi:https://doi.org/10.1097/jes.0b013e3181f45194.

Driver, Jon, and Charles Spence. "Multisensory Perception: Beyond Modularity and Convergence." *Current Biology* 10, no. 20 (October 2000): R731–35. doi:https://doi.org/10.1016/s0960-9822(00)00740-5.

Dubal, David. *Reflections from the Keyboard*. New York: Summit Books, 1984.

Dudai, Yadin. "The Neurobiology of Consolidations, Or, How Stable Is the Engram?" *Annual Review of Psychology* 55, no. 1 (February 2004): 51–86. doi:https://doi.org/10.1146/annurev.psych.55.090902.142050.

Dweck, Carol S., and Ellen L. Leggett. "A Social-Cognitive Approach to Motivation and Personality." *Psychological Review* 95, no. 2 (1988): 256–73. doi:https://doi.org/10.1037//0033-295x.95.2.256.

Eigeldinger, Jean-Jacques. *Chopin: Pianist and Teacher as Seen by His Pupils*. Cambridge, Cambridgeshire; New York: Cambridge University Press, 1986.

Ericsson, Anders. *Peak: Secrets from the New Science of Expertise*. Boston: Houghton Mifflin Harcourt, 2016.

Ericsson, K Anders, ed. *The Road to Excellence: The Acquisition of Expert Performance in the Arts and Sciences, Sports, and Games*. New York: Psychology Press, 2013.

Ericsson, K. Anders. "Deliberate Practice and Acquisition of Expert Performance: A General Overview." *Academic Emergency Medicine* 15, no. 11 (November 2008): 988–94.

Ericsson, K. Anders, Ralf T. Krampe, and Clemens Tesch-Römer. "The Role of Deliberate Practice in the Acquisition of Expert Performance." *Psychological Review* 100, no. 3 (1993): 363–406. doi:https://doi.org/10.1037/0033-295X.100.3.363.

Ericsson, Karl Anders. "Expertise and Individual Differences: The Search for the Structure and Acquisition of Experts' Superior Performance." *Wiley Interdisciplinary Reviews: Cognitive Science* 8, no. 1–2 (December 2016): e1382. doi:https://doi.org/10.1002/wcs.1382.

Fay, Amy. *Music-Study in Germany*. 1896. Reprint, New York: Macmillan Company, 1922.

Fink, Seymour. *Mastering Piano Technique: A Guide for Students, Teachers, and Performers*. Portland: Amadeus, 1999.

Forkel, Johann Nikolaus, and Charles Sanford Terry. *Johann Sebastian Bach, His Life; Art, and Work*. London: Constable, 1970.

Frank, Cornelia, William M. Land, Carmen Popp, and Thomas Schack. "Mental Representation and Mental Practice: Experimental Investigation on the Functional Links between Motor Memory and Motor Imagery." Edited by Cosimo Urgesi. *PLoS ONE* 9, no. 4 (April 17, 2014): e95175. doi:https://doi.org/10.1371/journal.pone.0095175.

Fraser, Alan. *The Craft of Piano Playing: A New Approach to Piano Technique*. Lanham, MD: Scarecrow Press, 2003.

Friedmann, Jonathan L. *Musical Aesthetics: An Introduction to Concepts, Theories, and Functions*. Newcastle-upon-Tyne: Cambridge Scholars Publishing, 2018.

Gát, József. *The Technique of Piano Playing*. 3rd ed. Budapest, Hungary: Corvina, 1968.

Gerig, Reginald R. *Famous Pianists & Their Technique*. Robert B. Luce, 1974.

Galembo, Alexander. "Perception of Musical Instrument by Performer and Listener (with Application to the Piano)." *Proceedings of the International Workshop on Human Supervision and Control in Engineering and Music*, (September 21–24, 2001) 257–66. http://www.engineeringandmusic.de/individu/galealex/Galambo-Paper.html.

Ghanamah, Rafat, Hazar Eghbaria-Ghanamah, Avi Karni, and Esther Adi-Japha. "Too Little, Too Much: A Limited Range of Practice 'Doses' Is Best for Retaining Grapho-Motor Skill in Children." *Learning and Instruction* 69 (October 1, 2020): 101351. doi:https://doi.org/10.1016/j.learninstruc.2020.101351.

Gieseking, Walter, and Karl Leimer. *Piano Technique*. 1932. Reprint, New York: Dover Publications, 1972.

Ginsborg, Jane. "'The Brilliance of Perfection' or 'Pointless Finish'? What Virtuosity Means to Musicians." *Musicae Scientiae* 22, no. 4 (November 13, 2018): 454–73. doi:https://doi.org/10.1177/1029864918776351.

Goebl, Werner, Roberto Bresin, and Ichiro Fujinaga. "Perception of Touch Quality in Piano Tones." *The Journal of the Acoustical Society of America* 136, no. 5 (November 2014): 2839–50. doi:https://doi.org/10.1121/1.4896461.

Goebl, Werner, Roberto Bresin, and Alexander Galembo. "Once Again: The Perception of Piano Touch and Tone. Can Touch Audibly Change Piano Sound Independently of Intensity?" *Proceedings of the International Symposium on Musical Acoustics, Nara, Japan, March 31 to April 3*, 2004, 332–35.

Goebl, Werner, and Caroline Palmer. "Temporal Control and Hand Movement Efficiency in Skilled Music Performance." Edited by Ramesh Balasubramaniam. *PLoS ONE* 8, no. 1 (January 3, 2013): e50901. doi:https://doi.org/10.1371/journal.pone.0050901.

Goldacre, Ben. *Bad Science*. London: Fourth Estate, 2008.

Guest, Steve, Caroline Catmur, Donna Lloyd, and Charles Spence. "Audiotactile Interactions in Roughness Perception." *Experimental Brain Research* 146, no. 2 (September 1, 2002): 161–71. doi:https://doi.org/10.1007/s00221-002-1164-z.

Hailstone, Julia C., Rohani Omar, Susie M. D. Henley, Chris Frost, Michael G. Kenward, and Jason D. Warren. "It's Not What You Play, It's How You Play It: Timbre Affects Perception of Emotion in Music." *Quarterly Journal of Experimental Psychology* 62, no. 11 (November 2009): 2141–55. doi:https://doi.org/10.1080/17470210902765957.

Hambrick, David Z., Brooke N. Macnamara, Guillermo Campitelli, Fredrik Ullén, and Miriam A. Mosing. "Beyond born versus made: A new look at expertise." In *Psychology of Learning and Motivation*, vol. 64, pp. 1–55. San Diego, CA: Academic Press, 2016.

Harari, Yuval Noah. *Sapiens: A Brief History of Humankind*. New York: Harper Perennial, 2015.

Harding, David C., K.D. Brandt, and B.M. Hillberry. "Finger Joint Force Minimization in Pianists Using Optimization Techniques." *Journal of Biomechanics* 26, no. 12 (December 1993): 1403–12. doi:https://doi.org/10.1016/0021-9290(93)90091-r.

Hart, Harry C., Melville W. Fuller, and Walter S. Lusby. "A Precision Study of Piano Touch and Tone." *The Journal of the Acoustical Society of America* 6, no. 2 (October 1, 1934): 80–94. doi:https://doi.org/10.1121/1.1915706.

Hassan, Aumyo, and Sarah J. Barber. "The Effects of Repetition Frequency on the Illusory Truth Effect." *Cognitive Research: Principles and Implications* 6, no. 1 (May 13, 2021). doi:https://doi.org/10.1186/s41235-021-00301-5.

Helding, Lynn. *The Musician's Mind: Teaching, Learning, and Performance in the Age of Brain Science*. Lanham, MD: Rowman & Littlefield, 2020.

Herrigel, Eugen. *Zen in the Art of Archery: With an Introduction by D.T. Suzuki.* Translated by R.F.C. Hull. 1953. New York: Vintage Books, 1971.

Hill, William G. "Noise in Piano Tone." *The Musical Times* 81, no. 1173 (November 1940): 458. doi:https://doi.org/10.2307/923870.

Howard, Jonathan. *Cognitive Errors and Diagnostic Mistakes.* Cham, Switzerland: Springer International Publishing, 2019. doi:https://doi.org/10.1007/978-3-319-93224-8.

Hyde, K. L., J. Lerch, A. Norton, M. Forgeard, E. Winner, A. C. Evans, and G. Schlaug. "Musical Training Shapes Structural Brain Development." *Journal of Neuroscience* 29, no. 10 (March 11, 2009): 3019–25. doi:https://doi.org/10.1523/jneurosci.5118-08.2009.

Igrec, Mario. *Pianos Inside Out: A Comprehensive Guide to Piano Tuning, Repairing, and Rebuilding.* Mandeville, LA: In Tune Press, 2013.

Ioannou, Christos I., Julia Hafer, André Lee, and Eckart Altenmuller. "Epidemiology, Treatment Efficacy, and Anxiety Aspects of Music Students Affected by Playing-Related Pain: A Retrospective Evaluation with Follow-Up." *Medical Problems of Performing Artists* 33, no. 1 (March 1, 2018): 26–38. doi:https://doi.org/10.21091/mppa.2018.1006.

Iott, Sheryl. *Thinking and Playing Music: Intentional Strategies for Optimal Practice and Performance.* Lanham, MD: Rowman & Littlefield Publishers, 2021.

Jain, Aditya, Ramta Bansal, Avnish Kumar, and K. D. Singh. "A comparative study of visual and auditory reaction times on the basis of gender and physical activity levels of medical first year students." *International journal of applied and basic medical research* 5, no. 2 (2015): 124–27.

Jain, Sanjiv, Kristy Janssen, and Sharon DeCelle. "Alexander Technique and Feldenkrais Method: A Critical Overview." *Physical Medicine and Rehabilitation Clinics of North America* 15, no. 4 (November 2004): 811–25. doi:https://doi.org/10.1016/j.pmr.2004.04.005.

Jost, Mack. *Yet Another Guide to Piano Playing.* Armidale, NSW, Australia: Allans Publishing, 1974.

Kahneman, Daniel. *Thinking, Fast and Slow.* London: Penguin, 2011.

Kantak, Shailesh S., and Carolee J. Winstein. "Learning–Performance Distinction and Memory Processes for Motor Skills: A Focused Review and Perspective." *Behavioural Brain Research* 228, no. 1 (March 2012): 219–31. doi:https://doi.org/10.1016/j.bbr.2011.11.028.

Kenny, Dianna T., and Bronwen Ackermann. "Optimizing physical and psychological health in performing musicians." *The Oxford Handbook of Music Psychology* 1 (2009): 390–400.

Keller, Peter E. "Mental Imagery in Music Performance: Underlying Mechanisms and Potential Benefits." *Annals of the New York Academy of Sciences* 1252, no. 1 (April 2012): 206–13. doi:https://doi.org/10.1111/j.1749-6632.2011.06439.x.

Kelley, Paul, and Terry Whatson. "Making Long-Term Memories in Minutes: A Spaced Learning Pattern from Memory Research in Education." *Frontiers in Human Neuroscience* 7 (2013). doi:https://doi.org/10.3389/fnhum.2013.00589.

Keysers, Christian, Evelyne Kohler, M. Alessandra Umiltà, Luca Nanetti, Leonardo Fogassi, and Vittorio Gallese. "Audiovisual mirror neurons and action recognition." *Experimental Brain Research* 153 (2003): 628–36.

Kimm, Dennis, and David V. Thiel. "Hand Speed Measurements in Boxing." *Procedia Engineering* 112 (2015): 502–6. doi:https://doi.org/10.1016/j.proeng.2015.07.232.

Kochevitsky, George. *The Art of Piano Playing*. Summy-Birchard Music, 1967.

Kohler, Evelyne, Christian Keysers, M. Alessandra Umiltà, Leonardo Fogassi, Vittorio Gallese, and Giacomo Rizzolatti. "Hearing Sounds, Understanding Actions: Action Representation in Mirror Neurons." *Science* 297, no. 5582 (August 2, 2002): 846–48. doi:https://doi.org/10.1126/science.1070311.

Kok, Laura M., Bionka M. A. Huisstede, Veronique M. A. Voorn, Jan W. Schoones, and Rob G. H. H. Nelissen. "The Occurrence of Musculoskeletal Complaints among Professional Musicians: A Systematic Review." *International Archives of Occupational and Environmental Health* 89, no. 3 (November 12, 2015): 373–96. doi:https://doi.org/10.1007/s00420-015-1090-6.

Koornhof, G., and Walt, A. "The influence of touch on piano sound." *Proceedings of the Stockholm Music Acoustics Conference (SMAC'93)* 79 (1994): 297–301.

Krakauer, John W., Claude Ghez, and M. Felice Ghilardi. "Adaptation to visuomotor transformations: consolidation, interference, and forgetting." *Journal of Neuroscience* 25, no. 2 (2005): 473–78.

Kullak, Adolf. *The Aesthetics of Pianoforte-Playing*. Translated by T. Baker. 5th ed. 1893. Reprint, New York: G. Schirmer, 1972.

Lakoff, George, and Mark Johnson. *Philosophy in the Flesh: The Embodied Mind and Its Challenge to Western Thought*. New York: Basic Books, 1999.

Lappi, Otto. "The Racer's Mind—How Core Perceptual-Cognitive Expertise Is Reflected in Deliberate Practice Procedures in Professional Motorsport." *Frontiers in Psychology* 9 (August 13, 2018). doi:https://doi.org/10.3389/fpsyg.2018.01294.

Leach, Stefan, and Mario Weick. "Can People Judge the Veracity of Their Intuitions?" *Social Psychological and Personality Science* 9, no. 1 (July 31, 2017): 40–49. doi:https://doi.org/10.1177/1948550617706732.

Leaver, A. M., J. Van Lare, B. Zielinski, A. R. Halpern, and J. P. Rauschecker. "Brain Activation during Anticipation of Sound Sequences." *Journal of Neuroscience* 29, no. 8 (February 25, 2009): 2477–85. doi:https://doi.org/10.1523/jneurosci.4921-08.2009.

Leow, Li-Ann, Welber Marinovic, Aymar de Rugy, and Timothy J. Carroll. "Task Errors Drive Memories That Improve Sensorimotor Adaptation." *The Journal of Neuroscience* 40, no. 15 (February 6, 2020): 3075–88. doi:https://doi.org/10.1523/jneurosci.1506-19.2020.

Leva, Paulo de. "Adjustments to Zatsiorsky-Seluyanov's Segment Inertia Parameters." *Journal of Biomechanics* 29, no. 9 (1996): 1223–30. doi:https://doi.org/10.1016/0021-9290(95)00178-6.

Levangie, Pamela K., and Cynthia C. Norkin. *Joint Structure and Function: A Comprehensive Analysis*. Philadelpha: F.A. Davis, 2001.

Levinskaya, Maria. *The Levinskaya System of Pianoforte Technique and Tone-Colour through Mental & Muscular Control*. London; Toronto: J.M. Dent and Sons, 1930.

Lewandowsky, Stephan, Ullrich K. H. Ecker, Colleen M. Seifert, Norbert Schwarz, and John Cook. "Misinformation and Its Correction: Continued Influence and Successful Debiasing." *Psychological Science in the Public Interest* 13, no. 3 (September 17, 2012): 106–31. doi:https://doi.org/10.1177/1529100612451018.

Lhévinne, Josef. "Good Tone Is Born in the Player's Mind." *The Musician* 28, no. 7 (1923).

Lhévinne, Josef. *Basic Principles in Pianoforte Playing*. New York: Dover Publications, 1972.

Li, Zong-Ming, Shouchen Dun, Daniel A. Harkness, and Teresa L. Brininger. "Motion Enslaving among Multiple Fingers of the Human Hand." *Motor Control* 8, no. 1 (January 2004): 1–15. doi:https://doi.org/10.1123/mcj.8.1.1.

Lin, Chien-Ho Janice, Ming-Chang Chiang, Barbara J. Knowlton, Marco Iacoboni, Parima Udompholkul, and Allan D. Wu. "Interleaved Practice Enhances Skill Learning and the Functional Connectivity of Fronto-Parietal Networks." *Human Brain Mapping* 34, no. 7 (February 22, 2012): 1542–58. doi:https://doi.org/10.1002/hbm.22009.

Liszt, Franz. *The Collected Writings of Franz Liszt. Volume 2, Essays and Letters of a Travelling Batchelor of Music*. Edited and translated by Janita R. Hall-Swadley. Lanham, MD: Scarecrow Press, 2012.

Long, Marguerite. *Le Piano*. Paris: Éd. Salabert, 1959.

Luft, A. R., M. Buitrago, T. Ringer, J. Dichgans, and J. Schulz. "Motor Skill Learning Depends on Protein Synthesis in Motor Cortex after Training." *Journal of Neuroscience* 24, no. 29 (July 21, 2004): 6515–20. doi:https://doi.org/10.1523/jneurosci.1034-04.2004.

Mach, Elyse. *Great Contemporary Pianists Speak for Themselves*. New York: Dodd, Mead and Company, Inc, 1991.

MacRitchie, Jennifer. "The Art and Science behind Piano Touch: A Review Connecting Multi-Disciplinary Literature." *Musicae Scientiae* 19, no. 2 (March 13, 2015): 171–90. doi:https://doi.org/10.1177/1029864915572813.

Maes, Pieter-Jan, Marc Leman, Caroline Palmer, and Marcelo M. Wanderley. "Action-Based Effects on Music Perception." *Frontiers in Psychology* 4 (2014). doi:https://doi.org/10.3389/fpsyg.2013.01008.

Mamizuka, Naotaka, Masataka Sakane, Koji Kaneoka, Noriyuki Hori, and Naoyuki Ochiai. "Kinematic quantitation of the patellar tendon reflex using a tri-axial accelerometer." *Journal of Biomechanics* 40, no. 9 (2007): 2107–2111.

Mark, Thomas, Roberta Gary, Thom Miles, and Barbara Conable. *What Every Pianist Needs to Know about the Body: A Manual for Players of Keyboard Instruments: Piano, Organ, Digital Keyboard, Harpsichord, Clavichord*. Chicago: Gia Publications, 2003.

Mattar, Andrew, Mohammad Darainy, and David J Ostry. "Motor Learning and Its Sensory Effects: Time Course of Perceptual Change and Its Presence with Gradual Introduction of Load." *Journal of Neurophysiology* 109, no. 3 (February 1, 2013): 782–91. doi:https://doi.org/10.1152/jn.00734.2011.

Matthay, Tobias. *The First Principles of Pianoforte Playing*. London: Longmans, Green & Co, 1922.

———. *The Visible and Invisible in Pianoforte Technique*. Oxford: Oxford University Press, 1932.

Menkes, C-J., and N.E. Lane. "Are Osteophytes Good or Bad?" *Osteoarthritis and Cartilage* 12 (2004): 53–54. doi:https://doi.org/10.1016/j.joca.2003.09.003.

Mohr, Franz, and Edith Schaeffer. *My Life with the Great Pianists*. Grand Rapids, MI: Ravens Ridge Books, 1992.

Morris, Tony, Michael Spittle, and Anthony P. Watt. *Imagery in Sport*. Champaign, IL: Human Kinetics, 2005.

Nagel, Julie Jaffee. *Managing Stage Fright: A Guide for Musicians and Music Teachers*. Oxford: Oxford University Press, 2017.

Neuhaus, Heinrich. *The Art of Piano Playing*. Translated by K. A. Leibovitch. London: Kahn & Averill, 1993.

Ng, Betsy. "The Neuroscience of Growth Mindset and Intrinsic Motivation." *Brain Sciences* 8, no. 2 (January 26, 2018): 20. doi:https://doi.org/10.3390/brainsci8020020.

Newell, Karl M., Gottfried Mayer-Kress, S. Lee Hong, and Yeou-Teh Liu. "Adaptation and Learning: Characteristic Time Scales of Performance Dynamics." *Human Movement Science* 28, no. 6 (December 2009): 655–87. doi:https://doi.org/10.1016/j.humov.2009.07.001.

Norkin, Cynthia C., and Pamela K. Levangie. *Joint Structure & Function a Comprehensive Analysis*. Philadelphia: F.A. Davis, 1992.

Ortmann, Otto. *The Physiological Mechanics of Piano Technique*. New York: Dutton, 1962.

Overduin, Simon A., Andrew G. Richardson, Courtney E. Lane, Emilio Bizzi, and Daniel Z. Press. "Intermittent Practice Facilitates Stable Motor Memories." *The Journal of Neuroscience* 26, no. 46 (November 15, 2006): 11888–92. doi:https://doi.org/10.1523/jneurosci.1320-06.2006.

Owens, Melinda T., and Kimberly D. Tanner. "Teaching as Brain Changing: Exploring Connections between Neuroscience and Innovative Teaching." *CBE—Life Sciences Education* 16, no. 2 (June 2017): fe2. doi:https://doi.org/10.1187/cbe.17-01-0005.

Palmieri, Robert. *The Piano*. New York: Routledge, 2003.

Papetti, Stefano, and Charalampos Saitis, eds. *Musical Haptics*. New York: Springer International Publishing, 2018.

Parncutt, Richard. "Piano Touch, Timbre, Ecological Psychology, and Cross-Modal Interference." *International Symposium on Performance Science.*, January 1, 2013. http://iwk.mdw.ac.at/lit_db_iwk/download.php?id=22058.

Parncutt, Richard, and Malcolm Troup. "Piano." In *The Science and Psychology of Music Performance: Creative Strategies for Teaching and Learning*, edited by Gary McPherson, 285–302. New York: Oxford University Press, 2002.

Pascual-Leone, Alvaro. "The brain that plays music and is changed by it." *Annals of the New York Academy of Sciences* 930, no. 1 (2001): 315–29.

Paterson, Mark. "Movement for Movement's Sake? On the Relationship between Kinaesthesia and Aesthetics." *Essays in Philosophy* 13, no. 2 (2012): 471–97. doi:https://doi.org/10.7710/1526-0569.1433.

Pease, Allan, and Barbara Pease. *The Definitive Book of Body Language: How to Read Others' Attitudes by Their Gestures*. London: Orion, 2017.

Piggott, Patrick. *The Life and Music of John Field, 1782-1837, Creator of the Nocturne*. Berkeley: University of California Press, 1973.

Plagenhoef, Stanley, F. Gaynor Evans, and Thomas Abdelnour. "Anatomical Data for Analyzing Human Motion." *Research Quarterly for Exercise and Sport* 54, no. 2 (June 1983): 169–78. doi:https://doi.org/10.1080/02701367.1983.10605290.

Platz, Friedrich, and Reinhard Kopiez. "When the Eye Listens: A Meta-Analysis of How Audio-Visual Presentation Enhances the Appreciation of Music Performance." *Music Perception: An Interdisciplinary Journal* 30, no. 1 (September 2012): 71–83. doi:https://doi.org/10.1525/mp.2012.30.1.71.

Ramachandran, Vilayanur S., and William Hirstein. "The Science of Art: A Neurological Theory of Aesthetic Experience." *Journal of Consciousness Studies* 6 (June 1, 1999): 15–41.

Rankin, Catharine H., Thomas Abrams, Robert J. Barry, Seema Bhatnagar, David F. Clayton, John Colombo, Gianluca Coppola, et al. "Habituation Revisited: An Updated and Revised Description of the Behavioral Characteristics of Habituation." *Neurobiology of Learning and Memory* 92, no. 2 (September 2009): 135–38. doi:https://doi.org/10.1016/j.nlm.2008.09.012.

Ranganathan, Vinoth K., Vlodek Siemionow, Jing Z. Liu, Vinod Sahgal, and Guang H. Yue. "From Mental Power to Muscle Power—Gaining Strength by Using the Mind." *Neuropsychologia* 42, no. 7 (2004): 944–56. doi:https://doi.org/10.1016/j.neuropsychologia.2003.11.018.

Rieger, Martina, Shaun G. Boe, Tony, Victoria, and Stephan F. Dahm. "A Theoretical Perspective on Action Consequences in Action Imagery: Internal Prediction as an Essential Mechanism to Detect Errors." *Psychological Research* 88 (March 24, 2023). doi:https://doi.org/10.1007/s00426-023-01812-0.

Rizzolatti, Giacomo, and Michael A. Arbib. "Language within Our Grasp." *Trends in Neurosciences* 21, no. 5 (May 1998): 188–94. doi:https://doi.org/10.1016/s0166-2236(98)01260-0.

Roberts, Jonathan R., Roy Jones, and S. J. Rothberg. "Measurement of contact time in short duration sports ball impacts: an experimental method and correlation with the perceptions of elite golfers." *Sports Engineering* 4, no. 4 (2001): 191–203.

Rosen, Charles. *Piano Notes: The World of the Pianist*. New York: Free Press, 2002.

Rosenbaum, David A. *Human Motor Control*. San Diego, CA: Academic Press, 2016.

Ruiz, María Herrojo, Hans-Christian Jabusch, and Eckart Altenmüller. "Detecting wrong notes in advance: neuronal correlates of error monitoring in pianists."*Cerebral cortex* 19, no. 11 (2009): 2625–39.

Russell, Daniel Allen, and T. Rossing. "Testing the Nonlinearity of Piano Hammers Using Residual Shock Spectra." *Acustica* 84, no. 5 (September 1, 1998): 967–75.

Safonoff, Wassili. *New Formula for the Piano Teacher and Piano Student*. Brighton, Sussex: J. & W. Chester, 1916.

Sándor, György. *On Piano Playing*. Boston: Schirmer Books, 1981.

Shadmehr, Reza, and Thomas Brashers-Krug. "Functional Stages in the Formation of Human Long-Term Motor Memory." *The Journal of Neuroscience* 17, no. 1 (January 1, 1997): 409–19. doi:https://doi.org/10.1523/jneurosci.17-01-00409.1997.

Schiavio, Andrea, Damiano Menin, and Jakub Matyja. "Music in the Flesh: Embodied Simulation in Musical Understanding." *Psychomusicology: Music, Mind, and Brain* 24, no. 4 (December 2014): 340–43. doi:https://doi.org/10.1037/pmu0000052.

Schiffman, Harvey Richard. *Sensation and Perception*. 6th ed. New York: John Wiley & Sons, 2012.

Schindler, Anton Felix. *Beethoven as I Knew Him. A Biography*. Translated by Constance S. Jolly. 1860. Reprint, Chapel Hill: University Of North Carolina Press; London, 1966.

Schlaug, G. "Increased Corpus Callosum Size in Musicians." *Neuropsychologia* 33, no. 8 (August 1995): 1047–55. doi:https://doi.org/10.1016/0028-3932(95)00045-5.

Schonberg, Harold C. *Horowitz: His Life and Music*. New York: Simon & Schuster, 1992.

Schumann, Robert. *Advice to Young Musicians*. Translated by H Pierson. New York: J. Schuberth & Co, 1860.

Schultz, Arnold. *The Riddle of the Pianist's Finger and Its Relationship to a Touch-Scheme*. 1936. Reprint, Frankfurt am Main, Germany: Fischer, 1949.

Schutz, Michael, and Scott Lipscomb. "Hearing Gestures, Seeing Music: Vision Influences Perceived Tone Duration." *Perception* 36, no. 6 (June 2007): 888–97. doi:https://doi.org/10.1068/p5635.

Schwartz, David J. *The Magic of Thinking Big*. 1959. Reprint, New York: Penguin, 2014.

Simonsmeier, Bianca A., Cornelia Frank, Hanspeter Gubelmann, and Michael Schneider. "The Effects of Motor Imagery Training on Performance and Mental Representation of 7- to 15-Year-Old Gymnasts of Different Levels of Expertise." *Sport, Exercise, and Performance Psychology* 7, no. 2 (May 2018): 155–68. doi:https://doi.org/10.1037/spy0000117.

Smith, Maurice, Ali Ghazizadeh, and Reza Shadmehr. "Interacting Adaptive Processes with Different Timescales Underlie Short-Term Motor Learning." Edited by James Ashe. *PLoS Biology* 4, no. 6 (May 23, 2006): e179. doi:https://doi.org/10.1371/journal.pbio.0040179.

Spence, Charles. "Audiovisual Multisensory Integration." *Acoustical Science and Technology* 28, no. 2 (2007): 61–70. doi:https://doi.org/10.1250/ast.28.61.

Stachó, László. "Mental Virtuosity: A New Theory of Performers' Attentional Processes and Strategies." *Musicae Scientiae* 22, no. 4 (November 13, 2018): 539–57. doi:https://doi.org/10.1177/1029864918798415.

Stephan, Marianne A., Carlotta Lega, and Virginia B. Penhune. "Auditory Prediction Cues Motor Preparation in the Absence of Movements." *NeuroImage* 174 (July 1, 2018): 288–96. doi:https://doi.org/10.1016/j.neuroimage.2018.03.044.

Stephens, G. Lynn, and George Graham. "Reconceiving Delusion." *International Review of Psychiatry* 16, no. 3 (August 2004): 236–41. doi:https://doi.org/10.1080/09540260400003982.

Suzuki, Hideo. "Spectrum Analysis and Tone Quality Evaluation of Piano Sounds with Hard and Soft Touches." *Acoustical Science and Technology* 28, no. 1 (2007): 1–6. doi:https://doi.org/10.1250/ast.28.1.

Svard, Lois. *The Musical Brain*. Oxford: Oxford University Press, 2023.

Swire, Briony, Ullrich K. H. Ecker, and Stephan Lewandowsky. "The Role of Familiarity in Correcting Inaccurate Information." *Journal of Experimental Psychology: Learning, Memory, and Cognition* 43, no. 12 (December 2017): 1948–61. doi:https://doi.org/10.1037/xlm0000422.

Talsma, Durk, Daniel Senkowski, Salvador Soto-Faraco, and Marty G. Woldorff. "The Multifaceted Interplay between Attention and Multisensory Integration." *Trends in Cognitive Sciences* 14, no. 9 (September 2010): 400–410. doi:https://doi.org/10.1016/j.tics.2010.06.008.

Taylor, Cynthia, and Bryan M. Dewsbury. "On the Problem and Promise of Metaphor Use in Science and Science Communication." *Journal of Microbiology & Biology Education* 19, no. 1 (January 26, 2018). doi:https://doi.org/10.1128/jmbe.v19i1.1538.

Tiedemann, J., D. Drescher, and E. Altenmüller. "Aus-Druck Beim Klavierspiel: Eine Untersuchung Zur Tastendruckdynamik." *Musikphysiologie Und Musikermedizin* 7 (2000): 13–21.

Toner, John, and Aidan Moran. "Enhancing Performance Proficiency at the Expert Level: Considering the Role of 'Somaesthetic Awareness.'" *Psychology of Sport and Exercise* 16 (January 2015): 110–17. doi:https://doi.org/10.1016/j.psychsport.2014.07.006.

Tsay, Chia-Jung. "Sight over Sound in the Judgment of Music Performance." *Proceedings of the National Academy of Sciences* 110, no. 36 (August 19, 2013): 14580–85. doi:https://doi.org/10.1073/pnas.1221454110.

Tullett, Alexa M, Mike S Prentice, Rimma Teper, Kyle A Nash, Michael Inzlicht, and Ian McGregor. "Neural and Motivational Mechanics of Meaning and Threat." *American Psychological Association EBooks*, January 1, 2013, 401–19. doi:https://doi.org/10.1037/14040-020.

Von Helmholtz, Hermann. *On the Sensations of Tone as a Physiological Basis for the Theory of Music*. Translated by Alexander Ellis. 1875. Reprint, London: Longmans, Green, And Co., 1895.

Walker, Alan. *Franz Liszt / Vol. 3, the Final Years, 1861–1886*. Ithaca, NY: Cornell University Press, 1997.

Walker, Matthew P., and Robert Stickgold. "Sleep-Dependent Learning and Memory Consolidation." *Neuron* 44, no. 1 (September 2004): 121–33. doi:https://doi.org/10.1016/j.neuron.2004.08.031.

Wang, Keming, Evan P. McGlinn, and Kevin C. Chung. "A Biomechanical and Evolutionary Perspective on the Function of the Lumbrical Muscle." *Journal of Hand Surgery* 39, no. 1 (January 1, 2014): 149–55. doi:https://doi.org/10.1016/j.jhsa.2013.06.029.

Weitzmann, Karl Friedrich, Otto Lessmann, and Theodore Baker. 1893. *A History of Pianoforte-Playing and Pianoforte-Literature*. From the 2d augm. and rev. German ed., by Dr. Th. Baker. New York: G. Schirmer.

White, William B. "The Human Element in Piano Tone Production." *The Journal of the Acoustical Society of America* 1, no. 3A (1930): 357–65. doi:https://doi.org/10.1121/1.1915190.

Whiteside, Abby. *Indispensables of Piano Playing*. 2nd ed. New York: Charles Scribner's Sons, 1961.

Whiteside, Abby. *Mastering the Chopin Etudes and Other Essays*. New York: C. Scribner's Sons, 1969.

Williamon, Aaron. *Musical Excellence: Strategies and Techniques to Enhance Performance*. Oxford: Oxford University Press, 2004.

Williams, Craig A., and Sebastien Ratel. *Human Muscle Fatigue*. London; New York: Routledge, 2009.

Williamson, Elsie B., Ronald Chamberlain, and N. Victor Edwards. "The Truth about Pianoforte Touch and Tone-Colour." *The Musical Times* 71, no. 1053 (November 1, 1930): 1021. doi:https://doi.org/10.2307/915441.

Wolf, F. Gregory, Martha S. Keane, Kenneth D. Brandt, and Ben M. Hiliberry. "An investigation of finger joint and tendon forces in experienced pianists." *Medical Problems of Performing Artists* 8, no. 3 (1993): 84–95.

Wulf, Gabriele, and Rebecca Lewthwaite. "Optimizing Performance through Intrinsic Motivation and Attention for Learning: The OPTIMAL Theory of Motor Learning." *Psychonomic Bulletin & Review* 23, no. 5 (January 29, 2016): 1382–1414.

Yamada, Chiharu, Yoshihiro Itaguchi, and Kazuyoshi Fukuzawa. "Effects of the Amount of Practice and Time Interval between Practice Sessions on the Retention of Internal Models." Edited by Karsten Witt. *PLOS ONE* 14, no. 4 (April 16, 2019): e0215331. doi:https://doi.org/10.1371/journal.pone.0215331.

Yin, Henry H., Shweta Prasad Mulcare, Monica R. F. Hilário, Emily Clouse, Terrell Holloway, Margaret I. Davis, Anita C Hansson, David M. Lovinger, and Rui M. Costa. "Dynamic Reorganization of Striatal Circuits during the Acquisition and Consolidation of a Skill." *Nature Neuroscience* 12, no. 3 (February 8, 2009): 333–41. doi:https://doi.org/10.1038/nn.2261.

Zatorre, Robert J., Joyce L. Chen, and Virginia B. Penhune. "When the Brain Plays Music: Auditory–Motor Interactions in Music Perception and Production." *Nature Reviews Neuroscience* 8, no. 7 (July 2007): 547–58. doi:https://doi.org/10.1038/nrn2152.

Zaza, Christine. "Playing-related musculoskeletal disorders in musicians: a systematic review of incidence and prevalence." *Canadian Medical Association Journal* 158, no. 8 (1998): 1019–25.

Zull, James E. "Key Aspects of How the Brain Learns." *New Directions for Adult and Continuing Education* 2006, no. 110 (2006): 3–9. doi:https://doi.org/10.1002/ace.213.

Index

Page references for figures are italicized.

aesthetics, 63–64, 66–77, 100; altering aesthetic experience, 218–33; percept-action alignment, 67–69, 71–74, 100–101, 194, 228–29
affective proprioception, 67–69, 74–75, 100
agogics, 55, 63–64, 76, 113, 156n35
anticipatory imagery, 166–70, 203n19, 203n20, 204n31
   arm-weight, 9, 15, 28, 37–39, 41, 53, 62, 68, 70, 75, 101, 107, 109–11, 122, 127–30, 142–43, 148, 155n25, 180, 232
assumed veracity. *See* beliefs
attention, 3, 63–64, 100–102, 105, 166, 171, 176, 182, 185, 187–88, 193, 214, 220

backfire. *See* beliefs
belief bubbles, 12–14, 28–29
beliefs, 1–30; associative coherence, 23–24, 44, 67–68, 75, 77, 100–101; assumed veracity, 8–9, 11, 21, 110–11; backfire, 10–11, 25; changing, 12–14, 29, 89–92, 223–25; cognitive dissonance, 25, 69; consequences for pianism, 3, 5, 5, 7–9, 17, 24–29, 36–37, 40–41, 67–69, 76–77, 89–92, 110–11, 144–45, 151, 182, 213, 217, 220; formation of, 3, 5, 21–22, 24, 68, 74–75, 100–101, 219–20; maintenance of, 8, 10–11; meaning threat, 10–11, 25; mismatch with reality, 5–6, *6–7*, 25, 67–68, 70–71, 90–92, 100–101, 110–11, 221–22
bias. *See* cognitive bias

Chopin, on technique, 26, 39, 70, 95, 97, 113–14, 128, 138, 142, 145, 214, 216–17, 242, 244–247
cognitive bias, 14–17; effect on pianism, 14–17, 22–23, 47n39, 63, 67–69, 110–11
cognitive dissonance. *See* beliefs
coordination. *See* mechanics of touch
cross-modal interference. *See* multimodal integration
cross-modal integration. *See* multimodal integration.

elements of music, 217–33
embodiment, 28, 42–43, 64–66, 67–68, 72–73

emotions, affecting touch, 85n81, 175–181, 205n44, 206n62
enslavement of finger independence, 141

finger movements. *See* hand
forces. *See* mechanics of touch

gesture and emotions, 40, 43–45, 63, 66, 72–75, 129, 175–81, 206n59, 206n62
gravity. *See* mechanics of touch

habituation, influence on technique, 3–4, 15, 21, 28, 72, 75, 145, 194, 200–202. *See also* beliefs
hand: anatomy and physiology, 130–34, 138–41, 145–49; arches, 130–33, 158n60; fingers, individual characteristics, 145–49; positions, 36–37, 39, 97
Hanon exercises, 17, 18n17, 28, 92–94, 164, 176, 201

ideation: motor skill development, 182, 213–16; creativity, 28–29, 217–20.
injuries, 15, 19n18, 29–30, 150–52, 159n75, 160n87, 161n92, 196, 207n65, 224, 245; forces contributing to, 57, 111–14, 123, 138, 147–48

learning. *See* practice
listening, importance of. *See* ideation
Liszt, on technique, 7, 97, 145, 182, 214, 216, 224–25

mass bridging. *See* momentum transfer
mechanics of touch, 95–149; coordination, 106–10, 112–14, 117–18, 123–28, 135, 137–38, 141, 149; efficiency, 96, 130–34, 136–38, *140*, 141–42, 147–49; forces, 57, 96–99, 110–12, 128–30; ideal mechanics, 125–28, *126*, 134–35, 158n54, 237–47; gravity, use of, 135, *135*; effect on technique, 95, 110, 123; inertia, management of, 111–14, 127–28;

window of opportunity, 99–100, 103, 106–07, *107*, 118, 123
memorizing. *See* practice
mental skills. *See* practice
metaphors and touch, 38–39, 42–44, 63, 65–66, 67–68, 70–71, 75, 176–77, 214
mirror neurons, 74–75
momentum transfer, 115–25; during touch, 104, 107, 115–18, 124–26, 133–35; ideal zone, *126*, 126–28; mass bridging, 107–11, 130–33, 155n32, 158n64; momentum chain, 115–16; m-v pairs, *126*, 127–28, 137, 145, 151, 237, 253; pedagogy, implications for, 120–22; posture implications, 143–45; touch angle, *116*, 116–19, 139, *140*, 141–42, *147*, 147–48. *See also* mechanics of touch
motor system: optimization of, 107–8, 110–11, 127–28, 141, 168–69, 177–78, 215–17, 223–25
multimodal integration, 53–56, 60, 64–66, 67, 74–77, 84n69, 98, 100–101, 110; learning, 101, 172–75
muscles, of hand and forearm, 138–40, 150–53; muscle fatigue, 57, 108–9, 112–14, 117–18, 123, 132, 141–42, 150
musical skills: development, 213–14, 217–18.
m-v pairs. *See* momentum transfer

neuroplasticity. *See* practice
noise. *See* tone quality

optimization of pianism: principles, 11–12, 28–29, 68–69, 89–94, 98–99, 101–2, 105–6, 110–11, 122, 126–28, 164–65, 171–72, 184, 197, 227–28; the 3 Ms, 89–94, 199, 201; 3M Triangle, *90*, 163, 197

pedagogy, assumptions, 9, 11–12, 29–30, 33–34, 36–39, 40–41, 44, 52–53, 55–56, 62–63, 67–69, 70–71, 74–75,

77, 97–98, 100–101, 105–6, 110–11, 115, 119–20, 129–30, 131–32, 134–35, 143, 163
perception. *See* cross-modal integration
piano action, and implications, 96, 96–106, *107*, *140*, 153n8, 154n9, 154n20, 157n44,
piano technicians, influence on tone quality, 41, 52–53, 76, 78n6
pleasure. *See* aesthetics
posture, 142–45, 157n48
practice: attention, importance of, 100–102, 182, 184, 193; memorizing, 170–75, 187–93; mental practice, 164–70; neuroplasticity, 170–75, 187–93; quality and quantity, 90–92, 182–93, *199–200*, 200–202, 216–17, 223–28
process optimization, 194, *216,* 216–17, 222–25; compounding gains, 195–99, 200–202; reward-to-risk ratios, 199–202

reward-to-risk ratios. *See* process optimization
rotation, of forearm, 114, 146, 149, 238, 241–43, 245, 247. *See also* mechanics of touch: ideal mechanics

thump. *See* tone quality; touch noises
timbre. *See* tone quality
tone quality: absolute or relative, 34–35, 62, 63, 77; altering perception of, 55–56, 63–64; arm weight, 36–39, 107–11, 129; hammer–string collision, 51–53, *56*, 56–59, 62, 78n6, 124–25; key and keybed noises, 58–62, *60*, *61*, 81n31, 103–4; noise, 39, 58–62, 125; perception, 27, 36–38, 43–45, 52–56, 59–60, 62–69, 72–75, 77, 98–102, 113, 129; piano influence, 41–42, 53, 58, 98; visual influence, 43–44, 72–73.
touch angle. *See* momentum transfer
touch-tone relationship: implications of (mis)understanding, 33–34, 52–54, 61–62, 67–68, 74–77, 97–98, 110, 115, 119–20, 125, 129–30, 132, 134–35
triple-stroke, 149, 237–41, *239,* 244–46

visualization, 164–67, 177–78. *See also* mental skills

window of opportunity, 99–102, 105–6, *107*, 118, 123, 125, 191, 238, 250. *See also* mechanics of touch

About the Author

Dr. Cameron Roberts (MBBS, FRCA, PhD, MMus) is a concert pianist who performs with many of the world's finest instrumentalists. He studied Medicine at the *University of Melbourne, Australia.* He also studied Music at the same (Masters), at the *National Academy of Music, Australia*, and internationally. Further, he holds a specialist degree in Anaesthetics (*Royal College of Anaesthetists, UK*). For many years, he taught at the prestigious *Reina Sofia School of Music, Madrid*, and, later, completed a PhD on the physical, perceptual, and pedagogical aspects of the touch-tone relationship (*University of New England, Australia*).

Cognizant of the fact that much of the teaching of piano technique is derived from traditions, metaphors of understanding, and mistaken assumptions about the relationship between touch and tone, Dr. Roberts applies science to the field of piano playing to establish a more objective platform upon which it can be discussed and developed. In *Optimizing Pianism*, he provides facts about the physical and psychological aspects of touch so that pianists can exploit such knowledge in their practice and avoid the musical and physical consequences of guessing wrongly about it.

To reduce the complexity of piano pedagogy into a simple practical framework, a *3M Model of Pianism* is proposed. It shows that while one's individual beliefs about what is important in pianism will influence what gets put into practice, it is the combination of the *Mechanical*, *Mental*, and *Musical* realities of one's playing that will determine its overall performance. Improving these areas using evidence-based perspectives is encouraged as being a safe and reliable way to optimize pianism.

www.ingramcontent.com/pod-product-compliance
Lightning Source LLC
Chambersburg PA
CBHW022010300426
44117CB00005B/112